REINVENTING LIBERAL CHRISTIANITY

Reinventing Liberal Christianity

THEO HOBSON

WILLIAM B. EERDMANS PUBLISHING COMPANY

GRAND RAPIDS, MICHIGAN / CAMBRIDGE, U.K.

Published 2013 by
Wm. B. Eerdmans Publishing Co.
2140 Oak Industrial Drive N.E., Grand Rapids, Michigan 49505 /
P.O. Box 163, Cambridge CB3 9PU U.K.

Printed in the United States of America

19 18 17 16 15 14 13   7 6 5 4 3 2 1

Library of Congress Cataloging-in-Publication Data

Hobson, Theo.
Reinventing liberal Christianity / Theo Hobson.
pages   cm.
Includes bibliographical references and index.
ISBN 978-0-8028-6840-4 (cloth: alk. paper)
1. Liberalism (Religion)   I. Title.

BR1615.H625   2013
230'.046 — dc23
2013014360

www.eerdmans.com

For Tess, my reinvention

Contents

—ↁↁↁ—

Acknowledgments

———⟋⟍⟋———

I am aware that, notwithstanding my care, nothing will be easier than to criticize this book, if anyone ever chooses to criticize it.

Alexis de Tocqueville, *Democracy in America*

In this book I am taking on rather a lot: sketching a huge proportion of modern religious and political thought in an attempt to show how there might yet be life in liberal Christianity. Such a broad canvas seems unavoidable if this argument is to be made. Let experts — and even nonexperts — find fault, but let them also engage with the argument.

I am grateful to Rupert Shortt for introducing me to the good people at Eerdmans (and for his editing me at the *Times Literary Supplement*); to Rev. Winnie Varghese, Rector of St. Mark's in the Bowery, Manhattan, and the other members of that church for introducing me to good contemporary Anglican worship; and to my wife Tess, who has once again been miraculously tolerant of my idea of work.

Introduction

—⟨ℓℓℓ⟩—

This is a book about liberal Christianity. Shall we begin by defining it? No, because the term lacks meaning. That is the problem. It is a serious problem, at least for those of us who are concerned that Christianity is dominated by fundamentalism, legalism, and reaction; by bad dreams of theocracy; and by donnish flirtation with it. To oppose these forms of Christianity, we must try to articulate their opposite. But there is something blocking the attempt.

One thing is clear enough about liberal Christianity: it had a huge role in the rise of modern Western ideology — of secular liberalism. And another thing is clear: it has been in decline for decades. Secular liberalism has no need of it (the clue is in the word "secular"), and it seems to be much less appealing than more conservative forms of Christianity — among theologians as well as generally. It has an aura of weakness, compromise, well-meaning muddle.

The stock of liberal Christianity sank as liberalism moved away from its religious roots, a gradual process that sped up in the mid-twentieth century. The overlap of religion and liberalism began to seem less natural. After the terrorist attacks of September 11, 2001, one might have expected liberal Christianity to recover its voice — in contrast to religious extremism. But no, the debate was between secularist voices, who warned against all of religion, and

1

conservative religious voices, who warned against the hostility of secularism.

Of course, there is still a certain amount of Christian culture that can be called "liberal." But it is in disarray. It has no coherent presence in academic theology, where the dominant forces are united by a dismissive rejection of the liberal theological tradition. Liberal theology is either dispersed among single-issue theologies, or it keeps a low profile. It can hardly summon the energy to reflect on its demise and fragmentation. Likewise, it still dominates a few gently declining churches. But these churches struggle to articulate a coherent vision, except in terms of particular causes. As in academia, identity politics has conquered all. Liberal Christianity has failed to separate itself from liberal humanism, to develop a robust account of its claim to religious truth, to insist that Christian authenticity lies here, not there. When it tries to talk tough and denounces reactionary religion, it only shows its affinity with secular discourse. It needs new depth and integrity, new rootedness in Christian language and practice. It needs to define itself.

So what is it? Why is defining "liberal Christianity" so problematic? Because it consists of two traditions. Consequently, this book is not a defense of liberal Christianity, but rather a choice of one of these traditions over the other — and, in fact, a call to repudiate the other. What are these two traditions? Let us introduce some flashy technical terms and call one *good* and the other *bad*. The *good* tradition affirms a deep affinity between the gospel and political and cultural liberty, meaning the liberal state. Indeed, it was liberal Christianity that first imagined the liberal state, in the mid-seventeenth century, by developing the antitheocratic emphasis of the Radical Reformers (chiefly Anabaptists) in a new way.

As soon as one has expressed enthusiasm for some form of liberalism, various possible misunderstandings pop up and must be bashed down, as in the game Splat-the-Rat. No, this Christian tradition is *not* dependent on a secular tradition called "liberalism" (or "political liberalism," or "philosophical liberalism"). And no, it does *not* entail uncritical affirmation of capitalism, or of America's foreign policy. And no, it does not affirm "secular liberal" culture, though it does affirm the secularization of political culture. It wants to see the flourishing of *Christian* culture within the *liberal* state. There is an element of paradox here, which makes this a frail tradition. Contemporary religion (and even erudite theology) seems reluctant to cope with this element of paradox.

The *bad* tradition of liberal Christianity is one that seeks to reform Christianity away from its "irrational" aspects and present it as the universal rational morality. Soon after the Reformation this ideal infected Protestantism (it also happened in the mid-seventeenth century, when everything really worth talking about happened). Critics are right to see this tradition as corrosive of Christianity, even when it means to defend it. For Christianity is a *religion,* a cultic practice proclaiming and performing the saving authority of Jesus Christ. It consists of language, and ritual action, that can no more be rationally justified than falling in love can. This cultic tradition *just is.* As Wittgenstein insisted — an insight that puts him into the first rank of theologians (though he was an eccentric, borderline Christian at best) — Christianity never ceases to be a *primitive* religion. Despite its involvement in rational civilization, it is as obviously primitive as the emperor is naked. It is, after all, a religion that makes regular use of (what might be called) fake blood, a ceremony that involves the *drinking* of fake blood! Authentic Christianity flows from ritual practice: it is clearly based in the worship of Jesus Christ. Christianity must be rooted in the primacy of ritual, which is its logic and oxygen. This performed myth cannot be rationally justified, smoothly squared with the assumptions of nonreligious contemporary culture. There is an irreducible particularity to Christianity that must not be lost sight of, because its neglect results in the gradual abandonment of Christianity for humanism.[1]

---

1. Is this "bad" tradition identifiable with "theological liberalism"? More or less, though the latter is imprecise — to the point of meaningless. It can refer to a theological method that is open to modern thought: for Ian Markham, "a 'liberal' believes that faith must be adapted in the light of the broad achievement of European thought and of contemporary culture" (quoted in J'annine Jobling and Ian Markham, eds., *Theological Liberalism* [Cleveland: Pilgrim, 2000], p. 1). But adapted how? Some argue for the rejection of anything contrary to rational humanism.

The aim of this book is to untangle the good and bad traditions of liberal Christianity. They grew up together, like the wheat and tares in one of Jesus' parables. A major initial task is simply to relate the good tradition, to show how a form of *Christian* idealism founded the liberal state. This is, perhaps unsurprisingly, neglected by secular thinkers, who suppose that liberalism is an essentially secular narrative. More surprisingly, the most influential theologians agree, for they see liberalism as an essentially anti-Christian tradition. This fairly simple narrative — that liberalism was a secular invention — suits both secularists and conservative theologians.[2] But it is false. Before the secular Enlightenment gained traction, specifically Christian idealism imagined the essential outline of the liberal state, and it remained the dominant force behind the development of the liberal state — into the nineteenth century. Liberal Christianity must regain pride in this narrative.

And yet, affirming this "good" tradition is not straightforward, for it was soon eclipsed, and intimately infected, by the "bad" tradition of liberal Christianity, which confused faith and rational enlightenment. Why did it succumb to this subversion? Because it had a major internal deficiency: it lacked an adequate grounding in Christian practice, ritual, sacramentalism, worship, church. It was seduced by rational humanism into forgetting the foundational role of faith and ritual. And so liberal Christianity became a hybrid in which the bad tradition dominated the good.

This means that the twentieth-century revolt against liberal theology was both right and wrong. It was right to say that liberal theology was riddled with rational humanism. But it was wrong to forget

2. E.g., Jonathan Israel argues that Protestantism produced a moderately liberal climate but that the really revolutionary work was done by secular thinkers, predominantly Spinoza (Israel, *Radical Enlightenment: Philosophy and the Making of Modernity, 1650-1750* [Oxford: Oxford University Press, 2001]). See also Mark Lilla, who argues that, mainly thanks to Hobbes, a "Great Separation took place, severing Western political philosophy decisively from cosmology and theology" (Lilla, *The Stillborn God: Religion, Politics and the Modern West* [New York: Knopf, 2007], p. 58). It is true that some thinkers sought such a decisive separation, but nothing so clear-cut actually happened.

the presence of the good amidst the bad: the tradition that affirms the affinity of Christianity and the liberal state. Today's dominant form of theology assumes that liberalism must be opposed in toto, that any theology that hesitates to do so is wet behind the ears, still in thrall to a past era. Does it not admit that the liberal state is on balance a good thing, or at least a less bad thing than any known alternative? (Does not every day bring fresh evidence of this from the Middle East, China, and elsewhere?) It evades the question, focusing on the deficiencies of the liberal state, fantasizing about the hypothetical possibility of a less secular modernity.

So the task is not to revive liberal Christianity but to *purge* it — by way of rejecting the bad tradition. This is perhaps better described as *reinvention*. For liberal Christianity must be reconceived, remade. And it must be reconceived because the only alternatives are a reactionary antiliberalism, or a perpetuation of flawed liberalism, or a muddled mix of the two. Only a reinvented liberal Christianity can substantially revive the cultural fortunes of Christianity in the West. It can speak to the two dearest ideals of modernity, which it helped to shape: freedom and the hope for a more harmonious future — indeed, for perfect social harmony. This reinvention takes the form of drastic surgery, the lopping off the large diseased limb that has caused us to stumble.

Am I really urging pride in the liberal state? Many readers will be surprised that news of the crisis and collapse of liberalism has not yet reached me. Surely, theology now knows better than to try to get in with liberalism; it's like trying to clamber aboard a holed *Titanic*. To this one must reply, with patient politeness, that the collapse of secular liberal theory is no indictment of liberal Christianity. Rather, the opposite is true: it suggests that liberalism, which remains our ideological reality despite the failure of theories about it, cannot do without its Christian basis. It is only *religious* liberalism that coheres. Only by returning to its origin in Protestant faith can liberalism acquire the thickness of a lived cultural tradition.

My argument takes narrative form: an account of liberal Protestantism's emergence — and its failure. (I make no apologies for using "liberal Christianity" and "liberal Protestantism" interchangeably in much of what follows, for only relatively recently has "liberalism" been substantially conjoined with Roman Catholicism or Orthodoxy. Only in the 1960s did Roman Catholicism agree that religious liberty was a good idea: a sector of Protestantism had been arguing this for over three hundred years.) I will first trace the complex roots of liberal Christianity. This entails a brief discussion of Christian origins. The New Testament obviously has no conception of modern political liberty, but it already contains the seeds of it: it detaches God from any form of state power, thereby rejecting theocracy. This insight, after a long Constantinian hibernation, is basic to the emergence of the liberal state. Also, Paul's theme of spiritual liberty, freedom from a religious law, finds very gradual cultural and political application. A sketch of the medieval era shows that various figures protested against Roman hegemony, and they urged secular rulers to keep the pope at bay. This is the origin of the modern state, including the liberal state. Luther was hardly a liberal, but his idea that religion should be subject to secular control was a step toward the liberal state. All the main Reformers took it for granted that a religious monopoly was necessary, that toleration was a dubious idea. A frail tradition of pro-toleration Protestantism arose, but for a century it was marginal.

And then, in the mid-seventeenth century, it gained a new clarity and force. It flickered into life and suddenly flared up, brightly. Let the state move toward complete toleration, said a few bold thinkers during the English revolution, and let it cease to uphold an official, established religion; only thus can a purer Christian culture emerge. They insisted that authentic Christianity entails the separation of church and state. Should the state become entirely neutral with regard to religion? Yes and no, according to John Milton (the most substantial of these radicals): it now has a sacred duty to protect liberty, and this duty is an expression of liberal Protestant Christianity. This paradox remains central to the liberal state: it is both a renunciation of ideological unity and a frail new *positive* ideology: liberty as the new national narrative. Crucially, this vision predates the Enlightenment anthropology launched by Hobbes, Spinoza, Locke, and others (though only just). Of course, the two traditions become deeply entangled, but this does not mean that they are one and the same.

This vision, rooted in the English revolution, was reframed by Locke. He presented toleration as natural to the rational state, which exists to protect citizens' material rights — a new theory of the state's purpose that he learned from Hobbes. Locke thus detached toleration from a specific religious motivation. And this move was part of something wider. Liberal Christianity became dominated by the early Enlightenment form of philosophy known as deism. (The next two chapters of this book are concerned with how and why that happened.) The essential question is this: Why did Milton's vision of liberty-loving Christianity fail to stabilize, cohere, or catch on? Why did it transmute into something else, that is, a semi-Christian rationalism with a merely pragmatic approach to liberty?

To answer this, we must explore the relationship between Protestantism and *sacramentalism,* meaning the cultural expression of religion, which is centered in ritual. For the new liberty-loving Protestantism was marred by its sacramental weakness, its fear of ritual. It inherited that fear from mainstream Protestantism, but the latter compensated for its rejection of Catholic traditions of ritual by developing a new kind of word-heavy sacramentalism, a focus on preaching, Bible-reading, prayers, hymns. The new *liberal* Protestantism made an even fuller break with sacramentalism. Its suspicion of established, empowered religion entailed a detachment from the practices of any institutional church, plus an assumption that all existing ritual was tainted by authoritarianism and superstition. It often treated Christian ritual, which is, of course, centered on the Eucharist, as a slightly shameful inheritance from the Dark Ages that could not quite be shaken off. A central complexity of my argument is that the new, politically liberal form of Protestantism was exceptionally prone to this massive theological error, this attempt to disown Christianity's cultic basis. It saw ritual as a tool of clerical power. Thus Milton saw both (Anglo-)Catholic and Calvinist worship as authoritarian. He advocated a sort of libertarian minimalism: households or similar small groups should worship as they saw fit; larger, showier, more "official" forms of religious expression were suspect, for they might open the door to the bad old institutionalism. But such minimalism was culturally weak: it gravitated toward an alliance with the rising rationalism and thus allowed Christian authenticity to remain defined by the other, older, less liberal forms. Liberal Christianity failed to become a robust religious tradition, for its essential locus was discourse rather than ritual practice.

The triumph of deism was the central intellectual event of the period — arguably, of all of modernity. This movement claimed to preserve the rational essence of Christianity while sidelining or dispensing with its outmoded "superstitious" forms. Liberal Protestantism was disastrously sympathetic to this project, even as it became more openly post-Christian. Chapter 4 below traces the rise of Christian — and post-Christian — deism and considers the ambiguous responses of Wesley and Rousseau. A critical account of deism raises the (very) large question of how liberal Christianity *should* relate itself to reason and philosophy. If excessive respect for rationalism is theologically corrosive, is the alternative to it *fideism,* in which the truth of Christian faith is simply asserted? I suggest that authentic Protestantism is skeptical of every fusion of faith and reason, but it does not quite opt for fideism, as normally understood. Instead, I suggest that the wisest Protestants take a *dialogical* approach to the issue: they see the necessity for an ongoing argument between faith and reason. This way, the most skeptical form of reason has a positive role in the dynamic of faith. Luther was the pioneer of this approach; unfortunately, it subsequently became marginal to Protestant thought. Its revival, I suggest, is an important part of the revival of liberal Christianity.

The chapters following chapter 4 are concerned with the era of the seeming triumph of liberal Protestantism. The American Revolution revived the liberal Puritans' thoroughgoing demand for religious liberty, and managed to establish this principle, though not as neatly as has often been assumed. Opposition to established churches became central to national identity, but this did not translate into full religious liberty — not, at least, until quite recently. And the breakthrough was ambiguous for another reason: in the heat of the Revolution, liberal Protestantism and deism were welded together as never before. A new ideology of rational liberal universalism emerged, with a providential aura. How could liberal Christianity detach itself from this ideological giant? Furthermore, the American Revolution tainted the ideal of Christian liberty — even as it put it into practice — by condoning the establishment of slavery.

In the late eighteenth century, a new form of Enlightenment emerged, more concerned with the social dimension of humanity and dissatisfied with a narrow instrumental view of reason. This gave rise to a new confident fusion of Protestantism and philosophy (which is largely my concern in chapter 6). It began with Kant's claim that the rational validation of religion was a category error: it was in *moral* terms that religion made sense. Adapting this insight, Hegel built a bold new form of religious philosophy, and Schleiermacher launched a new kind of systematic theology. And yet there was no clean break with the previous era: deist assumptions remained in place, under the surface. The new theology failed to see the need for a radical return to the particularity of Christian language and practice. Chapter 6 is also concerned with the changing face of political liberalism. In Britain especially, "liberalism" combined the demand for civil liberties with a belief in free-market economics and a demand for the franchise to be extended to all male property-owners. The central problem of liberal Protestantism remained the same: its open border with humanism (or a Romantically adapted deism). The mid-nineteenth century saw the first really modern responses to this problem. Tractarianism, or the Oxford Movement, exposed English liberal Protestantism as desperately sacramentally weak: the Church of England hurried to dust down Catholic habits, with various results (one strain of Anglo-Catholicism was decidedly theologically liberal). Another insight into its weakness came from Kierkegaard in Denmark: he complained that mainstream Protestantism was detached from the primal language of faith. Central to both attacks was the insight that Protestantism had drifted from its cultic basis. Its sacramental deficiency remained unrepaired.

The mid- and late nineteenth century saw a new interest in relating eschatology to history. Chapter 7 traces the rise of Christian socialism and considers the first liberation theology: abolitionism. But the meaning of eschatology was unfixed: to some, "the kingdom of God" meant a utopian heightening of "progress." But a few biblical scholars were noticing that Christianity's original vision was not so smoothly compatible with modern thought; it was based in an expectation of God's miraculous action. This insight was to be central to the twentieth-century attack on liberal assumptions. So eschatology plays a deeply ambiguous role in our story. On the one hand, it perpetuates the "bad" liberalism of humanist progress, and, on the other, it jolts theology into seeing the inadequacy of such liberalism.

Chapter 8 discusses twentieth-century theology — up to mid-century. After World War I, the Swiss theologian Karl Barth led a revolt against liberal Protestantism. He announced a purge of Enlightenment influence, a return to specifically Christian thinking. In a neo-Calvinist vein, he sought to reinvent theology around the proclamation of the Word. He constructed a huge dogmatic defense of this approach, whose aura of rigidity alienated most of his contemporaries. Barth was essentially right to take such a polemical and rigorous stand against theological liberalism, which persisted in contemporaries such as Bultmann. After centuries of humanist drift, an extreme corrective was needed. But the heroic prosecution of this necessary corrective led to a narrowness of vision. Barth's new approach was flawed on two grounds: his view of authentic theology was too narrowly verbal, cerebral, sacraphobic. And he overlooked the "good" strand of liberal Protestantism, its affinity with political and cultural freedom. Bonhoeffer, at the end of his curtailed life, attempted to question Barthianism on both of those grounds.

Chapter 9 looks at theological developments in the mid-twentieth century. Liberal theology seemed strong: thinkers such as Niebuhr and Tillich seemed to have learned from Barth's critique. But, in fact, they swerved it. In the 1960s the attempt to reinvent Christianity for modern minds gained much attention, but its shallowness shone through. Chapter 10 recounts the strong theological reaction against liberalism that has grown since the 1970s. It was partly rooted in Barth, yet was increasingly informed by the linguistic turn in philosophy, particularly Wittgenstein's work, and by Catholic thought. Secular postmodernism contributed to "post-liberal" theology, which is hostile toward any trace of Enlightenment universalism. This concerted attack on the remains of deism was a very good thing, but it soon emerged that its boldest proponents had a strongly negative view of liberalism. A new kind of high ecclesiology came to the fore, informed by post-Enlightenment philosophy as well as by Catholicism. The church should be seen as an alternative society, or polis, clearly distinct from the liberal state. This reflected a widespread denigration of liberalism as weak, thin, unable to produce robust ethical communities (Alasdair MacIntyre's communitarianism was particularly influential here). The overlap of liberalism and American nationalism came under attack from Stanley Hauerwas, and a similar antiliberalism was developed by Anglo-Catholic thinkers Rowan Williams and John Milbank. As archbishop of Canterbury, Williams repeatedly presented liberalism as alien to Christianity and threatening to all religious expression. It is no exaggeration to say that the common denominator of the dominant trends in theology over the last thirty years has been contempt for "liberalism." This cause united Left and Right, and high and low: it drew on Marxist Catholic thought, as well as neoconservatism, Anabaptism as well as Roman Catholicism. This ecumenical onslaught has continued to the present. There have been remarkably few attempts to challenge this climate, or to offer a fresh account of liberal Christianity.

This book is such an attempt. I have been motivated by the conviction that the fashion toward antiliberalism is bad for Christian proclamation. There needs to be new clarity that the liberal state is a good thing. There is sacred value in the transition from authoritarian theocracy, or secular totalitarianism, to a political culture that proudly guards people's freedoms (which is never a fait accompli but needs constant vigilance). The liberal state should be affirmed as the proper modern context for Christianity. And yet the task is not straightforward, for liberal *culture* must be criticized as empty and hubristic. It is good that people are freer than ever to choose how to live, and what to believe; but this good poses as *all good:* it eclipses the pursuit of fuller, more authentic community, and it tacitly scorns a religious narrative. Recent theologians are thus correct in saying that secular, liberal, market-driven culture is shallow, atomized, hedonistic, uncharitable. And they do not entirely exaggerate when they call liberalism nihilistic and when they detect in its worship of power, money, youth, sex, and spectacle a dark flash of fascism. To be Christian is to desire an infinitely better economic and cultural order, one that reaches into the kingdom of God — and to belong to a community that models this betterness. But what the postliberal theologians refuse to see is this: that modeling must occur *within* the liberal state. The church is indeed an embodied vision of Christ-based cultural order, but it does not seek to go back on liberalism but to go *on through* liberalism. There is no alternative. So the Christian's attitude toward liberalism is that of the responsible citizen's attitude toward freedom of speech: one can affirm it without thereby affirming whatever people feel free to utter. One can affirm it as context. This is a difficult balancing act: one must affirm liberalism's insistence on freedom, yet resist its pseudoreligious reverence for mere freedom and its subtle disparagement of a fuller, thicker account of the good.

My argument hinges on the claim that the liberal state is a good thing, that liberal Christianity is defined by affirmation of it. But what is it? On one level, it is a complex set of constitutional practices, each with its own history (thus "rights" has medieval roots, while "democracy" is a rather recent ideal, and so on). Of course, such complexity must be admitted; yet I suggest that a broad, narrative-based definition is also necessary. The central thing is a new attitude toward religion. The liberal state is the state that has moved away from theocratic religion (or "unitary theopolitics") for the sake of increasing liberty. It celebrates this narrative; it sees it as constitutive of national identity. Why make this transition so central? Because this is how it happened: this change was the lynchpin of a huge paradigm shift.

The objection to this narrative is obvious. The new national ideology of "liberty" becomes at least as dangerous as anything that preceded it. Look at Tudor England or Puritan England; look at revolutionary France; look at slaveholding America; look at Bismarck's Germany. And look at recent American history: Did not Kennedy's messianic promise to bear any burden in the global pursuit of liberty lead to Vietnam? And did not George W. Bush justify his invasion of Iraq, and his reinvention of the uses of torture, with rhetoric about freedom being God's gift to the world?[3] Is this narrative of holy liberty not dangerous? Yes, but it nevertheless remains worthy of celebration, for it is capable of reforming itself. To put it differently, the liberal state learns — only with painful slowness — what it has taken on, what it means to affirm liberty. And, alas, this learning curve is not a stable linear thing, for humanity does not become progressively less fallen: new advances can lead to new bursts of hubris. I am simply suggesting that Christians should affirm this complex, maddeningly slow-learning and tainted tradition rather than wash their hands of it. (As we shall see, some recent theorists see liberalism as "anti-tradition." This may be largely true of secular liberalism, but it is surely untrue of liberal Christianity. To be a liberal Christian is to be related to a long and rich tradition, from Martin Luther to Martin Luther King.)

Liberal Christians see the liberal state as integral to their religious identity; that is, they see themselves as part of this story. But another objection says, Doesn't the liberal state in today's world have a new *secular* character? Doesn't it seek to construct a common ideology through the marginalization of all religion? Whereas it once warned against illiberal forms of religion, doesn't it now call *all* religion illiberal? This danger indeed exists within liberalism, especially in the French tradition: there is an urge to create common culture around the rejection of religion in general. And Britain has recently shown itself to have a voluble atheist secularist minority that likes the idea of this. But the danger is likely to be exaggerated by religious conservatives (including "postliberals") who portray the liberal narrative as antireligious, which is to some extent a self-fulfilling description. If religion becomes more averse to liberalism, liberalism will become more suspicious of religion. The liberal state is not antireligious, but it is rooted in suspicion of illiberal religion. In its foundational phase, the liberal state is bound to curb some forms of religion. But as it becomes more secure, its approach naturally softens, which is likely to have a

---

3. Spreading God's gift of freedom is America's mission "across the generations," and "the calling of our time" (George W. Bush, Second Inaugural Address, January 20, 2005).

liberalizing effect on those religions, as they find it natural to belong to a liberal state. But there is no smooth progress to liberal pluralist harmony. Perhaps the central problem of our time is that the liberal state lacks a sense of purpose, lacks self-esteem. Liberal citizens (and less liberal ones) become more adept at criticizing than affirming their inheritance. On the Left, the idea of liberalism as a common social project is criticized as a veneer for capitalism; on the Right, it is criticized as weak and corrosive of real social bonds. This overlaps with the religious critique: liberalism means vapid secularism.

Is there a solution to this loss of nerve? I believe that there is a partial solution: the revival of the religious affirmation of political liberty as a sacred cause. (This might sound like the project of the religious Right, but it is absolutely not. The religious Right only affirms a limited version of liberalism, and it denounces the rest as secularist; furthermore, its theology is legalistic. Appropriately, it uses "liberal" as a pejorative.) In other words, liberal Christianity is the ideological ballast that the liberal state needs. In its absence, a culturally debilitating clash is inevitable between secular liberalism and liberal-fearing religion.

In Britain, all of this is complicated by the establishment of the Church of England, which is a strangely ambiguous phenomenon. It is rooted in an early form of *liberalism:* a national church was the way to ward off Catholic theocracy and be a free modern nation. But, of course, establishment was inhibitive of full religious liberty. The establishment is thus a kind of halfway house that is fraught with contradictory meanings. An important task of liberal Christianity (admittedly boosted by my own limited perspective on the world) is to untangle this, and to create at last a reasonably coherent form of liberal English Anglicanism.

The conclusion of this book proposes a new label for reinvented liberal Christianity: *cultic-liberal.* The cultic comes first. Christianity must first be understood as a strange, primitive business: worshiping this ancient murdered man as God. Faith must be understood as an aspect of the cultic. To have faith is to participate, on an individual level, in a cultic tradition. Theology's job is reflecting on this cultic- and faith-based tradition. Such reflection entails honesty about the clash between this tradition and rationalism. It does not help to claim that there is a higher rationality, compatible with faith, as Catholic theology does (and "philosophical theology" naturally gravitates in this self-aggrandizing direction). Nor does it help to overstate the quasi-rational systematic nature of Christian doctrine, as the Calvinist tradition does.

On a practical level, cultic-liberal Christianity will bring new energy to the task of creating surprisingly engaging Christian culture. Some of this will exceed the church setting, but ritual practice must naturally be rooted in church. Of course, most of the main churches already prioritize ritual, but in most of these traditions ritual is inextricable from dubious institutional authority. Their incense smells of reaction. Only a new liberal Christianity can liberate ritual from these ecclesiastical and political associations, and so present the sacramental core of Christianity to contemporary culture. It will do so through a new fusion of religion and "the arts."

The liberal side of cultic-liberalism means more than approval of political liberalism. It means a determination to show that the gospel opposes authoritarianism and legalism, and to accuse the strongest Christian traditions, Catholicism and evangelicalism, of flirting with the ghost of Christendom, a ghost composed of theocracy and legalism.

"Only connect": we must unite the cultic and the liberal. This means going against the grain of modern theology and of contemporary religious identity, which seeks cultic definition in opposition to liberalism. Only in this way can liberal Christianity be remade. It must exorcize its Enlightenment subversion, its dull urge to turn the gospel into humanism, wine into water. It must learn a whole new confidence in its cultic basis.

ONE

Roots

———*◊◊◊*———

A large part of my purpose is to restore some balance and tension to the tradition called liberal Protestantism. It wasn't so bad — not all of it. It was, at first, a vision of Christianity liberated from authoritarian error, refreshed for a new political era. Alas, this vision became entwined with — and eclipsed by — substantial error. So a single voice is insufficient to narrate this tradition. Because it has been excessively dismissed by recent theology, there is a call for an enthusiastic, almost triumphalist account of this stirring vision of liberty. But neo-Whiggish impulses must also be kept in check, for liberal Protestantism's core weakness must be acknowledged and carefully explored. Its failure can be put quite simply: it failed due to its neglect of Christianity's ritual basis, which led to an arid rationalism. Liberal Protestantism has been hobbled by this deficiency, and it stands in need of reform so basic that we can call it *reinvention*. This chapter and the next accentuate the positive, seeking to remind the reader that there is something of value — indeed, of sacred value — at the heart of liberal Protestantism.

Christian Origins

It is notoriously tempting to project liberal assumptions back onto the New Testament. Wasn't Jesus, in defying the fussy rules of the Pharisees, essentially like the modern liberal Christian who sees morality as far more important than church ritual? Wasn't Paul, in rejecting the rules of Judaism, also essentially like that modern liberal, preferring the general ethic of love to particular religious laws? Surely they were liberals *avant la lettre,* and surely they would have given their fullest blessing to the emergence of the liberal state, particularly when it foregrounds social justice.

This is dubious on two grounds. The historical Jesus was not a liberal universalist but an ancient Jew, steeped in some sort of apocalypticism. If he appeared before us now, we could no more understand him than we could understand a speaking lion. Also, appealing to "the historical Jesus" as the criterion of real Christianity is a category error, because Christianity is based on the assertion of his *divinity.* To praise his alleged moral and political opinions, and to suggest that he sowed the seeds of modern political enlightenment, is an evasion of the question of his divinity. The real, difficult question about him is why we think it worth talking about him at all. If one's purpose is to recommend a particular modern attitude or opinion, why not just cut the Gordian knot of an ancient Palestinian detour?

And yet we cannot avoid making connections between the New Testament and our contemporary reality. Nor should we. For example — with apologies for jumping straight to such an example — few would doubt the legitimacy of saying that Hitler's regime was at odds with the New Testament, more at odds than the liberal democracies around it. Indeed, any Christian who did not say this in the 1930s is generally agreed to have failed in his Christian duty (thus does the issue tarnish Pope Pius XII's reputation). If a modern political order can be notably at odds with New Testament principles, it surely follows that the question of an affinity between the New Testament and modern politics is a serious one. It is far beyond my scope to offer a detailed account of the New Testament; on the other hand, it would be strange if my account of liberal Christianity did not begin here.

Christianity originates in a break with an organic cultural tradition. God's "law" was now understood in the widest possible terms: the obligation of God's creatures to worship God and love each other. But it also had a new specificity: it was fulfilled in Jesus Christ.[1] What is striking about newborn Christianity is its minimalism, its insubstantiality. In place of the complex cultural system of the Jewish law, it offers . . . what? A new cult, a personality cult, centered on a ritual meal. Instead of a new set of moral rules, there was a vision of moral perfectionism, in expectation of the "kingdom of God," a sort of apocalyptic utopian cosmic revolution. Paul offered no stable creed: as one recent commentator says, Paul's new universal truth is "a truth remarkably without content."[2]

The two main ways in which Christianity broke from Judaism are central to its later affinity with liberalism. It rejected the theocratic impulse within Judaism, and it rejected its conception of religious law. Judaism was a political religion and was rooted in the historic experience of the Jewish people: their liberation from slavery and attainment of a homeland, a state. This state understood itself in theocratic terms: God directed its religion and politics, and every aspect of its moral culture, by means of his law. The state of Israel collapsed long before Jesus' time, but the aspiration to restore it remained central to Palestinian Judaism. Most Jews trusted that God would vindicate his people in due time by means of a heroic figure, a "Messiah" (the "anointed one"), and they accepted Caesar's rule as the provisional reality. In a sense, Judaism had become posttheocratic, for it no longer found full political expression. But there had been no clear break from that theocratic ideal.

---

1. Paul "opposes Jewish particularism, but introduces another kind . . . faith in Christ"; therefore, "the difference is not a black-and-white one between universalism and particularism" (E. P. Sanders, *Paul, the Law, and the Jewish People* [Philadelphia: Fortress, 1983], p. 160).

2. Dale B. Martin, "Teleology, Epistemology, and Universal Vision in Paul," in John D. Caputo and Linda Martin Alcoff, eds., *St. Paul Among the Philosophers* (Bloomington: Indiana University Press, 2009), p. 94. Martin explains that it is largely due to this near-contentlessness that the postmodern atheist readings of Paul by Alain Badiou and Slavoj Zizek are surprisingly pertinent.

Did Jesus present himself as the hoped-for Messiah who would restore Israel? Not explicitly, but this myth informed his ministry; he sometimes played with it, made irony of it. He announced a coming cosmic revolution that would be infinitely wider than a restoration of the Jewish state. The temporary rule of Satan was coming to an end; the utopian kingdom of God was breaking out. (On the other hand, Jesus generally restricted his ministry to his own people, and he showed no clear interest in founding a universal faith.)

Paul inherited this expectation of an imminent cosmic event, and he made it clear that this went beyond traditional Jewish hopes for a new theocratic state. He kept his distance from Jerusalem, where the Jesus cult retained stronger links with Judaism. He ministered to the Jewish diaspora in the Roman Empire. These communities were tolerated by Rome, granted exemption from the rising cult of the emperor. This cult had been hugely strengthened by Augustus in the previous generation, when the emperor was hailed as a living god, a savior figure. Judaism had long experience of living under alien empires, of seeing pagan rulers as temporary tools of divine providence. This was basically Paul's view of Rome. Therefore, he told the Roman converts that the state was a providential source of political order, within which the gospel could be spread, in the end-time. On the other hand, his relentless rhetoric of the kingdom and lordship of Christ may be seen as a rebuke to Caesar. And he sometimes applied the language of citizenship to this new form of community: "Your citizenship is in heaven," he told the Philippians (3:20). But we should not overstate this: the church did not seek to compete with secular politics for public space. Like diaspora Judaism, it accepted the necessity of a pagan empire, yet it was more fully detached than diaspora Judaism from any ideal of a restored Israel, a godly state. The Christian communities, of course, had no link to the state: they were born "disestablished" and had no idea of becoming established. I am not suggesting that this proves the illegitimacy of future developments, but it is important to clarify that it is the New Testament situation.

So the first point about the New Testament and liberalism, which is almost too obvious to note, is that Christianity rejected a unitary conception of religion and politics. Such a conception had been basic to Judaism, even though it had not found full realization for a while; it was also normal in some form, of course, throughout the rest of the ancient world. Babylonian and Egyptian rulers were living gods whose cult was the heart of religion; Greek city-states assumed a unity of militaristic politics and religious culture. Rome only differed in that its size and ethnic diversity made some degree of toleration necessary. Christianity, of course, was not sociologically unique: there were many other effectively apolitical sects within the empire. But it was *theologically* unique in its inheriting of posttheocratic monotheism and recycling it as a universal faith. It retained the *idea* of God's historical rule, his ownership of all of creation — including pagan politics — and yet refrained from the attempt to realize this idea through human power. This ability to separate the idea of divine sovereignty from worldly politics was surely unique to Christianity, and remained so into modernity. Islam's theopolitics imitated the Old Testament rather than the New. Does this have something to do with "liberalism"? Yes, because, as we shall see, the liberal state was first imagined by a frail minority of liberal Protestants who declared the illegitimacy of imitating Old Testament theopolitics.

Now I want to suggest that another crucial seed of Christian liberalism is the break with the Jewish law. Christianity was a strange new thing: a religion with an intensely moral-reformist vision eschewing specific laws that claimed divine warrant. This dynamic was rediscovered in early modernity; it enabled religious reformers to question the authority of religious institutions — and subsequently political institutions as well. It is a crucial ingredient of the liberal imagination: though it threatens disorder, the expansion of cultural freedom is a benign risk. This can be traced back to Paul's letters.

But naturally this issue is intensely problematic, because Christian (as well as post-Christian) anti-Semitism can also be traced back to this Pauline theme. There is a long dark history of Judaism being dismissed as legalistic, defined by the idea that salvation is a matter of following outward cultic rules. This dismissal was intensified by Luther, who contrasted the true means to salvation, "justification by faith," with Jewish "works-righteousness," which, he said, had been aped by Catholicism. This merged with a wider critique of Judaism as primitive, superstitious, and authoritarian. This attitude was inherited by liberal Protestantism, and also by much of the secular Enlightenment: Judaism seemed to embody the worst elements of religion. Most of Protestantism remained habitually anti-Semitic into the twentieth century.[3] After the Holocaust, it obviously had cause to rethink — to ask whether the polemic against Jewish legalism was really rooted in Paul's theology. Thus emerged a major revisionist movement in Pauline studies, something called the "New Perspective," which argued that Paul was not denigrating Judaism as legalistic, that his message was far more nuanced. This became the new orthodoxy — due in part to interfaith sensitivity. But maybe also due to something else: an aversion to the liberal Protestant emphasis on freedom from fixed moral rules, which is so corrosive of traditional ecclesiastical authority.

Maybe a nonexpert should steer clear of such a complex and controversial matter. But this matter is too theologically important to be politely evaded. What is beyond dispute is that Paul fiercely opposed the idea that Gentile converts should conform to the Jewish law, of which circumcision was the central totem, and that his winning of the argument allowed Christianity to become a universal faith. The question is this: Is the new faith thus defined in contrast to the Jewish law? Did Paul present antilegalism as the essence of Christianity? To Luther, of course, the answer was yes: Paul contrasts the true spiritual faith with the Jewish attempt to earn salvation, and he announces that Christianity is the dramatic inversion of Jewish religion (and, by extension, Roman Catholicism).

According to the recent revisionists, Paul was not accusing Judaism of being legalistic, but simply denying that observing the Jewish law was necessary for Christians. Thus E. P. Sanders says: "[O]pposition in Paul's letters between 'faith' and 'law' [has] to do with the

---

3. This continued into Bultmann's existential approach, which assumed that "human fallenness and alienation from God were definitively disclosed in the figure of the Pauline 'Jew,' with his 'works-righteousness,' his 'legalism,' his 'boasting of his own achievements,' his perversion of the law of God into a means to his own self-centered ends" (Francis Watson, *Paul, Judaism and the Gentiles: Beyond the New Perspective* [Grand Rapids: Eerdmans, 2007], p. 1).

central membership requirement, rather than with a whole way of life."[4] Instead of disparaging the law, Sanders explains, Paul implies that the Christian community must abide by it — on new terms. And far from seeing Judaism as intrinsically legalistic, he takes it for granted that it is a complex combination of faith and law. Where but Judaism did Paul's emphasis on faith come from?[5] Similarly, N. T. Wright explains that Paul's purpose in the passages that seem to contrast law and faith is to establish a new concept of "the people of God" that unites Jews and Gentiles in opposition to paganism, an opposition expressed in moral rigor. Faith is the means to membership in this new "Jew-plus-Gentile family," and such membership is what "justification" means: justification is not about "how I get saved" but "how I am declared to be a member of God's people."[6] In effect, being justified is being *kosher* [my summary rather than Wright's]. "Justified" is what the Jews traditionally are, through their fusion of faith and law. But God's new revelation suddenly boosts the role of faith over law. To remain "justified," the Jews must have a new kind of faith — in Jesus as Messiah. This is obviously an acute challenge to Judaism, but it is not a structural condemnation of it. For Paul, the story of Abraham shows that the radical priority of faith to law is latent within Judaism.

On one level this shift of emphasis is very welcome. It usefully moves us away from the idea that "justification by faith" is how Christians are saved. Salvation cannot be so neatly identified with a present event in the individual's soul. Instead, the Jewish model of salvation is retained; it is the eschatological hope of God's people (though there is a new anticipatory intensity). And this new emphasis rightly emphasizes Paul's deep conviction that the new faith is the fulfillment of Judaism, that it recycles rather than ditches the old covenant.

4. Sanders, *Paul, the Law,* p. 159.

5. Paul "believes two opposite things at the same time. One of them is that God called Israel and gave the law to Moses and the law is good and the people of Israel are chosen. The other is, God decided to [save] the entire world without reference to whether anyone was Jewish or obeyed the law" (E. P. Sanders, in Caputo and Alcoff, *St. Paul Among the Philosophers,* p. 176).

6. N. T. Wright, *Paul: In Fresh Perspective* (Minneapolis: Fortress, 2005), p. 122.

On the other hand, there is a danger that this shift of perspective would be used to downplay the radical postlegalism of the new faith. The fact is that Paul's polemical focus on this issue dominates his authorship. He is not just clarifying the fact that followers of Christ need not obey the Jewish law; he is insisting that this is *definitive* of the new faith. "Freedom from the law" is hardly a side issue in his theology. On the basis of whatever motive (fear of being accused of anti-Semitism, aversion to liberal antinomianism), today's most influential Pauline scholars seriously mitigate Paul's antilegalism.[7] I admit that there is nothing simple about this antilegalism: it coexists with deep respect for the inheritance of the law and an emphasis on moral rigor rather than libertarianism.

Let us briefly review some of the central evidence. In his letter to the Galatians, Paul recounts his dispute with the conservatives in Jerusalem. He expresses intense antipathy to the idea that the old cultic law should be binding on converts. Eating with Gentiles is no longer unclean, circumcision is unnecessary, the old holy days should not be observed. The new community is defined by "the freedom we have in Christ Jesus" (2:4): "It is for freedom that Christ has set us free" (5:1). This freedom takes the form of "faith expressing itself through love" (5:6), and it resolves not to "to indulge the sinful nature" (5:13). But the idea of law is not simply rejected: love is the fulfillment of the law (5:14), which is also called "the law of Christ" (6:2). Paul implies that the law's essence can only be fulfilled if its cultic prescriptions are defied. This brings up huge questions: Is the law's essence moral rather than cultic? If so, does the moral aspect of the law remain in place? He does not directly address these questions, but he implies that there is a new freedom from moral as well as cultic law. It is this that creates the huge risk of amoral libertarianism, which necessitates a new language of obedience to the abstract essence of the law (abstracted from specific laws).

This awareness of the possible abuse of freedom dominates

---

7. In Wright's case, the motivation is surely an aversion to liberal antinomianism. His book *Paul: In Fresh Perspective* contains no discussion wherein Paul's revolutionary move away from law-based morality is presented in a positive light.

Paul's first letter to the Corinthians. Paul condemns a member of the church for marrying his father's widow: this is subpagan behavior, an abuse of the new freedom. He then forbids any contact with sexually adventurous people. "'Everything is permissible,' but not all things are beneficial" (10:23). Because the law's specific moral restraints have been eschewed, a new moral vigilance is necessary. And Paul also addresses freedom from cultic law with a nuance. Although it is permitted to eat meat that has been sacrificed to idols, this freedom should not be flaunted over Christians who disagree. He repeats the point that he is not entirely outside of the law, being under "Christ's law" (9:21). He offers further specific directions: women should neither show their hair nor speak in church — "as the Law says" (14:34). (He surely does not mean that the authority of the law still obtains here, but that this is a matter that the law happens to be right about.) So he seems to row back somewhat from his excited rhetoric of freedom from the law (he had previously, we may presume, taught the Corinthians what he wrote to the Galatians), but without retracting the substantial message.

The letter to the Romans seems to attempt a fresh approach to the issue, then moves to a new complexity of reflection. The moral essence of the law is naturally known to all, on some level, but all disobey it, including the Jews who know it explicitly. There is now a new approach to righteousness: faith in Christ. It does not contradict the law but affirms its essence (3:31). So what is wrong with the law? If its essence is affirmed by the new faith, why can't Jews stick with the old faith? How is the new faith superior? Through various verbal diagrams, Paul struggles to explain that the new faith inherits the old narrative (of obedience to God's law) but also reinvents it. The old law defines God-obedience as contrary to human nature; it presupposes that our desire is to do what we are told we should not do. It is because we desire the wrong thing that we have to be told not to do it. The moral life is a sort of standoff, or draw, between "the sinful nature" and the attempt to follow the law. But this far it exceeds any pagan attempt at morality, so the best possible moral idealism is tainted by a kind of realism, an assumption that human nature is ungodly. (This dynamic is evident in the contemporary attempt to legislate morality.

For example, a law against racism implies that racism is naturally to be expected; in a sense, the law establishes it as a fact about us.)[8]

The new faith takes the ideal of obeying God's law of moral perfectionism and removes the negative presupposition. It says that moral perfectionism can be directly accessed by faith in Christ. This short-circuits the old dynamic of God's law defining us as morally limited. Does Paul claim that Christians are capable of obeying the essence of God's law in a way that Jews are not? He changes the subject: the new subject of morality is God's Spirit, who enables the miracle of full obedience. In a sense, he refuses to engage in the conventional discourse about morality, in favor of this new discourse of miraculous divine agency.

The complexity is that the law cannot simply be ditched as irrelevant, for the new faith inherits its narrative of obedience to God that transforms human life. Simply to reject this narrative is to descend into pagan normality: hedonism and violence. The old moral intensity of the law must be preserved and built upon, but framed by a new rhetoric of the Spirit. Therefore, when Paul engages in an urgent moralism, warning against sinful behavior such as anger and lust, is he not issuing new holy rules for living? In a sense, yes, he is insisting that the spirit of the law must be obeyed more conscientiously than ever, and that exhortation cannot really dispense with the language of rules. Most obviously, he rules out all forms of nonmarital sex, and even seems tempted to rule out marital sex as well, but thinks better of it. But this is a different discourse of moral rules, detached from the idea of a divine law written in stone. Also, it is important to note that he does not exercise the normal religious-moral authority of a priest enforcing obedience to a moral order, but he speaks from a distance.

Despite his moral conservatism, Paul detached religious morality from rules. The theme of Pauline liberty is of huge importance to modern liberalism. (It is also summed up in a sentence from the letter to Titus, though it was probably not written by Paul himself: "To the

8. There is an announcement on the New York subway that I find deeply annoying: "Ladies and gentlemen, a crowded subway carriage is *no* defense for unlawful sexual contact." This morally idealistic attempt to defend people from harassment entails a negative view of human desire.

pure, all things are pure, but to those who are corrupted and do not believe, nothing is pure" [1:15].) Overreacting against its associations with anti-Semitism on the one hand, and with theological liberalism on the other, recent theology has failed to foreground this theme of lawless perfectionism. No other religion has this dynamic, in which the absolutism of a perfectionist moral vision is affirmed — yet its dangerous rigidity is criticized. Christianity uniquely establishes freedom at the heart of moral idealism. Paul did not, of course, understand by "freedom" exactly what we do, but there is a substantial continuity: the modern idea of freedom was informed by the rejection of religious institutional authority, and this rejection appealed to Paul.

Is an emphasis on Pauline liberty offensive to Jews? Why should this question dominate? Pauline liberty is an implicit rebuke to *all* law-based religion, including most of Christianity, and, of course, Islam. Liberal Christianity sees legalism as the natural tendency of monotheism, not as a particularly Jewish thing. It could be said that the other forms of monotheism learned it from Judaism, but that is unilluminating. In a sense, all monotheism learned everything from Judaism. So I suggest that Christianity must reaffirm its risky postlegalism — risky in the sense that it offends other monotheists, but more importantly in the sense that it detaches morality from firm inherited structures and forces religious believers to improvise. And I suggest that this is a very basic ingredient of cultural liberalism.

The theme of freedom from the law clearly influenced the writing of the Gospels. Of course, it may also have been the other way around: Paul may have known of some of Jesus' sayings that were critical of the law, but if so, it is odd that he does not quote them. For example, Jesus' statement that a person is not defiled by what goes into his body but by what words and actions come out of it is seemingly influenced by Paul's thoughts on meat sacrificed to idols.[9] More generally, the stories of Jesus violating the boundaries between pious folk and sinners, and challenging the Pharisees' legal rigidity, while surely rooted in historical reality, are surely also enhanced by Paul's theol-

---

9. Incidentally, this saying can surely be logically cited by Christian defenders of male homosexuality, but I am not sure whether they have used it.

ogy. It is also notable that a rhetoric of freedom is presented as basic to Jesus' ministry: freedom from demonic possession and illness, freedom from inhumane interpretation of the law, and, according to John's Gospel, a sort of existential freedom — "the truth shall set you free" (8:32). Perhaps Jesus' most powerful expression of Pauline liberty, which seems to me to be particularly pertinent to the strange mystery of homosexuality, is "judge not" (Matt. 7:1). Does "antilegalism" settle the whole question of homosexuality — in the liberals' favor? Basically, yes: that is, it makes it illegitimate to treat the New Testament as moral law code, which is the natural habit of other forms of monotheism. But liberal Christianity has failed to place antilegalism in the foreground of the debate, and thus it has been open to the accusation that it simply agrees with the latest dictates of secular morality.[10]

Did early Christianity exhibit "liberal" characteristics? Did its rhetoric of freedom in Christ challenge religious and political coercion? To some extent, yes: it took the form of a radically inclusive community, in which slaves and women were accorded higher status than in the outside world. But Paul, of course, was neither an abolitionist nor a feminist. His approach to ethics did not call for immediate structural change, yet his theological framing of ethics planted the seeds of such change.

The Old Order

Soon after Paul, the new faith stabilized. The rest of the New Testament has a stronger sense of the church as a coherent, theoretically united movement to which loyalty is due. In the early second century, Ignatius, bishop of Antioch, taught that the church's unity depended on bishops, who were authorized to resist heresy. This development was a necessary defense against a proliferation of Gnostic versions of

---

10. On the other hand, a report by the Episcopal Church, "To Set Our Hope on Christ" (2005), did risk a discussion of the New Testament's questioning of fixed moral law; it referred closely to Paul's dispute with Peter as told in Acts 10–15.

Christianity that denied the goodness of the created world and idealized liberation from the evil of the flesh. And there is also something to be said for the respectability that the bishops gradually conferred on Christianity, allowing for a frail but developing relationship with civic society and also with philosophy. Without this, Christianity might have been too closely linked with marginal political forces, and thus more fully excluded from the empire. But the church's unity was still largely theoretical, virtual, an aspiration. An effective bishop might make it a local reality, but there was no central power to bring bishops into line. This changed in the early fourth century. The new emperor, Constantine, was deeply attracted to the warrior God of the Old Testament, and gradually showed favor to the Church (a capital *C* becomes appropriate with Constantine). When he built a new capital in the East, Christianity was at its heart. The ambiguity that Christians had felt toward the empire dissolved. And the apocalyptic eschatology of the New Testament was more completely sidelined by the rhetoric of Christian empire. A new level of doctrinal agreement was forged. The imperial Church banished the Arian heresy that denied the full doctrine of the incarnation. Bishops could now use political force against heretics in their midst. Augustine, bishop of Hippo, explained that it was the Church's duty to work with political power for the preservation of order — and heresy brought disorder. He interpreted a line from one of Jesus' parables to legitimate this: the lord who throws a banquet and is spurned by his official guests tells his servant to get people in from the streets. "Compel them to come in," he says. This hearty host became, for many centuries, a key excuse for state religious violence.

The new imperial unity of the Church, based in Constantinople, was gradually tested by the rise of the bishop of Rome, who assumed the name "pope." He soon resembled a new emperor of the West, a ruler who outsourced politics to barbarian rulers. In the mid-fifth century the papacy gained new confidence in its claim to originate from St. Peter, and it presented itself as the real defender of doctrinal orthodoxy. At the same time, it developed a bold new understanding of the relationship between spiritual and temporal power. Because it had been schooling barbarian rulers in civilization, it had come to assume that its own power was of a superior order to theirs. Over the following centuries the papacy became an increasingly effective monarchy. In the late eleventh century, Pope Gregory VII enforced clerical celibacy and tightened canon law. The papacy also claimed the right to demand regime change in the Holy Land — to channel the martial energies of Europe into crusading. And a new crusading zeal against enemies within was a fixture of European life. Gregory's revolution has been called "the formation of a persecuting society."[11]

Pope Innocent III stepped up the centralizing process even further in the early thirteenth century, and the papacy more closely resembled the universal monarchy it claimed to be. In 1215 the Church confirmed that heresy was punishable by death, a position that was soon strongly defended by its leading theologian, Thomas Aquinas. Crusading zeal was turned on the Neo-Gnostic Cathars in southern France: during this crusade, the Church used the first inquisitions to hunt down heresy. During this period of rising papal ambition — from around 1050 to 1250 — the Church developed a new emphasis on the Eucharist. Worship was centered on a guaranteed Church-controlled miracle, which proved the superior powers of the celibate clerical elite.

There were few explicit protests at the Roman monarchy, but signs of deep disquiet leaked out. In the early thirteenth century the philosophical thought of an outwardly loyal abbot, Joachim of Fiore, gained radical followers. He had taught that a new historical era was dawning, the Age of the Holy Spirit. Worldly institutions would gradually become unnecessary as humanity became directly enlightened by God before the Second Coming. This vision inspired the new Franciscan movement, which was suspicious of the power of the Church. It contributed to a wider movement that challenged a politically powerful papacy. Early humanists such as Dante took up the cause, accusing papal ambition of causing wars in the northern Italian city-states. In the 1320s, Marsiglio of Padua, in a book entitled *The Defender of the Peace,* offered a new systematic attack on the pope's claim to author-

---

11. R. I. Moore, *The Formation of a Persecuting Society: Power and Deviance in Western Europe, 950-1250* (Oxford: Oxford University Press, 1987).

ity. His central contention was that the church had no legitimate juris-
dictional or coercive power; indeed, Christ forbade his followers any
"coercive authority or worldly rule." The church should be a voluntary
society within the state; its ministers should be ordinary citizens, not
exempt from secular law. Religion should be ordered, not by the papacy or by a church council, but by "the faithful human legislator" —
the secular ruler.[12] Marsiglio anticipated Lutheran "secularism" in
the sense of the ideal of a state that excludes external religious institutions from political power. And he went somewhat further with his
idea of the church as a powerless voluntary association (this resembles the Radical Reformation). In the 1370s, John Wycliffe echoed
Marsiglio's antipapalism, thus giving rise to a frail resistance movement, the Lollards. Soon a Bohemian reform movement had more
success: after the Church's execution of its leader, Jan Hus, a defiant
new national church was established.

The Bohemian revolt sparked no wider movement. Instead, the
gentler reformism of the humanists dominated. The foremost of the
humanist reformers was Desiderius Erasmus. He was from the Netherlands, where a particularly strong lay reform movement had
emerged. In very readable prose he taught that the essence of Christianity — the teaching of Jesus and of Paul — had been obscured by
the church, which had allowed semipagan practices to clog things up.
He pointed out that the violent suppression of heresy had a questionable basis in the New Testament. In common with other humanists,
such as Nicholas of Cusa, he hoped for a new spirit of toleration; but
he assumed that the structures of Christendom needed repairing
rather than overthrowing. Indeed, any attempt at revolutionary
change would endanger the gradual reform movement that was underway and unleash violent forces — to no useful end.

His friend Thomas More agreed. The desire for reform should
not rock the boat, More believed. In one of the most famous acts of
displacement in literary history, More imagined a harmonious communist society called Utopia; one of its features was religious liberty.

---

12. Quentin Skinner, *The Foundations of Modern Political Thought*, vol. 1 (Cambridge, UK: Cambridge University Press, 1978), pp. 20, 21.

The state's founder saw that religious division was a cause of weakness and strife, and he established full religious liberty (except for campaigning atheists). He made a law "by which everyone was allowed to practice what religion he liked, and to try to convert other people to his own faith, provided he did it quietly and politely, by rational argument." He did this to keep the peace, "but also because he thought it was in the best interests of religion itself. . . . It seemed to him perfectly obvious that, even if there was only one true religion, and all the rest were nonsense, truth would eventually prevail of its own accord — as long as the matter was discussed calmly and reasonably." The narrator of *Utopia* notes that Christianity has recently been introduced to the island, but not entirely smoothly: one convert started attacking other religions. Such unpleasantness is abnormal in Utopia, where religious differences are friendly. Indeed, religious freedom leads to a very high degree of consensus, such that all can worship together in a broad official church. "Any ceremonies which are peculiar to individual sects are performed privately at home, and public services are so arranged as not to detract in any way from these private ones."[13]

More's point, of course, is that religion is not really like this. In the real world, religion is not sweetly reasonable, but is tied to intensity, extremity, rhetorical force. In the real world, religious freedom would lead to anarchy, not peace. In the real world, the various sects would not agree on a common form of public worship, and so the republic's harmony would be undermined. In the real world, the ideals of religious liberty and national unity are tragically at odds. (In his future career as Henry VIII's persecuting Lord Chancellor, More opted to defend the latter ideal of national unity.) The strange genius of *Utopia* is that it cannot see how competing goods can be reconciled, except in the realm of fantasy.

13. Thomas More, *Utopia*, trans. Paul Turner (Harmondsworth, UK: Penguin, 1965), pp. 119, 125.

The Reformers

Luther discovered that salvation could not be earned by human merit but was entirely God's gift. He tried to alert the church to the need for reform in the light of this message, and was rebuffed. So he began calling on Germany's secular rulers to reject Rome and reform their local portion of the church. This entailed a hostility to the idea of religious law — that is, law issued by a religious body. Only secular law is authentic. A religious version of law will not only create political tension; it will, more importantly, corrupt the gospel, turning it into legalism. This was a key part of Luther's teaching: the opposition between the slavery of religious law and the freedom of the gospel. On the other hand, he saw it as inevitable and right that the state should use religious rhetoric and identify its laws with God's will. He invoked a strong rhetoric of freedom ("a Christian is a perfectly free Lord of all, subject to none"), yet his idea of "Christian liberty" was confined to the spiritual sphere.[14] The Christian was freed from religious law, but had to obey the secular law, which entailed religious uniformity. For Luther, then, "Christian liberty" did not lead to the advocacy of religious liberty, though this connection was later made, as we shall see.

Luther hoped that the new pure church would spread the gospel by gentle enlightenment rather than coercion. In a tract he wrote in 1523 he told the magistrates not to get carried away with their new religious function: "The temporal government has laws which extend no further than to life and property and external affairs on earth, for God cannot and will not permit anyone but himself to rule over the soul. . . . Heresy is a spiritual matter which you cannot hack to pieces with iron, consume with fire, or drown in water. God's word alone avails here."[15] But this flirtation with toleration did not last, for heretical versions of reform were looking dangerously strong. Wittenberg itself was disturbed by iconoclastic radicals, and sectarians who denied the legitimacy of state-directed religion. In this initial turbulent

14. Martin Luther, *The Freedom of a Christian Man,* in John Dillenberger, ed., *Martin Luther: Selections from His Writings* (New York: Doubleday, 1961), p. 53.

15. Luther, *Secular Authority: To What Extent It Should Be Obeyed,* in Dillenberger, ed., *Martin Luther,* p. 389.

period, said Luther, the magistrate had to be strongly involved. If reform seemed disorderly, then what other rulers would risk defying pope and emperor? Luther's big breakthrough was the Farmers' War of 1525: he was such an eloquent propagandist for national security that the rulers began to look favorably on his religious alternative. Indeed, his revolution was attractive to princes who wanted to rule more absolutely, to make internal opposition less possible. Luther was complicit in this, and he was also notoriously supportive of anti-Semitic cleansing operations. So it seems that, in the mid-1520s, he took fright at what he had unleashed and began to emphasize order over freedom.

So Luther's revolution was scarcely politically liberal. And yet it prepared the way for the subsequent rise of political liberalism. For the liberal state arose from soil that had been plowed in this way — that is, on the basis of unitary political sovereignty, which rejected the claim of an independent religious institution to political and legal power. Similarly, Luther's revolution led to secularism, but at first only in a limited sense. Secularism in the full sense means the exclusion of religious institutions from power, including established churches. Luther created the state church, which inherits the monopoly of the old church of Christendom: it is still taken for granted that religious uniformity must be imposed. But the rejection of an imperial, suprastate church by the state is indeed a first stage in the story of secularism. So what Luther launched might be called *intermediate secularism*.

Just as Luther was beginning to appeal to Germany's rulers, Ulrich Zwingli was leading the reform of Zurich, persuading the city council to cut links with Rome. Because this city-state was run not by a hereditary monarch but by an elected council, there was an early form of democracy at work. But liberal democracy it was not. Zurich was a participatory theocracy: ancient Israel was the model, in which the unity of the community was sacred. The different political contexts of Wittenberg and Zurich created a major theological difference. Luther demanded a new *separation* of religion and politics; Zwingli demanded a new *unity* of religion and politics — along Israelite lines.

This meant a major divergence on the question of religious law.

34

Luther, following Paul, associated religious law with Judaism: that is, faith means liberty from the old concept of religion, and law is relegated to the secular sphere. Zwingli, by contrast, felt that a new, purified version of Christianity had to be based on a new legal rigor. The Jewish law is not revoked by Christ; rather, it is pared down to its essentials and is recycled for Christian use. The Ten Commandments retain sacred force, including the law against images. In a sense this becomes God's defining feature: his hatred of idolatry. The law against images becomes the synecdoche of all law: obeying it is the sign that one has moved to this new concept of religion. This is Zwingli's core difference from Luther. Diarmaid MacCulloch sums it up well: "Where Luther had contrasted law (bad) and gospel (good), Zurich now contrasted law (good) and idolatry (bad)."[16]

But both agreed that the state must preserve religious order — by imposing uniformity. This defines mainstream, "magisterial" Protestantism. The radical dissenters of Zurich (the first Anabaptists) were thus excluded — and executed — as heretical subversives. Can these radical dissenting Reformers be credited with a more liberal vision? Up to a point. The Anabaptists and similar groups rejected the whole Constantinian model of church, the idea that religion should be established. They believed that such a religion could not be true Christianity, which was necessarily countercultural, a gathering of the elect. They had the New Testament on their side, which irritated the magisterial Reformers. The Anabaptist rejection of establishment does indeed anticipate the rise of liberalism in the next century; but they did not imagine the possibility of a new kind of state.

It was universally assumed that toleration was a bad idea; society ought to be united in a common faith. Even progressive-minded Erasmus assumed that religious unity was the key to a healthy society. In 1516 he praised France as "the purest blossom of Christianity, since she alone is uninfested with heretics, Bohemian schismatics, with Jews and with half-Jewish marranos."[17] The Reformers did not di-

16. Diarmaid MacCulloch, *Reformation: Europe's House Divided* (London: Allen Lane, 2003), pp. 619-20.

17. Quoted in John Coffey, *Persecution and Toleration in Protestant England, 1558-1689* (London: Longman, 2000), p. 51.

rectly challenge this assumption that order depended on religious unity. But the religious division that they unleashed meant that in many states the old unity was a thing of the past. Thus did various rulers find themselves cornered into the distasteful necessity of partial toleration.

The Zwinglian tradition, which became known as "Reformed," was soon tightened up by the rising star of Protestantism, John Calvin. His reforming career started about fifteen years later than did Luther's, in the mid-1530s. In the intervening years, Protestantism had shown itself to be terribly unstable, difficult for rulers to keep control of. The starkest evidence was the seizure of Münster in Westphalia by an Anabaptist splinter group in 1534-35. For sixteen months the sect controlled the city, creating a messianic community to prepare for Christ's return. The local ruler, Prince-Bishop Franz von Waldeck, finally stormed the city amid scenes of horror. Heinrich Bullinger, Zwingli's successor in Zurich, used the episode as an excuse to persecute Anabaptists. Such rigor appealed to Calvin: he was desperate for reform to seem orderly — so that it would appeal to his king, Francis I of France. In the preface to *The Institutes,* he tells King Francis that the aim is the restoration of the church's dignity, purity, and truth. This grand, idealistic conception of the church is basic to Calvin's thought. It should not be attenuated or made subject to secular power, as Luther allowed. Reform should bring the church a new sense of confident autonomy. The Genevan church was subject to the city council, as was the case in Zurich. But since the city lacked a strong ruling class, the church soon eclipsed the secular council. It had the power to excommunicate offenders — in order to preserve its purity. It required the city council to do the dirty work of punishing these offenders, sometimes banishing them from the city. A reformed church should bring new social and political order. Calvin consciously set about creating a model that might be copied as widely as possible. The church's ruling body, the consistory, contained lay elders as well as ministers and deacons. It was a strong, largely democratic body that eclipsed the secular council. The democratic aspect of the church did not curtail Calvin: like an elected dictator, he successfully demonized liberal critics as "libertines." Like Luther, he talked of true faith in terms of liberty, but he saw no connection between this and toleration.

In a sense, Calvin's view of the church is close to the Roman Catholic view: it is an institution that exercises authority; it is a place of discipline, no less than the secular polis. Like a Roman Catholic, he insists that "the keys have been given to the Church": it is empowered to excommunicate the ungodly, to mediate divine judgment.[18] He also developed Zwingli's high opinion of Old Testament law, though he believed, of course, that it had to be adapted for the new Israel.

Rome was beginning its "Counter-Reformation" renewal, which entailed tightening its account of orthodoxy. For decades it had sought to keep humanists like Erasmus within the fold; now it rejected the spirit of liberal inquiry that had been gently mushrooming throughout the Renaissance. In the early 1540s the papacy cracked down on Italian humanists, many of whom fled north and defected. The Inquisition also pursued heretical humanists in France and Spain, many of whom ended up in Protestant refuges in northern and eastern Europe. These humanists brought a mystic rationalism with them that seeded the Enlightenment. Rome's new intransigence was exemplified by Ignatius Loyola, founder of the Jesuits. His style of dramatic authoritarianism is summed up in one of his "rules for thinking with the Church": "If she shall have defined anything to be black which to our eyes appears to be white, we ought in like manner to pronounce it to be black."[19]

Rome's crackdown posed a dilemma for the Protestant movement: Should it welcome the liberalism expelled by Rome, or should it imitate the intransigence? Calvin was clear. When the maverick Spanish theologian Miguel Servetus was being hunted by the Catholic Inquisition, Calvin decided to show that he was no appeaser of heresy. Servetus had been questioning the doctrine of the Trinity for about twenty years, advocating a mystical-rationalist form of Christianity,

---

18. John Calvin, *Institutes of the Christian Religion*, trans. Henry Beveridge (Grand Rapids: Eerdmans, 1989), 3.I, p. 298.

19. Quoted in David S. Katz and Richard H. Popkin, eds., *Messianic Revolution: Radical Religious Politics to the End of the Second Millennium* (Harmondsworth, UK: Penguin, 1999), p. 57.

which had clearly been influenced by the interfaith humanism that had recently flourished in southern Spain. He taught that all rigid orthodoxy was erroneous and that people ought to be free to follow their "inner light." In the 1540s he practiced medicine in Lyon under a false name. But the authorities were sharply reminded of his existence in January 1553, when he published a book entitled *The Restoration of Christianity.* Servetus sent Calvin a copy of his book, as well as some letters. Soon his cover was blown, and the archbishop of Lyon began to assemble a case against him. Calvin helpfully sent the Inquisition the letters Servetus had sent him, and the latter fled Lyon. But he made the strange mistake of stopping off at Geneva on his way. It seems that he was determined to debate his ideas with Calvin, come what may. Instead of offering him a debate, however, Calvin accused him of heresy and called his ideas "poison." Servetus was duly sentenced to death and was burned at the stake. Meanwhile, Calvin's fame as the tough guy of Protestantism reached new heights.

The execution of Servetus provoked the first serious debate about toleration within Protestantism. Calvin wrote a tract defending his actions, rhetorically asking, "How can religion still exist, how can the true Church be identified, what becomes even of Christ if the doctrine of piety is rendered insecure and doubtful?" He drew on the classic defense of persecution: "When religion is shaken to the core, when God is blasphemed in a most loathsome manner, when souls are led to perdition by godless and destructive teachings, then it is necessary to find the remedy which will prevent the deadly poison from spreading."[20] He claimed that it was appropriate to use the laws against false teaching that are found in Deuteronomy.

Calvin's main antagonist in the debate was his former friend Sebastian Castellio, a humanist reformer who had followed Calvin to Strasbourg and then to Geneva, where he taught alongside his master. In 1544 the two fell out. Castellio was accused of unorthodoxy, and he moved to Basel, where a degree of freethinking was permitted. He met

20. Calvin, *Defensio orthodoxae fidei de sacra trinitate contra prodigiosos errors Michaelis Serveti Hispani*, CO 8, pp. 461, 477, quoted in Hans R. Guggisberg, *Sebastian Castellio, 1515-1563, Humanist Defender of Toleration in a Confessional Age* (Hampshire, UK: Ashgate, 2003), pp. 78, 79.

Spanish and Italian humanists and also the Dutchman Sebastian Franck, of the quasi-rationalist Spiritualist movement, who had said that no organized community of worship is truly Christian. Castellio's book *Whether Heretics Should Be Persecuted* (1554)made him the leader of the liberal opposition to Calvin. Though Servetus's theology was false, he said, he was not deserving of death. He denied that Christians can use the Old Testament to authorize their laws, and he cited the parable of the wheat and the tares to insist that there can be no sure separation of truth and heresy in this world. He warned that the passion for doctrinal orthodoxy can eclipse the duty to love: "If you had not known [the doctrine of the Trinity], you would not have burned a man alive."[21] He accused the Genevan church of being worldly ("fleshly").

Despite his passion for toleration, Castellio's theopolitical assumptions were essentially traditional: he saw established religion as natural and did not argue that the state should grant full freedom to those it deemed heretics, just that its treatment of them should be less bloody. He was in this respect closer to Erasmus than to the major theorists of the next century.

The clear majority of Protestant leaders sided with Calvin rather than with his liberal critic. The English bishop John Jewel was proud that a Protestant rather than a Catholic had dispatched Servetus. Philip Melanchthon, Luther's prime heir, said that the church owed Calvin a debt of gratitude. Indeed, only a few Reformed theologians were sympathetic to Castellio's humanism: Bucer in Strasbourg, Bullinger in Zurich, and Jan Laski, a Pole who had moved to East Friesland and helped Reformed ideas spread to the Netherlands. But no coherent pro-toleration movement emerged. There were just a few pockets where toleration happened to be politically possible, such as the remote Alpine region of Switzerland, the Graübunden. The gen-

---

21. Franck exemplifies the link between antiauthoritarianism in religion and antisacramentalism: "I maintain against all ecclesiastical authorities that all outward things and ceremonies . . . customary in the church of the apostles have been done away with and are not to be reinstituted" (in Perez Zagorin, *How the Idea of Religious Toleration Came to the West* [Princeton, NJ: Princeton University Press, 2003], pp. 85-86, 88, 117).

eral assumption remained: uniformity was necessary, and the ruler had the right to decide on and impose this uniformity. This principle, known as *cuius regio, eius religio* (the one who rules the land decides its religion), had emerged in the 1520s, when the first magistrates opted for Lutheranism; it became more firmly established over the next century throughout Europe.

Part of the reason for Reformed hostility to Castellio's position was its affinity with Anabaptism. By the 1550s, the Anabaptist movement had stabilized somewhat, especially in the Netherlands. This was thanks to Menno Simons, who emphasized pacifism and congregational discipline, as well as the rejection of all politically established and empowered churches. He sharply condemned the cultic violence in Münster. The Anabaptists did not exactly advocate "toleration," because you have to exert political authority before you can be tolerant, and they denounced all Christians in authority. But the movement spread the idea that true Christianity was intrinsically opposed to persecution.

Calvin's model of reform became the dominant form of Protestant resistance to Catholic rule — in Scotland, France, the Netherlands, and elsewhere. It had the energy and rigor that a revolutionary movement needs. Unlike Lutheranism, it was capable of organizing without state supervision. Thus it had a slightly different understanding of establishment. It certainly wanted to be the established religion, but it was far less willing than Lutheranism (and the English Church) to be directed by a monarch. Consequently, the Calvinist Church of Scotland has always been far warier of the monarch's religious role than has its southern counterpart. This is not simply a matter of distance from London.

Toward Toleration

The dramatic beginnings of England's reformation need not detain us, except to note that Henry's reform followed Luther's model (without giving the German any credit; Marsiglio was given more). The Act in Restraint of Appeals (1533) defined the church not as a separate institution but as the spiritual aspect of the state, or "empire," whose ruler has comprehensive sovereignty. This exceptionally tight unity of church and commonwealth gradually caused a huge upsurge in cultural confidence, a sense of national vocation. When Elizabeth returned the nation to Protestantism in 1558, after her sister's bloody Catholic interlude (Mary burned more than 300 Protestants), England had a new image as the center of Protestant stability, for Lutheranism had suffered sharp reverses throughout the Habsburg Empire. Elizabeth's genius was to link the Church of England with the idea of liberty — without loosening the state monopoly. This was possible because England was at war with Catholic powers: it could define itself against Catholic tyranny. English Protestantism became deeply involved in a story about the heroic expansion of political freedom. A Protestant polity is humane, progressive, free — the opposite of an evil empire with a reactionary medieval ideology. This dynamic ideology was presented in religious terms by John Foxe in his *Book of Martyrs,* and later in more secular terms by Sir Walter Raleigh in his *History of the World.* And, of course, it pervades Elizabethan literature.

As soon as Elizabeth's reign began, it was easy to point to Roman tyranny: the Papal Index had been extended (Erasmus's works were now banned), and the Spanish Inquisition was at its height. Elizabeth enjoyed posing as the savior of humanism; she ordered every parish to keep a copy of Erasmus's *Paraphrases.* A decade later this narrative was deepened by the papal bull authorizing the Queen's assassination, and then by the Saint Bartholomew's Day massacre of Protestants in Paris. And in the following decade the defeat of the Spanish Armada sealed the impression that God approved. Elizabeth was adamant that English liberty depended on a strong established church, with orderly sacramentalism redolent of Catholicism — and a hierarchy answerable to her.

The Puritan (Calvinist-influenced) party within the church wondered why this powerful Protestant monarch allowed the church to retain a Catholic style, including episcopacy (bishops). The Anglican theorist Richard Hooker answered their question: he explained that, in the absence of a clear biblical blueprint for church organization, pragmatism is appropriate, and the English settlement worked. This episcopal establishment brings a stable unity of religion and culture. Such a culture is on one level liberal, for it only demands outward conformity, not precise assent to a theological system, as in Calvinism. Of course, the national church can coerce ("Will any man deny that the Church doth need the rod of corporal punishment to keep her children in obedience?"); but it is less likely to do so than any other kind of church.[22]

But this semiliberal approach did not extend to those who refused outward conformity. Many Roman Catholic priests were executed for treason, and a small but steady stream of radical Protestants were executed for heresy. The liberal Protestant ideologue John Foxe was particularly upset when some Anabaptists were burned in 1575. Those denying the Trinity were also regularly picked on. Only one or two voices dared argue for toleration: Sir Walter Raleigh defended the right of the sectarian Brownists to be allowed to worship in peace, and he spoke against compulsory attendance at the established church. A few humanists made pro-toleration noises: the Italian exile Acontius mediated Castellio's thought, which was in tune with the Erasmianism that Elizabeth claimed to favor.

A few bolder experiments in toleration occurred elsewhere. Eastern Europe was leading the way, partly due to the influence of Italian humanist exiles, but mainly due to a long tradition of ecumenism, arising from the proximity of Orthodoxy and Islam. The leading reformer in Transylvania, Ferenc David, abandoned belief in the Trinity and was allowed to establish a new church. In 1568 the Diet of Torda proclaimed full religious liberty, and the policy was a success for a few decades. This radical experiment influenced the new Polish-Lithuanian Commonwealth, where the monarchy's official allegiance to Rome was very loose. Various Protestant churches coexisted, and Trinity-deniers were tolerated here as well. Indeed, thanks to the Italian refugee Fausto Sozzini, Crakow became the anti-Trinitarian capital of Europe (for the next century, Trinity-denying Christianity was named Socinianism after him). In 1573 the Confederation of Warsaw attempted to rule out religious violence. Toleration lasted longer here

22. Hooker, in Coffey, *Persecution and Toleration,* p. 21.

than in Transylvania, but it was ultimately repealed by conventionally intolerant Catholicism.

France, meanwhile, was trying a degree of toleration, very much out of necessity rather than choice. In 1561, Catherine de Medici tried tolerating the Huguenots (French Calvinists), which provoked a slow-burning civil war. She sought to end it by eliminating the Protestant leaders at the Saint Bartholomew's Day massacre of 1572, where about two thousand Huguenots were murdered in Paris — and many more rounded up and killed throughout France. After two more decades of turmoil, Henry IV tried toleration again. The Edict of Nantes of 1598 acknowledged the presence of a Protestant subculture, which evoked papal fury. For most of the next century this worked well enough, but religious peace was rather superficial; the Huguenot subculture was not well integrated. There was a lingering sense that this large minority impeded France's unity. In 1685, therefore, the edict was revoked by an absolutist Catholic monarchy, and most of the Huguenots fled. The surprising thing is that a Roman Catholic state managed to tolerate a Protestant subculture for so long.

Among Protestant states, the most innovative was a new state, the Dutch Republic. It emerged from a bloody war of resistance against Catholic Spain in the 1570s. Calvinism was established, but the ruling class was liberally inclined and limited its powers: the constitution promised "freedom of conscience." But public dissent was banned (dissenting churches had to be hidden from street view). This was the "closest thing in early modern Europe to a disestablishment of religion."[23]

Almost no one questioned the need for an established church; liberals simply argued that it should become broader, so as to be a more effective agent of unity. The Dutch church refused to bow to such pragmatism. In the 1590s the eminent theologian Arminius joined the liberals in calling for a looser conception of orthodoxy — and particularly a rethinking of Calvin's teaching on predestination. The church condemned him, which led to a major political and reli-

---

23. Benjamin J. Kaplan, *Divided by Faith: Religious Conflict and the Practice of Toleration in Early Modern Europe* (Cambridge, MA: Harvard, 2007), p. 242.

gious rebellion in 1610. The Remonstrants demanded a new, broader religious settlement, but not complete toleration. After a six-year struggle, Arminius's movement failed, and the conservatives in the Dutch church began a purge of religious culture, expelling all traces of liberalism. At the Synod of Dordt (1616-18) they insisted that the doctrine of predestination was sacrosanct — and Arminius was a heretic. The Remonstrants went underground, and Calvinism became a tighter system than ever.

The Synod of Dordt seemed to prove that a liberal development of the Reformed tradition was a chimera, even in this relatively liberal setting, where Erasmian humanism flourished. Protestantism seemed to need to take fundamentalist form, partly to keep the Counter Reformation at bay and partly to harden itself against the semiagnostic rationalism that was springing up, partly thanks to Amsterdam's Sephardic Jews. Even the Arminian liberals equivocated on toleration. As Jonathan Israel says, "Neither Arminius . . . nor any Arminian leader, during the period down to 1618, tried to construct a general theory of toleration or argued for a general toleration on principle."[24] The leading Dutch liberal in the 1620s was Hugo Grotius. Like an Anglican (he admired the English church), he assumed that a state church was the necessary means to order. "As only the sovereign has the right to introduce the true religion, it is also his duty to suppress the false ones, either by lenient methods or by force."[25] This sums up the limited vision of the first phase of liberal Protestantism.

---

24. Jonathan Israel, "Toleration in Seventeenth-Century Dutch and English Thought," in John Marshall, ed., *John Locke, Toleration and Early Enlightenment Culture* (Cambridge, UK: Cambridge University Press, 2006), p. 350.
25. Hugo Grotius, quoted in Marshall, *John Locke,* p. 350.

TWO

The Frail Vision

—❦—

W as England incubating any kind of liberal Protestant movement? For some decades it had nurtured a rhetoric of national
Protestant liberty that was based on its rejection of Catholic absolutism. But its constitution remained basically theocratic: the arrival of
James I from Scotland in 1603 did not change this. There was no
strong liberal Protestant lobby urging reform. The Puritans were over-
whelmingly concerned to get their hands on the state monopoly of religion, but not to widen toleration, let alone jettison establishment.

Then, a few decades on, a new strength descended on this uncer-
tain tradition fairly suddenly. Instead of seeking an expansion of toleration, it demanded a revolution in toleration: the rejection of the
ideal of centrally imposed religious uniformity, of religious establishment. This strikingly new theopolitical vision emerged from the militant English Puritanism of the 1640s. It played a key role in the English revolution, and it greatly influenced Cromwell's regime. But, as
we shall see, this remarkable breakthrough for liberal Protestantism
proved disastrously counterproductive because, once the old order
was restored, such thinking was seen as intensely dangerous, linked
to regicide and chaos. After the failed revolution, liberal thought became careful, moderate, pragmatic, and its fuller vision went underground (and crossed the Atlantic).

Before the English revolution, the central struggle was between Calvinists and those with a more Catholic conception of the church (rather unhelpfully known as Arminians, after the Dutch anti-Calvinist thinker). Their leading thinker, Lancelot Andrewes, denied that the English Church had really become Protestant. By rejecting the pope, he said, it had come to a better understanding of its Catholicism. He and his tight group of followers looked for inspiration to the very first bishops, those who predated Roman hegemony. Puritans, of course, denounced these original Anglo-Catholics as crypto-papists.

Was there no liberal Protestant movement that was critical of both Calvinism and the authoritarian establishment? No, there was not. There were "separatist" Puritans, who rejected the Calvinist urge for establishment and were generally dubbed Anabaptists, or Brownists, after the main Elizabethan separatist sect. They were hardly liberals, but their rejection of the ideal of establishment was a crucial ingredient of the coming liberal vision. They did not preach toleration as a general principle, but their existence forced others to think about toleration in a new way. There were some Protestant intellectuals sympathetic to toleration, but they had very little impact until the English civil war.

The roots of the English civil war lie in the expansion of the high-church Arminian movement under Charles I. He allowed Archbishop William Laud to impose a Catholic interpretation of the Prayer Book, and to change the interior architecture of all churches: the altar was railed off, becoming the grand stage of the priest. Charles also revoked the partial leeway that Puritans who stayed within the church had pragmatically been granted. Catholic-style uniformity was strictly imposed, and opponents were shown zero tolerance. This had the effect of galvanizing Puritan resistance, including among members of parliament. Under the Tudors, Parliament had acquired a self-image as the defender of England's Protestant liberty. A strong lobby had learned from the trauma of Mary's reign that monarchs should not be trusted to defend England's Protestant identity. This lobby saw the high-church movement as crypto-Catholic, as opening the door to the Catholic absolutism on the Continent. It feared that England was constitutionally prone to such absolutism: it saw an established church, run by the monarch and his bishops, as gravitating in a Catholic direction. They observed with alarm that Charles was handing clerics local governmental powers that they had not enjoyed for a century. These members of parliament had grown up with the half-true Tudor rhetoric of Protestant liberty, and through believing it they made it truer.

Archbishop Laud showed signs of favoring Catholic absolutist methods, and he used the Star Chamber to repress dissent. In 1637, three high-profile dissenting ministers were punished with fines and ear-mutilation. The violence did not compare with Mary's zeal for burning her religious enemies, but the reaction it provoked was comparable. The dissenters' opposition to this semi-Catholic regime did not, of course, make the Puritans into liberals all of a sudden. The vast majority of them retained Calvin's suspicion of toleration. But a new emphasis within Puritanism did emerge. Laud's will to increase the church's political power by reviving church courts and seeking to rebuild the church's wealth led some Puritans to criticize the secularizing thrust of the Tudor reformation, to point out that an established church is not supposed to be independently powerful, but subject to lay control. Maybe an episcopal church could not be fully answerable to the laity and could not be held to Protestant principles. Maybe an episcopal established church gravitated toward Catholicism.

This was the conclusion of the Puritans who left for America in the 1620s. The most famous leader of those emigrées, John Winthrop, predicted that the new Massachusetts Bay Colony would be "a citty on a hill." Winthrop was adamant that he was not rejecting the Church of England; rather, he was creating a new pure limb of it that would guide the rest.[1] In this he was representative of the dominant form of English Puritanism, which didn't want to abolish establishment any more than an opposition party wants to abolish government. There was general enthusiasm for congregationalism, which held that authority lay in the congregation as a whole, and that a wider authority structure was unnecessary (the key difference from Presbyterianism). In practice, however, authority gravitated toward a priestly elite in this model

---

1. Francis J. Bremer, *John Winthrop: America's Forgotten Founding Father* (Oxford: Oxford University Press, 2003), p. 198.

also. Just as in Calvin's Geneva, the state was technically secular; but, in fact, it did the church's bidding. Officials had to be communicant members of the congregation, and the franchise was limited to full (male) members of congregations. In practice, church attendance was mandatory, and religious discipline was not a voluntary matter but was enforced. Drunkards and adulterers were whipped or banished; heretics might be mutilated, probably by having their ears cut off. This was the kind of discipline that Puritans had wanted to establish in England. They now did so with particular energy, a fear of the wilderness fueling their need for a tight community of moral order. To call such an order theocratic is not a vague liberal slur: they aimed it to be so. "Theocracy, or the aim to make the Lord God our governor, is the best form of government in a Christian commonwealth," declared John Cotton.[2]

In 1631 the colonists were joined by an intense young preacher from England named Roger Williams, a recent Cambridge graduate in his late twenties. He had studied under the jurist Sir Edward Coke, a major opponent of divine-right monarchism. He was probably also familiar with London's underground Baptist community, which may have influenced the bolder form of separatism that he espoused. The colonial church, Williams said, must explicitly reject the English church — and thus reject the logic of establishment. Williams called for the colony's theoretical congregationalism to be more strictly observed: there should be no wider authority than the congregation, and the church should not have any institutional existence beyond itself. Winthrop and his colleagues feared that this impulse was anarchic; they wanted to retain the official established aura of the English church, but to purify it. They also feared the political consequences of such a move. If they were to accept Williams's views, they would become tacit enemies of England rather than a vanguard, authorized by royal charter.

Williams moved on from Boston to Plymouth, where his ideas were tolerated — at least for a while. But he kept on objecting to the

2. John Cotton, quoted in Steven Waldman, *Founding Faith: Providence, Politics, and the Birth of Religious Freedom in America* (New York: Random House, 2008), p. 8.

new form of establishment that was emerging in the colony. In his view, the civil authority was wrongly trying to enforce obedience to the first table of the Decalogue, which was more about religion than public morality; and its demand for an oath of allegiance to the colony illegitimately used religious language to a political end. By making citizenship dependent on full church membership, the colony was encouraging — almost enforcing — inauthentic Christianity. The political community was one thing, he taught, and the church quite another. This was a more rigidly secularist viewpoint than had ever been put forward. The state should be completely nonreligious, and the church should renounce all political power. Only thus, he taught, could Christianity be pure, free of the taint of worldliness.

Williams also made himself unpopular throughout the Massachusetts Bay Colony by writing a pamphlet contesting the king's right to grant the colonists Indian land. He was the first settler to try to understand the Indians (and to study their language). He baffled his contemporaries by claiming that their religion should be tolerated (even though it was demonically false). Williams's ideas were tolerated while he lived in less populous Plymouth, but when he moved to Salem in 1633, he came under new scrutiny. The colony's leaders decided that his influence was subversive, and they prepared to send him back to England. Williams fled south and formed a new settlement in Rhode Island, where liberty of conscience was explicitly protected. In 1643, Williams returned to England to secure a charter for the new colony. As we shall see shortly, it was while he was back in England that he wrote the most complete advocacy of religious liberty to that point.

A few years later, Massachusetts faced another internal critic. Anne Hutchinson established a religious discussion group that began to focus on the relationship between grace and works. If God's grace was absolutely freely bestowed, why did preachers put so much emphasis on the moral law? It was a classic conundrum of Puritan theology: How could the antinomian spirit that Luther rediscovered in Paul be reconciled with a rule-based religious culture? Hutchinson was vilified for raising this intensely awkward issue and accused of undermining the theopolitical order, as Williams had been. Her suspicion of legalism was indeed closely related to his critique, for the close unity of church and state relied on the church's authority to mediate moral law. She was banished from Massachusetts in 1638, and soon thereafter was killed in an Indian attack.

The English Revolution

Charles I avoided calling a parliament for over a decade, knowing that it would be full of anti-Laudian clamor. He finally called a parliament in 1640, and it demanded impossible U-turns from him. The following year news of an Irish uprising led to a new level of Puritan militancy: the king could not keep England safe from popery, so parliament must. The decisive ingredient in parliament's defiance was Calvinist zeal, but as the conflict progressed, it became clear that a more liberal Protestant idealism was also present. Among the parliamentary rebels were many who hated the return of pompous bishops to local politics, but they had no clear desire for an alternative religious system. They basically wanted a Protestant established church that was tolerant. Because the actual established church was failing to be Protestant and tolerant, they felt obliged to reject its authority. In doing so, some of them began to question the whole ideology of an established church quashing dissent. This ideology now seemed outdated, because dissent had reached a tipping point, such that toleration seemed a surer path to peace and order.

So "Puritanism" should not be seen as a unified movement of illiberal, fun-banning Calvinism. The odd fact is that, within a generally intolerant movement that was pushing to be the new theocracy, there arose an unprecedentedly liberal movement that desired a new level of toleration. (This complexity remains generally overlooked, even after many decades of scholarly discussion about the nature of Puritanism. Most historians still seem to echo the traditional Tory view that Puritanism is defined by narrow religious extremism, and they fail to pay "liberal Puritanism" proper attention.)[3] Robert Greville, Lord Brooke

---

3. *The Cambridge Companion to Puritanism,* ed. John Coffey and Paul C. H. Lim (Cambridge, UK: Cambridge University Press, 2008) is, of course, mightily scholarly, but none of its contributors foregrounds this split within "Puritanism."

was one of these liberal Puritans. In an essay published in 1641, he argued that, by seeking to impose highly debatable doctrines on everyone, the bishops were creating disorder. The best hope for an orderly society was to allow various sectarian churches to exist. This need not lead to anarchy, for all churches would have to respect secular law: "I would gladly be shewed by reason, what there is in church government, why it may not derive itself into several corporations . . . still subscribing to those things which are left by Christ to the civil government, or monarchical power."[4] Previous attacks on the bishops had come from fiery preachers and pamphleteers, who had little interest in the constitution. Now a ruling-class Englishman was explicitly questioning the principle of established religion. The following year, Brooke was killed in battle. Had he lived, his intellectual leadership might have steadied the revolution. But his example was followed by other aristocratic radicals, including Oliver St. John and Sir Henry Vane.

Calvinist Presbyterianism had been dreaming of power for decades, and it was not going to be deflected by a new vogue for toleration. In 1643, with the old church abolished and the war half-won, a new religious authority was founded: the Westminster Assembly. It was strongly Calvinist; indeed, Scottish Calvinists came south to draw up a confession that retains wide respect among the Reformed churches today. Congregationalists, or "Independents," objected: they argued that congregations should be free from any centrally imposed orthodoxy, and thus did they advocate a degree of toleration. The Presbyterians successfully excluded the Independents, and it seemed that England was following Scotland. But the following year, this new religious order was shaken by a remarkable outpouring of objection. One can even make a case for calling 1644 the turning point of modern Christian and political history. For it was in that year that the strange new idea that a state did not need to uphold an official religious orthodoxy was suddenly trumpeted by many serious thinkers. The end of Christendom was announced.

4. Lord Brooke, *A Discourse Opening the Nature of That Episcopacie, Which is Exercised in England,* quoted in William Haller, *The Rise of Puritanism* (New York: Harper, 1957), p. 336.

One of the first anti-Presbyterian pamphlets came from William Walwyn, a London merchant and humanist. The new clericalism of the Presbyterians, he said, is "not so garish outwardly as the bishops, but is altogether as imperious and awful over men." All highly organized religion is suspect — a bid for power. The conservatives claim that religious variety leads to chaos, but in fact, he wrote, various Protestant sects can happily coexist: look at Holland, where they united against Spanish tyranny. Indeed, had not the English Baptists just proved their loyalty to Parliament?[5] The war shows a pluralist nation to be possible: it is not a dreamy theory but a new political fact. The following year, Walwyn joined two radical army leaders, John Lilburne and Richard Overton, in a new movement, the Levellers. They called for full religious liberty, and also for the expansion of democracy.

London's best-known radical minister was John Goodwin. He was a key spokesman for the new non-Calvinist party, the Independents, which led to his ejection from his parish in 1645. The essence of this movement, he explained, is that "it admitteth not of human prudence in church government. For the Church is a spiritual building, framed of such lively stones as are not of this world. . . ." A highly organized church will interfere with politics: "The bishops and presbyters, by their church policy, stand competitors with the magistrate." The war was caused by bishops "assuming to themselves that power which Christ never gave them, to wit, of compelling men to yield obedience to whatever they imposed. And men now are grown more various in their opinions than ever before, and will be as easily persuaded to forsake their meat as to relinquish their tenets. . . . Therefore there is not only a reason, but also a necessity, of toleration."[6] This was a common radical refrain: far from causing civil unrest, toleration has become the only means to civil peace.

Roger Williams was now back from his new colony, in England

5. William Walwyn, *The Compassionate Samaritane,* in David Wootton, ed., *Divine Right and Democracy: An Anthology of Political Writing in Stuart England* (Harmondsworth, UK: Penguin, 1988), pp. 254, 261, 267.

6. John Goodwin, *Independency God's Verity,* in A. S. P. Woodhouse, ed., *Puritanism and Liberty: Being the Army Debates (1647-49) from the Clarke Manuscript* (London: Dent, 1986), p. 186.

seeking a charter for it. He joined the attack with the passion of one who had recently suffered at the Calvinists' hands. His tract, entitled *The Bloudy Tenent of Persecution,* addresses the England and New England situations simultaneously. One of its basic theological principles is the absolute difference between the Old Testament and the New: Moses unified politics and religion, and Jesus reversed this.

> The state of the land of Israel is . . . no pattern nor precedent for any kingdom or civil state in the world to follow. God requireth not an uniformity of religion to be enacted and enforced in any civil state; which enforced uniformity, sooner or later, is the greatest occasion of civil war, ravishing of conscience, persecution of Christ Jesus in his servants, and of the hypocrisy and destruction of millions of souls. . . . An enforced uniformity of religion throughout a nation or civil state confounds the civil and religious, denies the principles of Christianity and civility, and that Jesus Christ is come in the flesh.[7]

The key phrase here is "ravishing of conscience": Willliams sees the sanctity of individual conscience as close to the essence of Christianity. The true church must be composed of people who absolutely freely decide to join it. Politics must assist by getting out of the way. In trying to protect and promote the true religion, politics taints it, makes it untrue. Thus the "unknowing zeale" of Constantine did more damage than Nero ever could.[8] His crucial move is to reimagine the state as concerned only with outward, practical, worldly matters: it keeps the peace, settles disputes, punishes criminals. It is the state in this capacity that Paul urged us to obey in Romans 13. With respect to religion, it must do nothing — beyond ensuring that various churches are allowed to exist. And these churches are entirely voluntary societies: "The church, or company of worshippers, whether true or false, is like unto a body or college of physicians in a city, like unto a

---

7. Roger Williams, *The Bloody Tenent of Persecution,* in A. S. P. Woodhouse, ed., *Puritanism and Liberty,* p. 266.

8. Williams, *The Bloody Tenent,* quoted in Perez Zagorin, *How the Idea of Religious Toleration Came to the West* (Princeton, NJ: Princeton University Press, 2003), p. 203.

corporation, society, or company of East India or Turkey merchants, or any other society or company in London." Such groups may "wholly break up and dissolve into pieces and nothing, and yet the peace of the city not be in the least measure impaired or disturbed. . . . The city was before them, and stands absolute and entire when such a corporation or society is taken down."[9]

Williams drew on his American experience in explaining what religious liberty entails: the state should ensure "that no persons, *Papists, Jewes, Turkes*, or *Indians* be disturbed at their worship (a thing which the very *Indians* abhor to practice towards any)." The state must allow no violation of "Conscience," which is God's "holy Light" in us. This emphasis seems to be influenced by Stoicism, which places great emphasis on being true to oneself, but he adds a decidedly Christian intensity. To interfere with another person's attempt to follow this light is a horrific crime, which he often calls "spiritual and soul rape."[10]

His whole approach to the issue is interestingly poised between deep suspicion of the state and a new kind of faith in the state. He is clearly influenced by the Anabaptist assumption that the state enforces a debased religious uniformity; it is a huge gushing source of false religion. Due to his experience of living in a new mini-state, Williams saw beyond this fatalism. He insists that this flow could be turned off. The state must simply stop corrupting religion; it must become neutral, empty of religious ideology. It must withdraw and simply hold the ring. This need not result in bloody conflict between religious groups, "if Men keep but the bond of Civilitie."[11] There is a hint of proto-Enlightenment trust in natural human goodness. He has a new kind of faith in the possibility of a minimal state that does not seek to unite people in a common ideology but lets them pursue their particular callings in peace. This seems naïve. Does not politics abhor an ideological vacuum? In effect, Williams calls for a new kind of

9. Woodhouse, *Puritanism and Liberty*, p. 268.

10. Williams, *The Bloudy Tenent*, quoted in Thomas N. Corns, "Milton, Roger Williams and the Limits of Toleration," in Achinstein and Sauer, eds., *Milton and Toleration* (Oxford: Oxford University Press, 2007), pp. 77-78, 51, 53.

11. Quoted in Zagorin, *Idea of Religious Toleration*, p. 205.

state, with a new ideology — of antitheocracy and of liberty protection. But he seems wary of placing any positive emphasis on this new phenomenon. All the emphasis is on the individual's freedom from coercion.

Emboldened by these pro-toleration pamphlets, but perhaps unimpressed by their literary expression, the poet John Milton entered the fray. He had already written a series of pamphlets against the bishops, in which he called for a pure, unworldly church. Before the war he had been more interested in poetry than religious politics. Then, while traveling in Italy, he had a glimpse of Rome's authoritarianism, and it sharpened his attachment to the Elizabethan ideal of Protestant liberty. That also led him to see Laudianism as a real threat. What is notable about his early pamphlets is not the attacks on Catholic-style clericalism but the deep, confident patriotism: God has chosen England to inaugurate a new Christian era, a fuller Reformation. At first he was vague about what such reform might entail; maybe the Presbyterians should be given a chance. But when he saw their hostility to free debate, Milton got off the fence and unleashed a uniquely eloquent attack on Calvinist intolerance. *Areopagitica* (1644) is rooted in the issue of freedom of the press, but it moves on to freedom in general. Christians should follow Paul's rejection of legalism, Milton says, and should be open to seemingly immoral forms of culture, as "to the pure, all things are pure." Now that the old religious order has gone, it is time to give serious consideration to various competing ideas, rather than hurriedly seeking shelter behind the new orthodoxy of Presbyterianism. We must develop a new expression of "reformation" rather than rush to accept that of the previous century. If we forget this, "we have looked so long upon the blaze that Zwingli and Calvin have beaconed up to us, that we are stark blind." It is rare for radical Protestants to dare call these great Reformers' authority into question in this way, but Milton is, of course, correct that religious liberty is a new concern that changes the rules of religious reform. He explains that the English have a special role to play in this new phase of reform: "God is decreeing [us] to begin some new and great period in his Church, even to the reforming of Reformation itself. What does he then but reveal himself to his servants, and as his manner is, first to his Englishmen?"[12] The phrase "reforming of Reformation" normally meant the introduction of a fuller Calvinism to the English Church. Milton, by contrast, is announcing a change of direction — toward liberty. Crucially, he seeks to marshal the spirit of Elizabethan Protestant patriotism so as to fuel this new phase of reformation.

This is what makes him a more substantial figure than Williams, Goodwin, or anyone else: his understanding that liberty must become a *positive* national ideology. Isaiah Berlin's famous distinction between negative and positive liberty is already relevant. The other radicals put the emphasis on a form of negative freedom: the state must stop imposing a flawed orthodoxy and allow people to worship freely. Milton intuits that the transformation of theopolitics requires that the state not just withdraw, but learn to play a new positive role. It needs to promote a new ideology of liberty. The true cause is not complete toleration but an inversion of the state's religious role. Instead of imposing religious uniformity, it must defend religious liberty. But it must do so, not in the postideological way that Williams seems to commend, but in a quasi-religious way. Only thus will this revolution *work.*

The radical manifestoes of 1644 made the Presbyterian Assembly determined to speed up its crackdown, and it hastily drew up new heresy laws. But Oliver Cromwell, now the leading general, came to the Independents' rescue. After his victory at Naseby in 1645, he promised to defend "tender consciences" from Calvinist ambitions, to protect the right of his ecumenical army to worship as they liked.

Like Milton, Cromwell was influenced by the idealistic and patriotic liberalism that Elizabeth had fostered: England had a special calling to model the compatibility of Protestantism and liberty. (Cromwell was influenced by Raleigh's *History of the World* — "the only book [he] is known to have recommended.")[13] Therefore, his instinct was to build a broad-based army, containing sectarian radical-

---

12. John Milton, *Areopagitica,* in Milton, *Collected Prose Works,* vol. 2 (New Haven: Yale University Press, 1955), pp. 512, 550, 553.

13. Christopher Hill, *The Intellectual Origins of the English Revolution* (Oxford: Oxford University Press, 1965), p. 2.

ism. He welcomed all soldiers who were keenly Protestant, who had "the root of the matter in them," in his phrase. Many were Baptists, which movement had been growing rapidly but was losing coherence, being split between those sympathetic to predestination ("Particular Baptists") and those hostile to it ("General Baptists"). His army was a microcosm of the state that could be, proof that different types of Protestants could unite in a common political cause. Most of his fellow generals were wary of this experimental liberalism; they felt he was playing with fire — and they had a point. But reformist preachers and thinkers were reassured by his army's steady rise.

Much of the army was sympathetic to the ambitious new political force, the Levellers, who called for a clear commitment to the ending of establishment by means of the abolition of tithes, and also for a charter ensuring the rights of ordinary people, and for democratic reform, including a wider franchise and salaried members of parliament. The army was divided over whether to pursue this democratic agenda, which threatened to lead to communist activism, as was briefly practiced by a dubious new sect, the Diggers.[14] The issue was debated in 1647 at a meeting in St. Mary's Church in Putney. Cromwell persuaded his colleagues that this wider agenda had to be shelved if the revolution were to stand a chance. However, he subsequently showed less patience: when the movement resurfaced two years later, he ordered the execution of some ringleaders. This intransigence damns Cromwell in the eyes of some, but it is facile to blame him for suppressing democratic ideas that England continued to resist for about two hundred years. It was hard enough trying to run a limited revolution, focused on religious liberty, without a new dimension opening up.

But how committed was Cromwell to religious liberty? In theory he agreed that a revolution in toleration was necessary. But should everything be permitted, even such heresies as Trinity-denying Socinianism, widely seen as a thin cover for atheism? Such questions be-

14. The Diggers had a rationalist edge: according to their leader, Gerald Winstanley, "the power of Christ" in us "judges all things according to the law of equity and reason" (Andrew Bradstock, *Radical Religion in Cromwell's England* [London: SCM, 2011], p. 58).

came moot in the Whitehall debates of December 1648: these detailed discussions of the relationship between Christianity and state power are remarkable evidence of the intellectual openness of the liberal Puritans. But there was a danger that such discussions would be merely academic. At this point the revolution looked like it was petering out; the Presbyterians in parliament were seeking peace with the defeated Charles, and royalism was rearing its head again. Cromwell launched a coup and expelled his opponents from parliament. He was determined that seven years of bloodshed should not be for nothing, that a new order should be attempted. The revolution could only regain momentum by removing the king, whose trial was set in motion. So began the paradox of the Cromwellian regime: it used tyrannical means to attempt a new era of toleration. The shocking violence of regicide was the only way to keep this experiment moving. So now the ideal of religious liberty had royal blood on its hands. Some prominent liberal Puritans now lost faith in Cromwell, accusing him of tyrannical egotism.

The Republic

The postregicide parliament had to decide what to do with the established church. Though episcopacy was abolished, the established church still stood — more or less. It was a shell that the Presbyterians had tried to occupy, and they still demanded the right to do so. Independency was now the officially favored form of religion, a fairly amorphous liberal Protestantism. Its radical wing wanted the established church to be decisively dismantled, but this was anathema to conservatives. Moderate Independency wanted an established church, but without either bishops or Calvinist ideologues. Of course, moderation prevailed. Establishment was retained but weakened: other Protestant worship was tolerated, within limits; sectarian radical groups were outlawed. To radicals such as Williams, Milton, and Vane, this was worryingly incomplete. They insisted that the state should completely stop worrying about "heresy" — unless it was politically subversive.

When Cromwell became head of state in 1653, assuming the title "Protector," he tried to renew parliament's commitment to religious liberty. In a debate the previous year he had declared, in opposition to a narrow Puritan colleague: "I had rather that Mahometanism were permitted amongst us than that one of God's children should be persecuted."[15] His new constitution promised liberty to "all who profess Faith in God by Jesus Christ," though this was "not extended to popery, prelacy, or [those who practice] licentiousness." He wanted toleration extended to all Protestants (except episcopal Anglicans), including even Trinity-deniers. He was adamant that religious persecution was a thing of the past; indeed, no heretics were executed during his reign. (In 1654 he managed to protect the Socinian philosopher John Biddle from Calvinist members of parliament, who were baying for his blood.) Did he also want the complete revolution in toleration that the radicals had proposed, a revolution that would do away with the established church altogether? It seems that he had pledged support for this vision, but once in power he sided with moderate Independency, and he called for the church to be reformed rather than dismantled. He played an active role in appointing and funding ministers, and in developing a new form of parochial quality control.

Cromwell's semiliberalism alarmed the Presbyterians, who remained a strong force in parliament. Their fear of the sectarians was undiminished. The Quakers had emerged alongside the Baptists and Congregationalists, and they were spreading fast. This movement combined vagueness with huge energy. Its theology was more liberal than that of the Baptists: for example, the inner Spirit had replaced the Bible. It had some of the political energy of the forbidden Leveller movement, but it lacked most of the latter's concrete demands. Yet its threat to the social order was real: it encouraged low-born people to defy their masters and form completely new types of social structure. Alarmingly, women were often allowed leadership roles. They also pursued a policy of direct action against the established church, for

---

15. Quoted in John Coffey, *Persecution and Toleration in Protestant England, 1558-1689* (London: Longman, 2000), p. 148.

example, heckling ministers and agitating against tithes. To the Presbyterians, these radicals were spreading poison, destroying the possibility of an orderly new church. Cromwell could not entirely dismiss such fears.

Another notable sign of Cromwell's liberalism came in 1655, when John Dury persuaded him to hold a conference discussing the readmission of Jews to England, nearly four centuries after their expulsion by Edward I. Cromwell made no official decree, but from that point on, London's Jewish community began to grow, led by Israel ben Manasseh.

John Milton had defended the regicide, and he was rewarded with a government job that involved writing official tracts in defense of the Commonwealth. He vigorously defended republicanism on Christian grounds, arguing that the new regime was opening a bold new chapter in Christian liberty. Already in *Areopagitica,* he had asserted a strong link between Pauline freedom and full toleration. He continued to ponder this. The gospel is "God's proclamation of our freedom," he wrote in 1651: "I do not speak of inward freedom only and omit political freedom. . . . Christ put our political freedom on a firm foundation."[16] There is tacit criticism of Luther here, whose loud rhetoric of freedom did not lead to advocacy of religious liberty. In a later tract he expanded on this. God, through Jesus Christ, frees us from religious legalism (from the very law he himself had earlier issued). It can hardly be his will that the state steps in and nullifies this breakthrough — by imposing religious laws on us. "As if God of his special grace in the Gospel had to this end freed us from his own commandments in these things, that our freedom should subject us to a more grievous yoke, the commandments of men!" Politicians must "meddle not rashly with Christian liberty, the birthright and outward testimony of our adoption."[17] In other words, the state has no right to try to impose any account of orthodoxy on the nation; its sacred duty is to defend liberty.

16. Milton, *A Defence of the People of England,* trans. Donald C. Mackenzie, in *Collected Prose Works,* vol. 4, p. 317.

17. Milton, "Of Civil Power in Ecclesiastical Causes," in Woodhouse, *Puritanism and Liberty,* pp. 227, 228.

A few years later, Milton wrote another tract defending the revolution so far, which includes some rather anxious advice to Cromwell to be bolder in separating church and state. This clear statement of principle is worth quoting:

> I would have you leave the church to the church and shrewdly relieve yourself and the government of half your burden (one that is at the same time completely alien to you), and not permit two powers, utterly diverse, the civil and the ecclesiastical, to make harlots of each other and while appearing to strengthen, by their mingled and spurious riches, actually to undermine and at length destroy each other. I would have you remove all power from the church (but power will never be absent so long as money, the poison of the church, the quinsy of truth, extorted by force even from those who are unwilling, remains the price of preaching of the Gospel).[18]

After Cromwell's death, Milton urged parliament to revive the cause of Christian liberty. In one tract he argued that Christianity is corrupted by compulsion: if a state tries to enforce the gospel, it falsifies the gospel. Of course, the Catholic ruler corrupts the gospel in this way. What is more scandalous is the way in which "the forcing protestant" imitates him: "[T]he more he professes to be a true protestant, the more he has to answer for his persecuting than a papist." It is a failure of trust in Christ to think that the gospel will wither away "unless it be enacted and settled, as they call it, by the state, a statute or a statereligion." Those who advocate a unity of church and state are reverting to the Old Testament model: "If church and state shall be made one flesh again as under the law, let it be withal considered, that God who then joined them hath now severed them." To rejoin them after their New Testament separation would be "presumptuous fornication."[19]

Another of Milton's tracts attacks a state-funded priesthood. While the practice persists, "I dare affirm that no model whatsoever

---

18. Milton, "Of Civil Power," p. 678.
19. Milton, *A Treatise of Civil Power in Ecclesiastical Causes*, in *Collected Prose Works*, vol. 7, pp. 256, 259, 261.

of a commonwealth will prove successful or undisturbed." The rot began with Constantine, "who out of his zeal thinking he could be never too liberally a nursing father of the church, might be not unfitly said to have . . . choked it in the nursing." The theologians of this era made Christianity into a worldly religion, "whereby thinking to gain all, they lost all: and instead of winning Jews and pagans to be Christians, by too much condescending they turned Christians into Jews and pagans." There is obviously no biblical warrant for the funding of clergy by the tithe system. The true church cannot be tied to a political territory in this way, for it consists "of many particular churches complete in themselves; gathered . . . by free consent." If the state controls religion, "how can any Christian object it to a Turk, that his religion stands by force only; and not justly fear from him this reply, yours by both force and money in the judgement of your own preachers? This is that which makes atheists in the land . . . : not the want of maintenance or preachers, as they allege, but the many hirelings and cheaters that have the gospel in their hands."[20] Milton thus predicts an era in which liberal opinion turns away from religion — through the dislike of a powerful church.

There is a kind of tragic nobility in Milton's persistent radicalism. The revolution had become a disappointing compromise with the old religious order, and its legitimacy was threadbare. But, even in its failure, it contained this sacred new idea of the separation of church and state. In reality, the vast majority of the English people had no sympathy with this idea; rather, they saw it as intensely dangerous, the source of chaos. The tragedy of the English revolution is that a new form of Christianity emerged amid chaos, and it was promptly buried. This new form of Christianity declared that full-scale reform entailed a commitment to freedom from established religion and thus a commitment to building a new kind of state. It announced that it is the Christian's duty to reform politics in the direction that we call "secular-liberal." This distinct new fusion of religion and politics failed to become a coherent, stable new force. This is

---

20. Milton, *Considerations Touching the Likeliest Means to Remove Hirelings out of the Church*, in *Collected Prose Works*, vol. 7, pp. 275, 279, 294, 293, 319.

principally because it was so closely associated with a political revolution that proved an unpopular failure. In a sense, the English have never recovered from this: they still see fully liberal Christianity (which entails the separation of church and state) as a dangerous, disorderly, ungodly idea.

Many recent commentators see Milton's commitment to toleration as more limited than that of other radical thinkers of the period, because of his insistence on the intolerability of Roman Catholicism. Perez Zagorin says: "His refusal to extend freedom to Catholicism, an oppressed religion in England, is explained by his Puritan background and the legacy of religious hatreds left by the Reformation conflict from which he was unable to emancipate his mind."[21] As I see it, his position on Catholicism was determined by his commitment to positive rather than negative liberty. Liberty had to become a new positive ideology, uniting the vast majority of the nation. It seemed to him that this project would be disabled by the presence of a large minority that lacked sympathy with it. To complain of Milton's anti-Catholicism is heedless of the political context. Liberty could not be extended to those who threatened to bring down the republic. This is perfectly in keeping with the practical assumptions of today: terrorists are not at liberty to plot. During the Interregnum, Catholics and monarchical Anglicans were justifiably seen as a political threat. Milton agreed that practicing Jews should be allowed back into the country, though he did not admire their religion; but they were politically unthreatening and hence tolerable. His position was surely consistent enough: religious liberty should not be extended to the avowed enemies of religious liberty, which were necessarily political as well as religious forces.

Restoration

Less than two years after Cromwell's death, the republic collapsed. In 1660, Charles II was invited back. There were scenes of mass rejoicing; the majority yearned for order, and they believed that only a mon-

---

21. Zagorin, *Idea of Religious Toleration*, p. 224.

arch could bring it. There was a violent reaction against the sectarian spirit. Puritanism in all its forms was suspect, seen as incompatible with national order. The Tudor and Stuart ideology was revived: England's Protestantism had to be stabilized by the strong return of the monarch-topped established church. Before his return, Charles II had promised to grant "a Liberty to tender Consciences." It turned out to be an empty promise. Dissenters were penalized under a new series of laws known as the Clarendon Code, and thousands of dissenting clergy were forced out. There were fines for attending nonconformist meetings, or "conventicles." Dissenters were prosecuted under the same laws used against Roman Catholic recusants: a statement that Protestant dissent was viewed as political sedition. This was unfair to the largest group of dissenters, the Presbyterians, who were at pains to show loyalty to the new regime and who hoped to be included in a new more comprehensive church. The charge of sedition had more substance with regard to the Quakers, who refused to compromise over the crucial issue of tithes. They were particularly harshly treated. According to one historian, "this was a persecution of Protestants by Protestants unique in Europe in its intensity and bitterness: another major question-mark against the complacent English boast of a national history of tolerance."[22] As another historian says, "Restoration England was a persecuting society."[23]

The Church of England had always been "intolerant," in common with every other form of official, established religion. But when it was restored to power, it was explicitly refounded on the denial of religious liberty. The nation had made a partial and awkward move in the direction of pluralism, and the church very decidedly quashed it and demonized it. But order had to be restored — by whatever means necessary, one might say. This was said at the time by Anglican apologists such as Edward Stillingfleet: toleration would lead to chaos, and then the stronger medicine of Rome might seem necessary. A "Wilderness

22. Diarmaid MacCulloch, *Reformation: Europe's House Divided* (London: Allen Lane, 2003), p. 531.
23. Mark Goldie, "The Theory of Religious Intolerance in Restoration England," in W. J. Sheils, ed., *Persecution and Toleration* (Oxford: Oxford University Press, 1984), pp. 331-68, esp. p. 331.

of Confusion" would lead to the "Abysse of Popery."[24] So the Anglican monopoly was refounded on the idea that a strong state-church was a necessary prophylactic against the worse tyranny of Rome. Indeed, the state-church could be seen as the expression of true, orderly *liberty*.

Like his father, Charles II wanted to augment the prestige of the royalty by imitating the lavish French model. This, of course, provoked Protestant anger, especially since he lacked his father's ascetic streak, having taken a series of Catholic mistresses. A moderate Protestant opposition emerged: the Whigs. They accepted the necessity of an established church — for the sake of the exclusion of Catholicism — but argued that Protestant dissenters were tolerable. (Many Whig members of parliament were dissenters who made themselves eligible for office via an annual attendance at the established church for the Eucharist.) To their alarm, the monarchy's gravitation toward Catholicism intensified. Charles seemed to be the vassal of Louis XIV; indeed, he was hugely indebted to the latter financially. And his brother James, heir to the throne, was openly Roman Catholic. In 1678 the Whigs tried to demand James's exclusion from the succession. This "Exclusion Crisis" resembled the early stages of the civil war: a lobby in parliament was determined to curb the will of the king. This challenge failed, and a Tory propaganda drive was successful in demonizing Protestant dissenters. They were witch-hunted and driven from their political posts. The laws against them were enforced with new vigor, leading to mass imprisonments and mass fatalities due to the grim conditions in the prisons. In response, the defeated Whigs flirted with coup plots, and some wrote fresh formulations of Whig theory: Algernon Sidney, for example, wrote his *Discourses,* and Locke began his major works.

The essence of the Whig case was that freedom depended on Protestantism. As the Earl of Shaftesbury put it in 1679, "Popery and slavery, like two little sisters, go hand in hand."[25] He warned that the partial toleration that existed in Catholic France was frail, and he was soon proved right. In 1685, Louis XIV revoked the Edict of Nantes, which had

---

24. Quoted in Coffey, *Persecution and Toleration,* p. 35.

25. Quoted in John Marshall, *John Locke, Toleration and Early Enlightenment Culture* (Cambridge, UK: Cambridge University Press, 2006), p. 31.

protected Protestant rights, and forced thousands of Huguenots into exile. (The Catholic Duke of Savoy followed suit and resumed persecution of the Waldensian Protestants.) This seemed proof that Catholic rulers were not to be trusted. England's hard-won Protestant identity would surely not survive a Catholic monarch in league with France.

But what was the logic of Protestantism's link to liberty? What kind of liberal Protestantism did the Whigs advocate? They fudged the issue, for they saw a clear and consistent liberalism that questioned the established church (and thus the monarchy) as subversive. The Whigs attacked Roman Catholicism with a vitriol that they dared not direct at the established church.

When James did succeed his brother Charles in 1685, England had its first Catholic monarch since Bloody Mary. Tory Anglicans had long argued that James's Catholicism was immaterial, that he would uphold the established church — and thus English liberty. But James could not keep his religion out of the picture. He pressed for the laws against Catholic recusancy to be relaxed; he even tried to form an unlikely alliance with dissenting leaders, promising them greater toleration if they backed his plans. "Toleration" now became rather paradoxical: a Catholic king was championing it as a cynical means toward the restoration of Catholicism, and thus toward the demise of toleration in the long term. When James's wife became pregnant, the Whigs plotted a Dutch takeover; when the child was born, the Dutch monarch, William of Orange, launched an invasion. He landed in Devon in November 1688, quickly gained support from the people, and James fled. Within a few months William was offered the crown.

The ensuing Glorious Revolution instituted a limited — or constitutional — monarchy. The possibility of a return to Catholic absolutism was blocked. It brought a new level of toleration for Protestant dissenters; of course, the Anglican establishment would not allow this to go too far. In a sense, the church was now supreme over the monarch: a new law decreed that the king and his wife had to be Protestants, that is, in order to be the heads of the (established) church. This "revolution" not only confirmed the Church of England's established status but put it on a stronger footing. Its dependence on a potentially Catholic-absolutist monarchy had jeopardized it; indeed, it was temporarily fatal. So England was now officially a nation of "liberty," but only in the sense that Catholic absolutism was made impossible and parliament's role in government was assured. We should not dismiss this as negligible: on this basis, England (soon Britain) became freer than any other major state. In the long run, however, this achievement made further reform very difficult. It enshrined the established church as a bulwark of liberty, and it justified the exclusion of dissenters — and Jews — from public office. So the Glorious Revolution allowed England to see itself as a nation of liberty, even though it had opted for a far more limited version of liberty than was glimpsed by the radical Puritans. And it allowed the established church to remain in place, with a new aura of modernity.

Hobbes and Locke

In his *Leviathan* (1651), Thomas Hobbes had launched a new scientific approach to politics — and a new kind of secular discourse. But his thought was not quite in tune with that of the liberal Puritans. In fact, it was largely a reaction against it. His basic thesis was that society is based on the idea of voluntary submission to sovereign power. Individuals are naturally at war with each other, until a strong ruler imposes order. Unless this power is single and unrivaled, the state will fall into the chaos of civil war. Because unitary power brings peace, and people want peace, its legitimacy can be understood as rooted in a primal contract. Crucially, religion must not disrupt civil order by setting up a rival power base. Therefore, the sovereign must control it — absolutely. He, rather than an independent church, must be seen as God's true prophet, and as the true judge of heresy. Hobbes thus applauds the Tudor "Exorcism" of Rome, "the Kingdome of Fairies."[26] His thought develops Luther's political theology (and that of Marsiglio) and provides a fuller theoretical basis for it. Crucially, however, his theoretical basis is at odds with Luther — and with the

---

26. Thomas Hobbes, *Leviathan,* ed. C. B. Macpherson (Harmondsworth: Penguin, 1978), 3.36, p. 469; 3.42, p. 605; 4.47, p. 714.

liberal Puritans — for it rejects a religious understanding of history. Hobbes exalts social order above religious truth; he favors whatever form of religion, or theopolitics, can keep the peace.

Hobbes, of course, was responding to the civil war. Why, according to Hobbes, did Anglican order fail? Because it failed to uphold its idea of establishment with full logical rigor. The principle of royal supremacy, and Hooker's unity of church and commonwealth, should have handed the sovereign a monopoly of power. But in practice the church retained some degree of separate existence; and this had grown under Charles I and Laud. The church started pursuing a divisive agenda, which a fully established church would never do. The Puritans were partly justified in resisting it. But their wider vision was also divisive — and muddled. The conservative Puritans' attempt to impose godly order would lead to endless friction; the liberal Puritans' idea of a new kind of tolerant state, on the other hand, was naïve, because some form of religion would dominate and cause division. Hobbes rightly judged that Cromwell's emerging regime was an unstable mix of these two impulses.

Hobbes's approach presents religion as intrinsically problematic: it threatens the peace-bringing monopoly of power. Even an established religion might develop in a divisive, dogmatic direction. The solution is the development of the established religion in a rationalist direction. This will naturally occur, Hobbes believed, as the hold of clericalist superstition weakens. For why should it be in the ruler's interest to foster credulity and enthusiasm, which is likely to cause civil unrest? So Hobbes wants a more fully nationalized and secularized established church, which imposes a very minimalist — an almost postclericalist — version of Anglicanism. This will lead to de facto religious toleration, which Hobbes admits is a good aim. At the end of *Leviathan* he seems to commend the virtual disestablishment of religion that the Glorious Revolution brought: "And so we are reduced to the independency of the primitive Christians, to follow Paul, or Cephas, or Apollos, every man as he liketh best. Which, if it be without contention . . . is perhaps the best."[27] But he insists that toler-

---

27. Hobbes, *Leviathan*, p. 741.

ation can only come in by the back door. Milton's vision of a state that rejects establishment and protects religious liberty cannot work. For religion abhors a vacuum, and it is an intrinsically power-seeking thing. A benign establishment must quash all power-seeking religious rivals. Only then is diversity possible — among forms of religion that have been politically neutered.

In a sense, this is close to Milton's vision. Though Milton rejects the establishment of any church, he might be seen as calling for a new kind of establishment: it would be the establishment of a new ideology, possibly called "Protestant liberalism," that must keep traditional forms of religious authority at bay via the government's stopping any religious institution from gaining political power. The difference is that Hobbes does not believe that this can be done: according to him, only an old-fashioned religious hegemony can keep order. Rather paradoxically, Milton's fuller belief in the separation of church and state is rooted in his sincere Christianity: that is, a broad, benign established church is not a sensible means to an end, for it falsifies the gospel.

Though Hobbes's religious skepticism was clear enough, his theory became central to the post-Restoration debate about the limitation of royal power. His Tory readers adapted his theory for the defense of royal absolutism: that is, the king should not concede power to parliament, nor should the church tolerate dissenters, for only a monopoly of power can secure peace.

John Locke was an academic from Oxford who became increasingly involved in Whig politics. In his first essay on toleration (1660) he expressed opposition to the idea. A policy of toleration would lead to anarchy, for it would encourage people and groups to demand exemptions from the law on grounds that they called religious — but were really self-interested. Why not claim that one's religion prevents one from paying taxes? And political rebellions will naturally claim to arise from religious principle: "None ever went about to ruin the state but with pretence to build a temple."[28] Uniformity is a necessary tool of the state.

---

28. Locke, "The First Tract on Government," in Mark Goldie, ed., *Political Essays* (New York: Cambridge University Press, 1997), p. 41.

Locke changed his mind, but he never really moved away from a spirit of Hobbesian pragmatism. He came to feel that toleration was a more effective means to social order. In 1665 he spent some time in Cleves in the Rhineland, an area that enjoyed a relatively high degree of toleration. He saw that it need not lead to disorder, but he still wondered whether it gave too much power to subversive minorities. He was soon drawn into liberal politics by his patron, the Earl of Shaftesbury, and he was radicalized by the events of the 1680s: the Tory reaction against reform, which led to his own exile in the Netherlands, and France's return to persecution in 1685. He saw an urgent need to rally English Protestantism against the threat of tyrannical Catholicism. These events provoked him to write his *Two Treatises of Government,* which followed Hobbes's contractual theory of the state's legitimacy but injected new liberal optimism into it. The social contract was not a response to humankind's natural violence; it was a development of humankind's natural goodness and rationality. Political society develops because people need laws — primarily in order to defend their property — and they give their consent to the creation of a new body, the state. Locke places far more emphasis than did Hobbes on the role of popular consent. The authority of the state, he believed, is absolutely dependent on the decision of the people. The people retain the right to decide how they are ruled; for example, they can choose to replace absolutism with mixed government, in which a parliament limits royal power. Therefore, no particular form of government has a divine warrant, because sovereignty belongs to the people, who have the right to rethink what they wish to.

In the same year, 1689, Locke published his *Letter Concerning Toleration.* It begins with the claim that toleration is "the principal mark of the true church."[29] To support this, he offers an account of the primitive church, obedient to Jesus' peaceful message. But human violence has colonized religion: the state claims that it must per-

29. Locke, *A Letter Concerning Toleration,* in *Locke on Toleration,* ed. Richard Vernon, trans. Michael Silverthorne (Cambridge, UK: Cambridge University Press, 2010), p. 3. Hereafter, page references to this work appear in parentheses in the text.

secute heretics in order to keep order; conversely, subversives claim religious grounds for their subversion.

> In order to avoid these things, I believe that we must above all distinguish between religious and political matters, and properly define the boundary between church and commonwealth. Until this is done, no limit can be put to the disputes between those who have, or affect to have, a zeal for the salvation of souls and those who have a real or affected concern for the safety of the commonwealth. (p. 6)

He proceeds to define the state in secular terms: it is "an association of people constituted solely for the purpose of preserving and promoting civil goods" (p. 6). And a church is "a free association of people coming together of their own accord to offer public worship to God in a manner which they believe will be acceptable to the Deity for the salvation of their souls" (p. 9). (As we have seen, Roger Williams said almost exactly that forty years earlier.) A church will have some internally binding rules, but cannot use force. It can excommunicate members, but this must have no worldly consequences. From this depiction, it seems that a dissenting church is normative and an established church is a mistake. But Locke the pragmatist does not press the point. He saw an established Protestant church as infinitely preferable to a resurgence of Catholicism, and perhaps a necessary bulwark against it.

For Locke, the civil power has no right to ban forms of religion that do no harm, according to an objective political understanding of "harm." The ruler cannot outlaw religious practice or belief that breaks no ordinary law. For example, "If a Catholic believes that what another man would call bread is truly the body of Christ, he does not hurt his neighbor" (p. 31). A religion is only dangerous if its practice entails the breaking of civil laws, or if it entails allegiance to a foreign ruler, as Locke says that Islam does. He implies that Roman Catholicism is also in this category. As the above example shows, he is keen to show that it is only on *political* grounds that Catholicism is intolerable.[30]

---

30. Jeremy Waldron points this out in *God, Locke and Equality: Christian Founda-*

Atheists, however, are explicitly beyond the pale: their rejection of an afterlife means that they cannot be trusted to abide by moral norms; nor can they swear trustworthy oaths. (This is at odds with Locke's general theory, that it is the breaking of secular law, rather than the holding of wrong beliefs, that makes one intolerable. His anti-atheist rigor is perhaps an attempt to reassure moderately conservative readers that he himself is not a dangerous radical.)

Locke builds on the common ground between Roger Williams and Hobbes: the state is really just a machine for the meeting of material needs. I suggest that this is a falsely scientific view of the state, abstracted from history. In reality, the state cannot be defined in such minimalist terms; it is also an imagined community, an inhabited narrative. Milton understood this. His account of the state sets it in a religious narrative: it is not a blank space, but is the arena of divine providence. A new era of reformation happens by means of the state that dares to reject theocracy. The new kind of state belongs to a positive religious ideology. Locke envisions it in terms of a reductionist, postmythological theory. What the state "really" is, once myths are removed, is the arena of rational self-interest. Both Milton and Locke advocate a secular state — in the sense of a state free of powerful religious institutions — but there is a gulf between the two discourses of secularism.

Locke renewed the cause of toleration, which had been set back by its association with republicanism. He was influential in claiming the rational high ground for it. But his advocacy changed the cause, weakening its affinity with a certain form of religion. This entailed a certain dishonesty. To present toleration as natural, rational, and enlightened was only possible in a culture that had been influenced by a liberal form of Christianity. Liberal religion must do the heavy lifting before toleration can meaningfully be called "natural." It was less natural in Spain or Persia. In a recent study of Locke's *Letter,* John Perry draws attention to this: Locke must first ensure a "harmonization of loyalties," meaning that the dominant religious culture must be

---

tions in John Locke's Political Thought (Cambridge, UK: Cambridge University Press, 2002), p. 221.

shown that there is no conflict between its religious presuppositions and toleration.[31] Only then can he show that his distinguishing of religion and politics works. This particular harmonization of loyalties, which reconciles Christianity and the tolerant state, is dependent on the rising presence of liberal Protestant Christianity. It surely follows that, at least in Locke's day, the coherence of liberal theory is dependent on liberal religious culture. A policy of toleration cannot be expected to work if the dominant religious culture demands state-backed uniformity. So Locke built on the liberal Protestant climate and identified it with political rationality. He thereby sought to lure, or cajole, conservative religion into reforming by showing that the rational state requires such reform. In other words, his account of the state as a secular phenomenon has religious roots that it downplays.

Locke's defense of toleration is generally seen as an advance on Milton's. This is largely due to its more secular character: it separates toleration from any particular religious position. It is the civilized duty of all, the proper modern attitude, whether one is Anglican, Catholic, or Calvinist. This enlightened view of the tolerant state is available to all theists. In effect, Locke announces a new separation of religion and politics. Good politics only needs the vaguest kind of religious basis: reasonable theism. We must make liberalism into a project that all forms of religion can sign up for. Its link with one particular religious vision must be broken. Locke thus moves away from Milton's assumption that a culture of political liberty flows from true Protestantism, from a passionately partisan interpretation of the gospel. Milton was offering a new fusion of religion and politics: *this* form of Christianity commits one to the liberal state. Anglicanism, Catholicism, and Calvinism do not have this intrinsic desire for liberty. They can only advocate toleration in a lesser sense, because it is external to their own inner logic. Only enlightened Protestants see religious liberty as a sacred cause. In a sense, the liberal state is their alternative to the sacred space of the church. Locke lacks this synthetic passion, this sense that the right political attitude comes out of the right theology.

31. John Perry, *The Pretenses of Loyalty: Locke, Toleration, and American Political Theology* (Oxford: Oxford University Press, 2011).

Locke's reformism was in tune with the spirit of the age. The Toleration Act of 1689 allowed dissenters to worship in licensed premises. But there were still major restrictions on dissenters: most areas of educational and professional life were closed to them by the Test and Corporation Acts, and marriage remained an Anglican monopoly. Despite much rhetoric about enlightened toleration, these restrictions did not melt away in a hurry, as we shall see.

Conclusion

Let's sum up the argument of these first two chapters. The main Reformers were not interested in fostering toleration, but in creating new forms of religious uniformity. There was a frail dissenting movement, but it only developed a radical new theopolitics in the mid-seventeenth century. It adapted the Anabaptist rejection of Constantinianism, the idea of an officially imposed church. It crucially removed the fatalistic element in Anabaptism and suggested that the state stop imposing one form of religion; rather, it should allow full freedom. For the most part, this vision was naively minimalist: it called for a postideological state. Milton, however, saw the need for a new kind of ideology. This new kind of state had to be made heroic, for which he borrowed the language of Roman republicanism (e.g., his sonnet to Henry Vane, whom he praised for knowing how to distinguish between "[b]oth spirituall powre & civill"). This is a vision of the gospel purified from state power — *by state power.*

Can the state that Milton envisioned be called "secular"? This raises a paradox. The state should promote full religious liberty (as far as politics allows), yet its motivation for doing so is decidedly liberal Protestant. Why can't the state simply be neutral, nonreligious, agnostic, secular (in the main contemporary sense of the word)? Milton would have found the question strange. Power is not exercised for no purpose. Rulers bloodily fight for it, as Cromwell did, and they are motivated by some grand religious vision or other. The right vision, which must naturally be shared by the majority of the nation if it is to work, is Protestant republican freedom, which entails religious liberty. So though he firmly called for the separation of church and state, Milton had no conception of nonreligious politics. The secularity of politics must be grounded on the liberal Protestant vision.

Hobbes, meanwhile, developed a supposedly scientific view of the state. Only through its unitary power, in his view, could a more civilized culture potentially emerge. And it would — because the natural rationality of humans would find expression. These two visions permeated Restoration England via underground means (Milton's was dangerously republican, Hobbes's dangerously skeptical, even atheist). Locke combined them, and in a publicly acceptable form.[32] This enabled the emergence of liberalism as an essentially secular and rational project, which proved massively problematic for theology, which was now sidelined — or rather, buried under a new sort of discourse.

So the real shift, between Milton and Locke, is the triumph of universalism and the demise of particularity. For Milton, liberty is rooted in a particular narrative, or myth: Christ brings freedom. Jesus' ancient opposition to Jewish assumptions about politics and law remains the pattern that liberty must follow. Liberty must be rooted in the narrative of obedience to God and personal transformation through Christ. The pursuit of abstract, unrooted liberty is the fate of Satan. Locke retains a role for religion but moves the entire discourse away from narrative particularity. Instead of needing to see liberty with respect to this particular story, we should see it as a natural human phenomenon. Jesus is transformed from the bringer of liberty to the best-known illustration of a universal principle. Suddenly, it is assumed to be *natural* that humans reject theocracy and legalism. It is in the interest of all humans, and so it must be what all naturally gravitate toward, once obstacles are removed. Of course, there is a sort of

32. Mark Lilla is right that Locke developed a liberal version of Hobbes's thesis, but it is too neat to say that Hobbes is the clear originator of the "subsequent consensus . . . around ideas of religious diversity, freedom of conscience, toleration, limited government, and separation of powers — liberal ideas, as they would later be called. Hobbes was no liberal; still, British and American liberalism stayed well within the philosophical orbit that Hobbes had circumscribed" (Lilla, *The Stillborn God: Religion, Politics, and the Modern West* [New York: Knopf, 2007], pp. 218-19). This overestimates abstract philosophy; in reality, Western liberalism owed more to liberal Christians.

universalism intrinsic to Christianity: the good news is for all human-ity. But this comes loose and dominates: if the aptitude for liberty is universal, then does it not make sense to start from that principle and sideline the narrative particularity? This is the great temptation of lib-eral Christianity (to which we shall return in chapter 4).

Why is such particularity necessary? Why can't liberal idealism simply be secularized? This is tricky, paradoxical territory. On a prac-tical level it can and should be secularized, detached from religious reference, for otherwise it privileges a form of religion. But its roots should be remembered (like a math student, it should show its work-ings). For this ideal only makes full sense in the context of a religious narrative. God wills the nation to reject coercive theopolitics and find unity in liberty. Away from this narrative, liberty lacks substance — it is thin. It lacks an account of new, posttheocratic cohesion. It at-tempts to find this in "reason," but this entails theologizing "reason," which leads to problems. Liberty is an ideal, and ideals are rooted in myths. Classical republican thought is no real alternative: it had only a weak idea of liberty, as the temporary absence of tyranny, and it lacked a vision of remaking politics around liberty.

I am suggesting that the liberal state not only has religious roots, as a matter of historical interest, but it can only be renewed by means of them.

THREE

The Sacramental Deficiency

———ᴐⁿᴐ———

H ere's the problem: just as this new, radically pro-toleration form of Protestantism emerges and begins to shape the liberal state, it more or less collapses, or dissolves. We have just seen a crucial instance of this: Milton's radically Christian advocacy of religious liberty is reframed by Locke as an essentially secular-rational project. Why does this happen? Because this emergent liberal Christianity is inadequately rooted in Christian practice. Its rejection of theological traditionalism is excessive. It rejects the major traditional forms of church because of their being implicated in preliberal assumptions; but it fails to see the necessity of the sacramental practices that they sustain. Because it detaches Christianity from its cultic basis, it leads only to an empty, bloodless form of Protestantism.

In order to explore this large issue, we must first look at the problem that sacramentalism posed for Protestantism in general. What I mean by "sacramentalism" is not confined to those rituals that a church calls sacraments; I also mean all the cultural stuff that makes up a religious culture, from a cross worn around the neck to a pilgrimage. What I mean is "the cultural expression of religion."

The Reformers, of course, objected to the culture of medieval Catholicism. They saw idolatry in the Catholic Mass, in the cult of saints, and in much else. Most of them were totally opposed to the use of images in worship. Aversion to images, or iconophobia, is commonly cited as the key cultural difference of Protestantism, but this is too narrow. Iconophobia is part of a wider phenomenon: aversion to the physical expression of religion, to nonverbal ritual performance. I am calling this *sacramentalism,* and the fear of it *sacraphobia.* Thanks to Zwingli and Calvin, the main form of Protestantism was highly sacraphobic. Of course, it did not dispense with ritual altogether. Its veneration of the Word of God produced new forms of ritual. And it managed to decontaminate and salvage the core ritual act, the Eucharist. Its fear of a wider sacramentalism was justified by referring to the Old Testament law against images. But why was it so keen to exhume this law — which is not clearly restated in the New Testament — and to widen its application beyond images to other forms of expression and performance? This theological reformism cannot be separated from a will to *regulate* religion with new rigor, to restrict its anarchic potential. This anarchic potential is present in all nonverbal representation; the meaning of an image or performance is less fixed than the meaning of a sentence.

In its reordering of religion, the main form of Protestantism strongly suppressed the anarchic potential of the visual and the performative. (This tendency was less marked in Lutheranism and in the Anglican Church.) But this suppression was balanced by the conviction that a limited, orderly version of sacramentalism was possible. God ordained a rigidly controlled form of ritual practice; he demanded that the core rite, the Eucharist, be performed in a particular way, that its meaning be understood in a particular way. The nonverbal aspect of the Eucharist had to be subordinated to the verbal aspect. It had to be understood as a demonstration of God's verbal authority, of his voice, his "Word." The church performed this rite because Jesus, at the Last Supper, had ordered it to be done. It was a sign of the communal obedience of the covenanted community. The reformed church showed its obedience by refraining from adding colorful packaging such as music and ornate vestments. Ritual became a performance of order, of obedience to the Word, of restraint. This new approach had a rationalist edge (taken from Erasmian humanism): Protestants considered Catholic sacramentalism not just un-

78

biblical; it was also an expression of primitive superstition, of delusion. Here, instead, was a dignified, orderly form of ritual. And, in a sense, it was a *rational* form of ritual, for it could be shown to conform to a verbal, cerebral account of God's revelation.

This new approach to sacramentalism entailed a heightened role for ecclesiastical authority. Of course, ecclesiastical authority upheld the old sacramental system, but the regulation was less complete. Because the Roman Church was unable to regulate the profusion of images, cults, and folk/religious practices, there was a vast amount of "leakage" beyond the official sacramental forms. The medieval church had little choice but to tolerate local variations on its official theme. A key aspect of the Reformation was a refusal to tolerate this; it brought a new tidy-mindedness to sacramentalism. Its meaning had to be fixed by the church, and unfixable forms had to be denounced as suspect. (This tidy-mindedness was soon imitated by Rome: the Council of Trent was concerned to define sacramentalism with new precision.)

The liberal Protestantism discussed in the previous chapter inherited this assumption that sacramental performance was dangerous, that it led to Catholicism and paganism. It favored the rationalist critique of ritual: it saw Roman rituals as empty superstition, spurious claims to magical power. But this liberal tradition was *also* suspicious of the new tightly controlled sacramentalism of Calvin and others. It questioned the claim of the Calvinist minister that God must be worshiped exactly thus. It objected to the new institutional authoritarianism. This was a basic aspect of its radical liberalism: no new priesthood had the right to lay down the law on correct worship (orthodoxy). All institutions claiming to define ritual orthodoxy were suspect.

This very modern attitude of suspicion toward both ritual and religious institutionalism brings a huge theological problem. How is Christianity to be expressed if not through institutionally regulated ritual? In a new aura of suspicion toward organized ritual, might not Christians lose the habit of celebrating the Eucharist, and allow religion to become disembodied, abstract? The liberals of the mid-seventeenth century failed to see this danger. They implied that a reformed Christianity was able to move away from institutionally regulated ritual practice, that Bible-reading and prayer were sufficient. This approach was inadequate: an ververbalized, anti-institutional, sacraphobic form of Christianity cannot sustain itself. This first wave of liberal Protestantism, therefore, lacked a positive sacramental character, a desire for the flourishing of new cultic practices. And so it failed to stand.

Origins of the Issue

Both the Old and New Testaments contain ambiguity concerning ritual. In the Old, it is rooted in antipathy to the religious practices of other tribes and nations. Jehovah is defined by his refusal to be worshiped alongside other gods, which he sometimes orders to be destroyed. What complicates this is that there is a huge overlap between Jehovah-worship and other older traditions. The Jews clearly adopted Babylonian and Egyptian myths and practices, yet remained ambivalent toward them. Abraham is depicted as leaving the gods of his fathers, in obedience to God's voice. This tradition is able to put a question mark over all ritual practices. God decrees them, which means that he is free from them — he is theoretically knowable apart from them, as he was to Abraham. But in practice he chooses to be known through rituals: an adaptation of the Canaanite sacrificial system, rooted in the agricultural year, and the new, specific rituals of commemoration of his liberating of his people from Egyptian slavery. So Judaism, though fully rooted in ritual practice, develops the ability to question this, to imagine God turning away from ritual. This largely occurs through the shamanic prophet figure, who is common to all Near Eastern religion but has a heightened role in Judaism. The prophet figure represents God's freedom from religious practice: God is dissatisfied with existing religious culture, and he means to launch a new kind of relationship with his people. Thus, in the Old Testament, God is expressed through ritual tradition *and* through voices that are semidetached from this ritual tradition. The Psalms are, to varying extents, cultically rooted: many of them refer to their use in public worship; others refer to public worship as the site of divine epiphany. Yet some also speak of God's detachment from any ritual system. God requires a devotion that cannot be wholly expressed through public ritual. The criticism of ritual continues in prophetic literature, where the inadequacy of mere ritual is often explicitly asserted. God requires a metaphorical, invisible sacrifice — a new spirit of devotion from his people. The noisy feast days are a distraction. But, of course, these prophetic voices supplemented rather than abrogated the cultic law that was attributed to Moses.

Jesus developed this prophetic criticism of ritual tradition as inadequate. Worship of God that is not accompanied by the pursuit of justice is empty, a form of idolatry. He derided those who prayed in public but lacked charity. His ministry was detached from organized Judaism, the cult of the Temple; yet, instead of rejecting it, he entered into dialogue with it. He criticized a strict interpretation of the law, but sought a fuller realization of its true meaning. At times, as in the parable of the sheep and the goats (Matt. 15), he implied that moral action was the true expression of religious piety. He sat very loose to public worship, but performed symbolic actions: theatrical exorcisms and healings, baptism, riding a donkey into the city, and so on. And he reportedly instituted a ritual through which his followers could remain in touch with his spirit, and (perhaps less credibly) urged baptism as an initiation rite. Despite his ambiguous relationship with traditional religious practices, his entire teaching and ministry is utterly dependent on the ritually rooted speech-forms of prayer and prophecy.

Whereas Jesus might seem to prioritize moral action over ritual observance, Paul might seem to prioritize faith over ritual observance, as we have seen. In both Romans and Galatians he makes his case with respect to Abraham: according to Genesis, the latter's trust in God's promises preceded any outward acts of religious allegiance, none of which had yet been instituted. As we have seen, this was a crucial argument against the role of the law: the danger is that it also seems to denigrate the role of ritual in Christianity. It falsely implies that Abraham's aloneness before God is normative. In reality, for Christians as well as for Jews, God's revelation is mediated by a cultural tradition. The believer acquires a sense of what it means to trust God — and indeed what the word "God" means — through participation in a ritual tradition, a tradition of stories, homilies, prayers, and sacramental actions. Abraham is a dubious model of religious identity, for most of us do not directly hear God's voice. If faith's dependence on ritual tradition is forgotten, there is a danger of overvaluing individual inwardness. Much of Protestant tradition has erred in this way, forgetting that individual faith is enabled by immersion in a cultural tradition. Faith consists in speech-forms that, though they must be individually appropriated, are essentially public-cultic. Again, the book of Psalms is the model for this blurring of individual and corporate-cultic faith. As we shall see, the Protestant emphasis on individual faith does not necessarily depart from this biblical model. Luther is particularly clear that faith is rooted in ritual speech-acts. But this awareness slips out of Protestantism, and individual faith becomes a way of breaking with ritual tradition.

For Paul, Christian identity is defined by participation in this new proclamation, of Jesus' divinity. This entails individual assent, membership in the new community, and participation in its ritual, the Eucharist. To outsiders, the new religion seemed naked. Christianity seemed so devoid of content that it could hardly be considered a religion at all. Its defining feature seemed to be a condemnation of more normal religion — hence it was called "atheist." The Jewish critic Trypho expressed his bafflement: "This is what we [Jews] can't grasp at all: that you want to fear God. Yet you do not withdraw from the pagans, you observe neither the festivals nor the Sabbaths, you do not circumcise." Pagan critics were similarly annoyed at the pretentious minimalism: "Why do they have no altars, no temples, no images?"[1]

As I briefly noted in chapter 1, early Christian ritual stabilized with the rise of the institutional church; the centrality of the Eucharist, and also of baptism, was intimately connected to the leadership of bishops. The stability was increased by the Constantinian revolution, which introduced royal splendor and pomp to worship, as well as further heightening the power of bishops. A very strong link between ritual and power was forged; indeed, the papacy became de-

---

1. Eberhard Arnold, *The Early Christians in Their Own Words* (New York: Plough Publishing House, 2011), pp. 89, 91.

fined by this overlap. The new kingdoms of Europe were drawn to the cultural richness that Roman worship offered. As Eamon Duffy writes, "The Catholic liturgy itself, with its exotic materials — the antique Latin of the chants and prayers, the silk and linen of the ministerial vestments, the ivory, jewels, and precious metals of the sacred vessels, the incense and wine used in the ceremonies of the mass — tied even the bleakest and most impoverished northern Christian outpost to the glamour and lavishness of the Mediterranean south."[2]

In a sense, the principal tool of the medieval church was pomp, the expression of power through ritual. Dissenting movements such as the Albigensians naturally called for the radical simplification of ritual. This reached a new phase with the Lollards, who saw ritual as the tool of clerical power and the pretext for worldliness and wealth (they allowed no image but a bare cross). Thus begins the key danger for Protestantism: in its struggle for new theological clarity and fidelity to Scripture, it is prone to see ritual in simply negative terms, as merely the tool of institutional power, and to forget that it is indispensable to faith.

As we have seen, the medieval church imposed an orderly pattern on Western Christendom, especially from the eleventh century. But this desire for uniformity was balanced by its fundamental acceptance of the fluidity of religious culture, its realistic awareness that purist uniformity was impossible. This was a matter of necessity: an institution based in an Italian city could hardly micromanage its spread throughout barbarian Europe. Mass conversion entailed an acceptance of syncretism, the coexistence of different religious systems. In 601, Pope Gregory told the missionaries in England to build churches on the site of pagan temples, to adapt the old traditions in a Christian direction. By such means the church had a porous relationship with paganism, a pragmatic openness to cultural otherness. Of course, the strategy worked: its myth became supreme, and old local myths bowed to its orbit. Ancient fertility cults and folk traditions were adapted. The old story about the local monster-slaying hero lived

---

2. Eamon Duffy, "The Rise of Sacred Song," *The New York Review of Books,* January 12, 2012, p. 44, a review of Christopher Page, *The Christian West and Its Singers.*

on in the new official story about the local saint. The old cult in which
the monster's defeat was performed could be grafted on to the saint's
day procession. The church's power grew on the soil of this syncretism. For example, it approved the magical aura surrounding barbarian kingship, and it developed this along Christian lines. It was similarly open to the old militaristic honor-culture. It confined its purism
in monasteries.

Once the church had secured its presence throughout Europe, a
desire for greater uniformity arose, and the result was a new focus on
the Eucharist. The church had always performed the Eucharist, of
course, but in the eleventh century it became more central to the
church's claim to universal authority. By performing this miracle,
the church could mediate God throughout Christendom. The role of
the priest was massively boosted. With the development of the theory
of transubstantiation, he was authorized to transform normal matter
into Christ himself. A complex theatrical liturgy was developed, centered on the moment when the priest raised the bread for the congregation to see (the "elevation"): "Bells pealed, incense was burnt, candles were lit, hands were clasped, supplications were mouthed."[3] This
liturgical moment was endowed with quasi-magical power. "In some
Italian towns a cult of pious women emerged who would spend the
day moving from church to church to watch elevations, which they
witnessed with ecstatic shouts and screams."[4]

The regular medieval Mass was not participatory in the obvious
sense. People were only invited to receive communion — and then
only bread — once a year, at Easter. Yet, according to some historians,
the annual event was such a powerful enactment of social unity that it
inspired the laity throughout the year, and made them satisfied with
secondary forms of participation: watching the elevation and also
kissing a wooden board from the altar called the pax-board.[5] The
church made Christ present, and it was enough to be present at this

3. Miri Rubin, *Corpus Christi: The Eucharist in Late Medieval Culture* (Cambridge,
UK: Cambridge University Press, 1992), p. 58.
4. Edward Muir, *Ritual in Early Modern Europe* (Cambridge, UK: Cambridge University Press, 1997), p. 163.
5. John Bossy has been the most influential proponent of this view.

miracle. "Before the Reformation the body of God in the mass and the bodies of the saints in their shrines were understood to be *present* in some quite literal sense."[6]

In the thirteenth century the desire for fuller participation in the Eucharist led to a huge new public festival: Corpus Christi. It originated in the vision of a Belgian nun named Juliana, who said that Christ told her to organize a feast focused on his eucharistic presence. The Dominicans took up the cause, and the feast was universally celebrated from the early fourteenth century. The interesting thing about Corpus Christi is that the Eucharist, which had become so closely bound up with ecclesiastical power, inspired a cultural event that was too large and diverse for the church to control. The feast day became centered on outdoor processions, whose prime aim was to show the eucharistic host. These became large parades, and most of the city wanted to participate in them. Unbidden by the church, new groups called fraternities arose to plan such things as *tableaux vivants* (floats with simple scenes performed) and street theater. In cities such as York the large-scale dramas were organized by the town council. The church then became wary of the festive monster it had created; in the 1450s it tried to put the event back indoors.

Of course, there were countless other public festivals in which a religious procession, displaying an image of the Virgin or of the local saint, was surrounded by more anarchic popular celebrations. The festival is a synecdoche of medieval sacramentalism. The authorizing heart of the event is the ritual of the church, but a wider cultural event exists in its wake. And the religious meanings made by this wider event cannot be neatly regulated. Even rigidly regulated rituals that occur within church buildings remain open to various interpretations: "It is the symbols which are conveyed in ritual which always contain a range of meanings."[7] The church understood that total control of sacramental culture was impossible; thus it allowed sacramental performance to spill out beyond its official rites.

A useful window onto the freedom contained in medieval sacra-

---

6. Muir, *Ritual in Early Modern Europe*, p. 151.
7. Rubin, *Corpus Christi*, p. 267.

mentalism is the mystical tradition that blossomed in the late four-teenth century. For example, the visions of Julian of Norwich are rooted in a personal appropriation of church-based sacramentalism. They begin when a priest, visiting her when she is ill, shows her a cru-cifix, which she alone can see is bleeding.[8] This is a good example of the fluidity of sacramentalism. Such a vision is pious, yet deeply un-settling to ecclesial structures. A religious institution that promotes the use of images, and the miracle stories attached to them, is inviting an unpredictable response of this kind. There is further evidence in the narrative of Julian's younger contemporary Margery Kempe. Jesus tells her to change her sacramental habits, to stop using a hair shirt and a rosary and, instead of eating meat, to eat his flesh and blood more regularly — more regularly than the church decrees. He prompts her to weep in public and to wear bridal white, in short, to make a spectacle of herself. Her visions are rooted in intense respect for church worship. For example, she has a vision of the wafer that a priest holds up at the Eucharist fluttering like a dove. Some of her vi-sions are inspired by seeing religious art; others occur while she par-ticipates in church processions.[9] To be so moved by church worship that a person hears the voice of Jesus addressing her is paradoxically more subversive than outright rejection of the church. For the church cannot easily refute such enthusiasm. Kempe's antics are a demon-stration of the looseness of the old sacramental system, the way in which it allows for anarchic appropriation.

The humanism that arose soon after the time of Margery Kempe was wary of such exotic, innovative sacramentalism. Erasmus, as I have briefly noted above, was suspicious of ritual on the grounds that it clouded understanding. People should read and ponder the New Testament, he believed, rather than beautify the shrines of fairy-tale saints. For example, he sneered at those who treated Saint George as a new Hercules: "They piously deck out his horse with trappings and amulets and practically worship it. Its favours are sought with some

8. Julian of Norwich, *Revelations of Divine Love* (Harmondsworth: Penguin, 1966), pp. 65-66.

9. *The Book of Margery Kempe*, trans. by B. A. Windeatt (Harmondsworth, UK: Penguin, 1985), pp. 51-52, 83, 214, 224.

new small offering, and an oath sworn by the saint's bronze helmet is fit for a king." Religious ritual is joined at the hip to pagan superstition; the church must keep it in check, subordinate it to spiritual meaning. Instead, Erasmus complained, scholastic theology buys in to the aura of ritual magic, offering complex explanations for it. The apostles felt no need for a theory of transubstantiation, he observed. He was also wary of scholasticism's justification of religious art: it would have baffled the apostles "that a mediocre drawing sketched in charcoal on a wall should be worshipped in the same manner as Christ himself, provided it had two fingers outstretched, long hair, and three rays sticking out from the halo fastened to the back of its head." His complaint was that the popularity of sacramentalism disrupted theology as an orderly cerebral system. Theology ought to point to the priority of the text, which counsels faith and love, and assumes the superiority of the spirit to the body. "The pious man throughout his whole life withdraws from the things of the body and is drawn towards what is eternal, invisible and spiritual."[10] This distrust of outward religious expression has roots in Plato and the Stoics as well as in Paul, as Erasmus would have gladly admitted. He taught the "philosophy of Christ" and saw philosophy's role as the exposure of mumbo jumbo. The core reform that the church cried out for was the *rationalization* of ritual, including in the modern business sense of drastic reduction.

In criticizing ritual, Erasmus and fellow humanists were launching a new form of Christian thought. Before, thinkers had spoken of the particular rites of the church, but had not marked off "ritual" as an aspect of religion. And the concept was at once pejorative. "Ritual" — and also "ceremony" — were typically preceded by the word "mere." To think about ritual was, in a sense, to declare detachment from it. This was partly the influence of Stoic philosophy on humanists: the wise thinker showed his detachment from popular supersti-

10. Erasmus, *Praise of Folly*, trans. Betty Radice (Harmondsworth, UK: Penguin, 1971), p. 126. Consider also, "if there's some legendary saint somewhat celebrated in fable (you can put George or Christopher or Barbara in that category if you need an example) you'll see that he receives far more devout attention than Peter or Paul or even Christ himself" (*Praise of Folly*, pp. 135-36, 157, 158, 205-6).

tion. A tension between ritual and reflection is very deeply rooted; abstract thought seems to emerge in opposition to ritual habit. Socrates was a threat to ritual practices. Stoic philosophy encouraged an enlightened detachment from popular credulity, yet saw limited ritual participation as a civic duty. Of course, Christianity was fully cultic, which seemed to be an immense weakness to its pagan opponents, such as Celsus.[11] Theology retained a certain awkwardness with respect to ritual, and the failure of Scholasticism to make sense of ritual provoked the rationalism of the humanists.

By rethinking the theological foundations of ritual, the Reformers massively expanded and radicalized the new culture of ritual-skepticism. This new attitude is definitive of modernity: enlightened modern people have freed themselves from the primitiveness of ritual and superstition. Only very recently, with Wittgenstein, has philosophy really begun to think about ritual with proper care — to guard against its own inbuilt prejudice against it.

The Reformers

It cannot quite be claimed that Protestantism was rooted in suspicion of ritual. Such suspicion was present in the Lollard movement, but the most important pre-Lutheran reform movement, the Hussites, showed a popular demand for frequent participation in the Eucharist. This reignited after Hus's being burned at the stake, with the added demand that both bread and wine be given to the laity, a practice that Rome had just explicitly banned. The rebellion was known as Utraquism, after the Latin word for "both." So far from rejecting the Eucharist as a tool of Roman power, the Utraquist movement proceeded to appropriate and democratize the ritual. Therefore, one im-

11. Celsus was annoyed that Christianity posed as a serious form of philosophy, and yet was plainly a primitive cult: "Christians claim to get some sort of power from pronouncing the names of demons or saying certain incantations, always incorporating the name Jesus and a short story about him in the formula" (Celsus, *On the True Doctrine: A Discourse against the Christians,* trans. R. J. Hoffman [Oxford: Oxford University Press, 1987], p. 53).

portant current within the Reformation was the desire for more involvement in the core ritual. This contributed to a transformation in how the Eucharist was understood. Daylight was let in, and the old sense of hieratic mystery receded.

Luther was not entirely opposed to the sacramental world of Catholicism. Like Erasmus, he wanted to see it subordinated to theological truth. But, whereas Erasmus's criterion for subordination was rather vague (Christian wisdom, the teaching of Jesus understood from a Platonic perspective), Luther's was clear and urgent: Paul's simple message about grace. Religious practice must reflect this message rather than obscure it. His attack on the sale of indulgences sharpened his thinking and led to his famous "tower experience," in which he saw faith to be at the heart of Christianity.

Luther was aware that inner faith should not eclipse the communal ritual basis of religion. The central ritual, the Eucharist, had to be reaffirmed; but it had to be purged of Roman errors, chiefly the idea that it is a sacrifice that the priest has special power to perform. Luther was adamant that Jesus was present in the bread and wine, not because of transubstantiation — a pretentious theory based on Aristotle's dubious concepts — but simply because he had promised to be. Both this ritual and baptism had to be rerooted in the power of the Word. Sacraments, he explained in a tract of 1520, are special presentations of God's promise. God decrees that his words of promise are ritually accompanied — in the two basic sacraments of the Mass and baptism. God's "speech-act," his transformative communication, attains a sort of amplification, a sort of solidity. He authorizes a theatrical presentation of his word. Luther was not averse to a bit of religious theater. He favored full-immersion baptism. It is not strictly necessary, he says, "but I consider it to be a beautiful act to give the sign of baptism as fully and completely as possible."[12] These rituals are meant to impress, to inspire, to be a spectacular focus for believers.

On the other hand, Luther says, Christian ritual tempts us to sideline and betray Paul's message. In another tract of 1520 he insists

12. Martin Luther, *The Pagan Servitude of the Church*, in John Dillenberger, *Martin Luther: Selections from His Writings* (New York: Doubleday, 1961), p. 302.

that no form of cultic action is the necessary means to the attainment of salvation. When people insist that "ceremonies" are necessary for salvation, the Christian must "offend them boldly, lest by their impious views they drag many with them into error. In the presence of such men it is good to eat meat, break the fasts, and for the sake of the liberty of faith do other things which they regard as the greatest of sins." But then he suddenly and sharply backs off from this iconoclasm, explaining that ceremonies and works are in practice still necessary, for the ordering of society, especially its young: "[T]he inexperienced and perverse youth need to be trained and restrained by the iron bars of ceremonies lest their unrestrained ardor rush headlong into vice after vice." Ceremonies are like architects' models, he says: necessary but provisional, not to be mistaken for real buildings, a means to an end. "Thus we do not despise ceremonies and works, but we set great store by them; but we despise the false estimate placed upon works in order that no one may think that they are true righteousness."[13]

He is walking a tightrope: individual faith is what really matters for salvation, but public religious culture is still of crucial importance. Neither of the two main sacraments confers grace, but he implies that it is necessary to treat them *as if* they confer grace, for people need public religious acts. And ritual uniformity is politically necessary. This is especially clear with regard to infant baptism, whose core function is to establish Christianity as socially normal. In effect, Luther proposes that Christianity occurs on two levels: in addition to the true inner level (justification by faith), there is a necessary outward level of shared ritual actions. Without the latter, it could not function as the official creed of society.

Luther was, therefore, a strangely conservative revolutionary. Religion must be reconceptualized and placed under new secular management, but what actually happens must in crucial respects stay the same. The whole community must join in officially sanctioned ritual action, and this ritual action only needs partial renovation. Luther

13. Martin Luther, *The Freedom of a Christian Man,* in Dillenberger, *Martin Luther,* pp. 82, 84.

saw no need for Zwingli's iconoclastic overhaul. He was mildly suspicious of visual art because of its role in the cult of saints and its connection to papal magnificence (the indulgence campaign that provoked him was raising funds for the building of St. Peter's in Rome). But he saw no reason to remove images of Christ or Mary from churches or to whitewash their brightly painted walls. When rival Reformers, led by Karlstadt, advocated iconoclasm in Wittenberg, he fervently opposed them. Though religious art may cause idolatry, iconoclasm is worse, for it turns the absence of images into a new law. Or, rather, it revives an old law — the second commandment, which forbade graven images. Luther duly dubbed the iconoclasts "Judaizers." He also warned that iconoclasm led to disorder, as the impulse was often accompanied by orgies of vandalism. Reform should be orderly, officially led, according to Luther. In 1525 he explained that religious images should be seen merely as "signs" that remind us of Christ. If images are so wrong, why is the Bible so full of verbal imagery? He defends the use of woodcut illustrations in his Bible translations, and then in a very interesting aside he imagines larger-scale illustrations of the Bible: "Would to God that I could convince the lords as well as the rich to have the entire Bible painted in detail on houses so that the eyes of everyone could see it; this would be a Christian work."[14] Elsewhere he defends depictions of the crucifixion and dramatic representations of the resurrection, including the defeat of Satan. A central aspect of his thought was the need to reflect on "Christus Victor," Christ as victorious hero (a theme he found in the church fathers). His preaching and writing often constructed a rhetorical icon of this. He saw no reason why visual art should not help to advertise it.

Luther wanted worship to be more engaging of the laity. The Eucharist should retain its theatrical aura, but include more participation. The congregation should not only eat the bread but drink the wine, which Rome had denied them. And the liturgy should be in the

---

14. Martin Luther, "Against the Heavenly Prophets," in *Works*, vol. 18, p. 83, quoted in Sergiusz Michalski, *The Reformation and the Visual Arts* (London: Routledge, 1993), p. 28.

vernacular, not Latin. He also gave new prominence to the rousing poetic sermon, in which the preacher should perform his dramatic struggle with Satan, showing how the power of the Word turns this nightmarish fiend into a mere pantomime villain. Preaching has a shamanic quality, and the preacher exposes himself, gives himself: "In the pulpit one should bare one's breast and give the people milk to drink, for every day a new church is growing up, and it needs the rudiments."[15] On top of all this, Luther introduced popular religious music: rousing hymns in which the sermon's themes could be appropriated by each member of the congregation. And worship was supplemented by religious education. In order that the congregation grasp these themes more soberly, each member was required to memorize a portion of the catechism.

Meanwhile in Zurich, Zwingli's reform was heavily centered on iconoclasm. This was primarily based on the Old Testament law, as we have seen, but it was partly molded by Erasmus's faith in the triumph of divine reason over empty superstition, that is, in the superiority of the spiritual to the corporal. Rome had polluted worship with empty rituals, which had to be pulled down — but not too rashly. (Indeed, Erasmus insisted that iconoclasts wait for the laws to be changed.) Once the city council passed a law, images were destroyed, and a purist minimalism was introduced to worship. Music was considered a kind of invisible idolatry, and thus organs were removed from churches. Processions were banned, since they featured the display of images. Pure worship follows Scripture, they believed, which rigidly resists introducing alien matter.

Like Luther, Zwingli saw the Mass as the centerpiece of Rome's idolatry: it was a theatrical conjuring trick in which priests pretended to have magical powers. But Zwingli went further. The whole aura of magic had to be denied, he said, including the doctrine of Christ's real presence in the bread and wine. The rite was reconceived as the pledge of the congregation's allegiance. He argued that the word "sacrament" derives from the military practice of swearing an oath of allegiance to the regimental banner, or flag. Hence it was a demonstra-

15. Quoted in Martin Marty, *Martin Luther* (New York: Penguin, 2004), p. 144.

tion of the community's identity. God had ordained this sign — and that of baptism — for the marking out of his people. But it was just a sign, not a miraculous event. Luther, following Augustine, had called a sacrament a special sign in which the thing signified is present. In Zwingli's view, this was muddled thinking that would open the door to idolatry. A sign is just a sign. Even a divinely commissioned sign is just a divinely commissioned *sign.* When Jesus said, "This is my body," he meant, "Let this stand for my body."

Nor did baptism have supernatural force. Zwingli argued that it should be seen as the Christian version of circumcision, the sign of God's covenant with his people. His theology of the sacraments was thus determined by his absolute belief in the Christian community. The sacraments were holy because they defined this holy community. They defined it as the new Israel, for both sacraments were new versions of the Old Testament identity-markers: baptism was the Christian circumcision, and the Eucharist was the Christian Passover. These signs were sacred, as ordained by Christ; but the fact remained that ritual was a lower form of religion than hearing and speaking, something crude, almost animal: "Christ has bequeathed," says Zwingli, "two ceremonies, two external signs . . . as a concession to our frailty."[16]

Because he rejected the doctrine of the real presence, it is tempting to think that Zwingli made the Eucharist into a dull rationalistic thing, devoid of holy spectacle. In fact, he rejected the old sense of theater in favor of a new sense of theater. Minimalism is not a rejection of aestheticism but a renewal of it — by inversion. This new style of sacramentalism rejected the idea that God is present in a visually rich performance; instead, it located him in the conspicuous renunciation of this tradition. Paradoxically, the renunciation of grand performance has to be impressively performed to show how much the renunciation matters. Ceremonial austerity becomes a performance of God's negative authority: it is God's way of saying "No" to sensuality, aestheticism, idolatry. This is indeed a feature of the Old Testament

16. Zwingli, in Euan Cameron, *The European Reformation* (Oxford: Clarendon Press, 1991), p. 158.

God, and Zwingli gives it unprecedented prominence. The community participates in this aspect of God in worship, by performing its obedience to his word.

This inverted sacramentalism has the effect of tightening institutional regulation. Worship is dangerous. In our fallenness, we are naturally drawn to a base, pagan form of it. True religion goes against the grain of religion in general. It must be regulated and supervised by a vigilant priesthood of scholarly experts. It is far too dangerous for amateurs to try at home. By contrast, in a religious culture that allows images, there will inevitably be an extensive gray area, an area of lay devotion that is not fully authorized by the church. If someone owns an icon of the Virgin, the church's monopoly on worship is slightly diminished. In Reformation culture there is less scope for religious activity beyond the priestly gaze. Therefore, though the Reformers rejected the idea of sacral power residing in the priest, they actually increased the priest's regulation of religious expression. In the old order, the two main sacraments had provided "leakage" into unofficial ritual practice. A literal example of such leakage is that the holy water used in baptism was often taken home by parishioners for use in a magical way: they would sprinkle it onto an ailing child or a crucial crop. So the old idea of priestly power allowed for a high degree of scattered sacramentalism that was embedded in daily life. The new, more rational approach isolated sacramentalism from the world around it, confined it within church walls.

A good example of the Reformed approach is provided by Zwingli's colleague in Strasbourg, Martin Bucer. In a tract he wrote in 1524, the latter explained that the rite of baptism had to be overhauled: "We pay no heed to the teaching about chrism, oil, salt, clay and candles. . . . Such magic tricks ill become intelligent and rational Christians, who ought to pay heed to the Word of the Lord, and follow it alone."[17] In this tradition, reform entails a war against idolatrous superstition, a war that opens the door to rationalism.

17. Martin Bucer, "The Reason and Cause . . . of the Innovations in the Lord's Supper . . . , Baptism, Images, and Song in the Congregation of Christ . . . Undertaken in Strasbourg," quoted in Susan C. Karant-Nunn, *The Reformation of Ritual: An Interpretation of Early Modern Germany* (London: Routlege, 1993), p. 54.

So the sacramental divergence of Luther and the Zwinglians is very substantial. The question of Christ's real presence in the Eucharist is just one aspect of it. The question is whether a whole new paradigm of sacramentalism is needed — that is, obedience to the anti-idolatrous Word. In Luther's eyes, this puts "Judaizing" legalism at the heart of reform. It is an overreaction that is worse than what went before. To put it mildly, Protestantism is awkwardly related to its sacramental inheritance, like a son who is torn between imitating his father and being his reactive opposite. The anxiety of influence is acute.

Calvin followed in Zwingli's wake, because Geneva had already been stripped of images when he arrived there. He developed an unprecedentedly rigorous iconophobic theology, a whole system of religious thought rooted in the rejection of idolatry. His writing continually emphasizes that God is known through his Word, that faith comes through hearing, not sight. It is the absolute priority of the verbal that enables Christianity to be orderly — and, in a sense, rational. If God communicated himself through a whole lot of images and performances, how could we be sure of receiving his essential message? Calvin was one of the greatest muddle-haters in history. He was horrified that the Catholic Church tolerated — and even promoted — religious muddle, mixing true teaching with superstitious chaff. In one of his image-bashing tracts he recalls a boyhood experience: watching the local celebration of the feast of Saint Stephen, in which statues were carried around the village. The religious meaning was totally lost amid the festive fun; all the images were decorated with the same garlands, including those representing Stephen's murderers. "So all was mixed up," he recalls with a shiver.[18] This is a good summary of his view of all of Catholic culture. Its great sin is to allow forms of sacramentalism that mix the gospel with pagan revelry, to bury its saving message in merry muddle.

Images incubate such a muddle, Calvin believed. A picture of Christ, for example, does not refer to Christ with the clarity that the

---

18. "An inventory of relics," in Henry Beveridge, ed., *Tracts and Treatises on the Reformation of the Church* (Edinburgh: Oliver and Boyd, 1958), p. 341.

word "Christ" does. One might be thinking of the figure's beauty, or of the artist's skill. Visual communication brings various possibilities of interpretation. The image has a freedom that the word lacks; it has a life of its own. Likewise, in a play about Christ, for example, one might be thinking what fun it is or how good the actor is. God cannot be communicated in this unstable, open, messy way. Only language really corresponds to the clarity of his message. Music in church is a dangerous distraction, unless Scripture is being sung in a clearly intelligible way. (The new practice of singing psalms thus became central to Calvinism.) Sacramentalism must not depart from unambiguous verbal communication. This relates to the Eucharist: the Roman Mass marginalizes speech, as the priests prance around "in pomps, ceremonies, and gesticulations. But there is not so much as a mention, an allusion, to the Word of God, without which sacraments themselves cannot be sacraments. Thus the Supper is buried, when it is turned into the Mass."[19]

Receiving the elements in the Eucharist became the badge of belonging to the people of God. Therefore, moral offenders had to be excluded. In a sense, Calvin combined the gathered church model with the magisterial Christendom model: everyone had to go to church, but only the keenly pious could receive communion. (His emphasis on predestination should also be understood thus: belonging to a Christian culture does not make you a true Christian. There is an elite of real Christians within Christendom, but it must remain humanly undefined.)

In addition to reinventing church ritual as an austere theater of obedience, the Reformed tradition launched a new kind of "everyday" sacramentalism. The emphasis on being God's people gave rise to a new alertness to God's will in every aspect of life. Also, the rejection of idolatry brought a new rhetoric of seeing God in his creation — and especially in the neighbor. The role of beauty in religion was not abolished along with images. Calvin often wrote of the beauty of Christian

---

19. Calvin, *The Institutes,* in Geoffrey Wainwright and Karen B. Westerfield Tucker, eds., *The Oxford History of Christian Worship* (Oxford: Oxford University Press, 2006), p. 322.

truth. His *Institutes* tries to show how the believer participates in the beautiful architecture of divine truth.[20]

The English Reformation lurched between a sacramental conservatism that outdid Luther's and the clarity-hunger of Zwingli and Calvin. Elizabeth finally brought some stability to the sacramentally traumatized nation. After a bout of iconoclasm, to clear the air of Bloody Mary, she launched her middle way. She left many Catholic rituals in place, such as the churching of women, the use of the ring in marriage, and the sign of the cross in baptism. She left "a framework round which a new ceremonial religion, with its own comforting rituals and much-loved routines, could grow."[21] A year into her reign she made a great show of forcing her new reform-minded bishops to wear the ornate vestments that they associated with Catholicism. She was putting her stamp on sacramentalism: the church's style should be in tune with that of the monarchy, which meant suppressing its Calvinist wing. A new liturgical magnificence was driven by royal ceremony.

Part of Elizabeth's genius was to see that England's Reformation enabled an increased religious role for the monarchy, that she could make herself into a focus for popular sacramental yearning. This entailed closing down other options for public festivity. She renewed the Edwardian ban on religious processions larger than the beating of the parish bounds. Various events, such as Saint George pageants, which had been revived under Mary, she now suppressed. "The town of Norwich was so reluctant to abandon its famous pageant that officials salvaged the production by banning St. George but allowing the dragon to march, unopposed, for the rest of Elizabeth's reign."[22]

Public festivity was channeled in a secular and royalist direction. Elizabeth's coronation involved unprecedented public religious theater, and Accession Day was celebrated for a decade (it was the first

20. See William A. Dyrness, *Reformed Theology and Visual Culture: The Protestant Imagination from Calvin to Edwards* (Cambridge, UK: Cambridge University Press, 2004), p. 67.

21. David Starkey, *Elizabeth: Apprenticeship* (London: Chatto and Windus, 2000), p. 287.

22. James Shapiro, *1599: A Year in the Life of William Shakespeare* (London: Faber, 2005), p. 168.

modern national holiday). To Catholics' disgust, the cult of Elizabeth stole aspects of the cult of the Virgin Mary (a Marian hymn was even adapted). And the very act of a monarch inventing a "holy day" to augment her power struck many as sacrilegious. A new festival, designed by leading dramatists in imitation of a Roman triumph, arose to celebrate the defeat of the Spanish Armada.

Puritans grumbled about all this pageantry, but at least it wasn't the traditional sort. New royal pomp was a price worth paying for the dismantling of traditional folk religion, the felling of maypoles. They were also glad to see the demise of the mystery play tradition, which had grown up around Corpus Christi processions in various cities. In Chester, for example, mystery plays were last performed in 1574, and there, too, processions were gradually tamed. In Chester in 1599 the spoilsport of a mayor banned the inclusion of the traditional "dragon and naked boys."[23] Dramatic spectacle migrated to the tighter confines of London's theaters, as well as its court. Because monarchs liked plays, the stage was largely protected from Puritan hostility. So theater had to keep alive many of the festive traditions that were being banned from other public spaces. This enraged preachers, who saw plays as concentrated bursts of otherwise proscribed festivity that made sermons look dull. One preacher complained, "Will not a filthy play, with the blast of a trumpet, sooner call thither a thousand, than an hour's tolling of a bell, bring to the sermon a hundred?"[24]

Shakespeare's unique place in English cultural history is closely related to the desacralizing tide that the Tudors unleashed. His plays often cherish the spirit of public festivity and preserve aspects of it. Whether or not he was a crypto-Catholic, he was clearly deeply attached to this aspect of Catholic tradition. In subsequent centuries, his work became a focus for England's regret at the sacramental losses of the Reformation. He allows us to imagine an alternative transition to modernity, free of the mechanistic crudities of Protestant "progress," more in touch with the social and celebratory past. He

23. Patrick Collinson, *The Religion of Protestants: The Church in English Society, 1529-1625* (Oxford: Oxford University Press, 1982), p. 226.

24. Shapiro, *1599*, p. 171.

hints at a fusion of merry organic English Catholicism and Protestant reforming clarity.

Under James I, public festivity continued in this national-royalist direction. A commemoration of the Gunpowder Plot, for example, became a focus for national Protestant identity. But he put the brakes on the Puritans' dismantling of public fun. His *Book of Sports* was a pledge that royal power would protect what remained of public festivity, a declaration that Puritanism had enjoyed too much cultural influence.

The Church of England gained confidence in its sacramental middle way: it prided itself in avoiding the gaudy excesses of Rome, but also in resisting the opposite extreme and stripping worship of beauty. This confidence is expressed in George Herbert's poem "The British Church," which pictures the church as a mother who is neither whorishly overdressed nor inappropriately naked, but a beautiful expression of "the mean." This middle way became a key part of the modern reasonability that Anglican culture modeled. The civilized gentleman should see the ceremonial aspect of life as a necessary thing, within limits. It should not be overdone; nor should one be fanatically opposed to it. Moderation — and a respect for convention — was essential. The essays of Francis Bacon exude this spirit of boat-stabilizing reasonability. Sacramentalism had become the realm of compromise and conformity. To be in communion with the established church was a matter of political common sense. As arch-pragmatist Richard Hooker had explained, outward conformity enabled a flexible and enlightened religious culture. But in practice a sensible middle way could not so easily be sustained.

Milton and Sacramentalism

As a youth, Milton seems to have accepted the ideology of the sacramental middle way, and he shared the assumption that Puritanism was an overearnest nuisance. He seems to have enjoyed worship at Saint Paul's cathedral. As we have seen, the success of Laud's movement provoked him into rethinking his position, and he became a pioneer of a new kind of Protestant radicalism that demanded a revolution in toleration — and an end to establishment. But our present concern is to look beneath this radicalism and to probe his view of religious practice. What was his proposed alternative to both Anglo-Catholicism and Calvinism?

Milton's polemical pamphlets against the bishops echo the conventional Puritan rhetoric of disgust at Catholic-style ritualism. In "Of Reformation in England" (1641) he attacks priestcraft's ancient corruption of the gospel: "[T]hey hallowed it, they fumed up, they sprinkled it, they bedecked it, not in robes of pure innocency, but in robes of pure linen, with other deformed and fantastic dresses, in palls and mitres, gold, and gewgaws fetched from Aaron's old wardrobe, or the flamins' vestry. . . ." The theater of high-church worship is a bid for power. By dressing their claim to authority in finery, they think it will go unchallenged. But why should "the rustling of their silken cassocks" command respect? Why shouldn't we laugh "to see them under sail in all their lawn and sarcenet, their shrouds and tackle, with geometrical rhomboids upon their heads"?

In another tract of that year, "Of Prelatical Episcopacy," Milton says that Protestants must not be intimidated by "all the heaped names of Angels, and Martyrs, Councils, and Fathers urged upon us," nor by the "Ephod and Teraphim of Antiquity."[25] This refers to the ornately bejeweled outfits worn by Israelite priests at a time when true worship was being forgotten. Milton acknowledges that there is something impressive — including aesthetically impressive — about Catholicism. But it must be resisted; the "beauty of holiness" is the secret weapon of reactionary clerics. The true Christian opts for minimalist plainness. Like the very first Christians, he gathers with his companions to read Scripture and pray, with no need for a grand institution, full of worldly pomp and power. Does the church need to be organized at all? Milton evades the question in these first tracts, but he gradually came out as a critic of all fixed forms of worship. In an attack on the Prayer Book, he argues that "constancy" is no virtue in

25. John Milton, *Collected Prose Works* (New Haven: Yale University Press, 1953-76), pp. 521, 611-12, 652.

worship: prayer should be fresh, new each time. In reaction against imperial orthodoxy, he advocates sacramental antinomianism, in which any worship rule is legalistic. So is the idea of doctrinal orthodoxy, an official body of belief; people should be free to come to their own doctrinal conclusions on the basis of Scripture.

So he became increasingly sure that highly organized religion was impressive but oppressive. Of course, he had a "high" conception of God's majesty, already expressed in his early poems; but it was strictly otherworldly, not to be expressed in worldly grandeur. This tension was central to his art. Poetry is the one form of expression that can communicate divine glory without the use of worldly power that is made by art, architecture, even most theater and music. Poetry is a form of aesthetic power that is not complicit in Catholicism, nor reliant on royal patronage. But a theological temptation lurked: the virtual reality of poetry is no substantial alternative to the communal bodily practices that root religion.

Yet Milton's poetry contains a yearning for the sacramental excitement that he renounces. "The Nativity Ode" imagines the sudden collapse of various pagan rituals when Christ is born, and Milton sketches the cults in a wistful, even romantic way. The bad old religion is dramatic and colorful, and true religion can enjoy representing this defeated color by means of poetry. Poetry, therefore, fulfills a complex function with respect to sacramentalism. It can appropriate the bad-but-impressive old religion for Protestantism. But it does so at the expense of overreliance on the virtual, verbal realm. This dynamic was perhaps established by Milton's hero, Edmund Spenser, an Elizabethan courtier and Puritan and the author of the epic fairy tale *The Faerie Queene,* which is partly about the danger of sensual appearances. One of the hero-knights travels to the epicenter of dangerous deception, the Bower of Bliss, a garden full of magically enhanced artworks. He surveys the scene, which is, of course, lovingly described, and then destroys it — "with rigour pitilesse" (II, xii, 83). Poetry allows Puritanism to be fiercely antiartifice, antiadornment, antiseductive excitement — while parading its defeated enemy in the manner of a Roman triumph. Of course, this parade is incapable of acquiring cultural substance, of becoming a new ritual practice. From this perspective,

Protestant poetry should have taken the form of liturgical drama (a possibility that Milton glimpsed in his drama *Comus*).

In his work as Cromwellian propagandist, Milton argued against the very deep-seated assumption that monarchy has an authentic religious aura. A hagiography of King Charles had appeared soon after his execution, *Eikon Basilike* ("The Image of the King"). Milton's response, *Eikonoklastes*, attacks "an inconstant, irrational and image-doting rabble" for idolizing a flawed king.[26] The need to exorcise the cult of royalism led Milton to intensify his sacraphobia. The problem he faced was that the Reformation had turned the English mind against sacramentalism, except with respect to the monarchy. The monarch remained a legitimate living saint; even Puritans such as Foxe had not contested this. Instead, they trusted in royal power to cement the Protestant direction of the nation. Such trust was misplaced, Milton says. Monarchy is necessarily in league with a Catholic-style church; absolutism is intrinsic to both institutions. A properly bold reform movement has to oppose monarchism. This, of course, contravenes the sacramental middle way of the English mind, which sees the monarchy as a natural part of a moderate and modern sacramental culture.

Milton kept his more theoretical religious opinions to himself; for example, his extensive theological work *De Doctrina Christiana* was not published in his lifetime. It gives fuller expression to his sacramental antinomianism. He also argues in this work that it is up to each individual Christian to worship as he or she sees fit. He describes the visible church in the broadest possible terms: it is all those "who openly worship God the Father in Christ either individually or in conjunction with others" (p. 362). Church membership is not absolutely required: "Although it is the duty of every believer to join himself, if possible, to a correctly instituted church . . . those who are not able to do so conveniently, or with a good conscience, are not therefore excluded from or destitute of the blessing which was bestowed on the churches" (p. 568). If the individual disdains all forms of church and misses out on the sacraments, it is no matter, for sacraments are just

---

26. John Milton, *Eikonoklastes,* in *Collected Prose Works* (1958), p. 452. Hereafter, page references to this work appear in parentheses in the text.

symbolic. "After all, he can give thanks to God and commemorate the death of Christ in many other ways every day of his life, even if he does not do so in the ceremonial way which God has instituted" (p. 557). Public ceremony is just one form of the "commemoration" of Christ that is required of us. Those Christians who opt for the Eucharist have no need for a presiding priest: the head of a family can do it, just as the head of a Jewish family presides at the Passover meal. Ritual should be low-key, do-it-yourself, devoid of pomp and fuss. It should be demystified, taken out of the hands of a clerical elite. Unlike in ancient Judaism, domestic worship does not have to be accompanied by large-scale temple worship: the quiet, homely scale is all that is needed. This is a departure from the Calvinist idea that the Eucharist, though merely symbolic, is the focus of the orthodox community, the place in which individualism is trumped by the common godly mind, as mediated by the minister. Ritual should not be an excuse, says Milton, for priests to exert authority; if it has become such, then we should stay clear of it.

Milton's suspicion of traditional religious practices is evident at the beginning of *Paradise Lost,* where the poet addresses God: "And chiefly thou, O Spirit, that dost prefer/Before all temples the upright heart and pure,/Instruct me, for thou know'st. . . ." A new kind of holy individualism is born in the claim that all forms of corporate Christian identity are dubious, that they betray God's pure, liberal revolution. (This holy individualism becomes a central ingredient of Romanticism.)

Paradise Lost is full of sacramental richness, safely virtualized in words. He outdoes traditional religious iconography, and even its recent baroque renewal, in the vivid imagining of heaven and hell, in the dramatic spectacle of fallen angels hatching plots and waging wars. Look how poetry can inherit the richness of traditional religion, he is saying. The new approach to religion may reject actual performances of pomp, but here is enough Platonic pomp for anyone. The problem is that Platonic pomp is not enough; virtual spectacle is no substitute for the real thing. *Paradise Lost* is a great epic poem, but its very greatness marks a fatal retreat of liberal Protestantism into the ether. Milton should have stuck to his original intention of writing a drama about Eden, thus implying the centrality of performance to religious art.

In a sense, the focus on Adam and Eve is an evasion of the question of religious practice. They do not need religion; they pray as naturally as they speak. For example, they do not "say grace" before eating but naturally remark on God's bountiful goodness. And they sing a spontaneous hymn of praise to God each morning, "[i]n various style" — no Prayer Book rigidity for them (V, 146). Their unadorned plainness is more divine than any cultural magnificence, we are repeatedly told. They are divinely natural. There is a cheeky hint that their lovemaking is a freestyle rite.

At the end, Adam watches a kind of film telling of the future of humanity, and the Archangel Michael explains it. After the apostles, says Michael, Christianity is corrupted by false leaders who "the truth/ With superstitions and traditions taint,/Left only in those written records pure . . ." (XII, 511-13). Established religion persecutes a frail minority "who in the worship persevere/Of spirit and truth. The rest, far greater part,/Will deem in outward rites and specious forms/Religion satisfied. Truth shall retire,/Bestuck with sland'rous darts . . ." (532-36). This is not a very satisfactory sketch of Christianity. What is "the worship . . . [o]f spirit and truth" exactly? Is it necessarily in conflict with "outward rites"? It seems that salvation consists in knowing that Satan's Edenic victory is temporary, that Christ defeats him eternally. Adam himself is saved by this knowledge: it allows him to recover a positive attitude as he begins his exile. But knowing — and believing — the story of Christus Victor is not a full recipe for Christian existence. We also need to participate in Christ's victory; we need practices that perform this plot.

Beneath Milton's grand confidence that the old sacramental order is worthless there is a half-conscious anxiety. In one early pamphlet he mocks the arrogant, complacent Laudian priest, who handles the communion wafer as if he's sitting in the tavern snacking on a biscuit.[27] This is a strange image, for he is ostensibly attacking the ceremonial grandness of Laudianism. So why attack it for a *lack* of dignity? It seems that anything less than perfect dignity in church ritual offends Milton: because it cannot be perfect, because human im-

---

27. Milton, *Eikonoklastes*, in *Collected Prose Works* (1958), p. 436.

perfection intrudes, it is better to have no ritual at all. Thus does he advocate plainness and cautious individualism. And a sort of agnosticism; maybe a new form of church order will arise. But for now we must do the rigid political work of creating a state that is bravely secular (that enforces a separation of church and state). Is there no positive vision of a new Christian culture?

There is one very interesting hint that a new deregulated Christian culture might be possible. In his tract of 1642, Milton ponders the role of a great national poet: he can "cherish in a great people the seeds of virtue and public civility," and also bring their religious stories to life. And then it emerges that he has a wider vision of the new Christian culture. The teaching of wisdom and virtue should be culturally central, he says:

> Whether this may be, not only in pulpits, but after another persuasive method, at set and solemn paneguries, in theatres, porches, or what other place or way may win most upon the people to receive at once both recreation and instruction, let them in authority consult.[28]

He proposes a new model of public religion, based on the Greek model of organic unity, in which religion and culture were one. There must be popular cultic events ("paneguries"); perhaps he envisions a revival of the medieval tradition of religious theater, which gave rise to the mystery play tradition. This passage is a brief high point in Milton's sacramental awareness, expressing, as it does, a sense that culture at large is called to a new kind of religious creativity. Of course, this hint of an insight is not developed in his work; he does not develop a new account of Christian practice for the new era.

A huge aspect of the failure of the liberal Protestant tradition can be summed up in our reflections on Milton. His clear, bold theopolitical vision is accompanied by deeply inadequate reflections on the church and Christian practice. He prepares the way for the deist

28. Milton, "The Reason of Church Government," in *Collected Prose Works,* pp. 816-17, 819-20.

subversion of liberal Christianity. His aversion to the main churches of his day blinded him to the necessity of organized sacramental practice, of an institution putting the Eucharist at the heart of Christianity. Not without reason did he associate sacramentally rich Christianity with authoritarianism, but failed to see that the association had to be challenged, broken.

Other Voices

What about this era's popular religious movements that denounced the established church: Did they have an understanding of the need to reconfigure, rather than reject, sacramental practice?

The Baptists were in many respects close to Calvinists: their distinctive difference was their rejection of religious establishment, of which infant baptism was a key support. Worship consisted of group prayer and informal preaching, with various people feeling inspired to speak. Because the Baptists did not normally celebrate the Eucharist, regular Baptist worship was sacramentally thinner than Calvinist worship; but the practice of adult baptism, a regular occurrence during its time of growth, made up for this. The full immersion of new converts in the local river was a conscious act of dramatic symbolism, an enactment of the believer's participation in the death and resurrection of Jesus. This often took place at night, due to the Baptists' fear of persecution. Opponents spread the rumor that initiates were naked, and that young women were sexually abused in the water. The underlying issue was that full-immersion baptism struck conservatives as an indecently physical form of religious expression.

The Baptist dynamic — of rejecting conventional sacramentalism yet reviving some form of primitive physical sign-making — was developed by the huge new religious movement of the 1650s, the Quakers (or Friends). Like the Baptists and other radicals, they denounced almost every aspect of organized religion. But they made less claim to scriptural orthodoxy, instead claiming direct *spiritual* authenticity — like the original apostles. During the civil war, George

Fox, a shoemaker from Lincolnshire, began to see the church as a life-less tool of the ruling class, and the dissenting opposition as little better. He sought confrontation by heckling preachers and attacking all religious rules, including the ban on women preachers. He inspired a movement of holy class warriors who refused to know their place, and he made bold claims about the presence of the Spirit and the arrival of the kingdom of God. Some of the Quakers disturbed church services by sitting in seats reserved for their betters and refusing to budge — à la Rosa Parks during the civil rights demonstrations.

In that it rejected established religion with great gusto, the Quaker movement was in tune with Milton's politically reformed vision. But, like the Baptists, it lacked a sense that politics had to be re-created, that a new kind of state had to be forged. Instead, the movement saw all politics as corrupt. Its antinomianism (rejection of rules) was more disorderly than was Milton's. Not only should one reject the rules laid down by religious institutions; the spiritually enlightened were entitled to reject all social and political rules, and to play at prelapsarianism, imitating the innocence of Adam. It was hardly surprising that a splinter group, the Ranters, advocated free love and fervent blaspheming.

Early Quakerism developed an anarchic sign-making of its own. One aspect of this is hinted at in the name Quaker, a pejorative nickname deriving from Fox's habit, imitated by his followers, of quaking in holy rapture, especially when his authority was challenged. The worship style seems to have been a strange mixture of enthusiastic testifying and eerie silence. A huge silent crowd was a discomforting threat to the local ministers and magistrates. And the cult grew around Fox's attention-seeking performance, his imitation of the wandering, preaching, authority-bothering, suffering Jesus. By putting himself in physical danger, he offered himself as a sacrificial scapegoat. The movement produced drama, spectacle, and controversy — especially when a few followers felt inspired to disrobe in public. This was usually an imitation of biblical prophets announcing imminent judgment, but it could also be a reference to the state of Edenic sinlessness that some Quakers believed the gospel bestowed. Such signs and actions can be seen as a reaction to the sacraphobia of

Protestantism in general. Having banished images and ritual performances, it seemed to be turning religion dull.

In 1656, however, the theatrical side of the movement caused a
scandal: Fox's sidekick, James Nayler, formed a splinter group that
decided to stage Jesus' entry into Jerusalem — in Bristol. They were
arrested and charged with blasphemy; the religious conservatives in
Cromwell's regime wanted to make an example of them. Fox dis-
owned them, probably because he saw Nayler's faction as a threat to
his own control of the movement. But he remained open to the use of
performed signs. Ten years later he claimed that the fire of London
was predicted by a Friend who scattered money in the street and ran
around half-naked. And this led to a wider defense of the phenomenon on Fox's part: "And many men and women have been moved to go
naked and in sackcloth . . . as signs of their [i.e., the people's] naked-
ness from the image of God and righteousness and holiness, and how
God would strip them and make them bare and naked as they were."
Yet in much of his *Journal* he sounds like a good Calvinist. For example he expresses his dislike of folk religion, such as "May-games,
sports, plays, and shows, which trained up people to vanity and looseness, and led them from the fear of God. . . ."

In general, the movement helped to weaken the idea that Christianity is rooted in particular ritual practices. It drew on the idea of
Pauline freedom from the law: we are no longer bound by religious
rules; God can be worshiped anywhere, at any time, by anyone. It also
often echoed the Protestant and rationalist critique of "superstition":
when he met Catholics, Fox enjoyed mocking transubstantiation. And
the Friends' creed pointed in a humanistic, world-affirming direction. The Spirit is potentially present in all people equally, including
women; oppressive traditions must be discarded. And all the traditional trappings of "religion" were treated with suspicion. For example, Fox reports: "And about this time many of the steeple-houses
were empty, for such multitudes of people came to Christ's free teaching and knew their bodies the temples of God."[29] The natural human

---

29. George Fox, *The Journal of George Fox,* ed. John L. Nickalls (Philadelphia: Religious Society of Friends, 1997), pp. 503, 37, 170.

dimension replaces the dogmatic-institutional dimension. Despite its propensity toward rational humanism, Quakerism, we must note, communicated aspects of the gospel that were neglected by other forms.

Conclusion

In his book *Divided by Faith,* Benjamin Kaplan tells a nice story. In 1628 the predominantly Catholic town of Gap in the French Alps arranged a jubilee procession. "Mothers made costumes for boys to appear as angels, girls as virgins." The Huguenot children demanded to join in, and their parents let them. Catholic priests tried to eject the heretics' children from the parade, but the bishop was wiser and allowed them: "That evening, returning elated to their homes, the Huguenot boys and girls told their parents, 'We too are Catholics!'" According to the Capuchin missionaries who recounted the event, Gap's Calvinist parents could not dissuade their children even by beating them. Many young converts had been "won that day to the Church." Kaplan comments: "In an age of the baroque, when tastes ran toward the grand and ornate, toward ceremony and drama, Catholicism had an aesthetic appeal no Protestant confession could match. Catholicism was also simply more fun; it offered more conviviality, more play. To a degree Protestantism never matched — indeed, purposefully avoided — it blended religious ritual with popular festivity."[30] It is surely unnecessary to limit this to "an age of the baroque."

Protestantism in all its forms was determined by its experience of sacramentalism as problematic, the site of danger — but an unavoidable site of danger. As Cameron puts it, the Reformers were "saddled with the sacraments."[31] The main Reformers weathered the crisis in their different ways and produced new styles of sacramentalism — which is to say, new styles of church. But this crisis of religious

---

30. Benjamin J. Kaplan, *Divided by Faith: Religious Conflict and the Practice of Toleration in Early Modern Europe* (Cambridge, MA: Harvard University Press, 2007), p. 266.

31. Cameron, *The European Reformation,* p. 418.

practice was heightened for the new liberal strain within Protestant-ism. It saw the traditional sacramental practices, including those of the new churches, as tainted by the clericalism that stands against religious liberty. The liberal strain was thus confronted by a huge question: How can Christian practice be liberated from the authoritarian habits of Christendom? Can Christianity recover its ritual core on new terms? The new liberal Protestantism evaded that question; it felt the need to step away from ritual practice in order to purify Christianity. And that evasion determined its fate — for centuries to come.

FOUR

The Allure of Reason

—◦◦◦—

We have traced the emergence of the "good" strand of liberal Christianity, defined by opposition to a state-enforced church and the desire for the separation of church and state. In describing Locke's adaptation of this vision, and also in exploring its detachment from sacramental practice, we began to anticipate the other side of the coin: the "bad" tradition of liberal Christianity. It argues that Christianity must undergo a rationalizing revolution: that is, it insists that we must dispense with all aspects of religious belief that offend natural reason. Christianity must be remade for a new enlightened age. What is so wrong with this? Why should we not seek a form of Christianity that harmonizes, as far as possible, with rational understanding? The problem is that such an approach departs, with remarkable speed, from the core "stuff" of Christianity, by which I mean the basic ritual acts involved in worship and the ritual-based language in which God's authority is acknowledged and the story of his salvation is told and performed. This whole side of religion — which is, in fact, not a side but its very base — is scorned by rational-liberal theology, treated as the business of a previous, less enlightened era. The new "Christianity" that it espouses is far too weak to stand; it collapses into post-Christian humanism.

Does authentic Christianity thus reject reason — from Greek philosophy through medieval scholasticism to the Enlightenment — in favor of counterrational fideism and a kind of primitive ritualism? Perhaps it does. It should certainly be deeply suspicious of any synthesis of faith and reason. On the simplest level, a clash between faith and normal rationality must be admitted. For commonsense rationality calls faith into question: it asks for evidence concerning divine action and faith's claims about Jesus. Faith must admit the force of this commonsense, everyday skepticism. And yet the tradition of divine reason cannot be entirely dismissed: If God is the source of all order and goodness, rationality cannot be alien to him. Though it is often in conflict with human reason, and though such conflict is integral to faith, divine truth is ultimately rational. Theology must hold on to both sides of this seeming contradiction. It is generally tempted to downplay, or deny, the former side: the conflict between faith and human reason. For it is natural to seek a harmonious, nondialectical solution to the problem. So the urge for synthesis dominated patristic and medieval theology; theologians acknowledged no real conflict between natural reason and faith. This emboldened humanists to pursue natural reason wherever it led, and then the collapse of a united Christendom allowed such inquiries to spread and develop. A new rationalism loomed that was no longer constrained by church authority and was skeptical of the role of revelation in religion. Protestant states were particularly receptive to this new religious rationalism, which naturally gave rise to postreligious rationalism that retained some concept of God (Spinoza) and eventually to explicit atheism.

This new theistic rationalism was particularly well received in England after the Restoration, where it gradually became a kind of orthodoxy, in which Christianity should strive to present itself as an essentially rational worldview, indeed, as *the* essentially rational worldview. This approach changed the nature of mainstream Protestantism. From one perspective, this was a happy development: it enabled the rapid scientific and cultural advances of the Enlightenment. But from a theological perspective, it was less happy. The confluence of Protestantism and rational humanism led to a severe loss of integrity within Protestant reflection. To put it bluntly, Protestant intellectuals found it difficult to remember that their religion was based in revelation — and in the cultic reperformance of revelation. Rational humanism was patently transforming the world. Should it not be baptized rather than shunned?

Why did Protestant theology open itself to rationalism and allow the very concept of revelation to get lost? Part of the answer lies in the events related in chapter 2 above: "politically reformed" Protestantism was too politically dangerous. Reformist energy was diverted into a safer channel. And part of the answer lies in the central point of chapter 3 above: the new liberal Protestantism lacked the inner resources to resist a secularizing mutation.

To criticize the overly cozy relationship between theology and rational thought in this era prompts the question of one's attitude toward the Enlightenment, which was largely enabled by that relationship. Was it regrettable? Or was it a necessary development despite the subversion of theology it entailed? Did it not ultimately provoke theology toward new honesty and self-criticism? Charles Taylor ponders a version of this dilemma:

> Some think that the whole move to secular humanism was just a mistake, which needs to be undone. . . . Others, in which I place myself, think that the practical primacy of life has been a great gain for human kind, and that there is some truth in the self-narrative of the Enlightenment: this gain was in fact unlikely to come about without some breach with established religion. (We might even be tempted to say that modern unbelief is providential, but that might be too provocative a way of putting it.) But we nevertheless think that the metaphysical primacy of life espoused by exclusive humanism is wrong, and stifling, and that its continued dominance puts in danger the practical primacy.[1]

In the concluding section of this present chapter, I offer a slightly different account of the providential nature of the rise of secular reason. I suggest that Protestantism requires the presence of a

---

1. Charles Taylor, *A Secular Age* (Cambridge, MA: Harvard University Press, 2007), p. 637.

sharpened rationality, even an outright skepticism. Authentic faith takes the form of a dialogue with reason; it benefits from the sharpness of its conversation partner. For this reason, a simplistic condemnation of deism, as inimical to the faith basis of Christianity, is inadequate. In fact, it contributed to a deepened conception of faith, as dialogical engagement with critical reason.

Some Background

The Hebrew Bible contains no abstract concept of reason, or of God or of anything. Religious truth is presented in the context of myth, poetry, sacred history. The God we meet here has little in common with the abstract divinity of later Christian philosophy. But that does not quite make him "irrational." His creation is orderly, the expression of a plan. He also has a plan for humanity. Humans struggle to grasp this plan, and to conform themselves to it, but it is assumed to exist. It is a process of cultic and moral education that goes against the grain of human nature, yet claims to express a higher rationality. Some of the most powerful parts of the Bible complain that the world very often seems devoid of divine order: this awareness dominates the books of Psalms and Job. But faith glimpses a higher rationality; it senses that God will reorder the world and bring justice. The irrational triumph of injustice is just a temporary thing. "The fool says in his heart that there is no God" (Ps. 14:1; 53:1): the unbeliever uses merely human reason, judging by appearances, and neglects the higher rationality that has been revealed. So there is a belief in a rational moral order; but this order is not naturally apparent (though it may be glimpsed in the grandeur of creation). One needs faith that this hidden order will overturn visible reality and triumph. Divine rationality is eschatological: it awaits full realization.

The New Testament inherits — and sharpens — the idea of a divine moral order that is becoming manifest: the kingdom of God. There is a quasi-rational aura to much of Jesus' teaching, but also a sense that its truth is hidden from the merely clever. This continues in Paul's letters: God's new covenant is the expression of God's wisdom, or higher rationality. Though he makes no attempt to prove the gospel by means of natural reason, he offers arguments about how the Christ event makes sense, how it consummates biblical revelation. Yet the dissonance with natural reason is more evident than ever. This is partly because of the new and shocking *specificity* involved: this particular vilified and murdered man is God's full revelation. The Jewish notion of God's transcendent wisdom is not easily squared with this particularity. Nor, of course, is Greek thought. Paul acknowledges that the gospel of Christ crucified is folly to the brainy Greeks; it should not try to seem rational, on their terms, in order to gain acceptance in educated pagan culture. On the other hand, however, it must be declared that this is the truth of *God,* the author of the universe, whom pagan philosophy yearns to understand — thus does Paul tell the Athenian philosophers (Acts 17:23). There is also a hint (in Romans 1) that universal moral conscience is an aspect of God's revelation.

After Paul, contact with Greek philosophy steps up. The clearest instance is the opening of John's Gospel: Christ is Logos, the rational-spiritual principle of Greek thought. Of course, this is not reason in the modern sense; the Greek sense was wider, more religious. Greek thought merged rationality (in our modern sense) with higher rationality — wisdom. For Plato, the philosopher trains himself to see the spiritual reality beyond mere appearances, which is a matter of moral conduct as well as intellect. Aristotle agreed that reason was existential — and practical: it could not be separated from a virtuous lifestyle. Because philosophy was not the dry business we know it as, but had this religious side, it was natural enough for Christianity to advertise itself as the true philosophy. Stoicism had become the dominant worldview among the imperial elite. It had developed the Greek idea of divine reason *(logos),* insisting that this was a universal human capacity (but especially suited to ruling-class males). Stoicism was soon incorporated into a wider intellectual system, Neo-Platonism.

To second-century theologians such as Justin Martyr, this tradition could be more or less baptized; it was compatible with revelation. An important feature of Greek philosophy was its skepticism toward pagan superstition: early theologians claimed to be continuing this tradition, with new rigor and authority. This infuriated some pagan thinkers, who insisted that Christianity was itself an irrational cult. It also raised the suspicions of some Christian thinkers, such as Tertullian, who insisted that the distance between Athens and Jerusalem was more than just geographical. But by the third century, philosophically influenced theology was a well-established tradition. This shift prefigured the Constantinian revolution, in which Christianity allied itself with imperial power. Christianity was making itself culturally respectable, in the academy as well as in courtly circles. In the fourth century, the Council of Nicaea made use of the Aristotelian concept of substance in its formulation of the Trinity.

This is not to say that philosophical rationality dominated Christian thought. Augustine's conversion, as recounted in his *Confessions*, does not hinge on philosophical enlightenment but on a sense that the church had authority — and also that God personally addressed him — through Scripture. On the other hand, however, his conversion does bring him a supra-Platonic participation in higher rationality. Increasingly, no real tension between faith and reason was admissible, for that would be to countenance the possibility of faithless reason — a form of rationality at odds with the gospel. Instead of tension, there was a strong narrative of progression, or ascent: faith takes one beyond normal rationality to the higher version.

Did theology get too close to philosophical reason and forget the other side of the coin? Yes, it glossed over the awareness that faith entails a sharp clash with natural reason. On the other hand, Christianity could not allow philosophy's pursuit of wisdom to seem distinct from the biblical God. So theology's colonization of philosophy was perhaps a necessary move, yet one that left it subtly wounded, forgetful of a major aspect of its own grammar.

Thomas Aquinas

The subsequent cultural dominance of the church meant that philosophy was fully subordinated to theology. It was not admitted that rational inquiry was a potential threat to church teaching. In a sense, it was not a threat, because an independent, skeptical rationality was unthinkable. Instead, reason was assumed to be a tool for the better understanding of theology: it offered a window onto the truth of doctrine. In about 1200, Aristotle's works spread from Muslim to Christian universities. Here was a complete system of knowledge — without reference to the Christian God. This forced theology to rethink its relationship with natural reason. Thomas Aquinas offered a nuanced account: reason, unaided by faith, gives an unreliable account of God.

> Therefore, in order that the salvation of men might be brought about more fitly and more surely, it was necessary that they should be taught divine truths by divine revelation. It was therefore necessary that, besides philosophical science built up by reason there should be a sacred science learned through revelation.[2]

Therefore, it is impossible to prove theology's truth by reason alone. Yet the traditional insistence is renewed: that reason belongs to faith, that true reasoning cannot challenge faith's claims. Recent followers of Aquinas insist that this is not an endorsement of rational apologetics (the claim that God can be *neutrally* rationally proved), for true reasoning must operate within the culture of faith. It is Protestantism, they say, that promotes such apologetics, which leads to a thin conception of God, and ultimately hands authority to atheists, who show that neutral rationality suggests God's *non*existence.

To some, Aquinas's renewal of the synthesis of faith and reason seemed too smooth. It came close to domesticating God within a form of human thought. For Duns Scotus, we cannot use reason to build a picture of God's nature and explain miracles such as the Eucharist. The Franciscan William of Ockham agreed. He accused rational metaphysics of overconfidence in abstract concepts. All we really have are sense perceptions, slippery signs, words. How can the concepts we build from these things be reliable? We can only know God by the miracle of his revealing himself; we must trust the authority of the church, which mediates this revelation. We should admit that Christian doctrines

2. Thomas Aquinas, *Summa Theologica,* trans. Fathers of the English Dominican Province (Westminster, MD: Christian Classics, 1948), p. 1.

defy rational explanation and hence rely on faith. Only thus can God's freedom and mystery be preserved; and thus did Ockham assert "nominalism" against the "realism" — or belief in essences — of Aquinas's system. The church was wary of nominalism, partly because it applied its deconstruction to politics. Ockham argued that worldly power belonged strictly to secular rulers, a position that was echoed by Wycliffe. But, in general, nominalism's critique was shrouded in academic complexity. When Luther studied theology, he saw it as just another branch of obfuscating scholasticism. In fact, however, Luther was very much in tune with the original theological impulse behind nominalism: he wanted to establish God's freedom, his dramatic otherness, from any philosophical system. The medieval synthesis of faith and reason clouded the essence of the gospel and overestimated natural human reasoning. Our rational and moral capacities are worth nothing (Luther would put it more vividly); salvation is utterly God's doing.

Luther and Erasmus

The Renaissance humanism that culminated in Erasmus was disdainful of the whole realist-nominalist debate — on different grounds from Luther's. It seemed a parochial debate beside the recovered philosophical landscape of the ancients, Platonism, and especially its Roman variant, Stoicism. Of course, humanists claimed that this classical rationalism was fundamentally in tune with Christianity. In Florence, Ficino boldly developed a Christian-Platonic rationalism, teaching that we participate in God through reason. It seems that almost no humanists espoused the thoroughgoing skepticism of Epicureanism. Questioning the basic teachings of the church put one so far beyond social acceptability that it was next to unthinkable. For the elite, as for the masses, God was so deeply implicated in the everyday rituals of social life that it was virtually impossible to doubt his existence. As Charles Taylor says, "God's power was there for you in the microfunctioning of your society."[3] And it was not just the credulous who

3. Taylor, *A Secular Age*, p. 43.

assumed the reality of demonic forces against which God's protection was necessary. The coherence of society depended on common belief. A freethinker was a kind of religious terrorist who threatened to unravel the web of society.

As we have seen, Erasmus hoped for a reformation in which faith-based reason would play a large role, alongside a fresh understanding of Jesus's teaching. The superstitious belief that surrounded church ritual had to be pruned back — on the dual grounds of reason and fidelity to the New Testament. It was important to keep these motivations united. The rise of Luther showed why. In Erasmus's eyes, Luther, by emphasizing the biblical-theological motive at the expense of the rational one, launched a dangerous new irrationalism. He was right to call grace God's gift, not something that could be ritually earned. But this led him in a hyperbolic direction: calling salvation completely and utterly God's gift and demonizing the idea of human participation in salvation through reason and morality. As Erasmus saw it, Luther fetishized this idea of dependence on divine action, and left no role for reason, except as antagonist and temptress. Luther did indeed take a polemical position toward Scholasticism. "The whole of Aristotle is to theology as darkness is to light," he declared early on.[4] And he persistently warned against the "whore Reason," urging believers to defy her, subdue her, do violence to her. But this is not the mark of some primitive irrationalism. Luther was a careful scholar, the equal of any humanist. His work is full of an impressive, energetic form of reasoning; like Paul, he is thinking hard about how God's salvation works. He is only opposed to reason when it casts doubt on God's authority. But even this "opposition" is nuanced: he takes it for granted that such skeptical reasoning is a necessary part of the picture. In a sense, it must be allowed its say, for its tension with faith is fruitful. Reason is a necessary player in the dialogism, or internal argument, of faith. (We shall return to this at the end of this chapter.)

---

4. Martin Luther, *Luther's Works,* vol. 31, ed. H. T. Lehmann and J. Grimm (Philadelphia: Fortress, 1957), pp. 112-13.

Calvin and Castellio

Calvin had a clearer sense that theology needed to acquire a wholly new logic (by contrast, Luther was not really interested in "theology" as a discipline). It must communicate God's orderly rationality, but in the mode of science rather than philosophy. The supposedly faith-based philosophy of Scholasticism gets God wrong from the outset, by overvaluing human reason. And it is limited to the realm of theory: it fails to put divine rationality at the heart of religious *practice*, which is still dominated by primitive ritualism and random traditionalism. But God is wholly rational, and everyone must know that, not just the professors. He is not a grand blur, or a huge baroque parade. He communicates himself as a wholly distinctive system of knowledge. He does not want to hide in mystery. If he did, why would he have bothered creating us and revealing himself to us? God is a rational extrovert; he wants to be known.

So theology is a rational (in one sense of "rational") system that rejects natural human reason. This is the central tension of Calvinism. Calvin's magnum opus has an aura of rational completeness; it presents the revealed Word as the supreme rational principle. Reformed theology has retained this emphasis on systematic exactitude, as if our salvation depends on the scientific formulation of every doctrine. In Calvin's day, and long after, the synecdoche of this system was the teaching that, because we cannot earn our salvation, God must predestine us to either salvation or damnation. The doctrine is indeed logical (it logically follows from the insistence that grace cannot be earned). But that is just the problem: it insists on applying logic to an area that is mysterious.

Although Calvin rejected the traditional synthesis of faith and reason, making clear that natural reason was corrupt, his system should be judged a new kind of synthesis of faith and reason: a rationalization of faith. Like modern fundamentalism, which it hugely influences, it sees no positive role for the skeptical gaze. It has a brittleness, a singleness of vision.

As we have seen, Calvin treated humanism that dissented from this rigorous theological system as demonically dangerous. His former colleague Sebastian Castellio, whose opposition to Calvin's intolerance I have noted (in chapter 1 above), exemplifies this tradition. After his defense of toleration, he wrote a wider defense of his humanist approach to theology, *On the Art of Doubting.* A major target of that work is Calvin's doctrine of predestination: its denial of free will made God the author of damnation and was at odds with the idea that all people are equal. More widely, it simply claims too much knowledge about the workings of God. There is a crucial theological role for what we now call agnosticism. "When I teach that one must sometimes doubt, I do not do so without great cause. For I see that no less evil arises from not doubting where doubting is called for, than from not believing where believing is called for." But how do we know when to doubt, and when not to? Castellio proposes a religion-rooted rationalism:

> Reason is, so to speak, the daughter of God. She existed before all works and ceremonies and before the creation of the world. . . . It was by her that God taught his people before there were any ceremonies or writings. . . . Finally, reason guided Jesus Christ, the son of the living God — who is called in Greek Logos, which means reason or word, which are the same thing, for reason is like an inner and everlasting word of truth within us. It was by her that Christ taught others and refuted the writings and ceremonies, to which the Jews attributed more authority than to reason.[5]

What is notable here is that "reason" has much in common with the agenda of the Reformation. Castellio continues the Erasmian tradition that influenced Zwingli: true reform requires a faith-based rationalism rather than a new doctrinal zeal. But Castellio goes much further than Erasmus did in judging religious teaching by rational standards. The Eucharist must be interpreted symbolically, he says, for otherwise it conflicts with reason. Indeed, "any statement . . . man-

---

5. Sebastian Castellio, *On the Art of Doubting*, quoted in Hans R. Guggisberg, *Sebastian Castellio, 1515-1563: Humanist and Defender of Toleration in a Confessional Age*, trans. Bruce Gordon (Hampshire, UK: Ashgate, 2003), pp. 220, 224-25.

ifestly contrary to reason or the senses . . . should be understood figuratively and interpreted so that it agrees with reason and the senses."[6] Castellio's influence was extensive: admirers included Fausto Sozzini, the founder of Socinian anti-Trinitarianism (who wrote an introduction to Castellio's works in 1578), the French skeptic Montaigne, and the Dutch spiritualist-humanist Coornhert, who influenced the theologian Arminius.

The Dutch Republic became the center of rational humanism. Writing in about the 1580s, Justus Lipsius influentially espoused a barely Christian Stoicism, with little role for sin and grace, and much talk of divine reason and providence, and a vague disdain for ritual practice. (Rather surprisingly, this appealed not just to liberal Protestants but also to French Catholic intellectuals, including some clergy. It seems that those Catholics saw such humanism as a way of regaining the intellectual high ground from the Reformers.) The Dutch Protestant Hugo Grotius was influenced by Lipsius to develop a new account of natural law, more rationally based than the Catholic version (indeed, it drew on the Stoic idea of natural law). Though natural law referred to God, Grotius claimed that it could be discovered *etsi Deus non daretur* ("even if God didn't exist"). Natural law thus becomes detached from a religious narrative and becomes a theory based on the empirical observation of human nature.

Another influential humanist was the Elizabethan Francis Bacon, a major pioneer of scientific experiment. He spread the novel idea that technology could substantially change the world for the better, even repair some of the damage of the Fall. His approach to religion was pragmatically reticent, but rationally inclined. Instead of contesting traditional doctrines as irrational, such thinkers accentuated God's positive affinity with reason, as we saw with Castellio. Bacon's legacy was continued by an aristocratic English tradition that included Lord Herbert of Cherbury, whose work *De Veritate* was published in 1624. This overlapped with a tradition of minimalist Anglicanism, whose leading figures were William Chillingworth and Jeremy Taylor. Christians could legitimately be agnostic on everything

6. Castellio, *On the Art of Doubting*, p. 231.

except the divinity of Christ, they said, which left huge scope for the exercise of reason. Hobbes, who knew these liberal Anglicans, echoed the point in *Leviathan*.

Descartes and Pascal

Christian rationalism found new systematic expression in the work of René Descartes, a French Catholic who settled in the Netherlands, where he came under Lipsius's influence. In the 1640s, Descartes launched a new kind of philosophical rationalism that claimed to defend Christianity. He was motivated by an anxiety that, after the Reformation's attack on the traditional source of authority, the church, theology would collapse amid skepticism. For the Protestant location of authority in Scripture was also open to question. The questionability of both the pope and the Bible seemed to be the root cause of the Thirty Years War, which was still ravaging much of Europe. To prevent such disputes, it was time for reason to take on a new and larger role in theology. The only thing that could not be corroded by doubt, said Descartes, was the rational subject, the thinking self. But the self cannot exist in isolation: it must be grounded in an objective rational principle, God. Reason was thus elevated into a divine principle — and the key to a new, more reliable kind of theology.

This was a clear break with medieval Catholic thought, in which reason was integrated with faith. And it was an even clearer break with Luther's thought, in which reason and faith were in dialectical opposition, and with Calvin's, in which the revealed Word was the supreme rational principle. And yet the new Cartesian approach to theology became increasingly mainstream; it seemed that much of educated opinion shared Descartes's desire for a more stable basis for thought and culture. Seeking this basis seemed a religious duty, and most of theology was soon dominated by this perspective. It was almost impossible to dissent from this juggernaut. The force of intellectual orthodoxy made it almost impossible to remember that Christian truth is not founded in the rational reflection of the individual, but in a particular ritual tradition and in the individual appropriation of this ritual tradition — known as faith.

Descartes's thought spread rapidly in his native France, despite official opposition from the church. Many Catholic philosophers saw it as the antidote to the skepticism that was winning over the elite. One of the few who dissented was Blaise Pascal. This rational divinity, he said, has very little in common with the God of the Bible, in whom we are supposed to have *faith*. Pascal was influenced by Jansenism, a recent Catholic movement that strongly resembled Protestantism: it foregrounded Augustine's belief in original sin and salvation by grace rather than moral merit.

Pascal's *Pensées* (unpublished notes toward a work of apologetics, which he was writing up to his death in 1662) is largely an internal debate as to whether Christianity can be rationally justified in any sense. The basic answer is no. Rationalism is pretentious: it claims to know that divine rational order pervades the universe, including the soul. This is the essential urge of philosophy, of which Descartes is just the latest expression. Its claim to be Christian is dubious, for its claim that there is a natural rational correspondence between us and God casts doubt on original sin. Pascal takes complete skepticism, or "Pyrrhonism," more seriously; it correctly sees that humans are ruled by convention and self-justification, and ultimately by animal passion. But skepticism is one-sided: it suppresses part of the picture, that the soul senses its need for God, its wretchedness without him. It also leads to atheism and despair. Christianity "teaches men both these truths: that there is a God of whom we are capable, and that there is a corruption in nature which makes us unworthy of him. It is equally important for us to know both these points, and it is equally dangerous for man to know God without knowing his own wretchedness, and to know his wretchedness without knowing the Redeemer who can cure him of it." The Christian God is known in a more than cerebral way — through faith, understood as God's miraculous gift. Pascal expands on this. Faith is learned through a psychological process of discovering one's need for God. In this process God is experienced as a suprarational reality. Reason and custom are necessary aspects of religion: we must "open our minds to the proofs" and "confirm ourselves in it through custom," but the crucial thing is that we "offer ourselves through humiliations to inspirations, which alone can produce the true and salutary effect."

There is a slight resistance to the role of "custom" in religion, meaning ritual practice. It is presented as a rather regrettable necessity that accompanies the private business of faith. "We have to resort to customs once the mind has seen where the truth lies, to immerse and ingrain in ourselves this belief, which constantly eludes us."[7] Despite his dissent from religious rationalism, Pascal shares the growing assumption that religion is essentially an individual cerebral matter.

In opposing religious rationalism, he was seeking to reverse a tidal wave: French philosophy was dominated by attempts to reconcile Descartes more smoothly with Catholic orthodoxy. The leading figure in the 1670s was Malebranche, who influenced the visiting German philosopher Leibniz with his idea that the fixed laws of nature should be seen as God's will, an idea that Leibniz would soon reframe in terms of God's creation of "the best of all possible worlds."

In the English revolutionary period, rationalism was largely eclipsed by the various forms of religious radicalism, but the distinction between these forces was often blurred. There was a rationalist element in the biggest new religious movement, the Quakers. Like Calvinists elsewhere, the vast majority of Puritans were intolerant of rationalist tendencies, which they saw in every other religious point of view, including ones that seem far from rationalist to modern eyes, such as Arminianism, which denied predestination.

Anti-Trinitarianism was a central feature of the new rationalism, though it remained largely covert. Difficulty with the Trinity was hardly new: this was the big problematic doctrine of the early church. The issue is inseparable from Christology: if Christ is fully God, then the concept of God has to accommodate him. The early church was beset by movements that resisted this, including Arianism, which was banished by the Council of Nicaea. But violent disputes continued for

---

7. Pascal, *Pensées,* translated by Honor Levi (Oxford: Oxford University Press, 1995), 688, p. 171; 655, p. 148; 661, p. 148.

another two centuries about how the fusion of humanity and divinity in Christ should be understood. Lingering dissatisfaction with the Trinity was a major factor in the rise of Islam, which passionately exalts God's unity. The doctrine became ever more central to the church. What complicates the issue is that the defense of the Trinity merges with the defense of ecclesiastical authority. The Cathar heresy was anti-Trinitarian; its association of this doctrine with ecclesiastical authoritarianism anticipated the post-Reformation era. In the late medieval period the West became increasingly aware of other religious and philosophical traditions — Islam, Aristotelianism, Judaism — that found this doctrine strange, indeed irrational. Christendom had to protect itself against this view. The main Reformers were at least as protective of Trinitarianism as their Catholic enemies were. Miguel Servetus embodied the threat: his anti-Trinitarianism was rooted in the southern Spanish mix of Islam, Judaism, and philosophy. And he exemplified a new spirit of confidence in the *obviousness* of God's rational unity. He seems to have supposed that even Calvin, having heard the arguments, would see the light. As I noted above in chapter 1, anti-Trinitarianism blossomed in Eastern Europe, in tandem with toleration, with the Italian exile Fausto Sozzini playing a central role.

To question the Trinity was not necessarily to take a rationalizing approach to religion. Milton advocated the Arian idea that the Son was subordinate to the Father. Though he called the doctrine of the Trinity irrational, his essential complaint was that it was unbiblical — and that it was a token of ecclesiastical authority. He did not share the wider anti-Trinitarian belief that religion should be comprehensively rationalized. He seems to have been largely motivated by an aversion to knee-jerk traditionalism: we should not passively receive doctrine from clerical authority, but should work it out for ourselves, Bible in hand. And yet, for many thinkers, the Trinity epitomized the irrationalism that had to be pruned away from Christianity. This stance could be presented as Protestant, since the doctrine has no explicit scriptural basis. But this, of course, was severely at odds with Reformation Protestantism, which firmly asserted the priority of revelation to reason.

After the Restoration of the English monarchy, there was a steady rise of cautiously rational theology. As long as it did not challenge church orthodoxy, this approach was positively encouraged. It was seen as far less dangerous than religious dissent, whether establishment-attacking Protestantism, or Catholicism. Indeed, rational religion was seen by clergy as an ally against bothersome religious extremism. "Latitudinarian" Anglicanism fully accepted the new emphasis on rational morality. The rejection of enthusiasm (we would say "extremism") became central to the rhetoric of Anglicanism and helped to legitimate its revived authority. The suppression of dissent was for the sake of a new form of civil order.

Writers who used reason in defense of religion were officially lauded, but those who used reason to criticize traditional doctrines were obviously seen as dangerous. In practice, the line between the two activities is blurred. To say that Christianity is essentially in accordance with natural reason is very close to saying that thus it must be purged of its other, irrational aspects. The latter position was vilified as "deism," which was seen as firmly on the road to atheism.

So deism might be defined as the call for the rationalization of Christianity, the claim that its reliance on revelation, and ritual practice, is now redundant. What complicates the picture is that most defenders of traditional Christianity strongly resembled the deists: they agreed that natural reason was central to religious truth, but added that traditional doctrines and practices were still defensible on these terms. So it might be useful to distinguish between *explicit* deism, which rejects revelation-based doctrine, and *implicit* deism, which defends traditional doctrine in rational terms. To add to the complexity, explicit deists often posed as implicit deists, "defending" Christianity in terms that were really intended to undermine it. Furthermore, many dissenters used deism as a coded way of attacking the established church (they also attacked Roman priestcraft, intending inferences to be drawn about the Anglican variety also).[8]

---

8. For example, the dissenting MP Robert Howard's *History of Religion* (1694) argues that Roman Catholicism is a continuation of paganism: saints and angels correspond to pagan demons and heroes, and "their Idol of Bread, Divinity infus'd into

Explicit deists were influenced by the new archheretic Spinoza, whose *Treatise* was published in 1670. To the anger of the Jewish community of Amsterdam — and subsequently of all traditional believers — Spinoza argued that science undermined all claims of revelation. He retained belief in a rational deity, or "supreme Being," but insisted that such a deity was incompatible with the endless irrationality taught by every revealed religion. He held that God has no existence outside of the rational universe he has created. In effect, the rational universe replaces God. Spinoza can be seen as the logically consistent deist, who dared to point out what has come to seem obvious, that a purely rational conception of God is strongly at odds with all traditional religion. Most deists, whether through timidity or sincere conviction, suggested that God should be understood in rational terms, and also that the core content of revelation remained credible.

Locke was an implicit deist; he was close to the Anglican Latitudinarians, such as Chillingworth. His *Essay Concerning Human Understanding* (1689) emphasized the role of reason in assessing the plausibility of claims to revelation, but did not dispense with faith in revelation. A few years later he seems to have become alarmed that explicit deists were making use of his thought, and he responded with *The Reasonableness of Christianity, as Delivered in the Scriptures* (1695). It begins by criticizing (unnamed) recent writers who "thought there was no Redemption necessary . . . and so made Jesus Christ nothing but the Restorer and Preacher of pure Natural Religion; thereby doing violence to the whole tenor of the New Testament."[9] Locke's aim is to present a simplified version of Christianity, based in the Gospels. He focuses on the moral teaching of Jesus, which is "conformable to that of Reason" (p. 153). And he proposes a minimal definition of Christianity's essence: one becomes a Christian by believing in God, and in Jesus as the Messiah. The term "Messiah," rather than divine Son, is

---

Crosses, Images, Agnus Dei's and Relics, correspond to the Pillars, Statues and Images consecrated by Pagan Priests" (quoted in S. J. Barnett, *The Enlightenment and Religion: The Myths of Modernity* (Manchester, UK: Manchester University Press, 2003), p. 90.

9. John Locke, *The Reasonableness of Christianity as Delivered in the Scriptures*, ed. John C. Higgins-Biddle (Oxford: Clarendon Press, 1999), p. 5. Hereafter, page references to this work appear in parentheses in the text.

justified by his focus on the Gospels: this is how Jesus was seen by the people who met him and had faith in him. To cover himself in the face of charges of heretical minimalism, he adds that, once one has become a Christian, one will naturally espouse various other doctrines. Nevertheless, focusing on Jesus as "Messiah" rather than the divine Son naturally brought charges of Socinianism.

He returns to the point that the essential content of revelation is compatible with reason: "Tis no diminishing to Revelation, that Reason gives its Suffrage too to the Truths Revelation has discovered. But 'tis our mistake to think, that because Reason confirms them to us, we had the first certain knowledge of them from thence, and in that clear Evidence we now possess them" (pp. 156-57). The stated aim is to assert the priority of revelation to reason, but if reason is capable of corroborating revelation, then the necessity of revelation becomes unclear. Surely it *is* a diminishing of revelation to say that anything important in its content is also available through reason. It makes it redundant.

A sacraphobic and anticlerical spirit often surfaces. Though the Jews had expected a Messiah who was prophet, priest, and king, Locke says, "yet I do not remember that [Jesus] anywhere assumes to himself the title of a priest, or mentions anything relating to his priesthood" (p. 120). After Jesus, worship needs no "magnificent temples" but "by a Pure Heart might be performed any where" (p. 160). (This seems to echo Milton's line about the only temple favored by God being "an upright heart and pure.") Religion becomes fundamentally inner: "all outside Performances might now be spared . . ." (p. 160). In practice, public worship remains necessary, but it can be decently restrained, even minimal: "Praises and prayer, humbly offered up to the Deity, was the worship he now demanded" (p. 160). There is no mention of the Eucharist. With this tract Locke seems to be meaning to contribute to the Latitudinarian tradition of Anglicanism, but in practice he demonstrates the closeness of that tradition to deism.

John Toland was the leading exponent of explicit deism (it was probably he to whom Locke was responding in his work). His anonymous tract *Christianity Not Mysterious* (1696) calls for Christianity to jettison its irrational elements and become a pure religion of reason.

In his account of Christian origins, the apostles "were employ'd to dispel Ignorance, to eradicate Superstition, to propagate Truth and Reformation of Manners." Unfortunately, irrational elements entered in from Judaism and paganism, traditions that are hopelessly respectful of ritual:

> Ceremonies never fail to take off the Mind from the Substance of *Religion,* and lead Men into dangerous Mistakes: for *Ceremonies* being easily observ'd, everyone thinks himself religious enough that exactly performs them. But there is nothing so naturally opposite as *Ceremony* and *Christianity.* The latter discovers Religion naked to all the World, and the former delivers it under mystical Representations of a merely arbitrary Signification.[10]

Toland insists that by this infection the Eucharist "was absolutely perverted and destroyed," and is "not yet restor'd by the purest Reformations in Christendom." (He implies that the Eucharist is theoretically a good thing, but its perversion was so deep that it remains untouchable, too toxic. This same idea was present in Sebastian Franck, and also surfaces in Milton.) Things became worse with Constantine, and the multitudes who joined the church from "politick considerations."[11]

It is noteworthy that Toland's skepticism is decidedly Protestant, an adaptation of the Calvinist attack on idolatry. He has a strong negative conception of God as the force of antisuperstition. It is tempting to think that he was "really" an atheist, using deism to seem more acceptable, but this is anachronistic: atheism entailed absolute skepticism rather than reformist confidence. Toland's book contributed to a sense of alarm. In 1698, Parliament passed an "Act for the effectual suppressing of blasphemy and profaneness" — mainly concerned with curbing Socinian deism. The threat was exaggerated by the High Church Party, to curb the power of the Latitudinarians, and

10. In Peter Gay, ed., *Deism, an Anthology* (Toronto: D. Van Nostrand, 1968), pp. 66, 76.

11. Toland, quoted in S. J. Barnett, *The Enlightenment and Religion: The Myths of Modernity* (Manchester, UK: Manchester University Press, 2003), p. 101.

the populist cry of "Church in danger" intensified over the next decade. And yet a real intellectual shift did underlie such machinations.

Toland's theopolitical posture was similar to Locke's. In theory, he saw establishment as inimical to religious liberty, but in practice he felt that Anglican establishment, after 1689, had enabled a strong form of national Protestantism, and that a strong Protestant England was crucial to the international cause of liberty. As long as the state continued to widen toleration for dissenters, establishment was compatible with the cause of republican liberty. Like Locke, then, Toland advocated reform (primarily meaning fuller toleration) from within — on the basis of acceptance of the new constitution. Such pragmatism had only limited success; progress toward fuller toleration for dissenters moved at snail's pace, for at least another century. In 1711, for example, a law was passed against dissenting schools. At the end of his life, Toland admitted that he had been overoptimistic about reform from within.

Implicit deism was fueled by science, especially that of Isaac Newton, and it became increasingly common to see God reflected in the laws of nature. The idea became prevalent that God had established the laws of nature, set the universe in motion, and retreated. The contrary idea, that Christianity was rooted in faith, worship, and revelation, was associated with ill-educated extremists and the wars of the previous generation. "The background assumption of the Deist standpoint involves disintricating the issue of religious truth from participation in a certain community practice of religious life, into which facets of prayer, faith, hope are woven."[12] Also consigned to the past was the sin-based anthropology that extended from Augustine to Calvin. Perhaps Calvin's overliteral interest in the workings of election can be partly blamed for the huge reaction against the very idea of original sin. According to deism, the sane, modern view was that human nature was capable of almost endless improvement. The new sin was error, especially the willful error of religious superstition. In the Netherlands, Pierre Bayle, son of a Huguenot minister, was a major proponent of the antidogmatic mood. His defense of toleration was

12. Taylor, *A Secular Age*, p. 293.

similar to Locke's: all sects should be tolerated unless they are provably politically dangerous. His *Dictionary*, published 1697, was famously irreverent toward Old Testament heroes, which it treated as strange tribal leaders. Yet he was detached from deism; for example, he called Spinoza's system "an absurd and monstrous hypothesis."[13] His passion for liberty was firmly rooted in his inherited Protestantism, which he never renounced.

Even avowed opponents of deism echoed many of its assumptions. In Daniel Defoe's novel *Robinson Crusoe* (1718), the nature of Crusoe's conversion reflects a mix of dissenting piety and the rational individualism of the age. The novel imagines a modern, practical, enlightened man who is suddenly plunged by shipwreck into solitude. In his new vulnerability he learns of his dependence on God's grace, thanks to a Bible salvaged from the wreck. His attitude changes from despondency to gratitude and enthusiasm. Despite his precarious situation, he now knows true spiritual happiness. Soon he meets a native, Friday, and he begins "to lay a foundation of religious knowledge in his mind." The two men constitute an idyllic minichurch that has avoided "all the disputes, wranglings, strife, and contention which has happened in the world about religion, whether niceties in doctrines, or schemes of church government." Here, in microcosm, is the civilized approach to religion: it is a divinely inspired form of knowledge that ought to be accepted in a flexible rather than dogmatic spirit, and that has no need of ritual expression. Indeed, the avoidance of religious expression is conducive to social peace, for there is no practice on which to disagree. Soon they are joined by Friday's father and by a Spanish sailor. Crusoe reflects that his three subjects were of three different religions: "My man Friday was a Protestant, his father was a pagan and a cannibal, and the Spaniard was a Papist. However, I allowed liberty of conscience throughout my dominions."[14] A peaceful society depends not on religious uniformity but on the dominance of a religious style that marginalizes sacramentalism.

---

13. E. A. Beler and M. du P. Lee Jr., eds., *Selections from Bayle's Dictionary* (New York: Greenwood, 1952), p. xxiii.

14. Daniel Defoe, *Robinson Crusoe* (New York: Signet Classic, 1960), pp. 212, 236.

If Crusoe were in the habit of considering the Eucharist a central part of Christianity, the separateness of these Christians from each other would appear less virtuous. Defoe thus reflects the assumption that ritual is the troublemaking side of religion, that social peace rests on inner verbal and cerebral religion.

In France there was a stronger post-Christian trajectory to deism, a response to the far greater official intransigence of the church. In the 1720s, Voltaire became the literary star of Paris, known for his daring freethinking as well as his verses and plays. His admiration for deism brought him to England in 1726, and he was impressed by the liberal culture he found. He was also fascinated by the Quakers, devoting four of his *Lettres philosophiques* (1734) to their seemingly post-superstitious form of faith. Back in France, he was chiefly concerned to attack pessimistic and superstitious Christian tradition (he particularly hated Pascal's distrust of natural reason). But he also opposed the atheist materialism that was beginning to surface: reason depended on divine order. Religion should be purged of superstitious error, but a rational remnant should remain, to inculcate popular morality (Latitudinarian Anglicanism seemed ideal). If one were not capable of rational faith, it was better to retain superstitious faith in divine order than to have no faith at all.

Voltaire's deism was irreverently post-Christian: he rejected the idea that Jesus, "the hanged man," had a unique role in showing us the rational God. In order to show that Christianity was not unique, Voltaire turned anthropologist: the various primitive peoples that were being discovered around the world were not demonic savages but were naturally moral, he suggested. And the Christless Chinese, he announced provocatively, "have perfected moral science."

Voltaire shows that deism is an alternative form of *faith* — in divine Reason — and that there is something contradictory about this conjoining of faith and nature.

God has given us a principle of universal reason, as he has given feathers to birds and furs to bears; and this principle is so constant, that it subsists despite all the passions which struggle against it; despite the tyrants who wish to drown it in blood; despite the impostors who would employ superstition to bring it to naught.[15]

But birds and bears do not need to preach about the efficacy of their feathers and fur. Reason sounds more like a saving cause, a new faith, than a biological property. There is a quasi-religious narrative about the persecuted truth that will ultimately be vindicated. This is the difference between deism and atheism, in the proper sense: atheism lacks this high view of reason; it is skeptical about whether reason is more than a messy human construction. Ironically, the faith element of deism, the sense that a better world is around the corner if only reason triumphs, is very basic to the "atheism" of our own day, that is, today's "atheism" is closer to deism than it understands. To Richard Dawkins and other atheists of today, deism is rather baffling: Why didn't Voltaire, and even Spinoza, reject "God" more completely? The fact is that the deists were more self-aware and honest than are today's atheists. They understood that their high view of reason as a redeeming, liberating force was essentially religious. They understood that atheism entailed the denial of ultimate purpose, that it was rightly associated with extreme skepticism, even nihilism. Today's atheists sternly deny God, yet they continue the deist tradition of faith in saving rationality.[16]

Deism helps us see beyond the master narrative of rational humanism. This has been called the subtraction narrative: once religious belief is taken away, the natural worldview is gradually uncovered. Deism suggests that humanism is a secularization of the Protestant Christian narrative, in which a rejection of superstition brings a new era of freedom and truth. It is also a secularization of the wider Christian narrative of the triumph of love, or *agape,* which some mystics had located within history.

It bears repeating that deism overlapped with authentically Prot-

15. In Henry Steele Commager, *The Empire of Reason: How Europe Imagined and America Realized the Enlightenment* (London: Phoenix, 1978), pp. 63, 43-44.

16. Thus John Gray: "Contemporary atheism is a Christian heresy that differs from earlier heresies chiefly in its intellectual crudity" (Gray, *Black Mass: Apocalyptic Religion and the Death of Utopia* [New York: Farrar, Straus and Giroux, 2007], p. 189).

estant impulses: criticizing an authoritarian church and seeking new freedom to study Scripture. For example, the classical scholar Conyers Middleton was one of the first to challenge the church's rigid insistence on a literal rather than allegorical interpretation of the Bible. In 1749 he argued that Protestants should be wary of the category of "miracle" because of its propensity for authoritarian abuse. He warned that the Church of England's stifling of free thought was against the spirit of the 1688 revolution, which made the established church answerable to lay rationality. "An ecclesiastical constitution not to be altered is a contradiction to Protestantism and to liberty, and can produce no other peace than what we see in popish countries, that of slaves."[17] Middleton thus argued that the critical study of Scripture was a Protestant right; the alternative was Roman-style authoritarianism. Naturally he was accused by high churchmen, such as William Warburton, the foremost theological policeman of the age, of being a dangerous deist. But, in fact, it is hard to separate Middleton's deism (which took the form of Ciceronian skepticism) from a seemingly sincere affirmation of the liberal spirit of Protestantism.

The most rigorous mid-century attack on deism did not come from a theologian but from the Scottish philosopher David Hume. He asked the question that now seems axiomatic: Why identify rationality and God? He revived the skeptical view, which Descartes had falsely claimed to bury (that reason is just a flawed human construct). Hume developed Locke's empiricism: we know things through the evidence of our senses rather than through something called reason. Philosophy cannot establish the supremacy of reason, let alone link this to God. Old-fashioned Christian orthodoxy is more realistic than modern philosophy about how God is knowable: that is, faith is needed. As Hume puts it:

> The Christian religion not only was at first attended with miracles, but even at this day cannot be believed by any reasonable person

---

17. Conyers Middleton, *A Free Inquiry into the Miraculous Powers which are Supposed to have Subsisted in the Christian Church*, in Hugh Trevor-Roper, *History and the Enlightenment* (New Haven: Yale University Press, 2011), p. 111.

without one. Mere reason is insufficient to convince us of its veracity: And whoever is moved by Faith to assent to it, is conscious of a continued miracle in his own person, which subverts all the principles of his understanding, and gives him a determination to believe what is most contrary to custom and experience.[18]

This statement is famously ambiguous: Is it a sarcastic dismissal of faith, or a Pascalian insight into the reliance of Christianity on faith? In the light of Hume's atheism, probably the former, but the insight nevertheless stands. (We shall see that Karl Barth says something very similar when he disputes the nature of faith with Adolf von Harnack.)

The strongest Christian response to deism arose from the new reform movement within the Church of England, Methodism. It was a variation on a Continental theme. In the early eighteenth century German Lutheranism spawned a new style of Protestantism, called Pietism. It emphasized the transformation of human life that faith brings, the moral idealism and energy. There was a significant overlap with deism: it shared the sense that too much emphasis on doctrines and sacraments and institutions was unhelpful (much of German Lutheranism was surprisingly antiquated). A new ecumenical era was possible if the simple message of love was prioritized. It had much in common with the mystical rationalism of the Quakers, and it was similarly democratic in spirit. The simple message could empower its humbler hearers. It was also anthropocentric and prone to the Pelagian downplaying of sin as an essential aspect of humanity. It combined a kind of rationalism with an emotional intensity.

In Britain this movement was channeled by John Wesley, who reacted against the Latitudinarian climate in the Church of England: Deism had made passionate individual faith seem outdated, Wesley complained. His style was simple, sincere, and emotionally open; yet he also restated the traditional Reformation themes of sin, grace, faith, and the power of the biblical Word. Though he remained a loyal

18. David Hume, *Of Miracles*, in Richard Wollheim, ed., *Hume on Religion* (London: Collins, 1963), p. 226.

Anglican, he warned that the hierarchical structure of the church was obscuring the essential Christian message, which is salvation by faith and the ability of ordinary people to live holy lives. (Wesley rejected predestination for an upbeat Arminianism; for him, salvation was universally available). The social Christianity that deists affirmed was not enough, according to Wesley; truly dedicated Christians would reject the ways of the world and embrace a simple disciplined life, sustained by prayer, Bible reading, and sermons. His movement spurned all dubious aspects of neopagan modernity, summed up by the theater. Wesleyan politics was ambiguous: it was a democratic movement in that it empowered low-born believers, yet it was strongly opposed to liberal reformism, which it saw as the tool of deism. It was one of the first popular movements to condemn the values of the "liberal elite," seen as a secular urban conspiracy whose real agenda was decadence.

Like the early Puritans, Wesley did not want to be outside the established church. He liked its orderly feel, and he had a high opinion of the Eucharist. Indeed, he encouraged a new level of lay participation in it. The main drawbacks of the church, in Wesley's eyes, were its laxity towards Latitudinarians and its anxious attachment to the parish system, which made an itinerant preacher into a virtual outlaw. In his journal he comes across as very much like a contemporary British evangelical: a middlebrow bourgeois, disappointed by faithless elitist culture and impatient with awkward theological issues, as if in possession of a religious version of common sense.

In France there was a desire for a new — richer and rounder — deism. According to Jean-Jacques Rousseau, the rationalism of the elite was stultifying: its excessive emphasis on the rational individual had produced a bloodless, mechanistic view of society and a narrow concept of civilization. A more holistic humanism was needed. The key was to understand humans as social animals. Of course, the deists had a positive account of society — as the arena of rational civility. But, according to Rousseau, their heart wasn't in it. Their emphasis on individual rights was at root opposed to the traditional idea of society as an organic unity. In 1750, Rousseau first announced that the conventional view of civilization was death to the soul. Thus he became the first postmodern French theorist, for he was rejecting the dominant idea of modernity, but in a nonreactionary way. Humans need a sense of social belonging, he believed. This is what religion is really about: the ecstatic membership of a holy body, which is simultaneously religious and political. This unity, natural to the ancient world, was severely damaged by Christianity — with its otherworldliness and its opposition of church and state. And the Enlightenment perpetuated the damage: its rational universalism pulls people away from their deepest cultural identity. Real social belonging is local, particular, and prerational. It consists of the myths and traditions that bind us together as tribe or nation. This will become a major component of modern nationalism, the sense that a precious mystical essence must be preserved from the rationalizing tide.

Rousseau makes a half-turn away from the sacraphobia of Protestantism and deism. Worship is an essentially human action; we create meaning through social celebration rather than cold thinking. But, instead of affirming Christian worship, he insists that a new, more effectively unitive cult is needed. For the first time in history, an affirmation of public worship is detached from allegiance to any particular religion. Humanist and Protestant thinkers had stepped back from ritual, but in order to condemn it rather than admire it — or to tolerate it as socially necessary, in the manner of Stoic philosophers. This fusion of Enlightenment with a new desire for social unity, performed through popular rituals, became central to the French Revolution.

Rousseau expressed his approach to public religion in his letter of 1758, in which he opposes Voltaire's campaign for the reopening of Geneva's theaters. Theater is an elitist and alienated form of culture, he argues. Instead of passively receiving culture in the dark, people should enjoy outdoor festivals.

> It is in the open air, under the sky, that you ought to gather and give yourselves to the sweet sentiment of your happiness. Let your pleasures not be effeminate or mercenary; let nothing that has an odor of constraint and selfishness poison them. . . . What will be shown in [such festivals]? Nothing, if you please. With liberty,

wherever abundance reigns, well-being also reigns. Plant a stake crowned with flowers in the middle of a square; gather the people together there, and you will have a festival. Do better yet; let the spectators become an entertainment to themselves . . . so that each sees and loves himself in the others so that all will be better united.[19]

It is worth noting that "liberty" does not seem to mean freedom from political constraint here; it means something more like "the free expression of the happiness-seeking human." This vision is rooted in an idealization of classical paganism as socially unifying, which entails a suspicion of Christianity as intrinsically antisocial, otherworldly. Rousseau, therefore, revived the pagans' complaint against the early Christians: that by refusing to join in with public festivities (which entailed sacrifice to the emperor), they disrupted common culture, which was ritually enacted. Of course, the Catholic Church had provided common culture, including public festivity, for centuries. But in Rousseau's eyes its power to do so was over, for it stood against the humanism that modernity had rediscovered. Christianity can only be revived if it fully embraces this humanism, if it begins with the holiness of the human heart. Rousseau ventriloquized this view through the Vicar of Savoy, a character in his novel *Emile* (1762). The vicar tells of his rejection of Calvinism and Catholicism in favor of an emotionally intelligent deism that has no interest in doctrine and a huge interest in psychology. This almost completely secularized pietism was a huge influence on Romanticism in the next generation.

In Germany (which was still divided into many states, of which Prussia was the largest), deism was vying with pietism for the allegiance of the elite. Deism was represented by thinkers, including the playwright Lessing, who produced a key sound bite of rational theology: "Contingent truths of history can never prove necessary truths of reason. That is the horribly wide ditch which I cannot cross, often and

---

19. Rousseau, Letter to M. D'Alembert, in Rousseau, *Politics and the Arts,* ed. Allan Bloom (New York: Ithaca, 1989), pp. 125-26.

earnestly as I have tried."[20] German deism was inclined to logical consistency: if God is rational, the irrationality of revelation must be rejected. As we saw, most British deism (implicit deism) evaded this either/or choice by claiming that revelation was compatible with rationality — a kind of truce underwritten by Latitudinarian Anglicanism. The Germans were less inclined to tolerate such muddle, but Christianity and the Enlightenment somehow had to be reconciled. The task fell to Immanuel Kant, who combined a passionate faith in the Enlightenment with a residual sympathy with the pietism in which he had been raised (though he abandoned actual pietist worship). His solution was to give new prominence to morality. He dismissed the proofs of God cited by deism, both the ontological proof (which holds that God is a logically necessary concept) and the cosmological proof (which holds that creation must have come from somewhere). It is only reflection on morality that grounds the idea of God, Kant argues in *The Critique of Practical Reason* (1788). We naturally seek happiness, and we feel a duty to be moral. The only imaginable way these impulses can be reconciled is if happiness comes from obeying the moral law. God must be the author of this law, and the soul must be immortal, so that happiness can come after death. Faith in these postulates is the only rational response to existence.

In 1793, Kant summed up his religious thinking in his book *Religion Within the Limits of Reason Alone*. Reflection on morality calls us to moral perfectionism, he explains. The discourse of morality only makes sense if absolute goodness is posited. "Morality thus leads ineluctably to religion, through which it extends itself to the idea of a powerful moral lawgiver, outside of mankind." And religion remains rooted in rational morality: "A moral religion . . . must consist not in dogmas and rites but in the heart's disposition to fulfill all human duties as divine commands." Does it follow that dogmas and rites are a distraction from true moral religion? Most deists would say yes; Kant's answer is subtler. In the real world, he says, this pure moral re-

---

20. Lessing, quoted in Karl Barth, *Protestant Theology in the Nineteenth Century: Its Background and History,* trans. Brian Cozens and John Bowden (London: SCM, 2001), pp. 237-38.

ligion only exists in the form of ordinary, messy religion: "A statutory ecclesiastical faith is associated with pure religious faith as its vehicle and as the means of public union of men for its promotion." This moral vision must be culturally strong rather than the theory of isolated intellectuals — thus religion. Of course, liberal Protestantism is the best possible vehicle: it minimizes the irrelevant packaging, and it understands its function — which is to be transparent to moral religion. It grasps that "the token of the true church is its *universality*."[21]

The deist rejection of myth-based religion is simplistic, according to Kant. Traditional religion is actually a necessary vehicle for the religion of moral reason. There are two levels to religious truth: the traditional myth-based form, known as "positive religion," and the rational-moral "kernel." Enlightened religion necessarily inhabits old-fashioned religion. But if religion is viewed as the means to a moral end, why not cut the Gordian knot and seek the moral end more directly? Why can't morality dispense with God? Because morality does *not* come naturally to humans. We must posit a divine authority telling us to be good, promising us eternal happiness through moral perfectionism. The problem with deism is its false optimism about the natural goodness of humanity. Kant's youthful pietism stayed with him: he argues that there is "radical evil" in humanity. On the other hand, in exalting a form of rationality and in assuming that religious practice is secondary, almost dispensable, he perpetuates deism. Kant's theory encourages the evolution, or dissolution, of religion into humanism — even if it is a specifically religious type of humanism.

The influence of this approach can hardly be overstated. Subsequent Protestant theology is deeply indebted to the idea that moral idealism is what Christianity is really about, and that myth and ritual are the necessary forms that such idealism takes. But in the end, Kant's approach was too subtle, too frail, and too dependent on waning Christian assumptions. In the next century it became less common to see morality as a crisis necessitating God. It was not rational

---

21. Immanuel Kant, *Religion Within the Limits of Reason Alone,* trans. Theodore M. Greene and Hoyt H. Hudson (New York: Harper, 1960), pp. 5-6, 79, 97, 105.

reflection on morality that led Kant to his view of the matter but the particular mythical structure he youthfully imbibed.

The era of deism was a profound disaster for Protestant theology: it drifted further away from acknowledging the rootedness of Christianity in particular cultural forms, cultic practices, and forms of speech. The sacraphobia discussed in chapter 3 intensified. Those who dissented from the deist drift, such as Wesley, neglected the link between Protestantism and liberty, the "frail vision" that formed in the previous century. As we shall see, Wesley offered a simplistic conception of faith. Protestantism, therefore, became a choice between deism on the one hand and Wesleyan reaction on the other, or high-church reaction, intellectually renewed by Samuel Johnson. (Deism was not Protestantism's finest phase, but again, its response to a reactionary church was largely justified. Many deists usefully began to subject religion to critical scrutiny, thus laying the foundations of liberal Protestant theology. For example, Gibbon was accused of treating Christian origins as if they were any other bit of history. In retrospect, this irreverence was a theologically virtuous move.)

Did things look up for theology with the advent of Romanticism?[22] Yes and no. Rousseau embodies the ambiguity: he seemed to announce a new post-Christian social humanism, yet his interest in ritual and primitivism helped spark a new direction in Protestant thought. The bridge was German Romanticism, which emerged in close dialogue with pietism. Goethe detached the cult of emotional sincerity from pietism and applied it to art, love, pantheism. He developed a new paganism, imbued with Christian eschatology. But other Romantics were more interested in theology. Foremost among them was Herder, who, inspired by the alleged rediscovery of the ancient Scottish poet Ossian and by the scholarly work on Homer during his time, developed a new understanding of the centrality of national culture — especially poetic culture. His book *The Spirit of Hebrew Poetry*

22. As Charles Taylor argues, Romanticism did not replace the Enlightenment; rather, it became its dialogue partner. This dialogue brought an ever-increasing expansion of options, new fusions of science and myth, including the antihumanist interest in heroism and tragedy that culminates in Nietzsche and fascism. Romanticism is "an immanent counter-Enlightenment" (Taylor, *A Secular Age*, p. 369).

(1782) launched a new approach to Scripture as consisting of poetry and mythology.

Did Romanticism help liberal Christianity rediscover its ritual basis? The answer is generally no. Instead, it largely enabled art, especially poetry, with its ecstasies and martyrdoms, to seem to be an alternative faith (Young Werther, Chatterton, Keats, and so on). It awakened Protestant *culture* to the value of sacramentalism — but in the arena of art rather than religion. Romanticism may be seen as a failed reform movement within Protestantism. It *should* have pointed Protestantism to its ritual roots and unleashed a new sacramental energy; but in reality the sacramental energy it unleashed was generally post-Christian.

The possibility of something different is tantalizingly evident right at the outset of English Romanticism. A differently gifted William Blake could have been a kind of new Luther, for he revived the liberal Christian vision of the civil war era in a potentially very fruitful way. Not only did he reject establishment, clericalism, and legalism — as many radical dissenters did — he also uniquely rejected the whole deist tradition of denigrating the primary speech-forms of faith. He saw that a revival of liberal Christianity had to be utterly rooted in revelation, faith. His prophetic approach to poetry announced that art should not be sundered from Christian truth; nor should political liberty. Though Blake was initially excited by the French Revolution, he rejected the secular radicalism of many of his friends. "The Bible," he says, "was the book of liberty, and Christianity the sole regenerator of nations."[23] Blake instinctively reached for a vision of liberal Christianity that had the virtues of Milton's (political liberalism, antilegalism) and that rejected the vices of the intervening period by putting faith in revelation first.

Blake's antilegalism is particularly noteworthy. It is often mistaken for a secular belief in self-expression and antipathy toward organized religion. But it is actually rooted in the Pauline theme that excited Luther and Milton: "To the pure all things are pure" and "All

23. Samuel Palmer, quoted in Alexander Gilchrist, *The Life of William Blake,* ed. Ruthven Todd (London: Dent, 1982), p. 303.

things are permitted, but not all things are beneficial." In *The Gates of Paradise,* Blake portrays Jehovah as writing the Mosaic law, and then thinking better of it: "[T]he Dead Corpse from Sinai's heat/[he] Buried beneath his Mercy Seat./O Christians, Christians! Tell me Why/You rear it on your Altars high." Not since Milton had an English thinker foregrounded Pauline liberty in this way. Of course, Blake was not interested in "Romanticism." He considered Wordsworth a nature-idolater, and he rejected the latter's idea of "Natural Piety" as deism in new garb ("There is no such thing as natural piety because the natural man is at enmity with God.") He was interested in proclaiming the gospel — a radically liberal version of the gospel — with new sacramental energy, by means of artistic creation ("Christianity is Art").[24] Of course, his immediate influence was next to nonexistent, which was hardly surprising given its fragmentary and eccentric character. But this character should not detract from its unique insight into the malaise of Protestantism. And as we shall presently see, Blake's conception of faith was more nuanced than that of other antideist believers.

The Dialogical Alternative

I have suggested that deism damaged Protestantism via its misconstrual of the relationship between faith and reason, by failing to see that Christianity is based in faith, and also in ritual action rather than reason. Deism posits an illegitimate synthesis of faith and reason — a rational faith. But what was, and is, the alternative? A return to the older integration of faith and reason, that of Aquinas? Or Calvin's pararational system? Or a rejection of rationality in favor of some form of fideism? Can fideism avoid narrow dogmatism and retain a form of rationality? How can Protestantism avoid its twin pitfalls, that is, excessive respect for the Enlightenment and angry reaction against the seduction?

I suggest that the authentic Protestant account of faith's rela-

---

24. Blake, *The Gates of Paradise,* quoted in Gilchrist, *The Life of William Blake,* pp. 87, 339, 326.

tionship to reason is decidedly nonsystematic, nontheoretical. The question is not how faith and reason interact, for this implies that the issue can be analyzed from a position of detached neutrality. And that subtly prioritizes reason: it supposes that we are looking down on something called faith. Instead, we must attend to the discourse of faith, asking how it speaks of reason. Does it claim to absorb and own reason? Or does it reject it as totally alien? Or something else? What is "the discourse of faith"? It is Christian speech that is rooted in its cultic source — prayer, praise, and proclamation. And, of course, the Bible is its pattern. As we have seen, there is a tension in the Bible between the idea that God is the supreme force of rational order and the idea that faith, or trust, in him exceeds material evidence, common-sense observation. This theme is not explicitly foregrounded in the New Testament; neither Jesus nor Paul seems to draw attention to it. But it is there in the background.

Luther rediscovers it: the idea of tension between faith and reason is central to his discourse. Anyone who reads Luther's works will quickly see that he rejects the abstract, impersonal style that theology generally shares with other discourses; or, rather, he subordinates abstract reflection to a polemical, poetic, performative style. His normative mode of discourse is the sermon, in which he performs the dramatic structure of faith. His tracts and biblical commentaries, his theoretical disputations (most famously his response to Erasmus on the issue of free will) — all revert to this mode. It is dramatic in the literal sense: it resembles a simple stage play, in which there are various characters, various voices. Because the plot is simple and repetitive, and centers on violent confrontation, it often resembles a Punch and Judy show more than anything else.

The reason for the dominance of this mode of discourse is Luther's desire to convey what it means to have faith. To have faith is to accept God's Word as authoritative: to accept that one is saved by his grace (and not by one's own moral or religious capacities), that what God promises is true. But this is not possible in a direct, straightforward way: faith is not a fixed condition one enters into and sits in. One can only have faith in the context of a struggle. The Devil must frequently be confronted, rebuked, reminded of his cosmic defeat.

First, of course, his voice must be represented. And there are other demonic characters, such as the law (or "Mistress Law") and demonic impulses within one's self that must be similarly addressed. To have faith entails confronting the pull of unbelief: one must kick against this and defiantly embrace the Word — "cling to it," in Luther's phrase. This structure is dialectical, an argument between two points of view. More precisely, it is dialogical — an argument between two voices. This is not just a way of presenting Christian faith, making it seem vivid. This structure is internal to faith. For the believer is *simul iustus et peccator* — both saved and a sinner. He exists in this state of psychological tension.

So Luther rejects the idea that faith is a stable, unified position. It is always argument-shaped. One's doubts must be rebuked, and so must other habits that belong to "the flesh," one's assumption that religion is centered on moral law, for example, or one's overvaluation of philosophy. This leads to scenes in which "Mistress Reason" is treated as a deceiver. In *The Bondage of the Will*, Luther warns that she "explains and pulls the Scriptures of God whichever way she likes . . . [but] I know that all her gabblings are stupid and absurd."[25] Elsewhere, he personifies philosophy similarly: "Let philosophy remain within her bounds, as God has appointed, and let us make use of her as of a character in a comedy, but to mix her up with divinity is not to be endured."[26] Such passages seem evidence of aggressive anti-intellectualism, but this is a superficial view. In fact, Luther stages a conflict in which skeptical rationality has a *necessary* role. It is a foil for faith's reliance on the Word. Without this dynamic, faith would be just a human point of view. It needs the presence of skeptical rationality so as to perform its otherness. It follows that the believer *should* acknowledge the rational absurdity of faith and *should* give voice to her doubts. For only thus can she express her need for the Word and keep in mind the otherness of faith, the fact that it is a divine miracle originating outside of herself, not a normal human option.

---

25. Luther, *The Bondage of the Will*, trans. J. I. Packer and O. R. Johnston (London: James Clarke, 1952), p. 152.

26. Luther, *Table Talk*, trans. W. Hazlitt (London: Harper Collins, 1995), p. 26.

This dramatic, dialogical conception of faith constitutes a radical new approach to the whole question of faith and reason. It dispenses with the idea that faith and reason are reconciled in a theological system, whether that of Aquinas or Erasmus (or soon, Descartes). Yet it is much less irrational than it sounds: under the guise of an aggressive fideism, Luther is showing how Protestant faith *includes* rationality.

Also, of course, Luther shows how faith is rooted in a ritual form of language. It is not an abstract cerebral affair but rooted in this primitive religious act: responding to the divine voice and rebuking its demonic opposite. Faith is rooted in prayer and in exorcism. And although its location is obviously the individual soul, it uses a common language, rooted in public worship. The self is centered beyond itself, in the hearing and reperformance of the Word, which is an essentially public phenomenon. So the idea that Luther's theology arises from his uniquely turbulent psyche is misleading.[27] His inner turmoil is only of interest in that he managed to express it in the idiom of dialogical faith, which he did not, of course, invent from scratch (he drew on the Rhineland mystics as well as the Bible). But he was the first to give such prominence to the voice of skepticism. Perhaps only after the Renaissance does the clash between faith and reason feel so intense. But before looking at the fortunes of this model of faith, let us look at its origins.

The idea that faith should be understood in dialogical terms — in terms of the conflict of two voices — is deeply rooted in the Bible. Its most basic ingredient is the concept of the divine speech-act: through speaking, God creates the world and defeats demonic powers and relates to humanity. His speech is "performative": he does things through saying things (blessing and cursing are good examples). Other aspects of religion gradually became sidelined by this intense verbal focus (sacrifice); or they are proscribed as rival sources of authority (religious art, sacred landscape, etc.). The believing commu-

---

27. "Luther's theology is radically existential — it grows out of his tortured personal experience" (Mark C. Taylor, *After God*, p. 47). To William James, Luther is the paradigmatic "sick soul."

nity relates to God through representing his primal action, remembering it. The psalmists often recall God's power-speech: "The foundations of the world were laid bare at thy rebuke, O Lord" (Ps. 18:15). The speaker seeks to conjure up this verbal power so that it might rescue him from his isolated, embattled predicament. Typically, he is surrounded by vague enemies, whose faithless attitude is ventriloquized; they deny God's justice, even mock at the idea of it. In Psalm 59, for example, "they say, 'Who can hear us?' But you, O Lord, laugh at them; you scoff at all those nations." The negative voices doubt God. Most famously, "The fool says in his heart, 'There is no God'" (14:1; 53:1). This is more than philosophical; it is an attitude of self-reliance and violent disregard for others. The speaker contends with this attitude, which seems supported by events: evil goes unpunished, and selfishness seems rewarded. Only the intrusion of the divine voice, which, of course, the speaker must represent, can dispel this impression.

God's voice most powerfully occurs in communal worship. The speaker typically recalls God's power and resolves to praise him in the assembly (e.g., Ps. 22:22). It is in communal worship that the speaker is assured of the fate of the wicked. As H. Kraus says, "The basic experience of the Psalms is that Yahweh speaks in the sanctuary."[28] The basic experience is also that the individual, having tasted the world's reality, *needs* to hear such speech. This is the original form of Judeo-Christian "faith." The Psalms show faith to be rooted in ritual dialogism. It is both an inner, individual phenomenon (the isolation of the speaker is often emphasized), *and* it refers back to communal worship, where God's voice is strongly performed. It cannot be over-emphasized that faith is a speech-act. God's chosen is he who "speaks truth from his heart" (15:2): "I say to the Lord, 'Thou art my Lord; I have no good apart from Thee'" (16:2). "But I trust in Thee, O Lord, I say, 'Thou art my God'" (31:14). To "have" faith is to perform this speech-act, which echoes communal ritual and returns to it.

God's word contends with what opposes it, resists it, neglects it.

---

28. H. Kraus, *Theology of the Psalms,* trans. K. Crim (Minneapolis: Augsburg Press, 1986), p. 33.

This tension is renewed by the shamanic isolation of an individual who moves outside of the existing habits of worship. In the book of Job, Job's friends have the "right answers": suffering should remind one of one's dependence on God; one should trust his justice despite everything. But such formulae are stale beside the individual's passionate demand for justice, which accuses all theological "answers" of inadequacy. The dialogical structure of faith is also apparent in biblical narrative: those addressed by God often enter a state of internal tension. They are somewhat resistant to the call, and certainly they are told things that seem absurd (Sarah will have a baby, Abraham must kill his son, shy Moses must lead a revolt, and so on).

Paul's concept of faith retains this dialogical structure. The psalmic idea of a conflict between divine speech and the worldly point of view determines his conception of God's new utterance; it "is foolishness to those who are perishing, but to us who are being saved it is the power of God" (1 Cor. 1:18). Faith is ever conscious of the faithless response, the commonsense view, and this view is not quite external to it. For truth is "veiled," is at odds with what is "seen" (2 Cor. 4:3, 18). Faith entails struggle against the doubting viewpoint: "We demolish arguments and every pretention that sets itself up against the knowledge of God, and we take captive every thought to make it obedient to Christ" (2 Cor. 10:5). The Christian, therefore, continues to see things from the worldly point of view *as well as* from the redeemed point of view. Paul does not generally dramatize faith in Luther's ventriloquistic way, but there is a seed of this in the famous taunt, "Death, where is thy sting?" And he often creates verbal icons of the new perspective (e.g., Rom. 8:38, "For I am convinced that neither death nor life . . ."), in which an assertion of divine power, in opposition to contrary forces, is sacramentally performed.

So in the Bible, God's power — and faith's trust in it — is largely expressed through vocal or rhetorical conflict. In the early Christian centuries this persists in the theme of cosmic struggle, of Christ's victory over demonic powers, which is particularly marked in the ascetic discourse of the Desert Fathers. This coexists with theology's philosophical turn, since there is a dialogical element in Stoic philosophy. A personification of wisdom contends with her adversaries, for example, in Boethius's *Consolations of Philosophy*. But monologic, single-voiced philosophical discourse gradually triumphs: it more safely communicates the singleness of ecclesiastical authority.[29] God's majestic oneness should be communicated through a stable, imperial discourse of authority, unclouded by any discernible tension between faith and reason. Nominalism questions this but cannot decisively challenge the monologic gravitation of Scholasticism. And humanism half-questions it by reviving Stoic psychomachia (conflict in the soul); yet this is really a means of asserting the triumph of orderly reason. Mystical discourse is freer to represent dialogism. The soul's unity with God is known only through conflict, struggle, self-opposition. It is by this means that Luther retrieves the patristic trope of Christus Victor, of conflict between God and Satanic powers.

Luther's genius was to defy the dominant tradition of theological discourse in favor of a form that reflected the primary religious language of prayer and worship. Theology must reject abstraction, he believed, in order to convey the dramatic structure of faith. So Luther did not invent a new theological theory about the inner experience of the individual; he revived faith as a dramatic speech-act, rooted in ritual language.

When the Reformation concept of faith is expressed in more abstract terms, this dynamic recedes. Calvin's idea of theology as "knowledge of God, and of ourselves," does not foreground this dynamic. He acknowledges that the sinful, rebellious point of view exists, but he does not existentially acknowledge it or build it into the structure of theological discourse. Rather, a too smooth discourse implies that faith directly reflects divine rationality and order. Calvin holds that humans have a natural awareness of the divine *(sensus divinitatis)*, though it is clogged by sin. And the era of confessionalism further buries the dialogical dynamic: faith becomes a series of propositions one subscribes to in order to show that one belongs to the right tribe.

29. My reflections are partly informed by the Russian theorist Mikhail Bakhtin, who argues that dialogism is central to the novel, particularly in Dostoyevsky, and deeply critical of every authoritarian system. See Theo Hobson, *The Rhetorical Word: Protestant Theology and the Rhetoric of Authority* (Hampshire, UK: Ashgate, 2002).

But Luther's account of faith did not disappear; rather, it interacted with the humanist conception of the self, which was indebted to classical Stoicism. In the latter model, there is an inner conflict in which the higher, rational part of the self subdues the errant passions. This kind of inner conflict is a natural aspect of being a civilized soul — rather than a matter of salvation or damnation. (Freud revived this model — we are naturally at war with ourselves — but his model entails no theological reference.)[30] The two models coexisted in the post-Reformation period, and they sometimes came into conflict. The poet John Donne experienced conversion as a rejection of the humanist model of selfhood, in which reason is a stable mark of the divine presence. In the sonnet that begins "Batter my heart, three-person'd God," the speaker complains that the old model has failed: "Reason, your viceroy in me, me should defend,/But is captiv'd, and proves weak or untrue." The *whole* self is subject to sin and in need of external divine intervention. This is a vote for Luther.

This drama underlies the stunningly psychological alertness of George Herbert's poems. The self is open to the world, wholly porous to its energies. Herbert refutes the humanist distinction between thought (good) and passion (bad); the opposition is between all of one's sin-infected humanity and the external Word. "The Pearl" is a good-bye to humanist self-understanding. Despite "knowing the ways of Learning, Honour and Pleasure," the speaker opts for the naïve childlike speech-act of submission: "Yet I love Thee." The tension is more dramatically expressed in "The Collar": a voice of atheist rebellion is performed, a voice of energetic humanity seeking autonomy. Then God's voice intrudes: "Me thought I heard one calling *Child!*" — and the whole edifice of rebellion collapses as the speaker simply responds, "My Lord." Faith has seldom been so acutely represented. It is a voice of prayerful assent that coexists with rational objection. Others of Herbert's poems administer very Luther-like rebukes to inner impulses. In "Conscience," the speaker violently confronts his negative, faithless attitude, referring to the violence of the Word. Many po-

---

30. Though on some level it is surely informed by the Jewish tradition of the inner division caused by moral striving to which Paul refers in Romans 7:15-22.

ems perform the need for God's intervention: they open up the self and display its brokenness. In that space the Word can be represented. As in the Psalms, faith is not a stable position, but is, instead, an awareness of the otherness of God's voice. Many poems conclude with a kind of divine ventriloquism, which must intervene like this (e.g., "The Quip," "A True Hymn," "The Sinner," "Love III," "The Collar," and "The Method"). In other poems, the voice of faith — rather than the divine voice itself — is finally performed (e.g., "The Discharge," "Denial"). But the distinction between the two is weak, for the voice of faith is always rooted in the reception — or anticipation — of the voice of God. They are two sides of the same coin, which always remains external to the self.

The basic anthropology is posthumanist in that one's natural disorder cannot be overcome by reason. Man is incapable of "settled peace and rest!/He is some twenty sev'ral men at least/Each sev'ral hour" ("Giddiness"). God must bring psychological order (see "The Family"); otherwise, the unity of the self is not possible. The assurance of salvation that the Word brings often feels formal or artificial; it is not assimilated into the self. In "Assurance," the speaker lacks resources to answer his tormenting doubt, and must appeal to God to do so. Of course, this is no deficiency but rather fidelity to the biblical grammar of faith; indeed, that grammar is here expressed with new depth.

There is a more philosophical echo of such psychology in Pascal. He keeps returning, as does a moth to flame, to the darkest skepticism. Rationalism is just an evasion of the fear of the void; we are primitives under the veneer of civilization. No amount or quality of thought can deliver us from this conclusion, so we must either despair or accept the absolute otherness of faith, which does not prove by argument but *tells* us that we are distinct from mere perishing beasts. We must ensure that this perspective becomes central to the inner dialogue of our thought: "[Man] carries on an inner dialogue with himself, which it is important to keep under proper control . . . we must keep silence as far as we can and only talk to ourselves about God, whom we know to be true, and thus convince ourselves that he is."[31]

31. Pascal, *Pensées*, p. 99.

Pascal was aware that the new philosophy of Descartes was based on a denial of the divided self that is capable of grasping the externality of faith. Descartes defines the self as the antidote to instability, a unitary essence, safe from all external forces. In Charles Taylor's phrase, the modern self is "buffered": "For the modern, buffered self, the possibility exists of taking a distance from, disengaging from everything outside the mind."[32] By contrast the traditional religious self is porous, open to forces beyond itself: the main Reformers had reaffirmed this model, with their insistence that sin naturally infects every aspect of one's life. On the other hand, however, they — especially Calvin — promoted the desire for orderly knowledge about God and humanity. This desire gradually triumphed, in the form of deism, and banished the unstable medieval self. It reaffirmed the assumption of Stoic-based humanism: reason is the divine power within the self. Faith should be seen as confidence in the power of reason rather than submission to some irrational authority.

Wesley, as we have seen, reacted against deism by placing his emphasis on faith. Yet I suggest that his concept of faith entailed a retreat from the dialogical complexity of Luther and Herbert. He echoed the deist desire for unity of self, even as he opposed rationalist autonomy. The religious restlessness of his youth was the desire for a fuller, stabler Christian identity. He recounted that he had a horror of "being half a Christian," and he determined to give God "all my soul, my body and my substance."[33] He sought to put sin behind him, to be morally perfect. But after years of struggle he realized that he was still not the kind of believer he saw presented in the New Testament, "freed from sin . . . freed from fear . . . freed from doubt."[34] His conversion — or further conversion — of 1738 was prompted by the teaching of the Moravian Peter Böhler. On hearing "that faith in Christ . . . had those two fruits inseparably attending it, 'Dominion over sin, and constant

32. Pascal, *Pensées,* p. 38.

33. In Roy Hattersley, *John Wesley: A Brand from the Burning* (London: Little, Brown, 2002), p. 82.

34. John Wesley, *The Journal of John Wesley: A Selection* (Oxford: Oxford University Press, 1987), p. 26. Hereafter, page references to this work appear in parentheses in the text.

Peace from a sense of forgiveness,' I was quite amazed, and looked upon it as a new Gospel. . . . I well saw, no one could . . . have such a sense of forgiveness, and not *feel* it. But I felt it not" (p. 33). Soon he received his assurance of salvation, and he sought to spread the experience. The key novelty in his approach was the idea of a sharp transition from uncertainty to certainty. Preaching a few years later, he reported that many responded with emotional groaning followed by thanksgiving, "being assured they now had the desire of their soul — the forgiveness of their sins" (p. 59). Wesley placed huge new emphasis on the emotional experience of God, which was universally accessible: everyone could have this saving sense of assurance, which was a clear new identity, a rebirth. He insisted that "whole Christians" were freed from sin "for ever more" (p. 140). "By Christian I mean one who so believes in Christ as that sin hath no domination over him" (pp. 142-43). In his *Plain Account of Christian Perfection,* written over thirty years after his conversion experience, he characterized faith as "salvation from all sin and loving God with an undivided heart."

Wesley proudly emphasized his difference from Calvin, attacking predestination in favor of an upbeat universalism, but the really telling comparison is with Luther. Despite foregrounding justification by faith, Wesley's conception of faith was at odds with Luther's. Of course, Luther had also sought certainty concerning his salvation, but his theology moved away from a rigid distinction between saved and unsaved, for faith inhabits a tension between the two states; to have faith is to accept a lack of finality, of a single identity, because one is *simul iustus et peccator.* Wesley shuns such a tension. To have faith, he says, is to be reborn into a clear new identity. He largely founded modern fundamentalism, which is about the need for certainty about individual salvation ("my chief motive is the hope of saving my own soul," he once said).[35]

His identification of faith with certainty entailed a bullish defensive attitude toward the rising tide of critical theological inquiry. One should not be diverted by mystical interpretations of Scripture, he warns; rather, "keep to the plain, practical written word of God" (*Jour-*

35. Quoted in Hattersley, *John Wesley,* pp. 90, 103.

nal, p. 59). Elsewhere, he urges Christians not to agree with skeptics that witchcraft is nonsense. Skeptics "well know (whether Christians know it or not) that the giving up witchcraft is, in effect, giving up the Bible." Science must be rejected at any point that it seems to undermine the "certainty" of the Bible. Wesley responds with the bullish assertion that traditional belief in the supernatural is more reasonable than "their vain imaginations" (p. 164).

By contrast, Blake's great works of the early 1790s express a dialogical concept of faith. His argument with philosophy was not simply that it elevated reason, but that it claimed to integrate faith with reason, to overcome any conflict. "Without contraries is no progression," announces *The Marriage of Heaven and Hell* (1790): one such opposition is "Reason and Energy." *Songs of Innocence and of Experience* (1794) is subtitled, "Shewing the Two Contrary States of the Human Soul." Faith is identified with an attitude of extreme trust, a childlike credulity. In many of the "Innocence" poems, a child (or animal, e.g., in "The Lamb") is being told about God's goodness. The suggestion is that God can be most purely described in a certain sort of voice, one used to soothe and delight a child. Mature faith must combine this with awareness of sin, which entails the ambiguity of religion and desire and the presence of deceptive rhetoric. It must learn to suspect as well as trust. Like Milton in *Paradise Lost* — and yet very differently — Blake externalizes or mythologizes the inner conflict of faith. The need to keep faith from the clutches of "Reasoning Power,/ An Abstract Objecting power that Negatives every thing," is a recurring theme in his work.[36] The alternative is not simply fideism, for faith will always contend with its opposite. Faith entails duality of vision. Blake thus pithily expresses it: "Pray God us keep/From Single vision & Newton's sleep!"[37] The theme returned at the end of his life: "Every man has a Devil in himself and the conflict between his Self and God is perpetually carrying on." "Men are born with an Angel and a Devil."[38]

36. Blake, *Jerusalem,* in Gilchrist, *Life of William Blake,* p. 207.
37. Blake, Letter to Thomas Butt, 22 November 1802, in Geoffrey Keynes, ed., *The Letters of William Blake* (London: Rupert Hart Davis, 1956), p. 79.
38. Quoted in Gilchrist, *Life of William Blake,* pp. 342, 347.

Other English Romantics develop poetry as a site of internal dialogism. Wordsworth and Coleridge often structure their poems by way of internal conversations. This is ambiguously related to the discourse of faith: it strongly echoes that discourse in which an external voice of divine affirmation is performed, yet it generally presents psychological unity as a natural possibility, though a mysterious one. Faith is not just a quarrel with ourselves, as Yeats has it ("out of our quarrel with others we make rhetoric, out of our quarrel with ourselves we make poetry"); it is our experience of the cosmic quarrel between God and Satan.

I am suggesting that liberal Christianity must rediscover this dialogical, psychomachic tradition that was marginalized by deism and secularized by Romanticism. Not only is it a basic aspect of primary Christian speech; it is also the key to faith's engagement with reason. It is a third way beyond the integration of faith and reason and the wrong kind of fideism that fears to engage with the discourses of skepticism, suspicion, and secular reason. The right kind of fideism combines an absolute respect for the primary speech-act of faith, rooted in ritual structures, with acceptance of the necessary presence of skeptical discourse. It turns skepticism to its advantage — with judo cunning. It does so by refusing the monotony of single-voiced speech. As we shall see, this tradition resurfaces in "dialectical theology," but it fails to secure a foothold in twentieth-century theology. This dialogical tradition is not quite the same as the common current view that faith and reason (or science) are "non-overlapping magisteria," that faith is concerned with narrative and value rather than hard facts.[39] This division is useful in some ways — for example, it rightly dissuades believers from creationism — but it is inadequate. It evades the fact that faith speaks in a way that provokes conflict with reason. It says things that initiate a skeptical response.

39. One expression of this comes from Nietzsche: "For this reason a higher culture must give to man a double-brain, as it were two brain-ventricles, one for the perceptions of science, the other for those of non-science: lying beside one another, not confused together, separable, capable of being shut off: this is a demand of health" (Nietzsche, *Human, All Too Human: A Book for Free Spirits,* trans. R. J. Hollingdale [Cambridge, UK: Cambridge University Press, 1986], p. 251).

FIVE

American Disestablishment

—◦◦◦—

O ur story so far goes something like this: liberal Protestantism had just begun unfurling its vision of political liberty and the separation of church and state when it became swamped by deism, which pursues quasi-Christian rationalism, and a less subversive form of politics, which was compatible with Britain's half-reformed constitution. In mid-eighteenth-century Britain there were almost no voices daring to call for disestablishment (which would, of course, entail challenging the monarchical constitution); but there were countless voices explaining that the essence of Christianity is rational civility, natural morality. So liberal Protestantism suffered a double diminution: it lost its full passion for liberty, and it deepened its association with sacraphobic post-Christian philosophy.

What happened next complicated this. The American Revolution dramatically revived the old call for the separation of church and state, and the cause largely succeeded. But what was the motivation for this movement? Was it still based in a radical understanding of Christianity, or was it now an essentially secular cause? The question goes to the heart of America's religious identity, and there is, of course, no simple answer to it. For the most part, the key American founders spoke the language of post-Christian deism: the language of rational liberty and divine reason. But they were far more rooted in the liberal Christian tradition than were their French revolutionary counterparts. Jefferson and Madison, who had most to do with disestablishment, considered themselves liberal Christians who wanted Christianity purified of the corruption of establishment. They saw disestablishment as good for religion as well as for politics. But, particularly in Jefferson's case, this idealism was joined to the bad strand of liberal Protestantism that wanted to rationalize the Christian faith. Therefore, the success of the American Revolution perpetuated the deficiency of liberal Protestantism: its overvaluation of rationalism and its alienation from ritual practice.

As we saw in chapter 2, New England was founded on rigid Puritanism. In most areas, dissent from Congregationalist orthodoxy was a civil offense. Toleration was seen as a fatal temptation that would reduce a godly society to anarchy. In 1644, just as English toleration was budding, the Massachusetts Bay colony banned Baptists. According to the Puritan minister Increase Mather, "the Toleration of all Religions and Perswasions, is the way to have no Religion at all."[1] Cromwell's attempt to create a tolerant Puritan state seemed to the colonists like a failure of godly nerve. But alongside this antiliberalism, an enclave of toleration was established by Roger Williams in Rhode Island. Religious liberty, including for the natives, was enshrined in the new colony's constitution, which made it a magnet for minority dissenting groups. From 1658 it hosted America's first Jewish community. The marginal approach of Rhode Island soon spread to the new Quaker colony, Pennsylvania, founded in 1681 by a grant from Charles II (in settlement of a debt he owed William Penn's father). Penn's determination to enshrine freedom of conscience for all monotheists, and the welcome he extended to Continental dissenters, established him as one of the most influential American founders (though he spent most of his life in England). A huge influx of Quakers and other dissenters made Philadelphia the second city of New England by 1690.

---

1. Increase Mather, quoted in Steven Waldman, *Founding Faith: Providence, Politics, and the Birth of Religious Freedom in America* (New York: Random House, 2008), p. 9.

Massachusetts stuck to its Puritan course, but with an increasing sense of insecurity. The unity of church and society became harder to maintain, as religious zeal cooled in the next generation. A looser form of church membership was invented for semidetached believers: the "halfway covenant." Fear that the godly society was weakening contributed to the Salem witch scare of 1692, which took twenty lives. To the south, the colonies of Virginia and Georgia had Anglican establishments. That traditional structure suited the new form of aristocracy that arose on the plantations, and the exclusion of dissenters smoothed the establishment of a slaveholding economy. There were almost no Quakers — or similarly minded dissenters — to suggest that the gospel meant liberty for all. Instead, the slaveowners welcomed — even accentuated — the feudal habits of Anglicanism. "The almost inevitable result was that the religion of Anglicanism became a prop for unusual social deference and the legitimization of the slave system."[2] Overall, the American colonies were a display of Protestant variety rather than a great advertisement for toleration. A radically tolerant middle was sandwiched between a Calvinist North and a conservative Anglican South.

In the early eighteenth century the colonies were increasingly receptive to the new style of faith that had originated in Germany — pietism. Its emphasis on emotional engagement over doctrinal and institutional correctness produced the Great Awakening, the first sign that American religiosity demanded to spill beyond the normal confines of organized religion, which seemed stuffy, undemocratic. The climax of the movement was the 1740 preaching tour of a wünderkind evangelist from England, George Whitefield. It was in some ways akin to a rock star's tour: he drew stadium-sized crowds with his gospel of emotional conversion. The old denominational allegiances were irrelevant, he said, and the old institutions were probably hindrances to faith. Like Methodism (he was a friend of the Wesleys), Whitefield's movement was deeply democratic: he insisted that Christianity was fully intelligible to ordinary people and had no need for the mediation of an elite

---

2. Mark A. Noll, *A History of Christianity in the United States and Canada* (Grand Rapids: Eerdmans, 1992), p. 90.

class. He was technically Anglican, but in spirit he was certainly anti-Anglican. Such preaching spread throughout the colony, significantly changing the meaning of religion. As Mark Noll puts it, "The Awakening marked a transition from clerical to lay religion, from the minister as an inherited authority figure to self-empowered mobilizer, from the definition of Christianity by doctrine to its definition by piety, and from a state church encompassing all of society to a gathered church made up only of the converted."[3]

Traditional Calvinism struggled to adapt. Jonathan Edwards sought to renew the Puritanism of the previous century, with new emphasis on personal conversion. Yet his response to the Great Awakening was ambivalent. He expressed the hope that the movement might herald humanity's progressive regeneration, culminating in Christ's return: "We can't reasonably think otherwise, than that the beginning of this great work of God must be near. And there are many things that make it probable that this work will begin in America."[4] On the other hand, he warned that revival conversions were often shallow, and were corrosive of Calvinist orthodoxy. He also faced the problem of whether Christian identity should be strictly defined or pragmatically flexible. If the boundaries of church and society are to overlap, pragmatism is needed. Calvin himself knew this: he taught that only God knows who belongs to the true, invisible church; the visible church is thus a necessary compromise. The "halfway covenant" was a version of this. But Puritanism wanted it all: a pure church, composed only of the saints *and* a culturally dominant church. Edwards reemphasized the first part of this: a model of church in which all members demonstrate deep inner commitment. "None ought to be admitted as members of the visible church of Christ," he said, "but visible and professing saints."[5] This caused a crisis in New England's soul. Was it still a "covenanted community"? Did salvation percolate down through the structures of society, as in ancient Israel? Or was society now to be un-

---

3. Mark A. Noll, *America's God: From Jonathan Edwards to Abraham Lincoln* (Oxford: Oxford University Press, 2002), p. 44.

4. Jonathan Edwards, quoted in Michael J. McClymond and Gerald R. McDermott, *The Theology of Jonathan Edwards* (Oxford: Oxford University Press, 2012), p. 237.

5. Jonathan Edwards, quoted in Noll, *America's God*, p. 45.

derstood as neutral space, and the church as a countercultural godly community? Though he sought to renew the old Puritan order, Edwards in effect opened the door to evangelicalism, which can be defined as Puritan-rooted Protestantism that moves away from reliance on traditional communal structures and presents faith as an unmediated response to revelation.

The colonies also became receptive to religious deism, seen by many in the clergy as an antidote to the excesses of the Great Awakening. A peculiarly American style of deism emerged, centered in Boston. A new breed of Congregationalist clergy echoed the "Latitudinarian" liberalism that had been a feature of English religious culture for a generation or two. Such thinkers questioned Calvinist dogma — not just predestination, but also the doctrine of the Trinity. Unitarianism was not yet a denomination, but its core ideas were present: God's rational moral law was supremely revealed by Jesus, who was in some sense divine but not the second person of the Trinity, which Unitarians characterized as a medieval superstition. Such views transformed Boston and Harvard. In the 1760s the dominant form of Christian deism was inspired by the Scottish philosopher Francis Hutcheson, whose "common-sense" philosophy rejected David Hume's skepticism, arguing that there is a universally knowable moral order that is in tune with Christianity. This moderate, practical deism was taught by John Witherspoon, the Presbyterian president of Princeton College. Through him and others it was hugely influential on Jefferson, Madison, and other founding fathers, who saw it as an updating of Locke's thought. This was the basic theological language in which America's identity would first be sketched.

It also influenced Benjamin Franklin, who rejected the Presbyterianism under which he was raised, but said "I never was without some religious principles. I never doubted, for instance, the existence of the Deity; that he made the world, and govern'd it by his Providence; that the most acceptable service of God was the doing of good to man; that our souls are immortal; and that all crime will be punished, and virtue rewarded, either here or hereafter." This is essential deism: to retain belief in providence and the soul's immortality.

When he occasionally attended church, he was disappointed that the preacher was more interested in dogma than general morality, and that his aim "[seemed] to be rather to make us Presbyterians than good citizens."[6] He found one preacher with what he thought was a proper emphasis on rational morality and ecumenism; but, to Franklin's bewilderment, this excellent Pelagian was accused of unorthodoxy. Did not the truth of Christianity lie in its ability to make people better citizens? He observed that American politics was being held back by squabbling sects, and his aim was to promote a common cause that would be capable of uniting all the colonies. This was a central ingredient of the new nation, this desire for a common denominator of vaguely Protestant idealism.

Franklin settled in Philadelphia, where he was impressed by the Quakers' emphasis on morality rather than dogmatism, and their habit of toleration. He was also gradually persuaded by their rejection of slavery. A crucial point about Franklin's deism, which separated it from that of Voltaire, and Europe generally, was that it had a democratic religious energy akin to the Great Awakening. He thus heralded Whitefield as a great broom that was sweeping aside religious tradition and inspiring people to a new faith in their own capacities. By opposing the old order, such religiosity was helping to launch a new one. Its supernatural error was almost irrelevant beside this, and people would grow out of that. Also, Franklin perceived that a huge rise in immigration was changing the nature of the colonies, making pluralism a reality. The formerly dominant churches, Congregationalist in the North and Anglican in the South, were losing their auras of natural preeminence. Franklin sensed that this would enable the rise of a new idea of the American people, one that might replace the old idea of the covenanted community rooted in Puritan orthodoxy. This ideological energy could be redirected to a secular end, Franklin intuited. It could provide the basis of a new national consciousness. And the big idea that could bind a new nation was obvious to all intellectuals — republicanism.

6. Benjamin Franklin, *The Autobiography of Benjamin Franklin* (Hertfordshire, UK: Wordsworth, 1996), p. 69.

Republicanism was fully enlightened politics: a state in which liberty was not constrained by monarchy, aristocracy, or established religion, but was allowed free rein. The state should be ruled by its citizens, who are elected to office. But as in classical times, there was a limited idea of democracy in this republicanism: only the property-owning class was capable of self-government (which left scope for a new, modernized aristocracy). There was also an idea that liberty depends on a culture of virtue, of the high moral standards of the ruling citizens. (As in classical Rome, the ideal politician was a gentleman farmer, unimpressed by courtly lavishness — in other words, a modest, responsible aristocrat.)

A huge vagueness surrounded republicanism, largely for reasons having to do with recent English history. As we have seen, this ideology was central to the English Revolution, and it partly lived on in the form of the "Real Whigs," who associated it with deism (it could be called "politically radical deism"). More widely, most English intellectuals were semirepublican in that they supposed that the essence of republicanism lived on in Britain's constitutional monarchy. For was not liberty steadily on the rise? So it was left unclear whether republicanism entailed a major constitutional overhaul, or whether its spirit was compatible with England's political order.

The American elite drifted toward a radical form of republicanism. American Puritanism had always contained the idea of opposing antiquated tyranny, of creating a new covenant of liberty. Semisecular Puritans could rediscover their grandfathers' holy purpose in republicanism. And once the idea of breaking with Britain was formed, a strong ideology was needed to distinguish the new nation. So mainstream Christians of all denominations — including the new breed of unrooted evangelicals — began to see the tenets of republicanism as deeply attractive rather than dangerous. The potentially antireligious deist component of republicanism was easily ignored; most chose to view republicanism as deeply compatible with Christian liberty.

One cause of new radicalism was war with France in the 1740s and 1750s. Fighting a Catholic power led the colonists to a new idea of themselves as defenders of Protestant liberty, and this was soon turned against the mother country, first in the 1760s, when plans to install an Anglican bishop were hotly opposed, then in response to the Stamp Act. In 1774 the British recognized Roman Catholicism as the official religion of Quebec. Thus, many Americans concluded, the British Empire could not be trusted to defend Protestantism and liberty.

At the heart of the cause was a conviction that Britain was acting tyrannically and that liberty must be defended. But few thought to define liberty with any precision. Did it mean religious liberty, and if so, did that mean the separation of church and state? This became central for some of the founders, but at first it was not a popular rallying cry. Religious liberty was not specifically mentioned in the Declaration of Independence of 1776, but it was implied in its famous opening sentence: "We hold these truths to be self-evident, that all men are created equal, that they are endowed by their Creator with certain unalienable Rights, that among these are Life, Liberty, and the pursuit of Happiness." The point is that these rights are not something that a king graciously bestows on his subjects, which is the Hobbesian version of the social-contract narrative. By implication, no state can legitimately limit the religious liberty of its citizens. But this was not spelled out. Most of the thirteen colonies had established churches, and suddenly announcing the illegitimacy of this would not have aided the cause of unity. In the Declaration, and even more so in the Constitution, as we shall see, ambiguity on the question of religious liberty was essential.

As the opening of the Declaration of Independence suggests, the influence of deism was acute. One of its main channels was Thomas Paine, who was quick to offer himself as the Miltonic voice of the revolution, its visionary intellectual. His pamphlet of 1776, *Common Sense,* attacked the alliance of throne and altar, and celebrated the ideal of religious diversity. Vague references to "the will of the Almighty" helped to conceal his militant opposition to organized religion. He wanted not just the separation of church and state but the establishment of a robust rationalism.

Thomas Jefferson, the prime author of the Declaration, wanted to put disestablishment at the heart of the revolution. He and James Madison were fellow campaigners against Anglican establishment in their native state of Virginia. It was largely through them that the ideal of the separation of church and state became central to the national ideology. But this happened gradually and uncertainly.

In 1776, Virginia began debating a new constitution. Jefferson and Madison were both adamant that it should go further than vague Lockean toleration: it should guarantee full religious liberty, which entailed disestablishing the Anglican Church. It was Jefferson's assistant, Madison, who insisted that "toleration" was an unhelpful term, that rights-based language about "free exercise of religion" and "liberty" was needed. For "toleration" implied the state's right to choose how tolerant to be. The issue was debated in Virginia's senate for ten years. Jefferson's "Bill for Establishing Religious Freedom" was finally passed in 1787. Its influence on other states, and on the ideology of the United States, makes it one of the most important bits of legislation in history.

Locke had argued that society needs a religious basis, however broad — that is, atheists should not be tolerated. The individual right to religious freedom should not totally override corporate religious order. Jefferson dispenses with this idea: he says that the individual's freedom to choose how to be religious, if at all, is absolute. Religion is a free choice, and so politics should be fully secularized. It is important to emphasize that this position, which is essentially that of modern secular-liberalism, flows out of the radical Christian position of Roger Williams, who had insisted that God is too precious to be used as a test of political allegiance. This was also a feature of Quaker thought: they refused to swear oaths because oath-swearing was an essentially political practice that used religious terminology. So Jefferson's approach to the issue of church and state builds on a radical Protestant tradition, that politics must be secular *so that* religion can be pure. Jefferson was more motivated by secular than religious idealism in taking up this cause, but it was a religion-rooted cause.

Jefferson's original speech calling for Virginian disestablishment, made in 1776, survives in note form. He argues that religious uniformity is necessarily violent and tyrannical. It also makes for religious complacency. It is good for the church to be independent of political "protection"; indeed, that is a return to early church purity. "[It] betrays want of confidence in doctrines of church to suspect that reason or intrinsic excellence insufficient without secular prop. Gates of hell shall never prevail [against the church]."[7] The latter quote from Matthew 16:18 is a challenge to conservatives: Do you not believe Christ's promise that the church will survive forever? He repeats the quote elsewhere in the speech. He also refers to the "glorious Reformation." Is he cunningly using radical Protestant rhetoric to achieve a secular aim? That oversimplifies the matter. Jefferson genuinely stands within the tradition that seeks the purification of religion through disestablishment, though he brings a new deist emphasis to this tradition. The bill that he wrote the next year follows this approach. Establishment had made the Virginian church lazy. He contrasts "false religion" with "our religion," meaning Protestantism.

In 1784, Virginia's conservatives proposed a compromise: lest disestablishment lead to the demise of religion, there should be a form of tithing, a tax for the support of clergy of various denominations. With Jefferson now in Paris, Madison took his place and launched a fierce attack on the plan. His pamphlet "Memorial and Remonstrance Against Religious Assessments" was the clearest argument for the separation of church and state of the revolutionary era. Echoing the Declaration of Independence, but with greater specificity, it calls *religious* liberty an "unalienable right." The problem with the state funding of religion is that it would entail the state defining "religion" and discriminating against certain marginal groups. Selective funding of religion amounted to a form of establishment, he insisted. "We maintain therefore that in matters of Religion, no man's right is abridged by the institution of Civil Society and that Religion is wholly exempt from its Cognizance."[8] That is to say, the state should not even *think* about religion. He repeated the arguments that state meddling was a hindrance to religion, that true believers trusted that religion needed no such support (wasn't the church purer before its establishment?). In the pamphlet Madison cleverly appeals to different groups: those who did not want to pay more tax, deists, and evan-

---

7. In Garry Wills, *Head and Heart: American Christianities* (New York: Penguin, 2007), p. 190. Hereafter, page references to this work appear in parentheses in the text.
8. James Madison, quoted in Waldman, *Founding Faith*, p. 120.

gelicals. His campaign succeeded, and Virginia remained on course for a thoroughgoing version of religious liberty.

So Jefferson's deism was clearly rooted in the radical Christian tradition of liberty. On the other hand, he stretched these roots to the breaking point as he moved ever closer to Paine. He became increasingly influenced by Joseph Priestley, the mastermind of English intellectual dissent. Like Locke and others, Priestley held that Jesus' unique moral teaching had been corrupted by supernaturalism and clericalism, especially by means of the doctrine of the Trinity. Priestley popularized a new label for such Christian deism: Unitarianism. Jefferson agreed that Jesus was a unique moral teacher, but not divine. Unlike most deists, he did not see this as a valid modern dilution of Christianity, but as the *true* interpretation. He was a passionate, if muddled, religious reformer. With a rather adolescent brand of idealism, he felt that Christianity was undergoing a reformation, away from divisive superstition and toward rational universalism. He had to conceal this from the public, but he often discussed it with friends. "I trust that there is not a young man now living in the U.S. who will not die an Unitarian," he said (Wills, p. 161). In retirement he kept on thinking about it: he carefully crafted a version of the New Testament from which he cut superstitious passages, leaving us with the pure moral teaching. (He cut the Last Supper, assuming ritual to be a force for reaction.) He echoed the conventional anti-Semitism entailed in deism, seeing Judaism as the source of Christian irrationalism. Moses had "bound the Jews to many idle ceremonies, mummeries, and observances, of no effect toward producing the social utilities which constitute the essence of virtue. Jesus exposed their futility and insignificance. The one instilled into his people the most anti-social spirit toward other nations; the other preached philanthropy and universal charity and benevolence."[9] So Jesus was essentially an anti-Jew, putting moral reason before superstition.

Madison, another Anglican, was more orthodox than Jefferson — and more wisely reticent. While a student in New Jersey, he saw

---

9. Thomas Jefferson, Letter to William Short, August 4, 1820, quoted in Waldman, *Founding Faith*, p. 79.

that parts of the north, especially Pennsylvania, had developed a healthier religious culture, and he resolved to bring reform to Virginia. Madison was taught by the radical Presbyterian minister John Witherspoon, a leading Christian deist who was influenced by Scottish Common Sense philosophy and who put much emphasis on religious liberty. Coming back to Virginia in 1774, Madison defended persecuted Baptists, who were demonized partly because of their interest in preaching to slaves. Madison wrote to a friend that an established, coercive priesthood "vexes me the most of anything whatever. . . . I have squabbled and scolded, abused and ridiculed so long about it, to so little purpose, that I am without common patience" (Wills, p. 204). But as to his own faith, he retained a typically Anglican reticence; he steered clear of Jefferson's earnest deist enthusiasm.

How much simpler American religious history would have been if the Virginian model had been replicated in all the other states — if the new nation as a whole opted for this strong clear version of religious liberty. In one respect it was representative: the disestablishment of the Anglican Church occurred in the six other states where it had been established. But these states retained restrictions on Catholics, or non-Christians, or non-Trinitarians holding office. In Massachusetts and Connecticut, Congregationalism remained established. Only Virginia and Rhode Island fully affirmed religious liberty. (Massachusetts' establishment was the last to fall, in 1833.)

So the Revolution entailed a move away from establishment toward religious liberty, but an incomplete move. And the states were far from united in their approach to the issue. This was reflected in the writing of the federal Constitution in 1787-89. Madison wanted a law defending religious freedom throughout the states, but he quickly perceived that it would be impossible. (The phrasing he wanted was: "No State shall violate the equal rights of conscience.") Almost all the other delegates were more religiously conservative, indeed were wary of Virginia's bold move toward the separation of church and state. Conscious of this, Madison felt that complete silence on religion might be better than any legislation, which was likely to set the current majority view in stone. But there was a desire for a bill of rights, so some kind of compromise had to be forged. The resulting compromise reads as follows: "Congress shall make no law respecting an establishment of religion, or prohibiting the free exercise thereof." The strange thing about the First Amendment is that it addresses a nonissue: whether any form of religion should be officially privileged by the new national government. No one seriously thought that it should be. Religious diversity was an obvious fact about the new nation. Yet within most states there was a dominant church. The real question was whether the federal government should push the cause of religious liberty, overriding the will of the more conservative states. And Congress evaded that question. If anything, the First Amendment seems to defend the right of each state to form its own religious policies. But it also contains a nod to the cause of religious liberty. It is in, effect, meaningless — intentionally so. It expresses a vague desire that religious liberty should be national policy, but the gesture remains limp. Nothing is said about whether the individual has the right to be protected — by the federal government — from the religious policy of the state.

What did the other Founding Fathers want? Benjamin Franklin was certainly a campaigner for religious liberty, but he lacked the rigor of Jefferson and Madison. When he chaired Pennsylvania's constitutional convention in 1776, he approved a clause excluding atheists from full citizenship. Pennsylvania's was the most representative position of the Founders: a desire for a new era of religious liberty, balanced by a belief that the state should uphold religion — or rather theism — in some general way. This describes George Washington, who was a calm, aristocratic Anglican deist. He seems to have felt a lofty detachment from church-based religion. When he attended church, out of public duty, he left before the Eucharist. When the priest questioned that, Washington stopped attending on days when the Eucharist was celebrated. This suggests a man quietly confident that religion is nonsense, except for its ability to teach the masses morality. His famous reference to God as "the Great Disposer of events" echoes Paine's sense of God as the providential guarantee of the rightness of his own secular cause. Washington was one of the numerous Founders who preferred Freemasonry to church. Freemasonry was a kind of natural-reason club: it featured a huge emphasis on friendly cooperation and moral progress, and had a bit of exotic mystery and ceremony thrown in. It had spread throughout the colonies since 1731. The men-only policy of Freemasonry partly explains why deism was so popular among aristocratic men, whereas their wives remained keen churchgoers.

John Adams was another deist, but, like Jefferson, he had a quasi-Protestant zeal for reform, a passion to free "real" religion from superstition. He was particularly scornful of the narrow orthodoxy of Massachusetts Calvinism, and also of Catholicism. His description of a visit he once made to a Catholic church is a good glimpse into the sacraphobia of the deists:

> The poor wretches fingering their beads, chanting Latin, not a word of which they understood. Their holy Water — their Crossing themselves perpetually — their Bowing to the Name of Jesus, wherever they hear it — their Bowings, and Kneelings, and Genuflections before the Altar. . . . But how shall I describe the Picture of our Saviour in a Frame of Marble over the Altar at full Length upon the Cross, in the Agonies, and the Blood dropping and streaming from his Wounds. . . . Here is everything which can lay hold of the Eye, Ear, and Imagination. Every Thing which can charm and bewitch the simple and ignorant.[10]

Like Jefferson, Adams favored the emerging creed of Unitarianism, and sometimes he expressed his creed with contempt for traditional doctrines, including the incarnation. Superstitious believers, he wrote, "all believe that Great Principle which has produced this boundless universe, Newton's universe and Herschel's universe, came down to this little ball to be spit upon by Jews; and until this awful blasphemy is got rid of, there never will be any liberal science in the world" (Wills, p. 166). It is worth noting the anti-Semitism: an incarnated God is unpleasantly involved in Judaism. (Such anti-Semitism is present in Voltaire, Montesquieu, and many other Enlightenment figures: they associate Judaism with irrational particularity.)

10. John Adams, quoted in Waldman, *Founding Faith*, p. 36.

The first presidents made great use of religious rhetoric — of a Christian deist nature. Washington made plentiful references to "Providence" and "Heaven" and "the Almighty" smiling on the new nation. Chaplains were appointed to Congress and the army, as had been the practice during the Revolution, and the use of the Bible for the ceremony of the inauguration was begun. Most of this new "civil religion" was uncontested. Indeed, far from opposing it, Madison wrote some of Washington's holy patriotic speeches. Even the greatest theorist of the separation of church and state thus saw the necessity of a theistic nationalism, a broadly religious sense of national unity (Washington explicitly included the Jews in this broad tent). But Madison and Jefferson were wary of overdoing this civil religion — of drifting toward a nondenominational Protestant establishment.

The new nation's balance of religion and secularism was deeply threatened by events in France, where a progressive democratic ideology was attacking religion. Was this the real agenda of Jefferson? That suspicion was strengthened by the increased radicalism of Thomas Paine, whose book *The Age of Reason* (1794), written in France, was more openly post-Christian than his previous writings had been. Such deism was increasingly at odds with popular opinion. There was a powerful new wave of evangelical enthusiasm, and, as in Cromwell's England, the new climate of freedom was oxygen to Protestant innovators. The forces of the Great Awakening were stirring again.

Despite being attacked as a dangerous democrat (democracy was still largely seen as inseparable from anarchy), Jefferson won the presidential election of 1800 by uniting evangelical energy with the republican ethos, reaffirming the very overlap that had enabled the Revolution in the first place. So he consolidated a national ideology, a faith-based democratic optimism. One ingredient of this was a new understanding of eschatology. Many of the evangelicals taught that a new era of utopian harmony was underway to precede Christ's final return (a belief known as postmillennialism, that is, Christ returning after the progressively utopian era). The new democratic nation was deemed a sign of this. In a sense, Jefferson's belief in rational progress was kept afloat by a highly irrational belief in *divine* progress.

He established a firmly antiaristocratic style of government. Instead of issuing holy national rhetoric and calling for days of prayer, as had his two predecessors, Jefferson took a sober, secular approach to the office, making the separation of church and state into a presidential duty. Most of the states were still lukewarm about religious liberty when he came into office. Jefferson could not directly change this, but he could signal support for the cause of separation, presenting it as a nation-unifying ideal. He most famously did this in 1802, when he replied to a letter from a group of Baptists who complained of persecution at the hands of the Congregationalist establishment in Connecticut. He expressed "reverence" for the First Amendment, which, he said, has the effect of "building a wall of separation between church and state." He did not claim that Connecticut's policy was hence illegal; instead, he implied that it was ultimately doomed, for the principle of separation was the nation's guiding star. In other words, the ideal of full religious liberty defines the nation, though it is presently hindered.

Jefferson was succeeded by Madison, who was just as keen to use the presidency to promote separationism. He was vigilant against the federal government promoting religion, even in minor, seemingly innocuous ways. He generally avoided presidential religious proclamations, though they were a popular new tradition: "They seem to imply and certainly nourish the erroneous idea of a *national* religion. The idea, just as it related to the Jewish nation under a theocracy, having been improperly adopted by so many nations which have embraced Christianity, is too apt to lurk in the bosoms even of Americans, who in general are aware of the distinction between religious and political societies" (Wills, p. 239). On one of the rare occasions when he did publicly thank God, he thanked him for the gift of religious liberty. In retirement he reflected that the danger of mixing religion and politics remained strong: "Every new & successful example therefore of a perfect separation between ecclesiastical and civil matters, is of importance. And I have no doubt that every new example will succeed, as every past one has done, in shewing that religion and Gov[ernment] will both exist in greater purity, the less they are mixed together."[11] Jeffer-

---

11. Madison, Letter to Edward Livingston, July 10, 1822, quoted in Waldman, *Founding Faith*, p. 180.

son and Madison established a strong tradition of presidential reverence for the First Amendment as a central national principle (despite varying interpretations of it at the state level).

Meanwhile, the Second Great Awakening had changed the religious landscape: the Methodists and Baptists were booming, and the revival meeting became the central religious event. Calvinism was effectively replaced by evangelicalism, which held that being saved was the individual's free choice, and which often overlapped with chiliastic visions of national renewal. This was more in tune with the democratic ethos of the new nation — but only up to a point. It left great scope for anti-intellectual illiberalism, particularly biblical literalism. And evangelicalism was the ghost of Calvinism in that it yearned to see the upholding of godly laws. Evangelicals believed that Christians should work to reunite society around biblical morality. The crucial complexity is that the evangelicals, due to their explosion in the revolutionary period, imbibed the rhetoric of religious liberty. But what they meant by it was that no distant English bishop or haughty Harvard cleric should tell them what to believe — or how to organize themselves. They shared Jefferson and Madison's rejection of official establishments, but they were fundamentally *unsympathetic* to the rights of non-Protestants, or of any dissenters from traditional morality. As David Sehat argues in *The Myth of American Religious Freedom,* the evangelicals wanted "a *moral establishment* that connected religion and the state." They successfully salvaged — and strengthened — state laws that privileged Protestant assumptions and excluded immorality and blasphemy, as well as minority religious rights. "After institutional establishment fell, the moral establishment became more important. . . . Protestant Christian moral norms needed the force of law because, proponents claimed, in the absence of Christian moral enforcement the nation would devolve into anarchy, licentiousness, and ultimate ruin."[12]

Therefore, even as the separation of church and state was becoming a central shibboleth of federal government, most states were

12. David Sehat, *The Myth of American Religious Freedom* (Oxford: Oxford University Press, 2011), pp. 5, 69.

strengthening their unofficial Protestant establishments. Evangelicalism had asserted itself as the new nation's ideological glue. Of course, liberals such as Madison could hardly contest this by seeking to limit the influence of evangelicalism. The huge new nation needed all the ideological glue it could get.

A kind of double-think was born. The principle of religious liberty through the separation of church and state was a nationally unifying principle, but the states were allowed to interpret this in a deeply conservative way. And they did so by guaranteeing the liberty of the dominant religion, as long as it was not officially established, to dominate through law. In effect, the nation contained two conceptions of religion and society, and it tacitly agreed to pretend that there was no real conflict between them. Such pretense was possible while the nation was young. But the Civil War changed that: the nation discovered the need for increased ideological unity. The Fourteenth Amendment limited the power of states to pass laws infringing on citizens' civil liberties. Yet the federal government did not challenge the religious conservatism of most states; Protestant hegemony was too strong. As we shall see, the First Amendment was not applied on a state level — as Madison had wanted — until well into the twentieth century.

Despite this limitation, the American Revolution was a huge step forward for the "good" liberal Christian tradition. After a century and a half of uncertainty, it was clearly announced that Christianity could move on from establishment, from the idea of an official national church that might or might not deign to tolerate dissenters. The compatibility of Christianity and religious liberty was a major new historical fact, despite its patchy implementation. But the American Revolution also hugely boosted the "bad" liberal Christian tradition. Jefferson separated the vision of John Milton and Roger Williams from its Christian roots. For Milton, the creation of a new kind of state, enshrining religious liberty, was one's Christian duty. But it was not one's *entire* Christian duty; a person still had to learn to understand himself as God's fallen creature, dependent on God's grace, and expecting his posthistorical eschatological consummation. In Jefferson's mind, such belief was dubious and backward, for surely the essence of Christianity lay in the project of creating a boldly liberal state, making America "the world's best hope."

Of course, there were also full-blooded Christians involved in the American Revolution, such as the liberal Baptist (and friend of Jefferson) John Leland, who helped sell the separation of church and state to the clergy, but they remained marginal.[13]

In the revolutionary era, secularized Christian eschatology coexisted with millenarian Christianity. Liberal idealism and supernatural chiliasm, which we are accustomed to seeing as starkly opposed forces, overlapped, producing a uniquely eschatological nationalism. An eschatological aura allows a nation to forgive itself for its violence. The new nation managed to overlook its genocidal relationship with the Native Americans, as well as to boast of liberty while allowing slavery. The Founders assumed that slavery was on the wane. Their trust in progress entailed the evasion of current injustice. If this nation was the world's best hope, then its crimes could be assumed to be temporary aberrations. Deism thus contained a fatal pragmatism. Slavery cannot suddenly be ended, the Founders said (particularly the Virginian trio of Washington, Jefferson, and Madison), for the economy is presently reliant on it. Hence moral urgency is unhelpful. Have patience — justice and reason will prevail. This confidence was illusory: slavery's roots gradually strengthened in the South rather than withering away.

One effect of this disastrous complacency was that it enabled American republicanism to be dismissed, particularly back in Britain. Instead of being forced to admit that the Americans had achieved a new constitutional clarity, Britons could dismiss their ideology as

---

13. Leland was perhaps the closest the Revolution had to a Milton figure: someone advocating religious liberty on primarily Christian grounds. In his tract *The Rights of Conscience Inalienable* (1791), he made various arguments reminiscent of Milton's, including this: establishment "has a natural tendency to make men conclude that *bible religion* is nothing but a *trick of state:* hence it is that the greatest part of the well informed in literature are over-run with deism and infidelity" (quoted in Matthew L. Harris and Thomas S. Kidd, eds., *The Founding Fathers and the Debate Over Religion in Revolutionary America: A History in Documents* [Oxford: Oxford University Press, 2012], p. 144).

self-righteous, as in Samuel Johnson's famous jibe, "Why do we hear the loudest yelps for liberty from the drivers of negroes?" Largely because of slavery, the semiliberal pragmatism of the English was unshaken by events across the Atlantic. And, as we shall see, the pragmatism was further deepened by events across the Channel.

The new American nation was the perfect arena for the triumph of capitalism, which is a certain form of belief in progress. The freeing up of markets will bring general prosperity, even if it increases inequality for the time being. This prospect justifies all social and ideological upheaval, as greed mutates into a virtue. This process shows us providence, or Smith's "invisible hand." In Europe this ideology had to fight against certain traditional structures; in America it seemed the natural expression of freedom.

Should liberalism and capitalism be condemned for failing to be perfect instruments of progress toward fuller human flourishing? Yes and no. It is dubious to criticize them on political grounds, as if one knows of a better ideology that could be implemented to take us to utopia quicker. On the other hand, yes, they certainly should be criticized for their aura of self-aggrandizement, for their "ideological" dimension (in Marx's sense). Which means that they should be criticized on theological grounds. The only grounds on which liberal democracy can meaningfully be criticized is on the grounds of failing to be, as it implicitly claims to be, divinely good. When this relatively good human tradition exalts itself, it is an affront to God, who is the world's best hope.

SIX

Golden Age?

—◦◦◦—

In the nineteenth century, liberal Protestantism spread like never before, mainly due to the British Empire and its American off-shoot, and also to the rise of Germany. But it did not gain coherence. For "liberty" became detached from Protestantism because of the French Revolution and its aftermath, and also because of the rise of economic liberalism — in Britain especially. In addition, of course, the theological problem that I have traced over the last three chapters remained: liberal Christianity continued to gravitate to some form of universal humanism (with Romanticism now supplementing ratio-nalism) and to gravitate away from the foundations of Christianity: faith, revelation, and ritual. Romanticism, as we began to see in chap-ter 4 above, brought some awareness of the deficiency of deist-influenced Protestantism, of its propensity to arid abstraction and in-dividualism; but instead of seeking theological reform, it proposed a new spiritually enhanced humanism. The advanced secularization of Protestantism provoked new reactions. We shall see that two very dif-ferent critiques sowed the seeds of twentieth-century theology.

Throughout the eighteenth century, Britain proudly claimed to be upholding Protestantism and liberty; indeed, the two were seen as one. Those who objected that the British constitution was somewhat at odds with liberty were easily dismissed, for where was a stronger realization of liberty? The American Revolution furnished an answer: here was a fuller vision of Protestant-based liberty, despite the blot of slavery (which most Northerners assumed was fading fast). British radicals hoped that this vision would filter back to the homeland; but something else happened instead. The French Revolution cried "liberty" in a decidedly post-Christian accent, and the old narrative — Protestantism nurtures liberty — was suddenly put in doubt. From the perspective of my argument, this was unhelpful. For attention was suddenly diverted to something far more spectacular than the frail independence of some distant colonies: the dramatic transformation of an ancient state. The idea of liberty was ripped from its Protestant roots and mixed with new forces: egalitarianism, militant secularism, and a new kind of state power.

The association of Protestantism and liberty did not end. It remained central to Britain's ideology (and of course America's), but it lost its axiomatic aura. That tradition was eclipsed by "liberalism," an ideology with strong secular associations due to its opposition to Catholic power. In effect, "liberty"/"liberalism" was redefined by the French Revolution. (In America, the liberal-Protestant connection remained axiomatic, but the Atlantic was very wide during this period.)

In Britain the new complexity surrounding "liberty" was particularly acute. Edmund Burke, in his *Reflections on the Revolution in France* (1790), used the French Revolution to redefine British liberty in opposition to the Jacobin creed, and in doing so he also attacked the British radical liberal tradition, the radical Protestant vision that had emerged during the English civil war and still haunted the national psyche. Burke powerfully implied that its vision, of full religious liberty in place of establishment, was cut from the same cloth as the reformist excesses of the French. He was responding to the sermon of a dissenting minister, Dr. Richard Price, who celebrated the French Revolution as a victory for liberty against monarchical absolutism and the papacy, and therefore as God's will. Instead, said Burke, a rigid ideology of freedom will imperil the actual freedoms enshrined in the existing order. This rigidity was shared, he says, by the French radicals and the English dissenting tradition, whom he refers to together: "Something they must destroy, or they seem to themselves to exist for no purpose. . . . They are aware that the worst consequences might happen to the public in accomplishing this double ruin of church and state; but they are so heated with their theories, that they give more than hints, that this ruin . . . would not be unacceptable to them."[1] Burke cites Priestley as a reckless opponent of, in his words, "this most unnatural alliance" of church and state. Having associated English and French radical traditions, Burke is emboldened to idealize the French Catholic monarchy, in terms that recall the "martyrdom" of Charles I.[2] There is a tacit rebuke to Milton's rejection of royal idolatry: religion legitimately blurs with the sublime sacramentalism that is the soul of "chivalry." Puritanism (both Protestant and deist) has tried to rob political attachments of beauty and feeling. Similarly, a manic opposition to "superstition" is destabilizing: the human mind has "many dispositions and many passions" that elude rational justification.[3]

Burke was one of the first critics of liberal Protestantism; he saw that it was an amorphous thing that was in some ways closer to post-Christian rationalist humanism than to authentic Christianity. And he influentially located Christian authenticity in tradition, popular devotion, the habits of the heart. He shows how Romanticism overlaps with a Catholic turn. Before returning to the British mutation of liberal Protestantism, let us look at the theology that arises from German Romanticism.

Hegel

Kant's thought surely did not lack boldness: he dared to suggest that the religion of the churches, what he called "positive religion," was a vehicle for the true universal rational-moral form of religion. But a re-

---

1. Edmund Burke, *Reflections on the Revolution in France* (Harmondsworth, UK: Penguin, 1986), pp. 147-48.
2. Marie Antoinette is depicted as a sort of goddess: "[S]urely never lighted on this orb, which she hardly seemed to touch, a more delightful vision" (Burke, *Reflections,* p. 169).
3. Burke, *Reflections,* p. 269.

lated theory now emerged that made Kant's look humble and reticent, that of G. W. F. Hegel. Before paying Kant serious attention,
Hegel was deeply influenced by the Romanticism of Goethe, Herder,
and others. His early view of religion was close to Rousseau's. Its remarkable first expression is an essay (1793) that he wrote when he was
just twenty-three. Religion is the thing that can unify a nation's culture; therefore, authentic religion is "folk religion," meaning nationally unifying religion. It must combine rational morality with affective
power.[4] There must be public "ceremonies," but they demand vigilance: "Nothing is harder to prevent than their being taken by the
populace at large for the essence of religion itself" (p. 54). They must
be carefully managed, so as to "intensify devotion and pious sentiments" (p. 55). Choral festivals would be good, he suggests, which
seems to indicate an awareness that Protestantism has reacted too far
against sacramentalism. Culturally rich religion must be nurtured to
ensure the popularity of rational-moral religion.

Very much like Rousseau, Hegel insists that religion must be
world-affirming: "A folk religion must be a friend to all life's feelings
. . . [it must be] supportive of their undertakings and the more serious
concerns of their lives as well as of their festivals and times of fun. It
must not appear obtrusive, must not become a nagging schoolmarm,
but rather initiate and encourage" (pp. 55-56). He then notes that ancient Greek religion permeated all of public culture. And the thought
of sunnier climes emboldens him to show his hand: whereas a folk religion "goes hand in hand with freedom . . . our religion would train
people to be citizens of heaven, gazing ever upward, making our most
human feelings seem alien" (p. 56). As we noted with respect to Rousseau, "freedom" means communal cultural expression, not just the
absence of restrictions. He opines that at the Eucharist (our idea of
public festivity!) we are gloomy black-clad isolates, nervous about

---

4. "The imagination must be filled with large and pure images, and the heart
roused to feelings of benevolence. . . . [Otherwise] both the heart and the imagination
all too easily strike out on paths of their own or let themselves be led astray" (Hegel,
"Religion is one of our Greatest Concerns in Life," in Peter C. Hodgson, ed., *G. W. F.
Hegel: Theologian of the Spirit* (Minneapolis: Augsburg, 1997), p. 49. Hereafter, page references to this work appear in parentheses in the text.

catching something from the chalice. "How different were the Greeks! They approached the altars of their friendly gods clad in the colours of joy, their faces, open invitations to friendship and love, beaming with good cheer" (p. 56).

In his mature thought, Hegel dropped his flirtation with Rousseau-esque Neo-Paganism; the course of the French Revolution had shown it to be dangerously anarchic. He decided that only Christianity can enshrine rational morality in a nation and culturally unify it. But he retained and developed the conviction that authentic religion affirms culture. He saw his own task as reinventing philosophy as the discourse explaining this. Amid the grand verbosity of his theorizing there is an exciting vision of Christianity's development. As Hegel's early essay already suggests, there is an understanding that Protestantism's rejection of Catholicism must be reappraised, for the older form has greater ability to bring Christianity to cultural expression. But Protestantism is ultimately superior. Its seeming negation of socially unifying religion ("It has imprinted on religion the whole character of *northern* subjectivity") is just a phase, for from this alienated position it imagines a new universal expression of Christianity.[5] And philosophy — meaning Hegel's own philosophy — plays a key role in this. It directs this consummation of religion.

The true philosophy reconciles faith and reason, but not as deism attempted to do — by emptying God of all content.[6] Its emptiness, Hegel says, makes it inevitable that people will return to reactionary forms of faith, or turn atheist, or affirm a vague pietism that overvalues "feeling" and "dependence on God" (a rebuke to his contemporary Schleiermacher).[7] Modern theology leaves us unable to say anything about its rational God, known through subjective feeling.

---

5. Hegel, "The Resumption of the World into One," in Hodgson, ed., *G. W. F. Hegel*, p. 90 (italics in original).

6. Hegel, "Introduction: On the Philosophy of Religion," in Hodgson, ed., *G. W. F. Hegel*, p. 179.

7. According to the subjective approach, "People have had various religions; but that does not matter, as long as they are pious. We cannot know God as an object, we cannot cognize God, and it is the subjective attitude that is important" (Hegel, "Christianity: The Consummate Religion" [1824], in Hodgson, ed., *G. W. F. Hegel*, p. 207).

Hegel wants to be able to say things about God. The task is to formulate "an objective content, a doctrine of faith [*Glaubenslehre*]." Theology and philosophy are united in this task: "Thus it was that *scholastic theology* came into being in the Middle Ages — a science that developed religion in the direction of thinking and reason and endeavored to grasp the most profound doctrines of revealed religion in thinking fashion."[8] Where is the enlightened Protestant version of this? he asks.[9]

Instead of saying that faith and reason are compatible, as deism (unconvincingly) does, he says that they are the same thing: the higher rationality is self-aware Christianity. How does this theory deal with the knotty problems of revelation, miracles, and so on? Very cleverly. God communicates himself through traditional religious forms. He does not just sit in the realm of pure abstraction, but he comes to "representational expression. Religion is universal and does not exist only for educated, conceptual thought. . . . [I]nstead, the truth of the idea of God is manifest for representational consciousness and it has this necessary characteristic: that it *must* be universally accessible for representation." It belongs to God's truth that he is represented in miraculous terms; for he would otherwise be limited to an intellectual elite. The educated believer does not disparage this representation as irrational; he affirms it as an aspect of the higher rationality, the story of Spirit.

Hegel sincerely saw himself as rejecting the secular drift of the Enlightenment, and as rerooting thought in revealed religion. "The Enlightenment — that vanity of understanding — . . . takes it very ill when philosophy demonstrates the rational content in the Christian religion, when it shows [that] the witness of the Spirit, the truth in the most all-embracing sense of the term, is deposited in religion. Thus the task of philosophy is to show forth the rational content of reli-

8. "Foreword to Hinrich's *Religion*" (1822), in Hodgson, ed., *G. W. F. Hegel*, pp. 161, 169 (italics in original).

9. This emptiness is inexcusable, since "the Christian community is supposed to be nothing other than the community into which the Spirit of God is sent and in which this spirit . . . is the thinking, knowing and cognizing of God, and leads its members into cognition of God" (Hodgson, ed., *G. W. F. Hegel*, p. 170).

gion."[10] Rather like a medieval Scholastic, Hegel argues that reason has to be rooted in a big religious narrative.

In his grand narrative, modernity was moving toward a new unity of religion and politics, a superior version of medieval unity. Religion must serve the state and promote an ideal of national culture, which is fortunately the inner desire of Protestantism. This is the modern liberal state, which values freedom, philosophy, the arts. And yet it has a new emphasis on positive liberalism, on a uniting vision. This is where existing liberal states fail: they provide insufficient common purpose, an insufficient sense of what freedom is for. They contain too many dissenters, who weaken the narrative of common purpose. Such groups should be tolerated rather than banned, says Hegel (this isn't the Middle Ages!), but they should not get in the way of the positive ideology, which might be summed up simply as belief in the liberal Protestant state, a fusion of national and religious pride.[11] There need not be one established church (Protestantism rightly celebrates freedom from that model), but the various churches should be state-affirming.

Hegel might be seen as developing a Hobbesian account of the liberal state. Individual freedom must be subordinate to a positive narrative of the strong united state. Positive liberalism must trump negative liberalism (to borrow Isaiah Berlin's terms). This is an authentic aspect of the political liberal tradition, but naturally it is open to abuse: "liberty" (tailored to the particular requirements of national character) might become the pretext for a new kind of state power.

This is often criticized as protofascist, but Hegel might simply be seen as describing the logic of the liberal state. It is not enough just to allow freedom: it needs a positive narrative in order to cohere, or liberty will devour itself and collapse. It needs the courage to promote

10. Hegel, "Christianity: The Consummate Religion" (1824), in Hodgson, ed., *G. W. F. Hegel,* pp. 222, 259.

11. In *Philosophy of Right,* Hegel explains that Quakers, Anabaptists, and Jews should not become too strong, and that it might be necessary to withhold full citizenship from them (Mark Lilla, *The Stillborn God: Religion, Politics and the Modern West* [New York: Knopf, 2007], p. 204).

positive rather than negative liberalism (to borrow Isaiah Berlin's terms), and to limit antiliberal forces. It should reaffirm Protestantism, as the freedom-promoting religion. To a large extent, this was already the logic of Britain and America, but the logic was muffled in certain ways (Britain's half-reformed constitution was at odds with liberal philosophy, and America was perhaps too large and diverse to promote common purpose effectively). In a sense, Hegel was reviving Milton's idea that, in order to promote religious liberty, a state must be motivated by religious idealism. Hegel was reframing this in more philosophical terms. The disaster that lay in Germany's future does not detract from the legitimacy of putting a robust nation-state at the center of political reflection.

Schleiermacher

Like Kant, Friedrich Schleiermacher was a product of pietism and the Enlightenment. In his case the pietism sank deeper. As a boy at school (as he later recalled), he developed a "mystic tendency . . . which has . . . carried me through all the storms of skepticism."[12] In the 1790s he became friends with writers, including Schlegel, and found himself defending religion against the rising Romantic humanism. This was the genesis of his book *On Religion: Speeches to Its Cultured Despisers* (1799). His approach can perhaps best be summed up in seemingly flippant fashion: religion is *deep*. Those who reject it as irrational are missing something — in a dual sense: they are failing to understand, and they are missing out. And they are underestimating the complexity of faith, which is capable of self-criticism and development.[13] Schleiermacher suggests that his audience habitually scorns religion, "as if

12. Schleiermacher, "Letter to George Reimer" (1802), in Richard Crouter, ed. and trans., introduction to *On Religion: Speeches to Its Cultured Despisers* (Cambridge, UK: Cambridge University Press, 1996), p. xiii.

13. Schleiermacher, "Letter to George Reimer," p. 8: "Religion helped me when I began to examine the ancestral faith and to purify my heart of the rubble of primitive times. It remained with me when God and immortality disappeared before my doubting eyes." Hereafter, page references to *On Religion* appear in parentheses in the text.

the sense for the holy, like an old folk-costume, had passed over to the lower class of people to whom alone it is still seemly to be gripped by awe and belief in the unseen" (p. 10). This hints that faith contains an exotic primitivism (a hint informed by Rousseau and Herder). His key move is to use Romanticism to offer a new account of religion: it "springs necessarily and by itself from the interior of every better soul, it has its own province in the mind in which it reigns sovereign" (p. 17). On the one hand, this approach ennobles religion — it is the *supreme* human activity; on the other hand, it naturalizes or humanizes it — the supreme *human* activity. So he assures his learned hearers that religion is wider than any dogmatic system: "[R]eligion does not strive to bring those who believe and feel under a single belief and single feeling" (p. 22). Roman Catholicism fails to grasp this; it corrupts religion with rigidity. By contrast, ancient Rome, "truly pious and religious in a lofty style, was hospitable to every god and so it became full of gods" (p. 28). He seems to go ever further in identifying religion with Romantic humanism: revelation is "every original and new intuition of the universe" (p. 49). "It is not the person who believes in a holy writing who has religion, but only the one who needs none and probably could make one for himself" (p. 50). Everything depends on creative subjectivity: "It is your imagination that creates the world for you, and you can have no God without the world" (p. 53).

But then he changes tack. Serious religious experience brings people out of isolation and into community. The believer will want "to communicate the vibrations of his mind to [others]" (p. 73). Such sharing will constitute a major cultural form: "People cannot toss religious views, pious feelings, and serious reflections upon them to each other in small snatches, like the ingredients of a light conversation. . . . The communication of religion must occur in a grander style, and another type of society, which is especially dedicated to religion, must arise from it" (p. 74). Organized religion does not quash individual creativity (the fear he seems to be addressing); instead, it arises from a pooling of individual creativity. It is an illusion to think that "natural religion" — the deism that spurns traditional practice — is superior. Such freethinkers only have "the freedom to remain unformed, the freedom from every compulsion to be, to see, and to feel something even remotely specific. Religion plays far too paltry a role in their mind" (p. 108). They have "no specific dwelling in [religion's] realm" (p. 109). "The essence of natural religion actually consists . . . in the most violent polemic against [religion]" (p. 110). The detached flâneur cannot understand religion: it "can be understood only through itself and . . . its special manner of construction and its characteristic distinction will not become clear to you until you yourselves belong to some one or other of them" (p. 113).

So Schleiermacher offers a new defense of religious particularity, but in rather general terms; and his defense of communal practice presupposes the priority of individual religious experience. These tensions continue with his dogmatic work of 1821, *The Christian Faith*. He first explains that dogmatics is a science internal to the Christian church; it rejects "the task of establishing on a foundation of general principles a Doctrine of God, or an Anthropology or Eschatology either, which should be used in the Christian Church though it did not really originate there, or which should prove the propositions of the Christian Faith to be consonant with reason."[14] This bold insistence on particularity is somewhat undercut by his next move: defining the concept of church in general philosophical terms. A church is an association based in "piety," which is a form of "feeling." His famous definition of piety as "the consciousness of being absolutely dependent, or, which is the same thing, of being in relation with God" seems to be a rebuke to Descartes: selfhood is based not on thinking but on recognizing one's dependence (p. 12).

Schleiermacher explains that Jesus possessed full and perfect God-consciousness. He redeemed humanity through imparting his God-consciousness to his followers, in whom it contends with normal sinful forces. We can access this saving God-consciousness through participating in the corporate mind of the church. There is a huge emphasis in Schleiermacher on "entering into fellowship" with Christ, which is clearly derived from pietism. This alone is the locus of salvation; other accounts are dubiously "magical." For example, some

14. Schleiermacher, *The Christian Faith* (London: T&T Clark, 1999), p. 3. Hereafter, page references to this work appear in parentheses in the text.

claim that the atonement effects a saving transformation independently of the believer's entry into church fellowship.

The church is a kind of corporate soul in Schleiermacher. Once
we are in fellowship with Christ, via the community, our consciousness has smoothly progressed to a new level. Schleiermacher seems to
ignore the whole Protestant *topos* of the clash of faith and reason. For
example, is there no ongoing problem of believing in the reality of the
resurrection? No, because one locates the reality of redemption in the
power of fellowship: belief in miraculous events is dubiously "magical" if it detracts from this fellowship emphasis. Schleiermacher does
not propose dropping supernatural belief; but he greatly downplays
it, and he approaches the issue as a church historian would. Doctrine
is a historically contingent expression of the church. (When formulating his new theological syllabus, he placed dogmatics within the category of church history.) There is surely an echo of Kant's division between the essence of the gospel and its outer forms, but here the
essence is not morality but Christ-consciousness — an end in itself.

Schleiermacher made a major turn toward particularity: Christianity is not an idea that merely makes use of the church; it takes the
form of church. He saw that the church, understood as spiritual fellowship, allows a liberal approach to doctrine. Because the real locus
of truth is community, there is no need for an anxious defense of an
intellectual system. Protestantism entails intellectual freedom. "If
the Reformation . . . has not the aim of establishing an eternal covenant between the living faith and scientific research, which is free to
explore upon all sides and works for itself independently . . . then it is
not adequate for the needs of our age and we require another Reformation, no matter how, and as a result of what struggles, it may develop" (p. 426). This sentiment gradually became axiomatic in liberal
Protestantism, and so one is likely to overlook its daring. At this time,
in both England and Germany, the churches were still deeply hostile
to the new critical approach to Scripture. Such openness was surely a
good thing; on the other hand, however, Schleiermacher enabled a
new spirit of cultural accommodation in the churches. It became difficult to identify where Christianity differed from the rising liberal
culture that was transforming Prussia.

A century later, Karl Barth insisted that Schleiermacher had failed to move theology on from humanism — that is, to reroot it. He was, says Barth, heretically focused on the human experience of religion at the expense of its divine content. Schleiermacher hoped for "the disappearance of even the semblance of the idea that the subject of dogmatics was anything else but human states of mind" (p. 443). No less seriously, he idolized modern culture: "The kingdom of God, according to Schleiermacher, is utterly and unequivocally identical with the advance of civilization." He was thus indirectly responsible for the nationalist abuse of the ideals of fellowship — unity and communion. Despite such criticisms, Barth insists that Schleiermacher put theology back on track by insisting that it was not an exotic form of philosophy but the reflection of the church. Because he subordinated intellectual inquiry to religious seriousness, Barth reversed Enlightenment assumptions: "We have to do with a hero, the like of which is but seldom bestowed upon theology."[15] Barth's point is that theology was so deeply corrupted by the Enlightenment that even a heroic figure could only half-repair it.

Kant, Hegel, and Schleiermacher created a context in which the critical study of the Bible became increasingly acceptable. It became possible to explore the role of mythology in Scripture, and to present the exploration as sympathetic to the latest theological approach. If the essence of Christianity was in some sense distinct from its outward forms, then the tall stories of Scripture could be probed with a clear conscience. The deists had long implied that Scripture was dubious; such questioning could now be presented as theologically motivated. Richard Strauss led the way with his *Life of Jesus* (1835), which denied the historical reliability of the New Testament, yet praised Jesus as the embodiment of perfect moral duty. His Tübingen colleague Baur launched a more careful study of the New Testament, and such critical inquiry soon became basic to the study of Protestant theology.

English theology was resistant to this innovation, as it was oblivious to German theology generally. Samuel Taylor Coleridge was one of the few intellectuals to follow it, and it left him isolated. He tenta-

---

15. Karl Barth, *Protestant Theology in the Nineteenth Century: Its Background and History* (London: SCM, 2001), pp. 421, 413.

tively proposed that the authority of the Bible should be detached from the question of its historicity. Instead, its authority lay in its literary sublimity and power, its existential hold on the reader. (Similarly he warned against seeking proofs of God in the external world; believers did better to "look into their own souls.")[16] Coleridge's influence prepared a few intellectuals for the shock that Darwin would unleash in 1859. But until then such discussion was more or less out of bounds in Britain. The high church and evangelical parties within the church were equally adamant that such inquiry led to atheism. The broad church party was not so rash as to champion the cause. (It was largely the absence of a firmly established church in Germany, and the independence of the universities from ecclesiastical control, that enabled the critical study of Scripture to get going.)

The Progress of "Liberalism"

After the fall of Napoleon, British radicalism came out of hiding. It had become decidedly secular. In the 1820s, James Mill and Jeremy Bentham announced the new reforming creed of Utilitarianism, or "philosophical radicalism." It inherited the politics of radical dissenting Protestantism — without the religion. Bentham had attacked the established church in a tract he wrote in 1818. Mill rejected his Scotch Presbyterian upbringing and taught his son, the philosopher John Stuart Mill, that religion was "a great moral evil" and that it detracted from the greatest happiness of the greatest number by spreading "belief in creeds, devotional feelings, and ceremonies, not connected with the good of human kind." The ghost of Protestant zeal clearly hung over this worldview. The younger Mill says: "He taught me to take the strongest interest in the Reformation, as the great and decisive contest against priestly tyranny for liberty of thought."[17] This is a

16. S. T. Coleridge, "Aids to Reflection,"in John Beer, ed., *The Collected Writings of Samuel Taylor Coleridge,* vol. 9 (Princeton, NJ: Princeton University Press, 1993), p. 408.

17. John Stuart Mill, *Autobiography* (Harmondsworth, UK: Penguin, 1873), pp. 50, 52.

good glimpse into the Protestant roots of the rising political radicalism that became influential on mainstream liberalism: Whig Liberalism. The cause partially triumphed in 1828 with the repeal of the Test and Corporation Acts, which had banned dissenters from public office. What complicates this cause is that it overlapped with the huge new ideology of economic liberalism, laissez-faire capitalism. The Whigs became dominated by the new interest of industrialists (many of whom were dissenters), insisting that they should be represented in parliament alongside land-owning aristocrats. The Reform Bill of 1832 secured that change.

So the cause of political liberalism (meaning religious liberty and the gradual expansion of democracy) got mixed together with the cause of industrial capitalism. From the perspective of my argument, this confusion was deeply unhelpful. Just as the cause of religious liberty finally began to triumph in Britain, after almost two centuries, its meaning was muddled. It seemed joined to a deeply ambiguous new strain of rational capitalism that lacked a vision of society as a whole. The established church, aided by Romanticism, fostered this impression: it spread deep resentment at the demands of nonconformists and their atheist allies. It became fashionable to see liberty as a mechanistic, soul-destroying force, motivated by the self-interest of dissenters and businessmen.

Thus, in the space of forty years or so, the idea of liberty went through two major changes. Through the French Revolution it became associated with antireligious zeal. And in Britain it then became associated with a divisive economic agenda — and with the perceived self-interest of an upstart class. These forces threatened to bury the older idea of liberty that we have traced: the idea of the (Protestant) state's duty to defend religious liberty. This suited the established church: it could spread the fear that the expansion of religious liberty was associated with French radicalism, on the one hand, and soulless capitalism, on the other. Both ideas affected Coleridge's thoughts on church and state: organic unity must be emphasized in defiance of the negative forces of the age. The young William Gladstone agreed that establishment must be defiantly defended. He gradually admitted that religious liberty must also be extended, even in Ireland, and that liberalism should be central to national ideology. But Gladstone's first impulse, in common with various great intellects, such as Carlyle and Matthew Arnold, was to distrust liberalism as an ambiguous cause: just and unstoppable, but corrosive of national unity. In rather the same way, they saw science as right and unstoppable, but corrosive of faith.

What had happened to the optimistic assumption that Protestantism and liberty were natural allies, and that this alliance could inspire national unity? It was in rude health across the Atlantic. America's distance from the French Revolution meant that it avoided the association between liberty and atheism that haunted Europe. It also avoided England's assumption that liberty was corrosive of national religious unity. A new paradigm had arisen in Europe: political progress seemed to threaten religion. In his book *Democracy in America* (1835), Alexis de Tocqueville sought to address this problem. His introduction explains that in Europe something has gone wrong: the democratic principle is steadily increasing its influence, but this is inducing a crisis. Despite its intrinsic belief in equality, Christianity has entered a deep alliance with reaction: "It is not unfrequently brought to reject the equality which it loves, and to curse that cause of liberty as a foe, whose efforts it might hallow by its alliance."[18] Advocates of liberty ought to invoke religion, but "they have seen religion in the ranks of their adversaries, and they inquire no further. . . . The religionists are the enemies of liberty, and the friends of liberty attack religion" (pp. 34-35). The reason to study America is that it has avoided this dynamic: "The spirit of Religion and the spirit of Liberty" have "been admirably incorporated and combined with one another" (p. 47). This fusion is paradoxically a product of separation: "Free and powerful in its own sphere, satisfied with the place reserved for it, religion never more surely establishes its empire than when it reigns in the hearts of men unsupported by aught beside its native strength." Liberty, in America, is not quite secular in spirit: it "regards religion

---

18. Alexis de Tocqueville, *Democracy in America*, ed. Richard D. Heffner (New York: Penguin, 1984), p. 34. Hereafter, page references to this work appear in parentheses in the text.

as its companion in all its battles and its triumphs — as the cradle of its infancy, and the divine source of its claims" (p. 48).

Tocqueville strongly implies that this is the model for Europe to follow, but he avoids sounding uncritically enthusiastic. Something gets lost, he believes, when the principle of equality is elevated so high. The absence of an aristocracy means "less splendor. . . . The nation, taken as a whole, will be less brilliant, less glorious, and perhaps less strong" (p. 32). He returns to the issue in the conclusion: "A state of equality is perhaps less elevated, but it is more just: and its justice constitutes its greatness and its beauty" (p. 315). Such a state is surely more pleasing to God, though not to many of us. Tocqueville's purpose seems to be to hold the hand of a Europe traumatized by rampant liberalism and democracy. Don't be too alarmed, he says, because these movements are rooted in the modern logic of Christianity. It is strange that no stronger — and more Christian — a voice was saying such things. Milton really should have been living at that hour, as Wordsworth had said in 1802. (But it was not Milton's theopolitical leadership that Wordsworth had yearned for; rather, it was his grand poetic presence. His sonnet was symptomatic of the fact that the strong voices of the day were in thrall to Romanticism.)

Romantic Faith

Romanticism had an open border with Protestantism: many of its exponents supposed that they were daringly discovering the true logic of Protestantism. And most assumed that Jesus was a Romantic humanist. For example, Jesus' character was "of a sublime humanity," according to Hazlitt, his religion "the religion of the heart." "He has done more to humanize the thoughts and tame the unruly passions, than all who have tried to reform and benefit mankind. . . . [R]egarding the human race as one family, the offspring of one common parent is hardly to be found in any other code or system."[19] Even

---

19. William Hazlitt, *Lectures on the Age of Elizabeth* (1820), in Hazlitt, *Selected Writings* (Harmondsworth, UK: Penguin, 1987), pp. 411-12.

those Romantics who hotly rejected Christianity echoed Protestant themes (e.g., Shelley on poetry as prophecy; Keats on the martyr-making religion of art and the world as a "vale of soul-making"). For a figure such as Carlyle, authorship was a prophetic endeavor. The age needed a new kind of faith, a post-Protestant spiritual heroism.

The basic Romantic view was that humanity should be affirmed — in place of God. Philosophy now moved in this explicitly humanist direction, led by Ludwig Feuerbach, who reacted against the idealism of Hegel, insisting that all value must be explicitly located in the material existence of humanity. And Feuerbach reacted against the claim of both Kant and Hegel that traditional religious forms must be preserved as the necessary vehicles of rational-moral truth. The old forms must not be preserved but upended, or turned inside out, he explained in *The Essence of Christianity* (1841). He was writing in opposition to "a superhuman, i.e., anti-human, anti-natural religion and speculation." This sounds like the deism of Voltaire or Paine, but it is subtly different. For it claims that religion tells the truth about humanity, in a back-to-front way: that it is sacred, "divine." God must be pulled down from heaven and located in the human. Atheism, in this specific sense, is the "secret of religion itself." For Christianity, "while lowering God into man, made man into God." So it is missing the point to say that Jesus was merely human: "I accept the Christ of religion, but I show that this superhuman being is nothing else than a product and reflex of the supernatural human mind."[20] Whereas the deists' idea of rational humanity was implicitly religious, inheriting an aura of salvation history without quite realizing it, Feuerbach's idea of divine humanity is explicitly so. The problem — or at least one problem — with this theory is the question of how such a humanism is to sustain itself: Does it continue to need the old idea of religion to kick against? This question was, at the same time, being tackled by Auguste Comte. He announced that the truth of rationalism, which he called "positivism," must not just be written and talked about. It must be enshrined in a new religion, the Religion of Humanity; de-

---

20. Feuerbach, *The Essence of Christianity*, trans. Marian Evans (New York: Calvin Blanchard, 1855), pp. xv, xviii, xxi.

tailed plans for temples and liturgies were made. This is in the tradition of Rousseau and the revolutionary festivals of the Supreme Being. In America, too, Protestantism blurred with the new kind of humanism. Ralph Waldo Emerson trained as a Unitarian minister, but he soon decided that even this form of religion was too rigid. After traveling to Europe in the 1830s, and meeting Coleridge and Carlyle, he set himself up as New England's Romantic-religious sage. In few other thinkers is it so clear that Romanticism is a sort of derailed Protestantism. True faith, he insists, opposes "pews, vestries, family prayer, sanctimonious looks and words" (May 14, 1835).[21] It must resist all inherited assumptions, including the idea "that Jesus was the perfect man," for there is more to humanism than he exhibits, such as "cheerfulness, . . . the love of Natural Science . . . [and] Art" (July 30, 1835, p. 29). A new belief in the divinity of the soul must refuse to fetishize tradition, or make a cult of any previous teacher. In 1838, Emerson addressed the graduates of Harvard Divinity School, telling them that "the idioms of [Jesus'] language, and the figures of his rhetoric, have usurped his truth," his message that "man's life was a miracle" (p. 252). "Historical Christianity has fallen into the error that corrupts all attempts to communicate religion. . . . [I]t is not the doctrine of the soul, but an exaggeration of the personal, the positive, the ritual. It has dwelt, it dwells, with noxious exaggeration about the *person* of Jesus" (p. 252). He exhorts each student to think of himself as "a new-born bard of the Holy Ghost," scorning all conformity (p. 262). Instead of creating new religious forms, the old forms can be revived through "soul": "A whole popedom of forms, one pulsation of virtue can uplift and vivify" (p. 264). This aversion to tradition surfaces in his essay "Self-Reliance" (1841). Great spiritual figures dared to think for themselves: "The highest merit we ascribe to Moses, Plato, and Milton is that they set at nought books and traditions, and spoke not what men but what they thought" (p. 267). With regard to the first two, this is of course questionable; with regard to Milton, it is particularly

21. Ralph Waldo Emerson, Journal, May 14, 1835, in William H. Gilman, ed., *Selected Writings of Ralph Waldo Emerson* (New York: Penguin, 2003), p. 27. Hereafter, page references to this work appear in parentheses in the text.

absurd. What great poet has been *less* original in terms of his subject matter? Emerson is struggling to make sense of his Protestant inheritance: Doesn't this tradition exalt courageous independence and innovation rather than ritual and doctrinal habit? "Man . . . dares not say 'I think,' 'I am,' but quotes some saint or sage. . . . These roses under my window make no reference to former roses or to better ones; they are for what they are; they exist with God today" (p. 279). Elsewhere he notes that when writers broach the question of immortality, "they begin to quote. I hate quotation. Tell me what you know" (p. 127). But Emerson's basic concepts — of the soul, and of God — are inherited: God is a quotation (as some French theorist has doubtless said). The true hater of quotation would be silent as a rose. In effect, he is trying to detach the Protestant idea of prophetic speech from its tradition (in which such speech serves the otherness of God's word rather than unearthing inner truth). The essence of his humanism is a denial of the distinction between God and the soul, and the fallibility of the soul: "Trust thyself" ("Self-Reliance," p. 268). He recalls that a friend questioned his rejection of "the sacredness of traditions" in favor of absolute self-reliance: "My friend suggested: 'But these impulses may be from below, not above.' I replied: 'They do not seem to me to be such; but if I am the Devil's child, I will live then from the Devil.' No law can be sacred to me but that of my nature" ("The Over-Soul," pp. 269-70). Emerson cannot accept the basic Christian idea of self-suspicion; thus authentic prayer does not appeal to "some foreign virtue." "It is the soliloquy of a beholding and jubilant soul. It is the spirit of God pronouncing his works good" (p. 285).

In a journal entry from 1848, Emerson predicts a "New Religion . . . founded on moral science, at first cold and naked, a babe in a manger again . . . but it will have heaven and earth for its beams and rafters, all geology and physiology, botany, chemistry, astronomy for its symbol and illustration, and it will fast enough gather beauty, music, picture, poetry" (p. 122). This is a very Romantic desire for the simultaneous rationalization of religion and reenchantment of nature — a new unity of meaning.

Why dwell on this Romantic humanism, which has little direct bearing on contemporary theology? Because liberal Christianity must find negative inspiration here. It must remember, with a shudder, that it can lead in this direction. There is substantial overlap between this and the tradition launched by Schleiermacher.[22] This is the true logic of a theology that departs from ritual particularity. Nevertheless, it must be acknowledged that the Romantic affirmation of human value was not simply wrong: it helped to bring out incarnational and eschatological aspects of the gospel that theology now takes for granted.

Oxford Otherness

In the early nineteenth century, evangelicalism was the rising force within the Church of England, but it was balanced by the Latitudinarian party, moderately sympathetic to Whig reformism. The high-church party seemed in decline; it was actually ripe for radical renewal. In the late 1820s a group of Oxford academics agreed that a premodern conception of the church was the true basis of Anglicanism, and that this basis must be reasserted against the liberal tide. This movement, called the Oxford Movement, or Tractarianism, is relevant to our argument because it was the first really serious critique of liberal Protestantism (the Methodist and evangelical critiques could be batted off, accommodated, or patronized). On one level this critique could also be dismissed as crypto-Catholic, but there was a gradual realization of the inadequacy of that familiar response.

The movement was prompted by horror at the church's being controlled by an increasingly liberal state. The concept of an established church was suddenly questionable, if it was subject to a government that lacked real respect for it. A sharp new rhetoric of high-church resistance came from John Keble and his pupil Richard Hurrell Froude, who jumped to the logical extreme of opposing establishment. They convinced John Henry Newman, a former evangelical,

22. Emerson's view of revelation closely reflects the early Schleiermacher's: "We distinguish the announcements of the soul, its manifestations of its own nature, by the term *Revelation*. These are always attended by the emotion of the sublime" (Emerson, *Selected Writings*, pp. 301-2).

that the church could only be saved from liberal infection by an extreme Catholic turn. Newman recalled: "I saw that if Liberalism once got a footing within her, it was sure of the victory in the event. I saw that Reformation principles were powerless to rescue her." Newman's antiliberalism was theological rather than political, he later insisted, but of course it was both, for he saw the church as imperiled by the Whig reforms of 1828-34 (also, he recalls his dismay at the "unchristian" revolt against the Bourbons in 1830).[23] Tory Anglican opposition to Whig reform was not new; what was new was the religious intensity of the group, and the boldness with which it linked Protestantism itself to corrosive liberalism. It had a strong new narrative: liberal theology was the natural consequence of the Protestant assault on ecclesiastical authority. This was an expansion of Burke's genealogy linking Protestant dissent and atheist radicalism: all of Protestantism gravitated toward liberalism, which undermined the authority of the church. And without an authoritative church, Christianity becomes a matter of arid abstraction rather than cultural vitality.

The movement gained traction largely through Newman's personality. He modeled a form of Christian identity that was in sharp contrast to cultural normality. Being a serious Christian was something beyond being a decent Englishman, he announced, to general bafflement. He had pledged himself to a celibate life, which already linked him to the sacerdotal otherness of Rome. He performed religious otherness with an intensity that fascinated many students, while others detected a strong element of posturing artifice. In an early sermon he suggests that it would be good for the country "were it vastly more superstitious, more bigoted, more gloomy, more fierce in its religion than at present it shows itself to be."[24] In another sermon he says that heretics should be dealt with as embodiments of evil."[25] He sees liberalism as "the anti-dogmatic principle." Religion,

---

23. John Henry Newman, *Apologia Pro Vita Sua* (London: Collins, 1959), pp. 119, 118.

24. Newman, *Apologia*, p. 130.

25. Looking back later in life he makes light of this: "Even when I was fiercest . . . I [could not have] even cut off a Puritan's ears, and I think the sight of a Spanish auto-da-fe would have been the death of me" (*Apologia*, p. 131).

he says, "as a mere sentiment, is to me a dream and a mockery" (*Apologia*, p. 132).

Once it became clear that the movement would not save the church from liberalism, Newman began to drift toward Rome, converting in 1845. The Anglo-Catholic movement, led by Pusey, remained highly influential, especially when it put the emphasis on ritual reform rather than ecclesiological theory. (Newman was scornful of an overly aesthetic Anglo-Catholicism, "the gilt-gingerbread school" [*Apologia*, p. 330].) Tractarianism should have provoked Anglicanism into serious theological reflection: it preferred to renew its attack on Roman Catholicism. In 1864, Charles Kingsley attacked Newman in an essay that is very revealing of Victorian Anglicanism. He focused on sermons published while Newman was still an Anglican, in which he had subtly disparaged Protestant culture. In one, Newman had suggested that Christians will naturally come across as different, and very likely as "artificial" and "wanting in openness and manliness," and "a mystery" to the world.[26] Such sentiments were deeply characteristic of Newman's charisma: "In proportion as young men absorbed [his teaching] into themselves, it injured their straightforwardness and truthfulness. . . . It spread misery and shame into many an English home" (p. 40). One wonders whether Kingsley is really talking about something else here, something unmentionable.

Kingsley goes on to discuss Newman's more recent Catholic sermons. The latter peddles superstitious belief in miracles that he cannot really believe himself, Kingsley says. He is particularly outraged by Newman's defense of nuns acquiring "miraculous" stigmata, through the institutional encouragement of hysteria: "I trust that it will arouse in every English husband, father and brother . . . the same feelings which it roused in me" (p. 55). And his sermons in defense of the "Marian cult should be read by any man who thinks it any credit to himself to be a rational being" (p. 57). Another sermon "tries to undermine the grounds of all rational belief for the purpose of substituting blind superstition" (p. 57). It is shocking that this comes from a

---

26. Charles Kingsley, "What, Then, Does Dr Newman Mean?" in Newman, *Apologia*, p. 39. Hereafter, page references to this work appear in parentheses in the text.

man "educated as an English gentleman and Oxford scholar" (p. 64). Newman's extremism, according to Kingsley, is feeding the worst prejudices against Catholicism, and damaging the cause of the Catholic gentry, who are "honest gentlemen and noble ladies" (p. 65). It is striking how firmly he assumes that true Christianity must be in tune with the "manliness," "rationality," and respectability of mainstream culture — and how threatening he finds an alternative perspective. He thus shows the key weakness of the liberal Christian tradition, especially when it takes the form of an established church: it cannot admit that the overlap of religion and modern culture is problematic, that a crucial aspect of Christianity gets lost. He fears that any departure from mainstream rationality will lead to medieval superstition.

In his book-length response, Newman is at pains to show that his religious career has been based in meticulous spiritual and intellectual reflection. He carefully narrates how he came to see the need for an institution that exercises authority, that determines doctrine, and upholds a sacramental system. At the end of the book he addresses the specific charges: that he submits himself to authoritarianism and superstition. On the question of authoritarian dogmatism, he explains that to take Christianity fully seriously is to be part of a culture that is larger than oneself and to trust its institutional aspect. It must strongly define orthodoxy, and censure dissent, so as to resist "a bottomless liberalism of thought" (p. 293). In practice, Catholic theologians do question tradition, and thus tradition gradually changes. With respect to the question of belief in miracles, he turns the tables on liberal Protestantism: it has no understanding of the nature of an organic religious tradition, in which popular piety plays a major part. Of course, there is a mythical element in traditional stories of saints and their relics, but that is how culture *works*. In the same way we allow legends about King Alfred to be mixed up with the sober facts; and we repeat the legend that some Anglo-Saxon jewel in a museum belonged to him. Myth arises when people are involved in a cultural tradition, when they care about it. "Why then may not the country people come up, in joyous companies, singing and piping, to see the Holy Coat at Trèves?" (p. 338) Newman cleverly turns to Queen Victoria (popular culture abounds with tall stories about her): "She roves about in the midst of tradition and romance; she scatters myths and legends from her as she goes along" (p. 338). Only the worst kind of cynic would not be "struck with this graceful, touching evidence of the love her subjects bear her." Just as she surely approves of such expressions of devotion, God surely approves of belief in miracles.

Newman's point is that religious belief is about allegiance to an *entire cultural tradition.* (In a sense, Kingsley, with his assumptions about Protestant manliness, has shown that he agrees.) Like patriotism, it is a comprehensive allegiance. Catholics may question aspects of official teaching, but they should respond to it "with those outward marks of reverence, submission, and loyalty, which Englishmen, for instance, pay to the presence of their sovereign" (p. 285). Protestantism, he implies, entails allegiance only to a culture of individualistic rationality. It is committed to the denial of comprehensive religious culture. As we shall see, this anticipates postliberal communitarianism.

By defending himself against reactionary medievalism, Newman points forward to major themes in subsequent theology, themes that come to full expression with postmodern theology. His central insight is that religion is located in communal cultural practices rather than the isolated intellect. Protestant thought was not capable of grasping this: it was too full of the individualism, rationalism, and antisacramentalism of the Enlightenment. Of course, some Protestant traditions challenged rational humanism (most of dissent and evangelicalism), but they did so in a way that strengthened individualism and antisacramentalism.

Partly thanks to Newman, liberal Protestantism acquired a muddled awareness that something was wrong. One expression of this came from Matthew Arnold, best known as the author of "Dover Beach" (the most tediously overquoted nineteenth-century poem). In his critical study *Culture and Anarchy* (1868), Arnold argues that national culture had been damaged by the narrowness of "Liberalism," which was dominated by puritanical Nonconformity. This force has disparaged "culture," meaning the great tradition of Western art and learning. Its reform of politics is perhaps necessary, but it has an unsettling cultural effect. This was the traditional Anglican view of Nonconformity: its obsession with religious liberty threatens common national purpose — and good culture. But Arnold implies that Protestantism itself contains this socially negative tendency; he controversially credits Newman with standing up to narrow Liberalism, daring to point out the inadequacy of "the Dissidence of Dissent and the Protestantism of the Protestant religion." But Arnold's motivation is more humanist than Catholic. He warns that Puritanism is illiberal: its "idea of human perfection is narrow and inadequate." Its traditional claim to liberalism is bogus; its "attitude of horror and holy superiority . . . towards Rome is wrong and false." It is not the force of liberal enlightenment that it thinks it is. The special calling of the established church, he argues, is to overcome the polarity between "Hellenising" and "Hebraising" impulses, to help people "towards culture and harmonious perfection." Without this integration, the absoluteness of the Judeo-Christian tradition will be rejected by educated people as backward. This would be a tragedy, for religion is "the greatest and most important effort by which the human race has manifested its impulse to perfect itself."[27] It supplies the energy and discipline without which culture is weak, effete. In effect, Arnold argues for a new kind of liberal religiosity, one that rejected Puritanism and sought to integrate Christianity with respect for high culture. Arnold's reflections suggest that Anglicanism found liberalism deeply paradoxical. By granting freedom to dissenters, it was undermining the nation's spiritual character (its vision of "positive liberty," in Isaiah Berlin's terms).

The complaint that liberalism had become narrow, lacking in social vision, should not be entirely dismissed as the gripe of the threatened privileged class. A strongly established church had united (most of) the nation in a certain liberal vision. If everyone is free to believe different things, won't common culture necessarily decline? The kind of liberalism that Arnold was wary of had been expressed a decade earlier by John Stuart Mill. His book *On Liberty* (1859) is dry and technical; it offers no rousing vision of political purpose, arguing — or rather assuming — that individual liberty is the natural state of

---

27. Matthew Arnold, *Culture and Anarchy,* edited by J. Dover Wilson (Cambridge: Cambridge University Press, 1963), pp. 62, 58, 31, 15, 47.

things once culture has become enlightened. Rational government will see that "the only purpose for which power can be rightfully exercised over any member of a civilized community, against his will, is to prevent harm to others." This is an aspect of political modernity: "Liberty, as a principle, has no application to any state of things anterior to the time when mankind have become capable of being improved by free and equal discussion." So how did humanity pull itself up into enlightenment? The power of religion was limited by thinkers who "asserted freedom of conscience as an indefeasible right, and denied absolutely that a human being is accountable to others for his religious belief." At first such thinkers were motivated by dissenting religion; yet only when people stop caring too much about religion does it become clear that "the only freedom which deserves the name, is that of pursuing our own good in our own way, so long as we do not attempt to deprive others of theirs." Mill repeats that an acknowledgment of the individual's natural right to liberty is made possible by "the separation between the spiritual and temporal authority (which placed the direction of men's consciences in other hands than those which controlled their worldly affairs)."[28]

Once politics is secular, the state's desire to restrict liberty falls away. And the British state must become more fully secular, for there are still many cases of religious intolerance. Mill carefully ignores the objection that a state needs some degree of common belief, that it is not just a collection of individuals. Similarly, he ignores the fact that England's progress to its relatively enlightened state was by means of a vision of positive liberty, of the nation united in a common story. In practice, liberty is defended by a liberal state, which must be understood in historical terms. Like Locke, Mill sees rational universalism as the only valid political discourse; but there are huge realities it misses. Mill was right to argue for a fuller separation of church and state, and to defend the secularization of politics and society as no necessary threat to religion.[29] Yet he was wrong to imply that negative

28. John Stuart Mill, *On Liberty* (London: Longmans, Green, 1922), pp. 10-15.

29. Defending secular education, he wittily put it this way: "To say that *secular* means irreligious . . . is very like saying that all professions except that of the law are illegal" (Mill, *Autobiography* [Harmondsworth, UK: Penguin, 1989], p. 210).

liberty — the individual right to be left alone — is the only real consideration. Liberty is also a narrative about the state. (Most recent thinkers criticize Mill in a different way, that is, for his assumption that one rational worldview will triumph over others.)[30]

Incidentally, Mill's view of Jesus as the greatest moral reformer in history is a good example of the Enlightenment approach: "The most valuable part of the effect on the character which Christianity has produced by holding up in a Divine Person a standard of excellence and a model for imitation, is available even to the absolute unbeliever and can never more be lost to humanity."[31] That last clause could almost be called the antithesis of authentic Christianity: it presents Jesus as a kind of scientific fact that it is more or less impossible to be ignorant of, if one belongs to Western civilization, rather than as someone known through faith. This brings us to a deeply contrasting spirit.

Kierkegaard

How extensive was the subordination of Protestantism to rationalism and Romantic humanism? On one level, it should not be overstated: pietism lived on in various forms, and high-church movements preserved some degree of skepticism toward rational theology. But in terms of intellectual discourse, the subordination was very extensive. Hegel's system was taken very seriously by Continental Protestant theologians. The fusion of Protestantism and Enlightenment was so strong that it was almost impossible to dissent and affirm the primacy of faith in revelation. Or rather, it was almost impossible to do this in an intellectually credible way. Such dissent looked like dissent from modernity — even from sanity.

---

30. Thus John Gray: [Mill] "relentlessly propagates a narrow, partisan ideal of rationalistic individualism and progressivism . . . the imposition of a plan of life in which the prejudices and anxieties of the late nineteenth-century intelligentsia are made mandatory for all" (Gray, *Post-Liberalism: Studies in Political Thought* [New York: Routledge, 1993], p. 260).

31. J. S. Mill, "Theism," in Mill, *Three Essays on Religion* (New York: Prometheus, 1998), p. 253.

Kierkegaard sidled his way into such a stance, by means of literature. As the son of a successful Danish businessman, he could afford
to work as a freelance writer and thus he assumed a wry, detached per-
sona. In addition to economic freedom, he inherited from his father a
religious melancholy, a sense of faith as suprarational obligation to
patriarchal authority. His early writing sketched contemporary aesthetic and moral psychology with the light touch of a flâneur. In the
pseudonymously written *Fear and Trembling* (1843), he experimented
with an intense, mesmeric voice, advocating faith's necessary defiance of reason: the believer must imitate Abraham, who rejects rational and moral norms in favor of trusting God, and who risks the most
extreme isolation for the sake of acquiring authentic faith. The story
explodes all of Enlightenment universalism, for it presents faith as
"the paradox that the single individual is higher than the universal."
The "knight of faith" who imitates Abraham is outwardly ordinary; his
world-defying faith is private, ahistorical.[32] All the theorizing of Kant
and Hegel about the relationship of faith to morality and history
evades and obscures the primacy of the individual's response to the
question of religious truth. And this response can only be hindered
rather than helped by such theorizing, for philosophy assumes that
the single individual only finds significance as part of a nation or historical movement. Modern theology follows suit; for example, the critical approach to the Bible is supposedly conducted "in order to understand God's Word properly — look more closely and you will see that
it is in order to defend oneself against God's Word." The Christian
must resist this slide to impersonal objectivity: "When you read God's
Word, in everything you read, continually say to yourself: It is I to
whom it is speaking, it is I about whom it is speaking."[33]

Kierkegaard also began publishing slightly gentler religious discourses in his own name. Thus did he gradually come out as an eccentric religious voice, intent on showing Christianity's basis in faith,

32. Kierkegaard, *Fear and Trembling,* ed. and trans. Howard V. Hong and Edna H.
Hong (Princeton, NJ: Princeton University Press, 1983), p. 55.

33. Kierkegaard, *For Self-Examination and Judge for Yourself,* ed. and trans.
Howard V. Hong and Edna H. Hong (Princeton, NJ: Princeton University Press, 1990),
pp. 34, 36.

meaning the individual's response to divine authority. This approach was rooted in his personal life. Shortly before publishing his first book, he broke off his engagement, apparently for fear of infecting his fiancée with his melancholy. His resulting singleness contributed to his sense of faith as defiant, tragic isolation.

His view of Denmark's established Lutheran church was incoherent. He generally implied that it was the proper arena for Christian communication — and he attended church. Yet he became increasingly critical of its worldliness, its admiration for modern enlightened thought, including critical theology. By making Christianity integral to culture, an established church falsified faith, obscuring its link to suffering, isolation, and martyrdom. But he seemed unsure what the practical alternative was. Like an English Tory, he was unsympathetic to the radical connotations of religious dissent. In the last few years of his life (he died in 1855), he became increasingly outspoken against the church: he was provoked by a fairly standard eulogy to the local bishop, in which he was praised as a "witness to the truth." Such praise should be saved for martyrs rather than wasted on comfortable bourgeois clerics, Kierkegaard said. (He resembles Newman in his willingness to import the shocking otherness of martyrdom into a civilized conversation about enlightened faith; unlike Newman, however, he sees no practical alternative to a culturally compromised Protestant church.)

He could not forgive the church for its marginalization of individual faith: it allowed people to think that they are good Christians, though "it has never dawned [on them] that they might have any obligation to God."[34] The pathos of divine authority and "majesty" had been undermined by modern thought, especially by Hegel's claim that God is known politically and culturally. The corresponding category of sin had also been effectively denied. "A person can relate to God in the truest way only as an individual, for one always best acquires the conception of one's own worthlessness alone."[35] His prioritization of the

34. Kierkegaard, *The Point of View for My Work as an Author: A Report to History and Related Writings*, trans. W. Lowrie (New York: Harper and Row, 1962), p. 22.

35. Kierkegaard, *A Selection from His Journals and Papers*, ed. Hannay (Harmondsworth, UK: Penguin, 1996), p. 336.

individual, or subjectivity, has nothing to do with secular "existential-ism"; it is rooted in a desire to assert the otherness of faith. Christian-ity is not an abstract idea; its vitality lies in the decision to affirm divine authority in defiance of normal rationality. He re-presents doubt not as sensible caution concerning truth claims, but as an expression of spiritual pride: "The misfortune of our age is disobedience. . . . And one deceives oneself and others by wishing to make us imagine that it is doubt. No, it is insubordination [rather than] doubt which is the fault in our misfortune and the cause of it."[36] The proper response to the detached modern attitude is not to argue on its secular terms but to display the particularity of faith-speech (meaning the dialogical drama of faith discussed in chapter 4). To have faith is to reperform the clash of divine authority with human doubt. Kierkegaard explicitly fol-lows Luther: "One must not offer reasons to doubt — not if one's inten-tion is to kill it — but one must do as Luther did, *order it to shut its mouth.*"[37] This Lutheran idiom repeatedly surfaces in the Journals, for example: "Off with all this world history and reasons and proofs for the truth of Christianity: there's just one proof — that of faith. . . . [T]here is nothing higher I can say than 'I believe.' . . . Reasons are reduced to the ranks and that, again, is the opposite of all modern objectivity."[38]

Kierkegaard's echoing of Luther's psychomachy highlights a cru-cial point about his idea of faith. Despite all the rhetoric of individual-ism, subjectivity, and inwardness, faith is determined by a tradition of speech that is somewhat external to individual experience. This tradi-tion must be individually appropriated, yet comes to the self from out-side. Faith is a ritual-based speech tradition. It derives from commu-nal cultic forms. So an intense assertion of the priority of faith always points beyond individualism, for faith is not a private language.

36. Kierkegaard, *On Authority and Revelation: The Book on Adler, or a Cycle of Ethico-Religious Essays,* trans. W. Lowrie (New York, Harper and Row, 1955), p. liv.

37. Kierkegaard, *For Self-Examination and Judge for Yourself,* p. 88.

38. Kierkegaard, *A Selection from His Journals and Papers,* pp. 388-89.

SEVEN

Beyond Progress

—❦—

Almost all Protestants — and all post-Protestant liberals — believed in "progress." Thanks to the spread of purified religion, enlightened politics, science, and economic growth, history was improving. During the mid-nineteenth century the concept of progress was complicated by the rise of socialism, which accused liberal progress of being detrimental to the lot of industrial workers, forcing them into a new form of servitude. Many liberals, such as J. S. Mill, were confident that this insight could be integrated into liberalism; he admitted that the greatest happiness of the greatest number entailed defending the rights of labor against greedy capital and establishing universal male suffrage. But most liberals were less sympathetic, and the integration of socialism into liberalism was not smooth. Socialism had its own logic and energy. Owing to its emergence in working-class communities, it had a communitarian, churchy feel. And these communities were largely suspicious of the main churches; only the Primitive Methodists had real success with British workers. From 1837, the Chartist movement demanded workers' representation, often framing the argument in terms of liberal religion. "Study the New Testament," urged a Chartist newspaper. "It contains the elements of Chartism."[1]

1. Michael Burleigh, *Earthly Powers: Religion and Politics in Europe from the French Revolution to the Great War* (London: HarperCollins, 2005), p. 242.

While sharing certain liberal assumptions, socialism also harked back to a medieval Catholic vision of social harmony, before the advent of capitalism. (This was particularly clear in France, where socialism was nurtured by sections of the Catholic Church.) It was also rooted in the biblical vision of the divine healing of history. Earlier I briefly noted Joachim of Fiore's interpretation of eschatology: in the final era, the era of the Holy Spirit, he said, history will gradually become worthy of hosting Christ's return. I have also noted the presence of such ideas in the Radical Reformers, as well as various radicals of the English civil war period. As we saw in chapter 4, the Enlightenment was influenced by a diluted version of this vision. Deism saw reason as a saving power, redeeming humanity from ancient error, which would enable a new era. (At the same time, American Calvinism was developing a progressive eschatological aspect, as I noted with respect to Edwards.) Rational liberalism secularized — and softened — Christian eschatology. Socialism inherited this postreligious belief in historical progress, but it reintroduced the drama of eschatology — the idea of a decisive transformation of history, ending injustice. This idea had surfaced during the French Revolution, but it was subsequently eclipsed by mainstream liberalism. It was also a feature of German Romanticism.[2] It was rekindled by radical followers of Hegel, who saw in his grand theory of history something more intense than normal liberal progress. Karl Marx proposed that history hinged on a dramatic process: the suppression of the proletariat would rebound on industrial capitalism. A total reversal was brewing, in which true justice would be established, and the wrongs of history would be righted. Marx insisted that socialism was not just the aspiration to human brotherhood; it was the science of this spring-like mechanism within history. Though he angrily rejected all religious and quasi-religious idealism, the science he spoke of naturally retained a deeply religious structure, which was indebted to Marx's Jewish roots and also to the Romantic human-

2. Thus Friedrich Schlegel: "The revolutionary desire to realize the kingdom of God on earth is the elastic point of progressive civilization and the beginning of modern history. Whatever has no relation to the kingdom of God is of strictly secondary importance" (Schlegel, *Athanaeum Fragments,* in Mark C. Taylor, *After God* [Chicago: University of Chicago Press, 2007], p. 85).

ism all around him. As we have seen, various thinkers were talking about a "religion of humanity," but such talk tended to fall into vagueness. By ostensibly rejecting religion and recasting politics as eschatological drama, Marx created a movement that really did have the energy of a new religion. (Marxism has a curious affinity to Calvinism in the idea that true rationality, or higher rationality, belongs to this particular, practical form of science.)

It is missing the point to declare that Marx secularized Judeo-Christian eschatology, as though it had been simply otherworldly and supernatural before he applied the mythical framework to human history. The more complicated reality is that the biblical vision itself mixes supernaturalism with historical realism. Isaiah and others in the biblical narrative seem to have hoped for a new era of historical harmony by means of divine intervention. The historical aims of peace and justice for the poor merge with a cosmic vision of creation perfected. The New Testament vision of the kingdom of God inherits this ambiguity, this mixture of historical realism and supernatural belief. In early Christian times the ambiguity was closed down; historical hope was eclipsed by otherworldly assumptions, and also by the assumption that the church was the expression of the kingdom of God. A crucial feature of modernity is the gradual (and tumultuous) rediscovery of the eschatological ambiguity of the Bible. As we have seen, various modern Christian movements hoped that God's kingdom was imminent, and mainstream post-Christian thought assumed a vaguely eschatological view of history. Marx's novelty was to intensify this post-Christian eschatology, to locate "salvation" in a final chapter of history. Of course, the majority of Christians were utterly opposed to this concept, insisting that salvation related to the afterlife of the individual rather than a transformation of history. But those Christians influenced by deism and humanism were more receptive; religious socialism began to seem both relevant to modernity and authentically biblical. Here was a way of combining the Enlightenment rejection of clericalism and superstition with the otherness of biblical faith.

It follows that religious socialism was, from the perspective of my thesis, a deeply ambiguous movement. It was, on one hand, the latest temptation of humanized theology, a new evasion of the otherness of faith; on the other hand, it was a genuine rediscovery of the eschatological ambiguity of the Bible, of the fact that material history is the arena of hope. Naturally it is intensely difficult to hold on to this ambiguity, to insist that the coming of the kingdom of God is both historical and more-than-historical — that it means the transformation of historical life but is not reducible to any account of progress. It is, in a sense, "utopian," for it envisions the perfection of history, yet it insists that only divine action can effect this. From the second half of the nineteenth century to the present day, this is a central difficulty of liberal theology: How can it affirm historical eschatology without lapsing into optimistic humanism? How can it affirm a utopian historical vision without dismissing ritual and faith as irrational relics of the otherworldly era?

At first, "Christian socialism" was essentially traditional. A group of Anglicans responded to Chartism by arguing that the church should accommodate the concerns of workers and style itself as the true site of human "brotherhood," to use F. D. Maurice's word. A high-church hatred of laissez-faire capitalism was the main motive. Newman's antagonist Charles Kingsley was a member of this group, which indicates its essential congruity with traditional liberal Anglicanism. Its main insight was that charity — and tentative legislative reform — was not a sufficient Christian response to poverty, that it left an aggressive capitalism untouched. The approach of the evangelicals was therefore criticized as too otherworldly, insufficiently humanistic. Charles Dickens was such a critic: his social vision was very close to that of the Christian socialists. And he exemplified the danger that passionate moral idealism would come to seem to be the essence of Christianity. His humanized theology is most clearly evident in the version of the Gospels that he wrote for children. "Remember! It is Christianity *to do Good* always. . . . If we do this, and remember the life and lessons of our Lord Jesus Christ . . . we may confidently hope that God will forgive us our sins and mistakes, and enable us to live and die in Peace."[3] His mes-

---

3. Charles Dickens, *The Life of Our Lord* (New York: Simon and Schuster, 1934), p. 34.

sage to adults was essentially the same. He implied that ritual tradition and supernatural faith were dubious accretions to the moral message of Jesus. Any character in any one his books who uses distinctively religious language is likely to be a Calvinist bigot. The "real" Christians are quiet Christ-imitators. One of his most developed characters, Arthur Clenham from *Little Dorrit,* rejects his native Calvinism in favor of real moral Christianity.

George Eliot went in the same direction, but she broke more explicitly with traditional Christianity. In her first book, *Scenes of Clerical Life* (1857), she depicts an evangelical parish, comparing narrow dogmatism with the "real" Christianity of moral action. She claims the ability to stand above religion and analyze whether or not it promotes the really meaningful thing, a deeper humanism. Dickens and Eliot suggest that one major function of the mid-Victorian novel was to celebrate the transformation of Christianity from a dogmatic system to a spur to humanist praxis. From midcentury, partly thanks to writers such as Dickens and Eliot, a sanitized Christian socialism became an increasingly central feature of liberal Protestantism in Britain. The same thing soon happened in Germany and, right at the end of the century, in America.

American Eschatology

Before the arrival of religious socialism, America had sharp experience of the eschatological side of religion — through its crisis over slavery. Thanks largely to the Quakers, there was an old link between abolitionism and eschatology (though Quaker eschatology is milder than most forms, close to that of rational humanism). In the 1730s, Benjamin Lay became a famously eccentric campaigner who revived the Quaker tradition of protest theater. In one famous stunt he stabbed a Bible that then "bled." In the next generation, Quakers like Anthony Benezet and John Woolman launched abolitionism as a cause that spoke in both Christian and general moral terms.

At the time of America's founding, abolitionism was eclipsed by the two powerful religious impulses of the day: deist-tinged liberal

Protestantism and evangelicalism. Both were optimistic, democratic, progressive, but both evaded the issue of slavery. As I previously noted, America was split between these two forces: the former gave rise to secular liberalism, the latter inherited Calvinist suspicion of it. Part of the pathos of the Civil War era is that abolitionism had the potential to unite these two forces, to unite America's soul around a powerfully effective liberal Protestantism that was rerooted in biblical faith. Of course, this possibility of ideological unity was confined to the North.

There could be no clearer evidence of the deficiency of the founders' deism than their toleration of slavery. Some deists were opposed to slavery, as Franklin became, but an attitude of pragmatism reigned. This unpleasant phenomenon, which the Constitution did not even deign to name directly, seemed necessary — for the time being. Only unrealistic extremists, such as Quakers, demanded its abrupt end; the enlightened citizens were more considered, more patient. Their view was that the gradual triumph of Reason should be trusted to resolve the issue in due time. Instead, slavery became more firmly rooted in the South. This fact effectively killed the founding ideology, exposed it as falsely optimistic and lacking appropriate moral energy. This energy came from a more authentic Christianity: it flowed from the Bible, not Lockean theories. According to one historian, "radical popular religion helped eradicate an evil with which socially liberal theological opinion had learned to coexist."[4] The Quakers and a few others had been saying it for a century: slavery was directly opposed to the gospel. A significant strain within the Second Great Awakening echoed this, and abolitionism gradually became a major form of Northern evangelicalism.

Abolitionism was a biblical cause; it was "liberation theology." The vision of liberation from slavery echoed ancient Israelite history and revived the idea that history was the arena of divine salvation. The slaves' own adaptation of Christianity, which foregrounded the hope for "a better day a-comin'," in the words of one famous spiritual, was

---

4. Henry Mayer, *All on Fire: William Lloyd Garrison and the Abolition of Slavery* (New York: Norton, 1998), p. xx. Subsequent page references to this book appear in parentheses in the text.

eschatological in a new sense. It announced the coming of a new historical era of justice. This reignited the chiliastic excitement that had surrounded the birth of the nation. Through abolition, the vision of a truly free nation could be made real; the rhetoric of the founders could become reality.

Abolitionist opinion was led by William Lloyd Garrison, who blended biblical and republican rhetoric in semisecular preaching, beginning in about 1830. The movement's basis was "Divine Revelation and the Declaration of our Independence," he announced (p. 176). The high idealism of American liberty must be rescued from hypocrisy — and be made real. He confronted the apathy of the churches and even implied that the movement was a sort of religious reformation, the emergence of a fuller Christianity. True Christians should dissent from both church and state, inasmuch as both urged conformity to a slave economy and a tainted constitution, a position that was dubbed "come-outerism in church and state" (p. 368). People were urged to come out into the prophetic wilderness of total reformism. Like European socialism, abolitionism saw the dominant liberalism as worse than inadequate. To abolitionists, it was collusion with evil to say that the slaveholders' constitutional rights must be respected and the Union protected from dissolution. Garrison insisted that reverence for the liberal state was misplaced: truth must be preferred to human law. He accused moderates of making a "golden calf" of the Constitution (p. 390). The only logical course for the North to take was to condemn a tainted Constitution and secede from the Union itself. Until it did so, it did not merit the individual's allegiance.

The freed slave Frederick Douglass offered very similar rhetoric: the American ideal of liberty for all must be rescued from falsity, and the Fourth of July must be made into a day worth celebrating. In his memoir (published in 1845) Douglass presented Southern Christianity as a kind of inversion of true faith: conversion had made his master crueler, for "he found religious sanction and support for his slaveholding cruelty." His pious readers would have been similarly horrified to hear that his attempt to start a Sunday school was violently suppressed. In his conclusion he rams the point home: "The man who wields the blood-clotted cowskin during the week fills the pulpit on

Sunday, and claims to be a minister of the meek and lowly Jesus. . . . He who sells my sister, for purposes of prostitution, stands forth as the pious advocate of purity." Douglass does not refer just to the South but to "this land." All of American Christianity is complicit in slavery, he insists. "'Shall I not visit for these things?' saith the Lord. 'Shall not my soul be avenged on a nation such as this?'"[5] As J. Kameron Carter says, Douglass "constantly sees his life against the grid of Scripture, countering the exegesis of white Christians who justified black enslavement through theories of the curse of Ham. . . . At the culmination of Douglass's story, we find an account of his struggle with the slave master refracted through the three holy days of Easter. Upon defeating the slave breaker, Edward Covey, he says, "I arose."[6]

Abraham Lincoln formed a coalition opposed to the spread of slavery, but he did not come out for abolition. What kept him on the fence was a deep uncertainty as to what should follow abolition, for he could not really imagine the harmonious integration of former slaves into postslavery white society. Like many of the nation's founders, he was interested in schemes to return blacks to Africa. Yet he increasingly echoed abolitionist rhetoric concerning slavery being at odds with America's liberal destiny and the sacredness of the principle of equality in the Declaration of Independence. In 1860, just before the war, he quoted Frederick Douglass: "It is written in the sky of America that the slaves shall someday be free."[7]

When the war began, the North was not fighting to end slavery but to preserve the Union, to put down a rebellion. In the face of mounting carnage, however, Yankee patriotism needed definition, and that was supplied by abolitionist evangelicalism, exemplified by the Brooklyn preacher Henry Ward Beecher. Such preachers were galvanized by the Southern claim that Northern liberalism was godless (the origin of the rhetoric of today's religious Right), and they sought

5. Frederick Douglass, *Narrative of the Life of Frederick Douglass, an American Slave* (Harmondsworth, UK: Penguin, 1982), pp. 97, 98, 154, 157.

6. J. Kameron Carter, in Rupert Shortt, ed., *God's Advocates: Christian Thinkers in Conversation* (Grand Rapids: Eerdmans, 2005), p. 240.

7. In James Oakes, *The Radical and the Republican: Frederick Douglass, Abraham Lincoln and the Triumph of Antislavery* (New York: Norton, 2007), p. 145.

to show the religious basis of their humanitarian idealism. Lincoln was reliant on this new civil religion (which effectively suspended the ideal of the separation of church and state); but he himself was hesitant in his rhetoric. No crusader for liberty has ever been so understated. He was a moderate who was shunted by history into launching radical reform. Even as Jeffersonian idealism was being revived all around him ("God is the great democrat of the universe," said Beecher), and even as the new black recruits to his army hailed him as the new Moses, Lincoln pondered the unknowability of God and implied that guilt for the war was universal.[8] His agnostic circumspection and his emphasis on divine judgment embracing all sides had the effect of deepening the national-eschatological narrative, importing Christic passion, the idea of sacramentally binding bloodshed.

On one level, the nation was reunited around the triumph of abolitionism and the eschatological Christianity that inspired it. This replaced the founders' deist belief in rational progress: America's vision of liberty was shown to be rooted in biblical absoluteness rather than in rational theorizing. But can such prophetic idealism really form the basis of national identity? In reality, most of the nation — even most of the North — was either skeptical about, or directly opposed to, a really new egalitarian society. Thus was the compromise of Reconstruction tolerated. In a sense, Lincoln was right to dampen claims about the renewal of America's divine purpose: it was too big and pure a vision to live up to.

So the Civil War showed that the founding ideology could only be rescued from hypocrisy by an eschatological form of liberal Christianity. The problem was that this form of Christianity proved to be relatively weak. As in Europe, liberalism became increasingly post-Christian. But what began to set America apart was the vigor of the religiosity of the defeated South, which was defined by the explicit rejection of liberal faith.

The Civil War did nothing to settle the ambiguity concerning the

<hr>

8. Henry Ward Beecher, quoted in George C. Rable, *God's Almost Chosen Peoples: A Religious History of the American Civil War* (Chapel Hill: University of North Carolina Press, 2010), p. 190.

separation of church and state. As we have seen, the Constitution allowed religious conservatives to retain huge power at the state level — power to exclude Catholics and atheists from office and to practice rigid moral censorship. On the one hand, the war revived the cause of Jeffersonian liberalism in the North; on the other hand, many felt that a newly united nation should make its religious allegiance clearer. Maybe it was time to rectify the omission of God from the Constitution. Others, including Lincoln, saw the possibility of fresh division in any such move. In addition, religious politics were soon strained by the arrival of huge numbers of Catholic and Jewish immigrants. Many Americans felt that Protestantism should be federally privileged, especially when Catholics were lobbying for state-funded faith schools. To some extent, the cause of religious liberty — and secular politics — became led by nonbelievers, such as the popular campaigner Robert Ingersoll. Soon secular Jews would also play an important role. But this should not be overstated; liberal Christians remained the main force behind the slowly emerging consensus: that the separation of church and state should be more boldly affirmed, and that only by highlighting this aspect of the Constitution could the nation find unity in its new radical pluralism.

Birth of a Nation

The unification of Germany brought a new association of liberal Protestantism and nationalism that was to have major repercussions. (In the next chapter I shall suggest that Karl Barth's excessive reaction against the liberal Protestant tradition, which has influenced contemporary postliberals, is largely rooted here.) Though dominated by Prussia, Germany remained disunited at midcentury; many of the old medieval principalities survived. Liberal political ideas spread throughout Germany, yet constitutional change was slow, especially in Prussia. Unlike in Britain, industrialization was not accompanied by the steady rise of the bourgeois principles of constitutionalism, civil rights, and a property-based franchise. Semifeudal militarism still held sway.

The gradual advent of liberal modernization was accompanied by a theological movement. Following Hegel and Schleiermacher, German theologians were drawn to a positive account of liberty as something more than the individual's freedom to worship as he pleases and get as rich as he can. True freedom includes social belonging, which must take the form of a homogeneous Protestant culture. Such thought, popularized by Richard Rothe and others, was boosted by the German Protestant Union of 1863, in which Luther's national-hero status rose to a new level. The central idea was that Protestantism was the key to Germany's cultural and political unity, and that the internationalism of Catholicism and the cosmopolitanism of Judaism were unhelpful presences.

This ideology, which Ernst Troeltsch soon named the "German Idea of Freedom," came to define German liberalism, eclipsing a more secular ("negative") view of liberalism. Bismarck's military victories over France and Austria in the 1860s led to the new German Empire, to which the huge majority of liberals gave their support. A strong consensus held that Germany should not simply imitate the modern politics of Britain or America, but should express its character, its soul. The influential writer Heinrich von Treitschke put it thus: "For us the state is not, as it is for the Americans, a power to be contained so that the will of the individual may remain uninhibited, but rather a cultural power from which we expect positive achievements in all areas of national life."[9] So the liberals swallowed their unease at rampant militarism and trusted that strength would lead to reform. Likewise, they got behind Bismarck's religious policy: the close control of all religion (sermons critical of the new constitution were made illegal in 1871), the privileging of patriotic Protestantism, and the curbing of Roman Catholicism, which was seen as a barrier to national unity. Bismarck's campaign to marginalize Catholics (and Jews who remained observant) was known as *Kulturkampf* — the struggle for cultural progress. Liberal Protestants judged that national unity was the means to a modern centralized state. Of course, some Protestants saw Bismarck's approach as heavy-handed, illiberal, counterproductive, and they warned

9. Quoted in Burleigh, *Earthly Powers*, p. 327.

of an "idolatry of the state." But Protestants in general — as well as agnostic liberals — went along with it, because the suppression of Catholicism's residual political power seemed necessary. The *Kulturkampf* was "a struggle for progress, to unlock the potential for social development and free German society's dynamism from the dead hand of superstition and archaic institutions. The resources and apparatus of the Catholic Church were thought to be obstructing this potential, so that any reordering of social priorities of the kind liberals desired necessarily entailed an attack on the church's traditional practices and privileges."[10] Bismarck's achievement was to unite Protestants and liberals in national feeling, and to agree that the state should be strong before it became liberal. Prussia "was a state whose ideology was simply its own power."[11]

In Germany, then, liberalism was a particularly fraught ideology. It denoted progress toward freedom and equality, as it did elsewhere, yet it also denoted a kind of Faustian pact with aggressive nationalism. It meant agreeing that the imposition of national unity was an excusable means to the end of progress. This pact should not be too hastily condemned. The fact is that states do need a certain degree of ideological unity, and that a mainly Protestant nation is bound to find a strong Catholic minority difficult to tolerate, just as today's liberal states find Muslim minorities (though far smaller) difficult to tolerate. It is facile to pretend that respecting minority rights is a straightforward matter, when the principal minority opposes the state's ideological direction.

This period of German history has strong echoes of the creation of Protestant hegemony in England under the Tudors. Then, too, politically strong Catholicism was felt to be intolerably backward, and an ideology of national liberty justified a new state aggression. The problem with modern German history is that too much happened too quickly, producing a dangerous caricature of the dynamic we have traced: the evolution of the Protestant-based liberal state.

10. Geoff Eley, "Bismarckian Germany," in Gordon Martel, ed., *Modern Germany Reconsidered, 1870-1945* (London: Routledge, 1992), p. 21.
11. Norman Stone, *Europe Transformed, 1878-1919* (London: Fontana, 1983), p. 174.

Tolstoy

A brief Russian excursion offers an interesting perspective on the fusion of liberal Christianity with eschatological radicalism. Leo Tolstoy, the great aristocratic novelist, had always wondered whether he should really be a great religious reformer. It occurred to him at the age of twenty-seven that he should seek to found "a new religion corresponding to the development of mankind: the religion of Christ, but purged of all dogma and mystery, a practical religion, not promising future bliss but realizing bliss on earth."[12] He repressed the impulse until he was in his fifties, when he remade himself as a radical sage. As the youthful diary entry suggests, his vision combined the rationalism of deism with an eschatological intensity. He was essentially a liberal Protestant who was surrounded by the almost medieval culture of Russian Orthodoxy. He was close to deism in his moral rationalism and hostility to clericalism and superstition; but he rejected the calm pragmatism of deism in favor of a sort of chiliasm. He agreed with revolutionary socialism that liberal progress was fraudulent, that it was happy to postpone justice for the poor. He was also influenced by American abolitionism, particularly by the anarchist and pacifist rhetoric of William Lloyd Garrison. It was necessary to dissent from the violence of the state, even if it claimed to be liberal.

In *The Kingdom of God Is Within You* (1893), Tolstoy identifies the teaching of Jesus with rational morality: it "did not need to be proved by miracles and needed no exercise of faith, because this [teaching] is in itself convincing and in harmony with man's mind and nature; but the proposition that Christ was God had to be proved by miracles completely beyond our comprehension" (p. 48). But this is not quite the moral rationality of deism or Kant: that is, following Jesus' teaching is a disruptive moral perfectionism entailing anarchism and pacifism. Such a political vision can spread through humanity and can create the kingdom of God on earth. There is a Manichean intensity:

12. Leo Tolstoy, *Journals,* in Introduction to Tolstoy, *The Kingdom of God Is Within You,* trans. Constance Garnett (New York: Dover, 2006), p. vii. Hereafter, page references to this work appear in parentheses in the text.

traditional religion is totally corrupt, but a totally pure alternative version is possible. Tolstoy's view of traditional religion falls right into the Protestant trap of associating sacramentalism with the institutional imposition of superstition. The Orthodox "worship of relics and icons" is a tool of power-hungry priests: "They teach it to the people in theory and in practice, using every resource of authority, solemnity, pomp, and violence to impress them" (p. 66). They manipulate believers "with their special lighting, gold, splendor, candles, choirs, organ, bells, vestments, intoning, etc." (p. 73). All this pomp is needed to prop up an otherworldly version of Christianity that is, seen in the cold light of day, impossible to believe. "For such sentences as that God lives in heaven, that the heavens opened and a voice from somewhere said something, that Christ rose again, and ascended somewhere in heaven, and again will come from somewhere on the clouds, and so on, have no meaning for us" (p. 71). Figurative interpretation is a muddled evasion of the issue, and it evades the fact that the vast majority will cling to literal supernaturalism.

Tolstoy needs clarity; every aspect of the old supernaturalism must go. Christianity is simply moral perfectionism, the means to the kingdom of God on earth. Other interpretations are evasions of this: "The man who believes in salvation through faith in the redemption or the sacraments, cannot devote all his powers to realizing Christ's moral teaching in his life" (p. 67). He somewhat departs from liberal Protestantism in his emphasis on Christ's law as more than an impossible aspiration. "The Sermon on the Mount," he says, "lays down the simplest, easiest, most understandable laws for the expression of love towards God, towards one's neighbour, and towards life itself; without acknowledging and fulfilling these laws one cannot even speak of Christianity."[13]

Of course, such simplicity is an illusion: to speak of the kingdom of God, and to insist on the uniqueness of Jesus (and to call him Christ), is to go far beyond a strictly rational approach. Sometimes in his journals Tolstoy wrestles with this: Does it make sense to pray to

13. Tolstoy, *Journals,* in A. N. Wilson, ed., *The Lion and the Honeycomb: The Religious Writings of Tolstoy* (San Francisco: Harper and Row, 1987), p. 141.

God? Was religious language the relic of superstition, or essential to the true universal moral vision? This is the ultimate stumbling block of liberal (humanist) theology: its use of religious language is muddled. It implies that religious language is a means to a moral end, but it cannot explain why such a means is necessary.

Jesus of Progress?

Late nineteenth-century German theology was dominated by followers of Albrecht Ritschl, himself a follower of Schleiermacher. The emphasis was on the ethical movement that Jesus launched, the kingdom of God, unfolding in history. It was held that historical research could substantiate the ideological uniqueness of this movement. All the complex problems of theology were sidelined by confidence in Christianity as a grand historical movement. This view was popularized by Adolf von Harnack, who, in his *History of Dogma* (1886-89), renewed Kant's idea that supernatural doctrine was the necessary packaging of the spiritual and moral "kernel" of Christianity. Some theologians, such as Herrmann, argued that this approach was too reliant on claims about history, and that theology should prioritize the Christ known to faith — a position that was closer to Schleiermacher. But a basic Kantianism was generally accepted: theology belonged in the realm of moral values.

Then an awkward new discovery disturbed the consensus, though at first no serious disturbance was admitted. Historical criticism led to a new understanding of the New Testament idea of the kingdom of God. In 1892, Johannes Weiss argued that the kingdom was not the stable progressive vision that Ritschl assumed; Jesus and Paul had expected an imminent eschatological event, a sudden miraculous transformation. The same point had been made not long before — but not widely communicated — by Franz Overbeck, an eccentric Swiss scholar and friend of Friedrich Nietzsche. Authentic Christianity was incompatible with modern thought, he argued, for it was utterly reliant on this eschatological vision. The only honest response was atheism. Weiss, by contrast, drew no strong conclusion from his insight. A few theologians began to admit that the issue was a serious threat to liberal orthodoxy. Albert Schweitzer, later famous as an aid worker in Africa, decided that the real, fiercely irrational historical Jesus made nonsense of the rational reformism of liberal theology, and he drifted away from academic theology.

For Adolf von Harnack, the new insight was no threat at all. It only proved that Christianity was originally swathed in mythical packaging that modern theology had to unpack. In *What is Christianity?* (1900) he explained that "primitive Christianity" was a necessary stage through which the gospel had to pass. The idea of an imminent apocalypse bringing God's rule was "an idea which Jesus simply shared with his contemporaries."[14] The more important point is that he gave this idea a new dimension, by locating the kingdom of God in the individual soul. "The kingdom of God comes by coming to the individual, by entering into his soul and laying hold of it" (p. 56). We can confidently reject that part of Jesus' teaching that is incompatible with modern ideas. In so doing, he claims, we are not watering down the gospel but *purifying* it. For its pure essence is contained in the ethic of love, and in "the sense of the eternal," and not in the particular, outward, doubtful forms it was first adorned with. "[T]he fact that the whole of Jesus' message may be reduced to these two heads — God as the Father, and the human soul so ennobled that it can and does unite with him — shows us that the Gospel is in nowise a positive religion like the rest; that it contains no statutory or particularistic elements; *that it is, therefore, religion itself"* (p. 63).

In effect, this is the same old deism that we encountered a few chapters ago, but Harnack subtly adds a Lutheran pathos: outward religion is a form of legalism; a truly spiritual faith does not cling to dogmas and rituals. Of course, this is far from faithful to Luther himself, who was firmly attached to certain dogmas and rituals. But Harnack presents it as true to his *spirit.* He presents Luther (very like Jesus) as a man of his time, full of irrational medieval assumptions, but never-

---

14. Adolf von Harnack, *What Is Christianity?* trans. Thomas Bailey Saunders (Philadephia: Fortress, 1986), p. 54. Hereafter, page references to this work appear in parentheses in the text.

theless able to point to the essence of the gospel ("he had enough superstition left in him to allow him to advance some very shocking contentions" [p. 279]). Luther sought to move public worship away from all dogmatic and ritual particularity, Harnack claims — tendentiously (p. 272). A good example of his approach is his treatment of the resurrection. The New Testament reflects various beliefs — in the empty tomb and in Jesus' appearances to his disciples. But what really matters, for Paul and others, is "Easter faith," which is wider than belief in any particular miracle. "Either we must decide to rest our belief on a foundation unstable and always exposed to fresh doubts, or else we must abandon this foundation altogether, and with it the miraculous appeal to our senses" (p. 162). Of course, "Easter faith" is rather vague: it is a belief in the "infinite value of the soul," the vanquishing of the power of death by "eternal life," and so on. Harnack makes a Protestant virtue of this vagueness: rejecting a dogmatic belief in particular miracles is the means to a *purer* faith. Such faith is associated with the "freedom" trumpeted by Paul and Luther: "Belief in the living Lord and in a life eternal is the *act* of the freedom which is born of God" (p. 163).

Harnack claims that the spiritual freedom announced by Luther is the crucial ingredient of modernity: "What do all our discoveries and inventions and our advances in outward civilization signify in comparison with the fact that today there are thirty millions of Germans, and many more millions of Christians outside Germany, who possess a religion without priests, without sacrifices, without 'fragments' of grace, without ceremonies — a spiritual religion!" (p. 268) The implication is that such religion is the basis of authentic liberty, that German liberalism is not secular but Luther-based. German liberalism is stamped with Luther's character: "Luther's warmth and heartiness in preaching, and his frankness in polemical utterance, were felt by the German nation to be an opening out of its own soul" (p. 283). It seems that, while more mundane nations have liberal ideologies, Germany has Luther, a liberal personality. The problem is that this makes a rigorous account of political liberalism unnecessary, indeed un-German. The implication is strengthened by Harnack's comments on church-state relations.

Following Hegel, he insists that the free Protestant churches are the vehicles of liberty (p. 286).

Another great popularizer of liberal theology was Ernst Troeltsch. He offers a slightly more nuanced account than does Harnack of the relationship between Protestantism and liberalism. He draws a distinction between "early" and "modern" Protestantism. The former echoed the medieval worldview of the marriage of church and state — and doctrinal rigidity. It thus warned against toleration and intellectual freedom. Then Protestantism underwent a major transformation, beginning in the seventeenth century. The rise of sectarianism and toleration in the English civil war period caused the first clear break with medieval assumptions; this was "the departure point for the modern world."[15] This is close to what I have argued in the first chapters of this book, but Troeltsch implies that the breakdown of the medieval order was somewhat accidental, a side effect of sectarianism. He neglects the radical liberal tradition that consciously sought a new sort of state — on religious grounds. For Troeltsch, this modern revolution only finds clarity with the Enlightenment, which he idealizes as a tacitly religious movement of intellectual and political liberation. Individual autonomy is the central category of this revolution, and it makes any return to traditional religious authority impossible. He thus presents modernity as an essentially unified revolution that is based in radical Protestantism but only finds full expression in the form of Enlightenment typified by Kant that emphasizes the free choosing of the individual, including in the religious sphere.

As Troeltsch puts it in *Protestantism and Progress* (1906), "It was not until modern Protestantism had lost sight of the idea of a universal Church-civilisation that it could characterize as genuinely Protestant principles, the duty of historico-philological criticism, the organization of Churches formed by voluntary association, independent of the State, and the doctrine of revelation by inner personal conviction and illumination." The rise of political liberalism is thus completed by the rise of religious subjectivism. The point is soon re-

---

15. In Mark Chapman, *Ernst Troeltsch and Liberal Theology: Religion and Cultural Synthesis in Wilhelmine Germany* (Oxford: Oxford University Press, 2001), p. 150.

inforced: the Enlightenment deprived Protestants of the naïve realism of Luther and Calvin. "Thus Protestantism became the religion of the search for God in one's own feeling, experience, thought, and will, . . . while trustfully leaving open all the further obscure problems about which the Dogmatics of the earlier Protestantism had so much to say. . . . In this modern view . . . the idea of faith has triumphed over the content of faith, and only escapes weakness and sentimentality because, when all is said and done, the iron of the Protestant conception of faith rings through."[16] This suggests a fetishizing of "faith": it necessarily becomes the dominant category of modern Christianity, and it necessarily becomes semidetached from the traditional dogmatic framework.

Troeltsch was aware that this triumph of autonomy was problematic, for humanity desires a social ideal beyond mere individualism, and modern Protestant ecclesiology can hardly play this role. But he was adamant that theology's first task is to be honest about the nature of modernity; it must respond to the new reality of humanity that has reached its "maturity," in Kant's phrase. This insistence was to influence two of the figures we have yet to consider, Bonhoeffer and Tillich.

Both Harnack and Troeltsch were moderately in favor of liberal reform, but neither challenged the subordination of liberalism to nationalism that we considered earlier. In prewar Prussia, Lutheranism remained dominated by a conservatism that saw "the existence of a parliament, democratic forces, socialist movements and a strong criticism of the Emperor and the Army . . . as revolutionary, which meant criminal."[17]

The Social Gospel

Religious socialism gradually became a central feature of liberal theology in Britain and Germany. Soon the same thing happened in

16. Ernst Troeltsch, *Protestantism and Progress: The Significance of Protestantism for the Rise of the Modern World* (Philadelphia: Fortress, 1986), pp. 37, 98.

17. Paul Tillich, *My Search for Absolutes* (New York: Simon and Schuster, 1967), p. 31.

America, but with greater completeness, leading to the splitting of American Protestantism.

American industrialists were careful to nurture a strong alliance with the nation's unofficial Protestant establishment. Preachers could be relied on to defend private property and condemn labor unions. Many unions had strong Catholic and Jewish elements, so their suppression was part of the preservation of Protestant hegemony. The increasing regularity of violent strikebreaking, plus the rising economic inequality, led some Protestants to break ranks and imitate European religious socialism. In the 1880s the liberal Congregationalist Washington Gladden called for a more Christian social order, and he also took up the cause of Southern blacks. He was little heeded until the first decade of the new century, when liberal Christianity sprung into life. The key figure was Walter Rauschenbusch, a Baptist who ministered to New York's poor. He echoed the assumptions of the dominant liberal Protestantism, but added a new prophetic tone. He was deeply averse to the "priestly religion" of Catholicism, and when he visited England he was baffled by ritualist religious socialists. He presents Jesus as a straight-talking activist who was horrified by ecclesiastical pomp and fully focused on making the kingdom of God into historical reality. In *Christianity and the Social Crisis* (1907) he popularizes a spirit of this-worldly hope and predicts a new religious era: "For the first time in religious history we have the possibility of so directing religious energy by scientific knowledge that a comprehensive and continuous reconstruction of social life in the name of God is within the bounds of human possibility."[18]

As the foregoing suggests, Rauschenbusch's emphasis was on human capability rather than reliance on divine action. Like Harnack, he argues that Jesus wanted to move away from supernatural apocalypticism, but was somewhat thwarted by his followers. It seems that "the Church spilled a little of the lurid colors of its own apocalypticism over the loftier conceptions of its Master." Very like Tolstoy, he wanted eschatology without supernaturalism. Conventional liberal

18. Walter Rauschenbusch, *Christianity and the Social Crisis* (Louisville: Westminster John Knox, 1992), p. 209.

Protestantism was guilty of evading eschatology, though conservative evangelicals did at least have a form of eschatology — an overly literalistic obsession with the Second Coming. "They have [eschatology] in bizarre form, but they have it," he says. The question is, did Rauschenbusch have it? Does a new focus on the kingdom of God, as a possible human goal, constitute authentically biblical eschatology? No, because to soften the scandal of our reliance upon divine miracle is to perpetuate deism, despite a rhetoric of prophetic intensity. Such a theology implicitly denies the need for the otherness of ritual practice and faith. "Ethical conduct is the supreme and sufficient religious act" is how Rauschenbusch expresses it.[19] Like all the deists we have considered, he collapses Christianity into humanism. Religious socialism may be seen as a particularly dangerous form of deism, for in its utopianism it half-grasps the otherness of the gospel and thus stubbornly fails to see its essential humanism.

The Social Gospel movement became incorporated into theological liberalism. Rauschenbusch's radicalism was diluted in the promise of a vaguer transformation of society, through a new spirit of benevolence. Its rising star was Harry Emerson Fosdick, a liberal Baptist. He increasingly avoided contentious economic issues and depicted religion as the art of nurturing "the infinite worth of human personality."[20] Another liberal Baptist, Shailer Mathews, wrote popular explanations of the compatibility of Christianity and rational progress. Both strongly warned against the rising conservative movement, which had been galvanized by *The Fundamentals: A Testimony to the Truth,* a series of pamphlets published between 1910 and 1915. Eschatology was a crucial battleground; premillennial dispensationalism, the pseudoscience of interpreting signs of the Second Coming, was a major feature of fundamentalism. Liberals became more insistent that supernatural interpretation was dangerous error. According to the historian Martin Marty, "the tearing apart of Protestantism in

19. Rauschenbusch, *Christianity and the Social Crisis,* quoted in Gary Dorrien, *The Making of American Liberal Theology,* vol. 2 (Louisville: Westminster John Knox, 2001), pp. 100, 93, 99.

20. Fosdick, quoted in Dorrien, *Soul in Society: The Making and Renewal of Social Christianity* (Minneapolis: Fortress, 1995), p. 67.

the twenties . . . is one of the major incidents of American religious history. Its full consequences for culture and society keep revealing themselves differently with each passing decade."[21] In the short term, the liberals won the struggle: they achieved huge influence over an increasingly strong central state. A new era of the dominance of liberal Christianity began, which enabled Roosevelt's expansion of social democracy and decades of socially liberal legislation. As we shall see in chapter 9, such dominance was theologically frail, leading to its swift collapse.

---

21. Martin Marty, quoted in Mark A. Noll, *America's God: From Jonathan Edwards to Abraham Lincoln* (Oxford: Oxford University Press, 2002), p. 430.

EIGHT

The Reaction

———✥———

The reaction against liberal Protestantism was the one of the most important intellectual events of the twentieth century. This tradition had been a central component of the strongest powers of the West — Britain, America, Germany — and its demise had consequences.

It happened in two stages. In the first, modern theology was challenged by an updated Calvinism. Yet, despite its critical force, it lacked wide appeal as a positive alternative vision for theology. In the second stage, the weakness of liberal Protestantism was confirmed from various new angles, including Catholic-influenced philosophy. This second wave of attack decisively transformed the theological landscape. Much was gained, but much was also obscured and evaded.

The first stage has a clear hero figure, Karl Barth. What a strange figure he increasingly seems, with his prophetic impersonation, his old-fashioned aversion to ritual (rooted in a masculine disdain for that whole side of religion, as well as in Reformed theology), his eloquent obsession with authoritative speech, his shelf-long book, and his beautiful young assistant. Perhaps his life is best summed up in the title of the journal he started, *Between the Times (Zwischen den Zeiten)*. He announced the death of the old theological era, and it began to occur; but it was unclear whether his positive vision could provide for the future.

Barth was born, in 1886, into a fairly conservative Swiss Calvinist family. His pastor father reluctantly allowed him to study theology at the liberal University of Marburg, in Germany, where the dominant theology viewed Christianity as a historical movement, gradually bringing the kingdom of God, and prized historical criticism as the key means to understanding this movement. Barth's main teacher, Wilhelm Herrmann, was semidetached from this; he sought to stick closer to Schleiermacher, emphasizing the suprahistorical immediacy of faith, mediated by the community, and argued for theology's autonomy from other disciplines, including philosophy. He taught Barth to be wary of apologetics, the attempt to express faith in external terms. His approach was widely dismissed as dated, pietistic, and quaint alongside the more scientific-seeming liberalism, whose leading figure was Ernst Troeltsch.

In 1909, Barth began to serve as a pastor in the Reformed Church, first in Geneva, then in a rural working-class Swiss parish. In both places he was dismayed by the church's unpopularity, and he struggled to translate his liberal theology into sermons. He became drawn to religious socialism, partly by the rhetorical force of the movement's leading figure in Switzerland, Hermann Kutter. His theology teachers were broadly sympathetic to religious socialism, but they dismissed its strident expression as prophetic posturing. Barth dissented on this very point: theology needed a new injection of prophetic intensity, he believed, not more anemic academic discourse. He began to find his voice by echoing Kutter's, insisting that socialism was the true expression of Christianity — just as Rauschenbusch was saying in America at that time. Then came World War I. Germany's leading theologians not only failed to criticize the war; they actively signed up to it. Liberalism's captivity to nationalism was confirmed. And the German Social Democrats also fell into line. Both parts of "religious socialism" seemed flimsy. Was there any firm core to it? Barth edged away from the practical-political side of religious socialism, as he was increasingly drawn to its bold, colorful, prophetic fringe, which was embodied by the Lutheran preacher Christoph Blumhardt, the son of an even more colorful figure, who was defiant of modern thought and trusted in God's imminent eschatological action.

Barth's crucial insight in these years was that God must be spoken of with a kind of primal force. Authentic Christian discourse is *other* than normal discourse. To speak of the coming of the kingdom of God is not a normal bit of speech; it is to speak of a cosmic miracle, and to participate in that very miracle. The elder Blumhardt's (very Lutheran) mantra, "Jesus is Victor," was for Barth a kind of icon of theological authenticity. (He was fascinated by the story of Blumhardt's performing an exorcism, in which the expelled spirit had uttered that phrase.) So Barth acquired a new dramatic concept of Christianity: the point was not to explain a worldview to skeptical outsiders but to perform this cultic rhetoric. The priority of preaching to theology was absolute.

Only thus could eschatology be taken seriously, Barth believed. He was the first theologian to make real use of the insight of Overbeck, Weiss, and Schweitzer, that the original vision of the kingdom of God is at odds with rational humanist hopes, at odds with the ideology of progress — whether gradualist or revolutionary socialist. He did so by means of Kierkegaardian counterrationalism: our hope for the transformation of history is in human terms absurd, beyond comprehension, and Christianity is not a sensible modern viewpoint. When we speak Christianly, we are speaking in a strange, primal way. We are essentially in the same position as an Old Testament prophet, taken over by the Word.

Barth dared to reinvent himself, in his early thirties, as a performer of this prophetic eschatological rhetoric, a rhetoric whose template was the Bible. He braved the scorn of those academics who mainly saw his approach as a kind of exotic posturing. But a significant minority, particularly in Germany, saw his iconoclastic intensity as a valid response to the cultural crisis that had accompanied the war. One address that he gave, at a religious socialist conference in Germany in 1919, made his name. The core theme of that address was the need to avoid secularizing Christ by aligning him with this or that cause. In 1921 he revised a book that he had written two years earlier, a commentary on Paul's letter to the Romans. It was an impressive, hyperactive performance, an attempt to show that Paul's letter only makes sense insofar as we acknowledge the Word of God's agency as it speaks through Paul and through us. The Romans commentary was a manifesto: theology must reject its subordination to neutral critical methods and become a handmaid to Christian performance — preaching, proclamation. Barth did not reject the liberal approach to Scripture in the manner of fundamentalism; but he announced that it could be utterly sidelined (this had also been Kierkegaard's approach).

Part of Barth's abiding appeal is that his break with liberalism is expressed in a discourse that is both intellectually and poetically compelling. In order to argue for — and perform — the Word's agency, he analyzes religion and culture with a frank, critical, passionate voice that echoes (and quotes) Nietzsche, Marx, and Dostoyevsky, as well as his most obvious theological influence, Kierkegaard. He is bitterly critical of the self-righteousness, sentimentality, and political evasions of religion. He thus distinguishes the Word from all human ideas and endeavors, and he emphasizes the universality of sin. The Romans commentary is a surprising fusion of a reactionary theological voice that castigates modern forgetfulness of the basic Protestant categories of sin, grace, and miracle, and of a modern critical intelligence that is sharply suspicious of ideological evasion. It shows that, as I noted with regard to Luther, faith entails a searching skepticism: human capacities must be deconstructed to convey reliance on the Word. Barth's literary style is also strikingly modern, echoing as it does the "expressionist" urge to attack surface impressions in order to gesture toward a deeper reality (an urge with dubious political associations).[1]

So Barth's presentation of faith is directly in the "dialogical" tradition of Luther and Kierkegaard. He repeatedly stages an argument between skepticism and defiant submission to the Word. In faith we assert what is humanly impossible to believe. The themes of presumption, daring, and imposture are often present. For example, God calls us his children, as Paul writes. Barth comments:

1. "The various strains of German expressionism were united by a disdain for the materialist trappings of bourgeois life and an apocalyptic longing for a spiritual breakthrough to what its partisans called the 'new man'" (Larry Eugene Jones, "Culture and Politics in the Weimar Republic," in Gordon Martel, ed., *Modern Germany Reconsidered, 1870-1945* [New York: Routledge, 1992], p. 78).

We — God's children! Remember that, in daring this predication, we are taking the miraculous, primal, creative step which Abraham took; we are taking the step of faith, the step over the abyss from the old to the new creation, which God alone can take. . . . There is — not, of course, as an experience — a seeing and hearing which puts all our questioning to silence, and which remembers only the decision which has been pronounced.[2]

This is how faith works, Barth insists: we admit our inability to believe what we nevertheless confess. "We speak 'as though' there had come into our heart what no human heart has contained."[3] This sense of inauthenticity points to the agency of the Spirit. This approach to faith was central to Barth's public clash with Adolf von Harnack in 1923. Barth made Christianity seem alien, irrational, impossible to believe in, the older man complained. Barth replied in a very Kierkegaardian vein: "But is it not included . . . in the *concept* of revelation (and really not only in *my* concept!) that it is not possible to 'believe' in it?" The claims of Scripture are "unheard-of, unbelievable, and of course offensive. . . . The acceptance of these incredible testimonies I call faith. . . . Let no one deceive himself here concerning the fact that this is an unheard-of occurrence, that the Holy Spirit must now be spoken of."[4] Harnack's reason-friendly "simple Gospel" was worse than atheism, he said, with refreshing rudeness.

The theme of the radical difference between God and humanity in Barth's *Romans* led to the labels "crisis theology" and "dialectical theology." The latter term principally referred to the idea of a clash between the human and divine viewpoints — that it is in the negation of all human meaning that God is knowable. The term "paradox" was also often used. Such phrases are rather unhelpful, and Barth himself soon repudiated them. His aim was to change the rhet-

2. Karl Barth, *The Epistle to the Romans,* trans. E. C. Hoskyns (from the 6th German ed.) (Oxford: Oxford University Press, 1968), p. 299.

3. Barth, *Romans,* pp. 238, 304.

4. Barth, "An Answer to Professor von Harnack's Open Letter," in J. Robinson, ed., *The Beginnings of Dialectical Theology,* vol. 1, trans. K. R. Krim and L. de Grazia (Richmond, VA: John Knox, 1968), pp. 178-79.

oric of theology so as to give huge new prominence to the primary cultic speech form of proclamation. Theology should serve Christian speech, reflecting on the fact that Christianity is rooted in this utterly distinctive linguistic practice: proclaiming the Word of God, which cannot be domesticated but must be accepted (or rejected) in all its "otherness." And yet the terms "crisis" and "dialectic" are important, for they express the nature of contemporary interest in Barth. He quickly found allies who focused on the "existentialist" theme of external illusions being stripped away in the decision of faith. It seemed to Friedrich Gogarten and Rudolf Bultmann that Barth had restated the Protestant (especially Lutheran) idea of faith in contemporary terms — as a decision in favor of authentic existence. All religious and philosophical systems must dramatically collapse in this moment of heroic freedom. Bultmann was influenced in this direction by his colleague Martin Heidegger. This philosophy, Bultmann felt, could renew Luther's master-concept, justification by faith, for modern understanding.

Barth was wary of the Lutheran focus on faith, which had dubious Germanic as well as liberal echoes (as we have seen with regard to Harnack).[5] Yet he was glad about the aura of a movement; he allowed such ideas to grow up around him. But his own agenda was different. He was now a professor of Reformed theology (he accepted a job at Göttingen in 1921). From then on he was concerned to reframe and defend his breakthrough in systematic terms. Seemingly wary of his own rhetorical creativity, he was determined to put substance before style. The discipline of dogmatics had to be revived; it had to be restructured around the priority and agency of the Word. He quickly gravitated toward Calvin's pararational, scientific concept of theology. The Word, he explained, is threefold: it is revelation, it is Scripture, and it is preaching. But in practice the last of these has primacy, for it must animate the other two. "Preaching" extends to all Christian witness, including "whatever we 'preach' to ourselves in the quiet

5. In 1922 he was glad to get a friendly review of *Romans* from Bultmann, yet "'faith' and 'faith' again was at the center of his interest in my book and his approval of it" (Eberhard Busch, *Karl Barth: His Life from Letters and Autobiographical Texts*, trans. John Bowden [Philadelphia: Fortress, 1976], p. 136).

of our own rooms."[6] But, of course, its essential form is the preaching of the church. "The phenomenon of Christian *speaking* . . . is as it were the *raw stuff* of dogma and dogmatics."[7] This sums up Barth's entire theology: Only by starting from the phenomenon of *Christian speech* can theology be a really rigorous system of knowledge, and only thus can it move away from all the humanist vagueness of the liberal era.

Along with launching his dogmatic project, Barth continued to explain the need for it — to insist that the spirit of liberal theology had corrupted everything. As in a police corruption movie, he found rot right at the top: the archvillain was Schleiermacher himself, whom Barth had revered as a student. Authentic theology, he felt, had to fully reject the former's compromise with humanism. This is well expressed in a lecture Barth gave in 1926. He identifies "an ancestral line which runs back through *Kierkegaard* to *Luther* and *Calvin*, and so to *Paul* and *Jeremiah*," but does not include Schleiermacher. These names "are all characteristic of a certain way of speaking of *God* which Schleiermacher never arrived at."[8]

By the late 1920s, Barth had done something remarkable: he had followed his bold rhetoric of the Word's priority, and of the failure of liberal theology, with a robust alternative vision for theology, as ambitious as Calvin's (and very close to it). It was to focus on the special linguistic practice of Christian communication, and it was to do so in the form of dogmatics. It should utterly resist the temptation to explain itself in external terms — that is, to find common ground with some form of philosophy. Authentic theology serves the proclamation of the Word. Its job is not to persuade outsiders that this discourse is meaningful or true; it is to make sure that it is done properly. This approach seeks to defend the honor of primary Christian speech. It must be protected from normal discourse, which casts doubt on it,

---

6. Barth, *The Göttingen Dogmatics*, quoted in Gary Dorrien, *The Barthian Revolt in Modern Theology* (Louisville: Westminster John Knox, 2000), p. 78.

7. Barth, *Göttingen Dogmatics: Instruction in the Christian Religion*, vol. 1, ed. H. Reifen, trans. G. W. Bromiley (Grand Rapids: Eerdmans, 1991), pp. 23-24.

8. Barth, "The Word of God and the Task of Ministry," in Barth, *The Word of God and the Word of Man*, trans. D. Horton (London: Hodder and Stoughton, 1928), p. 197 (italics in original).

demands that it explain itself, and offers to lend it more respectable clothes.

This project alienated most of those who had cheered Barth's early work. Though he had become the new big name in theology, he found himself with very few real allies. His approach seemed otherworldly, abstract, Scholastic. To the dismay of many, he now wanted to debate obscure doctrinal points with Roman Catholics, who, he said, had a better grasp of theology than Protestants. His announcement of a return to theological realism (the claim that the doctrinal entities are the supreme realities rather than projections of individual piety) seemed too stark a departure from liberal tradition. It seemed to be a fideistic attempt to wall theology off from intellectual culture. Barth responded that such critics were clinging to liberal assumptions, and he was generally right; on the other hand, his critics were right to worry that something was being lost in an overly hasty dismissal of liberal theology (though they failed to identify what that something was). Such critics were confirmed in their opinions when he published the first volume of his *Church Dogmatics* in 1932 (it was to be the first of fourteen volumes). It announced that theology was "the scientific self-examination of the Christian Church with respect to the content of its distinctive Talk about God."[9]

The complexity of Barth is that his reorientation of theology must be judged revolutionary, heroic, and climate-changing. But it is also too narrow. His achievement was to locate the essence of Christianity in the primary practice of Christian communication — the speech of faith. And yet his concept of this was too systematic, too tidy. It was also too verbal and too fixed on the idea of the Word of God speaking through human words. This is the core cultic event, and theology must be the science of it. Strict focus on the Word, and asserting its priority to nonverbal communication, makes theology a logical system that reflects the ordering agency of God. If God is supremely known as authoritative speaker, a coherent conceptual system is possible. What Barth finds in the Reformed tradition is a correspondence

9. Karl Barth, *Church Dogmatics* I/1, ed. G. W. Bromiley and T. F. Torrance (Edinburgh: T&T Clark, 1956), p. 3.

between divine authority and theological clarity. It is because God is known through speech "that the testimony of prophets and apostles comes to us in the form of *words,* and it is for this reason that permission and demand come to us — not to babble, not to mime, not to make music, but rather — to *speak* of God."[10] An idea of God that departs from order-giver, commander, dictator he suspects of vagueness and effeminacy (the implied link between order and manliness is pervasive).

Barth moves toward this from a more poetic, unsystematic idea of divine authority, a more Lutheran idea of God's living voice that needs no conceptual system to explain it. He seems to feel that this initial approach is frail. It may seem to be a local, angst-ridden version of Christianity, hatched in time of war and cultural crisis. But it needs to be rooted in a rigorous logical and theological system.

What is wrong with moving toward greater conceptual stability? It entails seeing primary Christian practice in strictly verbal terms, and sidelining its stubborn, mysterious ritual core. The Reformed tradition reveres the Eucharist in its way, but it demands its subordination to verbalism. And it forgets that linguistic communication has a more-than-verbal context; it decontextualizes the Word. In practice the cultic event in which the Word is credited to speak is an event in time and space. Consider the phrase, attributed to the elder Blumhardt, that excited the young Barth in about 1916: "Jesus is Victor." As I have already noted, he was fascinated by the story that Blumhardt had performed an exorcism in which the expelled spirit had uttered this phrase. This is a good example of primary Christian speech being rooted in a form of ritual action, involving bodies as well as minds and

---

10. Barth, *Göttingen Dogmatics,* p. 63. This emphasis demotes all forms of non-verbal ritual: "We are not told to light candles" by God, but to speak his Word (Dorrien, *Barthian Revolt,* p. 181). He once reflected on his detachment from church ritual: "Even during my youth I had an antipathy to all ceremonial in worship. I was aware of always being clumsy before the 'altars' of the German churches where I had to preach" (Busch, *Karl Barth,* p. 235). It seems that Nazism reinforced this suspicion of sacramentalism; he hints that its reliance on pagan spectacle contributed to German theology's seduction: "We were in danger of bringing, first incense, and then the complete sacrifice to [Nazism] as a false god" (Dorrien, *Barthian Revolt,* p. 136).

voices. All primary Christian speech is rooted in such action: it comes from bodies, and it is received by bodies. Or the same phrase, "Jesus is Victor," might be uttered by a dying martyr, leading the community to associate the phrase with his memory, which gives it great power. The point is that words acquire force from contexts, from past associations and present settings. The Word operates through cultural as well as purely verbal events. The cultic force of Christian verbal proclamation derives from cultural practices and settings.

To the Reformed tradition, a wider than verbal conception of Christian proclamation leads to confusion. If the Word is thought to be expressed through images and performances, its agency is too diffuse to be defined or regulated. It becomes impossible to say what cultural forms are of primary importance. For example, it can be claimed that a particular icon has as much communicative power as Scripture; there is no grounds on which to deny that. Who is to say how the Word functions? If the monopoly of the verbal Word is denied, then the concept of divine authority will be dissipated, as in liberal Protestantism, or it will be mediated by institutional authority, as in Roman Catholicism (which Barth saw as the most serious existing form of Christianity).

So Barth was right to seek a new basis for theology in the particularity of Christian communicative culture, but he had a narrowly verbal conception of such culture. He also moved toward an overly systematic idea of *theology*. The amazing thing about his Romans commentary is that it really did open the possibility of modern theological discourse following the logic of Paul's discourse. This is a discourse that combines careful reflection with primary Christian speech. This hybrid discourse destabilizes theology as a system, for it keeps pointing out that primary Christian speech is prior to any systematic reflection on it. It rejects the idea of a gulf between primary Christian speech and the discourse that reflects on it. Barth moved toward affirming this gulf as a necessary thing. But in a sense he wants it both ways: theology is not wholly distinct from preaching, he insists; therefore, it must express the authority of the Word — and thus perform godly style — in its systematic rigor. The voice of *Church Dogmatics* is gently performative: the implicit claim is that the Word has been incorporated into a form of systematic reflection. I consider this a dubious departure from the authentically hybrid discourse of Paul (and Luther), in which systematic reflection is not taken so seriously.

The next phase of Barth's career was determined by the rise of Hitler. He revived his reputation as a prophetic figure by helping to organize opposition to the "German Christians" in 1933, which numbered his days of living in Germany. In a sense, this heroic episode was bad for his theology in that it confirmed him in certain assumptions that he might otherwise have reconsidered. We must approach the issue in the context of his wider engagement in politics.

Above Politics?

Barth's early breakthrough came when he echoed the religious socialists' rejection of liberal politics and then insisted that socialist politics was just another form of fallen politics, not to be confused with the kingdom of God. Most importantly for our purposes, his mounting polemic against liberal theology entailed a suspicion of the old idea of a deep positive affinity between Protestantism and political freedom. Although he did not directly criticize political liberalism, he failed to distinguish it from the theological liberalism that he attacked so sharply.

As a student he was broadly accepting of the idea that political and cultural liberalism was an expression of God's will, an idea put forward by Ritschl, von Harnack, and Troeltsch, and contested by very few. In rejecting the theological liberalism of his teachers during the war, was Barth also rejecting *political* liberalism? The issue is complicated by the history sketched in the previous chapter: Germany's liberal tradition was deeply tied up with the Protestant hegemony promoted by Bismarck. To the German mind, liberalism demanded a strong state in which the Protestant churches played a major role. Barth's protest, beginning in 1914, was partly against this German tradition — of the fusion of religion, liberalism, and nationalism (sometimes dubbed "culture Protestantism"). But, instead of arguing for a new and better political liberalism, he implied that *all* political liberalism was part of a tottering old order, and that theology had better things to do than shore it up. He moved toward a simplistic view of politically liberal Protestantism as the expression of a secular Enlightenment agenda.[11]

The first edition of *Romans,* written in 1918, was particularly wary of idealizing any sort of state. So-called democracy is "the devilish art of the majority"; Christians should remember that their "State is in heaven," and they should reject "Monarchy, Capitalism, Militarism, Patriotism and Liberalism."[12] This largely persists in the rewritten version: the eschatological reality of God is distinct from all ideas of liberal progress and all humanitarian idealism (e.g., the gospel must not be equated with "the love of foreigners and negroes"). The idea that a "good" state is substantially better than a "bad" state is a distraction from the fact that the kingdom is other than all human possibilities: "Is there anywhere legality which is not fundamentally illegal? Is there anywhere authority which is not ultimately based upon tyranny?"[13] Such comments were balanced by other statements on the need to pursue morality as far as we are able; but the negative, skeptical comments, echoing Marx and Nietzsche, gained far more attention.

It was an interesting time to be flirting with the rejection of political liberalism. In 1919, a frail new liberal state replaced the defeated German Empire: the Weimar Republic. For the first time, liberal politics was clearly distinct from the old Protestant hegemony; a new separation of church and state was effected. What did Barth think of that when he returned to Germany in 1921? If he had objected to the nationalist bent of German liberal Protestantism, he would surely approve of the new, more secular state. But he was too focused on attacking liberal theology to think of defending liberal politics. He was focused on placing himself within Reformed tradition. He had not closely studied Calvin before moving to Göttingen, and he

11. "Karl Barth's vigorous postwar polemic failed to distinguish between types of liberty, regarding culture Protestantism as an ideological legitimation of an antireligious secularism with its origins in the Enlightenment" (Mark Chapman, "Protestantism and Liberalism," in Alister McGrath and Darren Marks, eds., *The Blackwell Companion to Protestantism* (Oxford: Blackwell, 2004), p. 325.

12. Barth, quoted in Timothy Gorringe, *Karl Barth: Against Hegemony* (Cambridge, UK: Cambridge University Press, 1999), pp. 44-45.

13. Barth, *Romans,* pp. 452, 480.

was keen to show his allegiance to the Reformer (having shown more rhetorical affinity with Luther). He presented Calvin as admirably focused on God's Word, amid the vagaries of human politics, and yet also as a practical, realistic figure who was no blinkered authoritarian but an architect of modern democracy.[14]

When Barth noticed the prevalence of reactionary sentiment among colleagues in 1923, he renewed his affirmation of socialism. A few years later, he expressed unease at his colleagues' disparagement of the "poor" Weimar Republic.[15] But his own theology was subtly contributing to such disparagement. It contributed to a climate in which political liberalism seemed weak, inauthentic, of the past. Much of the appeal of "dialectical theology" was its aura of apocalyptic instability. Like Nietzsche's work, it gestured at the total breakdown of modern enlightened values. On one level, it reflected the trauma of the Great War; yet, on another level, it prolonged the aura of that trauma and implied that the Weimar Republic was no real relief from it. At the risk of exploiting the benefit of hindsight, what was called for in Germany in the 1920s was an affirmation of Weimar liberalism, which Protestants were inclined to see as secular, banal, foreign, somehow American. A form of theology that implied that all values and ideas were still in a state of crisis was complicit in the mood of apocalyptic restlessness that grew over the decade and provided good soil for fascism.

Mark Lilla argues that Barth had much in common with his contemporary Franz Rosenzweig, who advocated Judaism in polemically postliberal terms: he says that both underestimated the political ramifications of such radicalism.

> Their books did nothing to cause [Nazism], which had much deeper sources. But they did unwittingly help to shape a new and noxious form of political argument, which was the theological celebration of modern tyranny. For all their complacency and blindness, the liberal theologians of the nineteenth century at least understood the basic distinction between freedom and tyranny.

14. Gorringe, *Against Hegemony*, p. 87.
15. Busch, *Karl Barth*, p. 134.

Seen in the light of "thoroughgoing eschatology" and "utopian hope," that distinction no longer seemed so clear, at least to some of those inspired by Barth's and Rosenzweig's writings.[16]

Klaus Scholder agrees: Barth's ideology critique "hit the attempts to establish and to preserve the Republic on the basis of feelings of Christian responsibility just as hard as the designs of the opponents of the Republic."[17]

Barth seems to have become half aware of this. In the late 1920s it began to bother him that his allies continued to be strangely fascinated by "dialectical theology" and the idea of the individual's "existential encounter" with "authentic life." Such rhetoric began to seem sinister. Bultmann kept badgering him to read Heidegger, whose philosophy was supposedly the framework that allowed people to make sense of the New Testament. Barth tried to explain that his Word-centered approach precluded such a use of philosophy.[18] In 1930 he included two other major sympathizers, Gogarten and Brunner, in his criticism: all were embarking on "a large-scale return to the fleshpots of Egypt," he said.[19] When Bultmann sought to repair relationships, Barth told him that his work was still subject to "the old and shameless dictatorship of modern philosophy under the new banner of that of Heidegger."[20] Soon it became more obvious that the attraction of dialectical theology was politically dubious. Some of those who took an interest in it, such as the Lutheran Paul Althaus, were now arguing for a new "natural theology," in which a powerful state belonged to the "orders of creation." Gogarten soon went in this direction: in 1932 he claimed that God had given "no greater gift" to humanity than the

16. Lilla, *The Stillborn God: Religion, Politics, and the Modern West* (New York: Knopf, 2007), p. 278. Timothy Gorringe is among those who disagree.

17. Klaus Scholder, *The Churches and the Third Reich, 1918-1934*, trans. J. Bowden (London: SCM, 1987), p. 51.

18. Barth, Letter to Bultmann, June 12, 1928, in Bernd Jaspert, ed., *Karl Barth/ Rudolf Bultmann Letters, 1922-1966*, trans. and ed. Geoffrey W. Bromiley (Grand Rapids: Eerdmans, 1981), p. 41.

19. Barth, quoted in Dorrien, *Barthian Revolt*, p. 97.

20. Barth, Letter to Bultmann, May 27, 1931, in Jaspert, *Karl Barth/Rudolf Bultmann Letters*, p. 58.

authority of the state.[21] Bultmann's guru Heidegger followed suit. In fact, Barth was surprised that Bultmann himself was anti-Nazi.

The rise of Hitler was cheered by most German Protestants. This allowed Barth to form a very simple narrative, which he held onto very hard in the years to come. The whole tradition of theological liberalism was complicit in National Socialism. Modern Protestantism was preset to admire this secular nationalist ideology; it was the outcome of a century or two of putting humanity before God. This reading of events was tenuous. It ignored the possibility that German Protestantism voted for Hitler because it wasn't liberal *enough*. Its defining feature was its nationalism. It thus felt deeply insulted by the secular modern aura of the Weimar Republic. It wanted its hegemony back. Though it talked about freedom, it lacked an understanding of the affinity between Protestantism and the liberal state. Perhaps most importantly, Protestant Germany was deeply shocked by the sudden advent of cultural liberalism — jazz, feminists, cabarets, and so on. These cultural changes that happened too fast made liberalism seem nihilistic. "To those who still identified themselves with the basic values of the bourgeois humanist tradition . . . it seemed as if their very culture was collapsing around them."[22]

In Barth's narrative, Protestantism had overinvested in the liberal state and failed to stand apart from all modern ideologies. The reality was that, in Germany, the liberal state was tainted by nationalism, and Protestantism failed to critique this and demand a more robust liberalism. It suited Barth to believe that 1930s Germany revealed the truth about politics: it was a confrontation between the godless state and the Word-based church, and political liberalism was but a veneer that falsely legitimated the state and obscured the *church* as the true site of freedom. In 1932 he wrote:

> The proclamation of the church is by nature political in so far as it has to ask the pagan *polis* to remedy its state of disorder and make

---

21. Dorrien, *Barthian Revolt*, p. 115.

22. Jones, "Culture and Politics in the Weimar Republic," in Martel, ed., *Modern Germany Reconsidered*, p. 86.

justice a reality. This proclamation is good when it presents the specific commandment of God, and not good when it puts forward the abstract truth of a political ideology.[23]

The implication is that the church should not assert the goodness of liberalism or democracy, that this is a bad old habit of theological liberalism. Surely, as Hitler came to power, Barth saw the virtue of political liberalism — as espoused by most Western powers. To admit that would have been to weaken his theological narrative; it would be to admit that political liberalism, despite its closeness to theological liberalism, must be taken theologically seriously. Barth's narrative is cleaner if political liberalism is removed from the picture. And so over the next decade he repeatedly insisted that Nazi-friendly "German Christianity" was the logical outcome of liberal Protestantism. Having lost any anchorage in the Word, liberal Protestantism naturally drifted to supporting national paganism. Barth effectively implied that any Protestants who disagreed with his neo-Calvinist rigor were tacitly pro-Hitler.

It was plain enough that nostalgic nationalism motivated the German Christians. When Hitler came to power in 1933, he created a unified Reich church, strongly under the state's control. This was a return to the effective establishment of old, created by Bismarck. It was so alluring to the German Christians that they accepted the Aryan clause, which banned those of Jewish origin from church jobs. The Pastor's Emergency League was set up to protest against this. This soon became the Confessing Church, whose central document, the Barmen Declaration, was drafted by Barth in May 1934. It was centered on the insistence that the church should obey Jesus Christ alone and should not recognize "other events and powers, figures and truths, as God's revelation." This idea of a heroically autonomous church is an understandable emergency measure, but it evades the fact that some political traditions are preferable to others, that the authentically liberal state is not a subtle enemy but an ally.

23. Busch, *Karl Barth*, p. 216.

So events in Germany led Barth to espouse a boldly postliberal ecclesiology. In 1934 he told a student conference in Switzerland, largely attended by Americans, that only a thoroughly Word-based theology could really oppose fascism. A theology infected by humanism might seem politically benign or harmless, but it was powerless to resist fascism and was thus complicit in it: "If you begin to take the pious man seriously . . . you will reach the same end before which the official German Church stands today."[24] Such rhetoric alienated many Protestant theologians who had considered themselves Barth sympathizers, such as Reinhold Niebuhr and Paul Tillich (a German who relocated to America). The rise of Hitler seemed to have provoked a corresponding authoritarianism in Barth. This "counter-extremism" was understandable under the circumstances, but no model for normal peacetime theology.

Did he really see liberal theology as complicit in Nazism? If it was, why did other liberal Christian nations not turn fascist? Why did most fascism arise on Catholic soil? He seems to have felt that the church needed to take a strong line against all of secular modernity. Of course, Hitlerism was particularly demonic, but to condemn it in isolation was to imply approval of normal modern culture and politics. He was seemingly influenced by the confidence with which Roman Catholicism castigated secular modernity in general. Why should Protestantism not speak in such lofty, sweeping tones? Why should it muddle its message by implying that contemporary liberal democracy is somehow an indirect expression of Christianity?

Nontheologians might assume that Barth's link between modern autonomy and Hitler is now seen as eccentric, hyperbolic. In fact, it is one of the foundational ideas of recent theology, as we shall see.[25] This seems to be a category confusion, a will to see too direct a con-

24. Dorrien, *Barthian Revolt*, p. 106.
25. Thus George Hunsinger, writing in 1987: "It was [the autonomous] self which secretly lurked in wait behind what Barth rejected so vehemently as 'natural theology,' which reached demonic culmination in Adolf Hitler, and which reaches new culmination, potentially worse than the first, in the nuclear-weapons state today" (Hunsinger, *Disruptive Grace: Studies in the Theology of Karl Barth* [Grand Rapids: Eerdmans, 2000], p. 102). We shall see that Rowan Williams is also fond of this link.

nection between theological error and political evil. It is surely driven by a desire to endow a theological idea with urgent political relevance.

Significantly, Barth showed a more nuanced approach to political liberalism when he left Germany (he returned to Switzerland in 1935), and especially when the war began. Back in a more stable democracy that faced a very immediate threat, "liberal" had a different ring; he even called it "so fine a word (outside theology)."[26] This little aside points to one of the huge deficiencies of his theology. When things became serious he had to admit, though only in passing, that political liberalism — even if associated with liberal theology — was rather an important force in the world. He was surely influenced by the mettle of the British resistance to Hilter.[27] But this more nuanced view did not really penetrate his work.

After the war, his lofty approach to politics continued in a new context. The descent of the Iron Curtain led most Western intellectuals to reaffirm the value of liberal democracy and to condemn communism. Addressing the World Council of Churches in 1948, Barth warned the churches not to get too close to this new consensus. The real task was proclaiming the Word of God, which was distinct from any worldly system. Communism should be resisted on political grounds, he said, but a Christian crusade against it was overblown, idolatrous. He persisted in this stance, declaring in 1958, "I regard anticommunism as a matter of principle an evil even greater than communism itself."[28] On one level, he was right to warn America of anticommunist crusades. But the issue also shows his inability to affirm political liberalism on Christian grounds. It was crucial to his lofty theological position to present all politics as flawed, as unworthy of association with the true ideology of the Word.

26. Busch, *Karl Barth*, p. 308.

27. In 1945 he expressed the hope that the defeated Germans would learn the "meaning of democracy, freedom, loyalty, humanity" (Busch, *Karl Barth*, p. 325). He also admitted that he had been "shy," as a Swiss, of speaking out against right-wing tendencies during the Weimar years (Gorringe, *Against Hegemony*, p. 84).

28. Dorrien, *Barthian Revolt*, p. 137.

The Reaction Questioned: Bonhoeffer

Barth was joined in the struggle against German Christianity by a young Lutheran theologian, Dietrich Bonhoeffer. He is a difficult figure to assess, since his thought was clearly in transition when he was executed for plotting to kill Hitler in 1945. But his curtailed career nevertheless casts unique light on the theological issues of the period. He was strongly drawn to Barth's approach, but he tenaciously questioned its adequacy.

Like many Lutherans, Bonhoeffer was excited about Barth's opposition of the gospel to religious culture, moralism, and religion as a human phenomenon. Was this, he wondered, a post-Nietzschean rediscovery of Paul's and Luther's rejection of "the law"? But Bonhoeffer also entertained a seemingly contradictory thought: maybe Protestantism needed more sacramental weight, a more Catholic concept of the church as the site of Christ's presence. Maybe Barth was too individualistic. Bonhoeffer had briefly worked as a pastor in Spain; he admired the cultural presence of Catholicism there, and he wondered how Protestantism could compete. In the early 1930s the specter of Nazism made him increasingly respectful of Barth's dogmatic rigor. But where Barth was confident, even bullish, Bonhoeffer was anxious, unsatisfied, conflicted.

He was seeking a more nuanced version of Barth's antiliberalism, in a fuller affirmation of ecclesiology: theology, he thought, must be rooted in the distinctive life of the worshiping community, which is wider than "the Word." For example, he said in 1933 that an understanding of Christ must be rooted in "the humble silence of the sacramental congregation offering its worship."[29] Bonhoeffer was attracted to a Catholic sensibility in a way that Barth was not — partly a reflection of his Lutheranism. He wanted to argue that the new postliberal theology must be rooted in the church; but he also worried that an assertion of the priority of church would lead to self-importance, rigidity, legalism. Barth's approach to theology was more

---

29. Andreas Pangritz, *Karl Barth in the Theology of Dietrich Bonhoeffer*, trans. Barbara and Martin Rumscheidt (Grand Rapids: Eerdmans, 2000), p. 104.

rooted in a big idea than in sacramental practice, and yet it was also developing a rather rigid ecclesiology — which could be seen as the worst of both worlds. The Confessing Church also seemed guilty of lacking political force, of being vague where it really mattered (the Barmen Declaration did not even denounce anti-Semitism).

Bonhoeffer's involvement in the Confessing Church continued, but his doubts remained, and his commitment to resistance was channeled elsewhere. He joined a plot to kill Hitler, and he was arrested in 1943. During his time in prison his theological attitude slowly changed. Because of his recent involvement in a secular conspiracy, and his current situation among secular-minded prisoners, he experienced a new wariness of religiosity. During air raids, when his fellow inmates were terrified, he found that he had no religious words for them. What was needed then was normal secular companionship. He began to wonder how Christianity could be communicated to those who were utterly indifferent to church and theology. The vast majority of people seemed not to need religion in the old sense — that is, a set of beliefs, allegiance to an institution. His thoughts kept dwelling on the world-affirming side of the gospel: the Old Testament's this-worldliness and Luther's affirmation of worldly vocations and ordinary happiness.

So began his famous theological prison letters, his fumbling grasping after "religionless Christianity." He falteringly suggested that the attempt to *explain* Christianity to people seemed self-defeating: "The time when people could be told everything by means of words, whether theological or pious, is over, and so is the time of inwardness and conscience — and that means the time of religion in general." Barth had launched a bracing criticism of "religion," he reflected, but his subsequent pursuit of doctrinal correctness was another form of alienated religiosity. The question remains: How do we speak of God — without religion, that is, without the temporally conditioned presuppositions of metaphysics, inwardness, and so on? How do we speak (or perhaps we cannot now even "speak" as we used to) in a "worldly" way about "God"? The old conceptual language of religion gets in the way of communicating God. There is a need somehow to break with the assumption that "religion is a condition of salvation," just as Paul broke with circumcision.[30] But this equation of "religion" with "the law" raises the question of what the pure other of "religion" is. *Faith* will no longer do; Barth was right to question pious subjectivity. What about "the Word"? In Barth's hands this leads to a brittle authoritarianism, a system that "must" be accepted — all or nothing. It lacks any nuance: in its quasi-scientific comprehensiveness it fails to see that there are "degrees of significance" within Christian faith, and it also lacks a feel for "the *mysteries* of the Christian faith."

The way forward, he falteringly suggested, was to affirm modernity's secular turn, the fact that this was now "a world come of age." Did this mean freeing Christianity from supernatural belief? Not quite: Bonhoeffer did not condone the "demythologizing" approach that Bultmann had recently proposed, agreeing with Barth that this was in tune with the old liberal Protestantism. But, in a sense, he wanted to go further than Bultmann had. "It's not only the 'mythological' concepts, such as miracle, ascension, and so on (which are not in principle separable from the concepts of God, faith, etc.), but 'religious' concepts generally, which are problematic. You can't, as Bultmann supposes, separate God and miracle, but you must be able to interpret and proclaim both in a 'non-religious' sense."[31] Bonhoeffer's dilemma is that Christianity must be presented in a new way that is meaningful to the modern person who finds traditional religion irrelevant. But the liberal paradigm for such renewal is bankrupt: its concepts might be free from supernatural belief, but they leave people cold. Bonhoeffer admits that he does not have the answer. Ultimately he can only hope — it is essentially a messianic hope — that the answer will come; that "men will once more be called so to utter the word of God that the world will be changed and renewed by it. It will be a new language — perhaps quite non-religious, but liberating and redeeming — as was Jesus' language; it will shock people and

30. Dietrich Bonhoeffer, Letter to Eberhard Bethge, April 30, 1944, in Bonhoeffer, *Letters and Papers from Prison* (London: SCM, 2001), pp. 91-93.

31. Bonhoeffer, Letter to Bethge, May 5, 1944, in *Letters and Papers from Prison*, pp. 94-95. Hereafter, date and page references to *Letters and Papers from Prison* appear in parentheses in the text.

overcome them by its power; it will be the language of a new righteousness of truth, proclaiming God's peace with men and the coming of his kingdom" (May 18, 1944, p. 105).

Explaining what Bonhoeffer "really" meant in his prison letters is a dubious exercise; one is probably trying to adorn one's own ideas with his radical-martyr aura. But there are grounds for thinking that he objected to Barth's revolt on the dual grounds already discussed: its conception of Christianity was too narrowly verbal and systematic, and it was too dismissive of political and cultural liberalism. As we have seen, Bonhoeffer argued, long before his imprisonment, for a more sacramental and ecclesial concept of the Word. In prison, expressing this more negatively, he said that Barth was erecting an unhelpfully abstract, conceptual system. In a fascinating aside, he tells Bethge that he has started making the sign of the cross when he prays: "There is something objective about it, and that is what is particularly badly needed here" (November 21, 1943, p. 29). It is strange that he does not say more about ritual as a possible alternative to the barren conceptualism of religion. Despite years of affirming the priority of the sacramental community, Bonhoeffer still seems deeply affected by the liberal Protestant suspicion of ritual — compounded by Barth's sharper-edged suspicion of ritual — and perhaps also by the pagan ritualism of the Nazis. These forces perhaps made it impossible to imagine a new central role for sacramentalism.

And his sketch of modern "autonomy" might be seen as an attempt to rescue the political and cultural aspect of liberal Protestantism from Barthian censure. Protestantism must reaffirm its secular affinity, remembering that Luther "wanted the establishment of a genuine secular social order free from clerical privilege" (October 31, 1943, p. 21). Elsewhere he suggests that modern worldliness is authentically Christian "even if it is anti-clerical" (March 9, 1944, p. 74). Theology must affirm this secularization, find a way of proclaiming God that is in tune with it, rather than associate God with cultural nostalgia. It must resist "the *salto mortale* [death leap] back into the Middle Ages. But the principle of the Middle Ages is heteronomy in the form of clericalism; a return to that can be a counsel of despair, and it would be at the cost of intellectual honesty" (July 16, 1944, pp. 133-

34). This relates to his critique of Barth and the Confessing Church: They "have encouraged us to entrench ourselves persistently behind the 'faith of the church,' and evade the honest question as to what we ourselves really believe. . . . To say that it is the church's business, not mine, may be a clerical evasion, and outsiders always regard it as such. . . . We cannot, like the Roman Catholics, simply identify ourselves with the church" (August 3, 1944, p. 144). Protestantism must refuse to erect a barrier between the church and honest liberalism. "Honest liberalism" is not Bonhoeffer's phrase, but it seems to be what he is seeking to defend: the awareness that liberal idealism is a healthy force, that it must be seen as central to Christianity — rather than its other. He knows that no return to the old liberal Protestantism is possible, but this essential openness must be preserved. At the risk of twisting Bonhoeffer into agreement with my thesis, I suggest that he was seeking to salvage the good in liberal Protestantism (its affirmation of political and cultural freedom, its suspicion of clerical subculture, its intellectual honesty) from the flawed theology. His emphasis is repeatedly on honesty, and his plea might be expressed this way: Let us admit that our urge to communicate Christ, beyond the confines of theological liberalism, is not working, that we must go, as Barth did in 1914, back to the drawing board.

Barth was not pleased to be told this. He even declared the publication of the *Letters and Papers from Prison* a mistake. It seemed to him that a promising young theologian had lost his nerve, had come to doubt the value of theology. He was extremely annoyed when Bonhoeffer became a name for liberal theologians to conjure with in the early 1960s, and he particularly disliked John Robinson's use of Bonhoeffer in *Honest to God*. As we shall see, Barth had a point.

NINE

The Collapse

—◈◈◈—

The mid-twentieth century was the crucial period of opportunity for liberal Protestantism. It had the chance to attend to Barth's critique, and to confront the infection it contracted from deism, or humanism. It should have busily begun to sort out what I am calling the good liberal Christian tradition from the bad. On the surface it seemed to be on the right track: the most influential thinkers claimed to have learned something from Barth's revolt, without following his dogmatism. A more moderate postliberal turn was possible, they claimed, one that rejected aspects of liberal Protestantism without recourse to Barth's drastic reactionary methodological revolution. In fact, however, they were evading the full depth of Barth's radicalism and thus perpetuating a flawed liberalism. In this chapter I will be investigating Niebuhr and Tillich, but I must also acknowledge the background presence of Bultmann. As we saw, Bultmann was convinced that he and Barth were kindred spirits, both pursuing the same eschatological emphasis in different ways. The difference was that Bultmann had found a way of making it intelligible to modern people: existentialism. (Heidegger's dalliance with Nazism did not deter him.) "Demytholigizing," the term that he unveiled during the war, had a compelling simplicity: here was a clean break with the supernatural past. Unlike Harnack and Troeltsch, he

had a biblical focus that gave his thesis a greater aura of authenticity. His declared aim was not to fuse Christianity and liberalism but
to uncover the real meaning of the New Testament. He tried to explain the distinction to Barth when he wrote to him in 1952: "We
need liberation from the mythological world-view of the Bible, because this has become totally alien to people today, and because the
link with it constitutes an offence — a false one — and closes the
door to understanding. . . . At root nothing matters more than that
the situation of man requires an existential interpretation of proclamation."[1] To Barth's dismay, Bultmann's influence steadily rose:
"demythologizing" became a major buzz word in theology over the
next two decades. We shall shortly return to its influence on some
works of the 1960s. But first we must attend to the figure who dominated theology across the Atlantic.

Niebuhr

It says much about the American religious scene that the foremost
Christian thinker of the time was not principally interested in theology, but in politics. In the 1940s, Reinhold Niebuhr became a major
political pundit, the preeminent voice of American Protestantism (he
subsequently also became a government insider). His concern was
not so much to preach the gospel, or reinterpret it for a new age, as it
was to channel America's religiosity into the strengthening of democracy. Though he had an aura of speaking for Protestant America, this
was rather illusory: as we have seen, American Protestantism was split
between the liberalism of the ruling class and a populist antiliberalism. But for half a century this split was largely obscured by the confidence of the ruling liberalism — and its investment in a unifying nationalism. Niebuhr could thus claim to speak for Christian America

---

1. Bultmann, Letter to Barth, November 15, 1952, in Bernd Jaspert, ed., *Karl
Barth/Rudolf Bultmann Letters, 1922-1966*, trans. and ed. Geoffrey W. Bromiley (Grand
Rapids: Eerdmans, 1981), pp. 88-89. In Barth's view, Bultmann offered "a Christian in-
stance of the general human encounter with some Other" (*Letters*, p. 142).

well into the cold war era, even though the appeal of his theological liberalism was more limited than it seemed.

Niebuhr emerged from the Social Gospel movement, which dominated liberal theology in the 1920s. As a pastor in an inner-city Detroit parish, he developed a sharp antipathy toward capitalism, having seen Henry Ford's development of it at first hand. His rejection of the Social Gospel movement was largely rooted in an attachment to Marxist realism: it underestimated the power of corporate selfishness and put too much trust in liberal humanist optimism. It neglected the basic Christian category of sin. Niebuhr was partly echoing Barth's invective against liberal Protestantism, and he was quick to understand that there was a new appetite for such rhetoric. In *Moral Man and Immoral Society* (1932), he noted the persistence in America of "the illusions and sentimentalities of the Age of Reason." "In spite of the disillusionment of the World War, the average liberal Protestant Christian is still convinced that the kingdom of God is gradually approaching . . . [and] that the wealthy will be persuaded by the church to dedicate their power and privilege to the common good. . . ." The liberal state is not an early stage of God's kingdom; it is a normal enough political tradition in which different interests must still clash. For example, "the white race in America will not admit the Negro to equal rights if it is not forced to do so." (He expressed the hope that nonviolent resistance would emerge, and that influenced Martin Luther King Jr.) He still advocated an essentially liberal theology that would inspire people to this-worldly engagement, but Christians must know that the final triumph of love and peace is *humanly* impossible: it waits on the intervention of God. "A sentimental generation has destroyed this apocalyptic note in the vision of the Christ."[2]

The problem with Niebuhr's whole theology is that it is unclear whether he himself really believes in this "apocalyptic note" as anything more than a necessary aspect of a more robust political vision. He later called the kingdom of God the "impossible possibility," an

---

2. Reinhold Niebuhr, *Moral Man and Immoral Society* (New York: Charles Scribner's Sons, 1960), pp. xxv, 79, 253, 82.

ideal by which human life should be judged. When theologians spoke of it in more biblical terms — as something really to be expected — he was dismissive.[3]

The big difference between Niebuhr and Barth is that the former did not move to a fundamental rethinking of theology. He did not want to topple modern Protestantism; he just wanted to attack one aspect of it — its excessive optimism. His aim was a more rigorous form of progressive Christianity, with a Marxist hardheadedness and a post-Enlightenment consciousness of sin. By attacking just one aspect of liberal theology, he implied that it was otherwise sound. His theological assumptions were essentially those of Harnack and Troeltsch, which is clear in one of his early books, *Does Civilization Need Religion?* There he explains that Christianity contains, in symbolic and mythical form, the ideals that humanity needs. "Its optimism is rooted in pessimism and it is therefore able to preach both repentance and hope. . . . Its adoration of Jesus sometimes obscures the real genius of his life but cannot permanently destroy the fruitfulness of his inspiration. . . . The idea of a potent but yet suffering ideal which is defeated by the world but gains its victory in the defeat must remain basic in any morally creative world view."[4]

In the early 1930s, Niebuhr remained strongly left-wing, criticizing Roosevelt's New Deal as timid. The rise of fascism led him to direct his fire at the strong pacifist lobby within liberal Protestantism, and to edge away from his socialist radicalism. The key issue was now the defense of democracy, in which he thought that Roosevelt should be strongly backed. He became well known during World War II by forcefully arguing that a robust liberal democracy, one capable of standing up to Hitler and Stalin, and also capable of pursuing the common good in peacetime, depended on "Christian realism." In his book *The Children of Light and the Children of Darkness* (1944), he ar-

---

3. Much later, in an interview, he expressed a desire to eliminate the language of the kingdom from Christianity altogether, as a recipe for unhelpful utopianism (see Gary Dorrien, *Soul in Society,* p. 144).

4. Niebuhr, *Does Civilization Need Religion?* quoted in Hauerwas, *With the Grain of the Universe: The Church's Witness and Natural Theology* (Grand Rapids: Brazos, 2001), p. 109.

gued that the doctrine of original sin "makes an important contribution to any adequate social and political theory, the lack of which has robbed bourgeois theory of real wisdom."[5] As this suggests, his focus was not a new forceful proclamation of the gospel but a wiser form of bourgeois theory.

After the war he powerfully argued that American power was the least worst kind of power, as long as it kept Christian realism in mind. It could pursue noble humane goals, with wise restraint. In political terms, he was surely a force for good, for such rhetoric helped to move the nation in a broadly progressive direction. In theological terms, his achievement was to perpetuate the old liberalism, adapting it to the civic religion of the 1950s, when anticommunism became a kind of national faith. (This civic faith led to the addition of "under God" to the pledge of allegiance in 1954, and to the creation of a new national motto, "In God we trust," in 1956.) Niebuhr's very limited critique of liberal Protestantism served as inoculation against real rethinking. Instead of grappling with Barth's critique of theology's humanist assumptions, he implied that such grappling was unnecessary. Surely all sensible people agreed that religion inhabited the realm of "myth."[6] Too much navel-gazing would be counterproductive.

Niebuhr's desire to toughen liberal theology was essentially worldly. Liberal theology, he thought, should lose its aura of wetness and be practical, responsible, manly, unafraid of the exercise of power. His rejection of liberal idealism was tied up with a fear of effeminacy, and the same fear stopped him from overanalyzing the basis of faith.[7] When such analysis loomed, Niebuhr protested that he was a social ethicist, not a theologian. To focus on primary theological matters, he implied, is divisive, and is likely to lead to some form of dogmatism. After

---

5. Niebuhr, *The Children of Light and the Children of Darkness* (London: Nisbet and Co., 1944), p. 19.

6. We can no longer "believe in the virgin birth, and we have difficulty with the physical resurrection of Christ," he wrote in "Coherence, Incoherence, and Christian Faith," quoted in Hauerwas, *With the Grain*, p. 129.

7. Dorrien quotes Niebuhr's biographer, Fox: "What annoyed him most of all about liberal Protestantism was its effeminate, namby-pamby faith in goodness and love" (Dorrien, *Soul in Society*, p. 160).

the war he acknowledged that he had next to nothing in common with Barth, whose work seemed to him to be full of old-world obscurantism, and whose reluctance to condemn communism he called irresponsible. Barth's form of religion, he said, is "fashioned for the catacombs and has little relation to the task of transfiguring the natural stuff of politics by the grace and wisdom of the gospel."[8] The problem was that Niebuhr underestimated the proximity of the catacombs — or, rather, the fact that the Western mind was rapidly becoming post-Christian. He was concerned to persuade nominal Christians to remain sympathetic to religion; he failed to see that nominal Christianity was fragile and that a more fundamental account of faith was needed.

Just as Barth's approach seemed extreme, so did that of Catholics and Anglo-Catholics. Niebuhr's thoughts on sacramentalism were few, and rather crass: he warned against allowing symbolism to lapse into the "magic" of Catholic ritualism and showed little awareness of the ritual basis of all religious language. (In an essay written in retirement, he admitted that he had only just begun to see the point of ritual. He began to see that preaching struggled "to explicate and symbolize [God's] majesty and mystery. . . . For the first time I ceased to look at Catholicism as a remnant of medieval culture.")[9] His main thought on ecclesiology was that authoritative churches denied the universality of sin, seeing themselves as already redeemed, and thus turned the gospel into "legalistic systems."[10] Roman Catholicism was especially guilty of identifying its preferred forms of culture with the kingdom of God: "It refuses to the very last to admit that the civilization which it has built is something less than a Christian civilization."[11] This is a valid warning against ecclesial power, but it is not

---

8. Robert McAfee Brown, ed., *The Essential Reinhold Niebuhr: Selected Essays and Addresses* (New Haven: Yale University Press, 1986), p. 231.

9. Niebuhr, "A View of Life from the Sidelines" (1967; unpublished in his lifetime), in Brown, *The Essential Reinhold Niebuhr*, p. 254.

10. Niebuhr, quoted in Wendy Dackson, "Reinhold Niebuhr's 'Outsider Ecclesiology,'" in Harries and Platten, eds., *Reinhold Niebuhr and Contemporary Politics* (Oxford: Oxford University Press, 2010), p. 92.

11. Niebuhr, *Beyond Tragedy*, p. 33, quoted in Harries and Platten, eds., *Reinhold Niebuhr and Contemporary Politics*, p. 94.

balanced by any account of what the church is for. He implies that the church ought to dissolve into Christian culture.

What ultimately makes Niebuhr less than a serious theologian is that he assumed that Christianity did not need fundamental advocacy. There seemed little need for a basic account of what it was, how it was credible. He seems to have assumed that, like the poor, it would always be with us, so the question was how to relate it to politics.

Despite his deficiencies, one might expect Niebuhr to provide a good account of the Christian basis of the liberal state. But he is disappointing on that score as well. In a sense, he assumes that his audience already knows the virtue of the liberal state, and so he sees his task as introducing the less familiar idea that all worldly politics is flawed. He wants to move Americans away from a complacent pride in the role of religious liberty in their story, and to see the role of ordinary murky power struggles. Even in midcareer he still echoes the broadly Marxist account of the rise of Protestantism, as the ideology of the new middle class. In *The Children of Light and the Children of Darkness,* he speaks very soberly of the rise of toleration as in the best interests of an essentially secular ruling class after the breakdown of religious unity: "[M]odern democratic toleration was made possible, partly because a bourgeois culture had created a spirit of indifference toward the most characteristic affirmations of historic forms of religious faith." But he seems to have second thoughts, and he adds that the "real foundation of Anglo-Saxon toleration lies in the religious experience of seventeenth-century England," and he mentions Milton as a supreme example. He also implies that a stable liberal state requires religiously inspired liberalism, full of humility and charity: "Whenever the religious groups of a community are incapable of such humility and charity, the national community will be forced to save its unity through either secularism or authoritarianism."[12] But this suggestion that liberal Christianity is the real basis of the liberal state is hardly clear and bold: he seems almost embarrassed to be thinking this, as though it might show him to be still in thrall to naïve Jeffersonianism.

12. Niebuhr, *Children of Light,* pp. 91, 94, 95.

This timidity is unfortunate, for a strong defense of religious liberty was needed during this period. Ironically, it was needed not because religious liberty was under threat, but because it was beginning to triumph as never before. It was only in the late 1930s that the Supreme Court began to endow the separation of church and state with legal force. As I noted in chapter 5, the issue had been evaded ever since the Revolution; major pockets of Protestant intolerance had been tolerated. As David Sehat has recently shown, huge confusion was sown by the pretense, in the mid-twentieth century, that religious liberty had always been a nationally unifying principle. In effect, the vision of Jefferson and Madison was only now finding full political expression, but instead of celebrating a breakthrough, liberals were understated, perhaps for fear of alerting conservatives to what was going on. In retrospect, this was unwise. The nation needed to hear a strong defense of the compatibility of religious freedom — in the full sense (which includes freedom *from* religion) — and Christianity. It needed to be shown that there was a vital link between the vision of Jefferson and Madison and the new era of secular liberalism. It needed to hear that full religious liberty was the proper context for the Christian gospel, rather than a threat to it. Niebuhr surely believed in this vision, but he was complacent about it; he vaguely assumed that it was almost universally accepted and that advocacy of it would seem naively whiggish. (On the other hand, like Barth, his early religious socialism perhaps damaged his faith in the adequacy of the liberal state.) Late in his career he seems to have partially understood this omission. Only in the late sixties did he realize that Billy Graham was not the harmless throwback to revivalism that he had first thought, but was stirring a major political force who challenged basic liberal assumptions. In 1969, a few years before his death, Niebuhr criticized the cozy relationship between Nixon and Graham.[13]

So what was really needed in midcentury was not "Christian realism" but liberal Christian idealism, a strong account of the Christian roots of religious liberty. For America can only be ideologically unified

13. Niebuhr, "The King's Chapel and the King's Court," *Christianity and Crisis,* August 4, 1969.

by this vision. In its absence, the narrative of the religious Right gained traction: the liberalism of the federal government was essentially atheist, inimical to traditional religious liberty. Perhaps the main thing that Niebuhr did have in common with Barth was this failure to defend the affinity between Protestantism and the liberal state.

Tillich

Paul Tillich was another major figure in mid-twentieth-century liberal Protestantism. Like Niebuhr and Bultmann, he claimed to have incorporated something of Barth's revolt, but this did not really extend beyond a few rhetorical touches. His thought was fundamentally in keeping with the theological liberalism of old. He was a German Lutheran, born in the same year as Barth, and was also involved in religious socialism during World War I. He imbibed existentialism and some of the rhetoric of dialectical theology before fleeing Germany in 1933 and heading for New York (Niebuhr recruited him to teach at Union Theological Seminary). His thought fit perfectly with American liberal Protestantism, for he combined old-world Protestant pathos with liberal-arts-college humanism. He mastered this hybrid discourse, centered on a spirit of courageous doubt, criticism, and openness. He presented this as the essence of the Bible as well as of humanism. In 1936 he criticized "Barthian supranaturalism" as a denial of the "Protestant principle":

> For Protestantism will continue to be something more than a weakened version of Catholicism only so long as the protest against every one of its own realizations remains alive within it. This Protestant protest is not rational criticism but prophetic judgment. It is not autonomy but theonomy, even when it appears, as often happens, in rationalistic and humanistic forms.

Theology must not be ashamed of affirming the "great, and truly human liberal principle of autonomy." "The modern trends of thought which are rooted in the Enlightenment are substantially Christian, in spite of their critical attitude towards ecclesiastical Christianity." So Tillich claimed that the Christian humanism that was wary of the church was in some ways more Christian than church-based Christianity. On the other hand, he admitted that only a tightened institutionalism was currently capable of showing any resistance to Nazism.[14] By baptizing the Enlightenment as indirectly Christian, Tillich was exactly conforming to Barth's script.

He continued to expound the idea of Protestant theology as a bridge between the flawed but necessary realm of religious institutions and the secular realm. Theology has a mediating role; it should explain what religious folk really mean by their symbolic doings. In the tradition of Kant, Tillich believed that an enlightened discourse must explain what religion is really about. But for the latter, like Bultmann, this "real meaning" is not so much morality as authentic human existence. He boldly used existential terminology to assert the compatibility of faith and reason. Thus, in the 1940s he defined God as the "infinite and inexhaustible depth and ground of all being." "That depth is what the word God means. And if that word has not much meaning for you, translate it, and speak of the depths of your life, of the source of your being, of your ultimate concern, of what you take seriously without any reservation."[15]

In a series of books in the 1950s, Tillich tirelessly reiterated these concepts. His *Dynamics of Faith* (1957) begins this way: "Faith is the state of being ultimately concerned: the dynamics of faith are the dynamics of man's ultimate concern." He then presents biblical faith as the quintessential instance of a general existential phenomenon: daring to relate oneself to the infinite (whatever that means). The sympathetic reader is flattered to hear that this takes great courage. Tillich explains that "faith is certain in so far as it is an experience of the holy" (whatever that means). But because we are finite beings, a sense of uncertainty haunts this experience, and "the element in faith which accepts this is courage." Over the next few pages he repeats the

---

14. Paul Tillich, *On the Boundary* (New York: Charles Scribner's Sons, 1966), pp. 41, 44, 60-61, 67.

15. Tillich, *The Shaking of the Foundations* (New York: Charles Scribner's Sons, 1948), p. 102.

words "courage" and "risk" — and also "doubt" — many times. Is this existential experience "Christian faith"? The answer is rather paradoxical: the pure, authentic form of Christian faith is semidetached from any account of orthodoxy. True faith kicks against particular creedal forms, though it understands the necessity of a shared symbolic language. Its discomfort with the formulae of corporate orthodoxy is a mark of authenticity. So faith must be "on the boundary" (one of his favorite phrases) between belonging to a community and rejecting its orthodoxy as stifling. Complete belonging in a homogeneous faith community removes the need for "the risk and courage which belong to the act of faith."[16]

This should not be entirely dismissed as existentialist posturing, for there is in authentic Christian faith a tension between submission to a common ideology and skepticism (the "dialogical" dynamic I explored in chapter 4). The problem is that Tillich treats this dynamic as a general human phenomenon rather than something particular to Christian faith. In effect, he exalts "faith" over Christianity and thus secularizes it, because it must be separate from religion in order to be above it. The heroic attitude is one of semidetachment from religion. He presents this move as intensely Protestant, but it is really a denial of the priority of Protestant faith. It exalts an existential attitude (learned from Protestantism but detachable from it) over the particularity of Christianity. Thus he begins an article of 1958: "Being religious means asking passionately the question of the meaning of our existence and being willing to receive answers, even if the answers hurt."[17] Again, the claim to courageous vulnerability obscures the banality of the humanism.

Tillichian faith fetishizes tension, doubt, difficulty, but this is superficial: there is no possibility of a really sharp clash with reason, or one's sinful nature, for faith is an expression of one's natural deepest self, one's real humanity, one's ultimate concern. Despite quoting

16. Paul Tillich, *Dynamics of Faith*, in F. Forrester Church, ed., *The Essential Tillich: An Anthology of the Writings of Paul Tillich* (New York: Macmillan, 1987), pp. 13, 22, 29.

17. Paul Tillich, "The Lost Dimension in Religion," *Saturday Evening Post,* June 14, 1958, in *The Essential Tillich*, p. 1.

figures such as Kierkegaard, Tillich's key fault is to make the question of belief too easy, to extract the scandal from it. His understanding of myth and symbol removes any real otherness from religious language; it is just the expression of an innate capacity: "Man's ultimate concern must be expressed symbolically, because symbolic language alone is able to express the ultimate."[18]

Tillich is perhaps more to blame than Niebuhr is for perpetuating the bad old theological liberalism in midcentury, for he was more extensively concerned with fundamental theology. Instead of admitting the importance of Barth's revolt, he effectively encouraged theology to dismiss it as just another manifestation of organized religion turning inward. And his affirmation of the affinity of Protestantism and liberalism was far too vague (it was too indebted to Troeltsch's conflation of liberal Protestantism and the Enlightenment). Tillich associated theology with a certain cultural mood — an earnest postwar humanism that wanted to affirm both Christianity and liberalism without making any hard choices. Like Niebuhr, he overestimated the strength of liberal Protestant culture, failing to see that liberal Christian allegiance is superficial, that the theologian's task is to strengthen it. He proudly saw his work as a bridge between Christianity and secular humanism, failing to see that this bridge was not keeping two cultures in healthy dialogue but leading people from one side to the other. It encouraged people to suppose that they were Christian enough if they affirmed human existence and were opposed to ecclesiastical control.

On the other hand, Tillich was in some ways an acute analyst of Protestantism. He explained that it was rooted in the protest against idolatry — but that this protest was ultimately self-defeating. Protestantism is suffocated by its sacramental deficiency:

The decrease in sacramental thinking and feeling in the churches of the Reformation and in the American denominations is appall-

---

18. *The Essential Tillich*, p. 41. Also: "Religious symbols . . . open up a level of reality which is otherwise not opened at all, which is hidden" ("Religious Symbols and Our Knowledge of God," *Christian Scholar* [September 1955], in *The Essential Tillich*, p. 49).

ing. . . . [T]he sacraments have lost their spiritual power and are vanishing in the consciousness of most Protestants: the Christ is interpreted as a religious personality and not as the basic sacramental reality, the "New Being." The Protestant protest has rightly destroyed the magical elements in Catholic sacramentalism but has wrongly brought to the verge of disappearance the sacramental foundation of Christianity and with it the religious foundation of the protest itself.[19]

The problem is that Tillich fails to see that his own approach continues the erosion of the sacramental basis of faith by perpetuating humanist assumptions. What he calls "the Protestant principle" is really an assortment of principles dressed as a coherent unity. "It was the Protestant principle" that inspired historical criticism of the Bible and that "enabled liberal theology to realize that Christianity cannot be considered in isolation from the general religious and cultural, psychological and sociological, development of humanity," which "is deadly for ecclesiastical and theological arrogance." Also, it was the Protestant principle that led "orthodox theologians (both old and new)" to assert the "otherness of God against all human pretensions, and to insist on the sinfulness of humanity."[20] This evades the need to think about the conflict between humanist-inclined theology and orthodoxy.

In the end, Tillich must be accused of wanting to found Protestantism on a new kind of rationalism. To present God as an indubitable existential reality, a name for what all humans believe in — whether they know it or not — is stifling to the grammar of authentic faith.

The Sixties

The early 1960s was the high-water mark of liberal Christianity — especially when Roman Catholicism is included in the survey. In America, the election of the first Roman Catholic president, a paragon of clean-

---

19. Tillich, *The Protestant Era* (1957), in *The Essential Tillich*, p. 80.
20. Tillich, *The Protestant Era*, pp. 84, 85.

cut optimism, seemed a major victory for the separation of church and state. "I believe in an America where the separation of church and state is absolute," Kennedy said while campaigning in 1960.[21] Perhaps American liberty was transforming Roman Catholicism, whose leading thinkers largely agreed with Kennedy that the church should not interfere in politics.[22] The launch of the Second Vatican Council added to this impression (its Declaration on Religious Freedom in 1965 seemed to mark a new era, an impression that subsequent popes have tried to repair). Above all, the gospel-based civil rights movement was promising to repair the great impediment to national harmony.

As a student at Pennsylvania's Crozer Theological Seminary and Boston University, Martin Luther King Jr. was influenced by the Social Gospel movement and Niebuhr. He learned to speak to the cultural Protestantism of the nation at large, as well as to his own congregation.[23] His nonviolent tactics won over cautious liberals, and the mainline churches joined the cause. His famous speech of 1963 might be seen as the high point of the progressive Christian era: liberal Protestantism seemed capable of healing the nation's worst wound. The biblical vision of justice and final peace on God's holy mountain was shown to underlie American politics. Major reforming political legislation followed in the next two years. It surely seemed that this religious-based movement was renewing the cultural strength of liberal Protestantism. But the opposite happened: young people were increasingly drawn to secular political activism and away from religious allegiance. Public Christianity became increasingly defined by the religious Right, which was born of resentment at the federal imposition of liberal policies.

21. Quoted in Damon Linker, *The Theocons: Secular America under Siege* (New York: Anchor, 2006), p. 66.

22. The Jesuit John Courtney Murray popularized the view that there is a deep affinity between the American Constitution and Catholic natural law tradition, for which he was indebted to Jacques Maritain.

23. Judging from his writings, King's "theology seems broadly Kantian with biblical overtones. God, freedom, and immortality constitute the explicit articles of faith, with Jesus as little more than a moral example, and the cross a moral symbol" (George Hunsinger, *Disruptive Grace: Studies in the Theology of Karl Barth* [Grand Rapids: Eerdmans, 2000], pp. 3-4).

Partly influenced by the political mood, liberal Protestant theology continued on its humanist course. One must probably agree with Barth that the influence of Bonhoeffer's prison writing was detrimental, at least to thinkers of this period. It emboldened them to put forward simplistic accounts of nonliteral belief and of secularization. It allowed them to endow the thought of Bultmann and Tillich with the aura of that very rare thing — a recent Protestant martyr.

Bishop John A. T. Robinson's popular book *Honest to God* (1963) was an expression of this trend. It convincingly combines the three thinkers — Bultmann, Bonhoeffer, and Tillich — in a common position. Their concern, Robinson explains, is to make the gospel available to those who cannot accept supernatural belief. Echoing Bultmann in particular, he argues that insistence on supernatural belief is a false form of "scandal"; it gets in the way of the real matter of Christian commitment. And he explains that Bonhoeffer seems to agree, in his remarks about treating "religion" as Paul treated circumcision. But what does Robinson present as the real scandal, the real difficult essence of Christian identity? Lacking the Teutonic existentialist rhetoric of Bultmann and Tillich, he puts the emphasis on morality, or the spiritualized morality of total self-giving love, in imitation of "the man for others," as Bonhoeffer referred to Christ. The conviction that love is the deepest reality

> takes an almost impossible amount of believing. It is frankly incredible *unless* the love revealed in Jesus is indeed the nature of ultimate reality, unless he is a window through the surface of things into *God*. Christianity stands or falls by revelation, by Christ as the disclosure of the final truth not merely about human nature (that we might accept relatively easily), but about all nature and all reality.[24]

This is how faith should be understood: as the willingness to see love as the ultimate reality. Christ is the model of this, but supernatural

---

24. John A. T. Robinson, *Honest to God* (Louisville: Westminster John Knox Press, 2002), p. 128. Hereafter, page references to this work appear in parentheses in the text.

belief in the resurrection or any other miraculous event is not necessary. The problem is that Robinson leaves it unclear why Christ is
needed: surely one can claim to believe in love as the ultimate reality
without him. Hence such faith is not really distinguishable from a humanism that happens to have a high opinion of Jesus (except in its
claim that it retains the "depth" of traditional religious belief). The
true otherness of Christian faith needs *cultic* definition: it rests on
particular linguistic and ritual practices. Robinson is wary of such
particularity, and he wants to present worship in humanistic terms.
The Eucharist is an exceptionally strong expression of "communion,
community-life." It reveals fellowship as "the ground and restorer of
our whole being" (p. 86). Robinson implies that to focus on the particular content of the rite is a barrier to grasping the rite's real meaning.
Like Tillich, he presents Christianity's real meaning in general humanist terms but retains just enough references to God and Christ to
seem motivated by a new sort of Christian piety.

Only on one issue does Robinson's liberalism pass from "bad"
to "good" (to use the schema of our introduction): his critique of traditional religious morality. Jesus opposes the rule-based morality of
the Jews and teaches the absolute authority of love. "It is, of course, a
highly dangerous ethic and the representatives of supranaturalistic
legalism will, like the Pharisees, always fear it. Yet I believe it is the
only ethic for 'man come of age'" (p. 117).

Robinson's motivation seems to have been anxiety at the prospect of a mass exodus from the Church of England. He wanted to keep
skeptics within the fold, to tell them that their attraction to the morality of Jesus mattered more than their difficulties with supernatural
belief (and organized religion). He wanted to tell them that "while
they imagine they have rejected the Gospel, they have in fact largely
been put off by a particular way of thinking about the world which
quite legitimately they find incredible" (p. 8). Such critics of traditional forms are very necessary "defenders of the Faith" (p. 9). This is
grounded in a belief in the established nature of the Church of England: "Anything that helps to keep its frontiers open to the world as
the Church of the nation should be strengthened and reformed: anything that turns it in upon itself as a religious organization or episco-

palian sect I suspect and deplore" (pp. 139-40). Robinson was far from alone in his belief that the retention and renewal of establishment entailed this affirmation of semi-Christian humanism.[25]

Robinson's book helped to launch an American trend. The next two years saw similar books by Gabriel Vahanian and Paul van Buren, and then Harvey Cox. In *The Secular City* (1965), Cox argues that "secularization . . . is the loosing of the world from religious and quasi-religious understandings of itself, the dispelling of all closed world-views, the breaking of all supernatural myths and sacred symbols . . . [it] is man turning his attention away from worlds beyond and toward this world and this time." There is a passing acknowledgment that "secularization" can have more limited reference — to "the passing of certain responsibilities from ecclesiastical to political authorities." But this is assumed to be one aspect of the wider phenomenon: "Secularization implies a historical process, almost certainly irreversible, in which society and culture are delivered from tutelage to religious control and closed metaphysical world-views." Christianity must learn to affirm this process: "The Gospel . . . is a call to a mature secularity. It is not a call to man to abandon the problems of this world but an invitation to accept the full weight of the world's problems as the gift of its Maker." But Cox leaves it unclear why we should persist with even a demythologized religious vocabulary. On what grounds, other than inherited prejudice, can it be supposed that talk of Jesus is particularly worthwhile? Cox offers the paradoxical idea that only the gospel can teach us rigorous secularism: the church "will continue to be a cultural exorcist, casting out the mythical meanings that obscure the realities of life and hinder human action."[26]

The proposal is not entirely absurd: in recent years a few atheists

---

25. In an article on the radical Anglican theology of the sixties, Mark Chapman explains that "English Bonhoefferism" tried to move away from the institutional church in order to make English Christianity truly integrated into society. It was "a kind of clergy-led anticlericalism" that tried to reinvent the tradition of establishment for a new era (Chapman, "English Bonhoefferism," in Jane Garnett et al., eds., *Redefining Christian Britain: Post 1945 Perspectives* [London: SCM, 2007] p. 112).

26. Harvey Cox, *The Secular City* (Toronto: Macmillan, 1965), pp. 2, 19, 20, 83-84, 162.

have praised Christianity as a crucial resource for a humane radical-ism that sees through the myths of modernity (Eagleton, Zizek). But, of course, Christianity could not be sustained by this kind of position; it would be eroded by the logic of "secularization," which denies the privileging of any narrative rooted in mythical language. Another fla-vor of secular-friendly theology emerged at that same time. Thomas J. J. Altizer's book *The Gospel of Christian Atheism* (1966) expanded an aspect of Hegel's thought: the death of Jesus marks the Christian God's move from transcendence to immanence. Nietzsche's procla-mation of the death of God should be seen as the key to a new Chris-tian humanism. Both Robinson's and Altizer's books are just dated footnotes to Feuerbach. But this approach was able to claim an aura of freshness, due to its ability to draw on new forms of secular philos-ophy. In the 1980s, Don Cupitt and Mark C. Taylor continued in this theologically barren direction — with "deconstruction" now supply-ing the semblance of freshness.

The mid-1960s saw a revival of interest in historical eschatology, though it was mostly detached from religious-socialist politics. It was partly influenced by the Old Testament scholar Gerhard von Rad. At midcentury he emphasized the historical-eschatological character of the religion of Israel, its expectation of the future action of God, his transformation of history. This emphasis helped to inspire the theolo-gies of Pannenberg and Moltmann in the 1960s. The single most in-fluential book of the movement was Moltmann's *Theology of Hope: On the Ground and the Implications of a Christian Eschatology* (1964). Moltmann was a Barthian who felt that Barth had moved too far from his early eschatological emphasis. He was influenced by the messi-anic Jewish thinker Ernst Bloch, who proposed a utopian form of Marxism. With some cause, Moltmann felt that this was the aspect of theology that could speak to the young idealists of the day, and that it should be foregrounded.

> From first to last, and not merely in the epilogue, Christianity is eschatology, is hope, forward looking and forward moving, and therefore also revolutionizing and transforming the present. The eschatological is not one element *of* Christianity, but is the me-

dium of Christian faith as such, the key in which everything in it is set, the glow that suffuses everything here in the dawn of an expected new day.

Moltmann criticizes Bultmann for reducing eschatology to an existential idea, and Barth for consigning it to a "transcendental eternity."[27] But he was predictably vague on the relationship of eschatology to reason and history. His book reflects a desire for theology to be fully involved in the political idealism of the day. The hope for a better world should not be left to secularists and Marxists but should be absolutely central to the Christian vision. It also reflects frustration at the difficulty of communicating this vision. With the youth of the world dreaming of love and peace, it should have been easy; but in fact all the old conceptual problems remained. And it was becoming clear that reactionary theopolitics was far more attractive to most people.

The culture war that emerged in America at the end of the 1960s was symptomatic of the failure of liberal Christianity to make itself understood, to present itself as simultaneously Christian and liberal. The basic claim of the religious Right was that liberal reforms were driven by a secularist agenda, a desire to weaken the role of Christianity in public life. The reality, of course, was complex: the liberal mood was largely Christian-based, and yet it did strongly overlap with secular liberalism — as authentic liberal Christianity should. Martin Luther King Jr., with his passionate public preaching, was hardly a secular figure, yet he did insist that the pursuit of justice should be framed in terms of individual rights rather than in terms of a religious conception of society. He was clearest on this point in the public letter he wrote from the Birmingham city jail in 1963. In effect, he affirmed secular liberalism as the proper framework within which to pursue the biblical goal of social justice. He was implicitly affirming the Supreme Court's recent decision to remove religion from public schools. Over the next decade, the Court would continue on its reformist course, culminating in the *Roe v. Wade* decision of 1973. As I

---

27. Jürgen Moltmann, *Theology of Hope: On the Ground and the Implications of a Christian Eschatology*, trans. James W. Leitch (London: SCM, 1967), pp. 16, 39.

suggested with respect to Niebuhr, there was a failure of liberal Christianity to speak up at this point and to clarify that the compatibility of the gospel with political and cultural freedom was central to the American idea.

Instead, the religious Right was allowed to dominate the discussion — in the intellectual as well as the popular realm. It was allowed to drum home the message that Christian values were being dismantled by secular liberalism. Billy Graham was the drummer-in-chief: it was he who transformed a neoevangelical movement into a huge political force. This movement was galvanized by resentment at the civil rights movement and the federal government's backing of it; but naturally the movement could not directly voice such resentment. Defense of prayer in public schools became the ostensible rallying point, and then abortion. In 1968, President Richard Nixon taught the Republican Party how to benefit from all this anger, and a new theopolitical landscape was formed. Could a liberal Christian countermovement not have challenged this restructuring? The problem was that the core liberal causes, civil rights and the separation of church and state, were more secular than religious. Also, a more radical strain of liberalism began with opposition to the war in Vietnam (in which King himself was a major player in the last two years of his life). So liberal Christianity was subsumed by the secular movements that it rightly supported. To some extent this was inevitable, and yet it was exacerbated by the rise of humanist theology.

This continued with "political theology," a term coined by Johann Baptist Metz in 1966. And soon after that, the movement for eschatological theology took Roman Catholic form: liberation theology. Gutiérrez's A Theology of Liberation: History, Politics and Salvation (1971) acknowledges the importance to his project of "the rediscovery of the eschatological dimension in theology" in recent German thought. It combines Marxism with liberal Protestant-style suspicion of the traditional church: "Today the seriousness and scope of the process which we call liberation is such that Christian faith and the Church are being radically challenged. They are being asked to show what significance they have for a human task which has reached adulthood." The echo of Bonhoeffer is sustained: "To announce the Gospel is to proclaim that the love of God is present in the historical becoming of mankind."[28] Like Bloch and Moltmann, Gutiérrez implies that human history is innately liberation-shaped. Even theologians who are highly sympathetic to socialism have tended to see liberation theology as a wrong turning; its strident modernism strengthened the hand of religious conservatives.[29]

The effect of this movement was rather paradoxical, given its bold universalism: it contributed to the rise of identity politics in theology. Mainstream theology was not transformed by such radicalism, but (perhaps rather patronizingly) began to reserve space for the voices of the marginalized at the seminar table: black theology and feminist theology became established presences just as a coherent liberal theology was collapsing, and gay theology would soon join them.

The early 1970s is perhaps when the demise of liberal theology became obvious: secular-affirming radicalism was looking tired, and as we shall see, there was a new world elsewhere. It was also becoming clear that liberal Christian denominations were losing members very fast. And, as we shall see in the following chapter, a coherent alternative to liberal theology was forming.

A useful perspective on the wilting of liberal theology comes from the late novelist John Updike. Many of the characters in his early fiction have been raised in liberal Protestantism, but find it inadequate. Now that most of their peers do not believe, they need a stronger account of why they themselves should. Religion has lost its force as a social duty, so it must become some kind of countercultural personal commitment. And the liberal version is not suited to such a role; its humanist ethos is too close to secular normality. Reverend Eccles, the Episcopalian priest in *Rabbit, Run,* is an example of this. A rival minister with Barthian tendencies tells Eccles that people need

28. Gustavo Gutiérrez, *A Theology of Liberation: History, Politics and Salvation,* trans. Sr. Caridad Inda and John Eagleson (London: SCM, 1974), pp. 10, xi, 268.

29. George Hunsinger is a good example. All recent liberation movements, he says, "forced the church to choose between progressive politics and traditional faith.... Each failed to see that, confronted with a forced option, the church will inevitably choose not to abandon traditional faith" (Hunsinger, *Disruptive Grace,* p. 3).

to hear God's word, not just receive humanitarian care. In a couple of later novels the narrator explicitly praises Barth's robust style — as a token of the kind of faith worth retaining. "I became a Barthian in reaction against [my father's] liberalism, a smiling, fumbling shadow of German Pietism," one recounts.[30] Another character finds his wavering faith revived by one of Barth's books. He marvels at Barth's "magnificent seamless integrity and energy in this realm of prose — the specifically Christian — usually conspicuous for intellectual limpness and dishonesty."[31] Part of Updike's agenda, into the 1980s, was to announce that the era of cultural Christianity's gently conversing with humanism was over. A starker decision between belief and unbelief had to be faced.

30. John Updike, *A Month of Sundays* (Harmondsworth, UK: Penguin, 1976), p. 24.

31. John Updike, *Roger's Version* (Harmondsworth, UK: Penguin, 1986), p. 40.

TEN

Postliberals

─══◦◦◦═──

Of course, liberal Protestantism was not routed by a single, coherent force. From the 1960s, Barth's stock steadily rose in the academic realm. In the wider cultural realm, liberal Christian idealism ceded ground to the religious Right — and, at the same time, to secularism. Other factors include a revival of Roman Catholic and Anglo-Catholic theology, rooted in the early twentieth century. Another was the rise of philosophy that criticized Enlightenment assumptions, which was related to the "linguistic turn" in philosophy. These intellectual forces enabled theologians to put new emphasis on the church as the site of distinctive cultural and linguistic practices. In the 1970s a new perspective was emerging that said that Barth had been right to reject liberal methodology and to root theology in its distinctive subject matter, but that his positive vision for theology should be supplemented by this new focus on Christian practice. This was a major revolution that changed the landscape of theology; and, of course, it overlapped with the secular postmodernist assault on Enlightenment rationality. This was a highly positive revolution that enabled theology to reject the stubborn errors of liberal Protestantism and to acknowledge the primacy of ritual practice. But it had a blind spot: the "good" side of the liberal Protestant vision became even more neglected than before.

Theology in the second half of the twentieth century was determined by developments beyond the habitual scope of Protestantism. An important factor was a new overlap of Catholicism and art, which was rooted in an appreciation of the centrality of liturgy and sacramentalism. This was related to the modernist revolution in the arts, especially its interest in ritual, from Wagner's neopagan operas to the Celtic ritualism of W. B. Yeats. And a new chapter had begun with Picasso's fascination with African masks, beginning in 1907. This primitivism challenged the notion of high art: maybe all authentic art was rooted in basic human needs (Freud's new approach to anthropology powerfully reinforced the suggestion). Maybe the new science of anthropology could do more than explain the exotic practices of "savages"; maybe it could show that civilized humans are not so different, that all culture conforms to primitive structures. This perspective was taken more seriously after World War I. Paris became fascinated by the primitivism of jazz music, and a related primitivism marked Stravinsky's *Rite of Spring* in 1913. In literature, *The Waste Land* introduced a sort of primitivism to serious poetry: Eliot drew on anthropological studies, including James Frazer's *The Golden Bough.*

This artistic trend slowly seeped into religious reflection. Of course, Catholics and Anglo-Catholics had been reflecting on ritual practice throughout Christian history; but a new perspective entered such reflections around the 1920s, when the monastic-based Liturgical Movement contributed to a new emphasis on the Eucharist as the vital essence of the church. Henri de Lubac, for example, argued that Roman Catholic ecclesiology was founded on the Eucharist. At around the same time, Russian Orthodox thinkers such as Florensky were influential in their reflections on their tradition's liturgical basis and its relationship to art, and Anglo-Catholicism followed suit.

In Britain the cultural presence of Roman Catholicism was rising from the 1930s, partly thanks to G. K. Chesterton, whose engaging style made Catholic sensibility seem to be a central aspect of Englishness. With Whiggish assumptions still strong, the indirectness of literature provided a way in for Catholicism: the rarified aspect of Catholic sacramentalism was being celebrated by Evelyn Waugh, and a grittier side by Graham Greene. Greene's novel *The End of the Affair* (1951) contains an excellent passage on the otherness of Catholic sacramentalism. The protagonist enters a Catholic church and is taken aback by the sheer physicality of its theology: on one level the images seem cheap, tacky, but, on another level, they speak of religious devotion being a real practical force in the world. Another influential Catholic convert was the artist Eric Gill, who in turn influenced the Welsh artist and poet David Jones. Jones saw a deep connection between modernist art and Catholic sacramentalism: "The insistence that a painting must be a *thing* and not the impression of something has an affinity with what the Church said of the Mass."[1] His essays of the 1950s reflect on material sign-making as the common ground of art, religion, and morality.[2] He notes that the Catholic Church "commits its adherents to the body and the embodied" and has a "certain mistrust of the unembodied concept."[3] This perspective would soon become central to theology — by means of philosophy.

After Wittgenstein

Perhaps the most important — certainly the most enigmatic — contributor to late twentieth-century theology was Ludwig Wittgenstein. In the decades after his death (in 1951), Wittgenstein's philosophy, or an aspect of it, began to percolate into theological consciousness, and it proved to be a powerful acid against liberal Protestant assumptions.

Before World War I, when he came to Cambridge to study under Bertrand Russell, Wittgenstein seemed to share the logical positiv-

1. David Jones, quoted in Rowan Williams, *Grace and Necessity* (London: Continuum, 2005), p. 59.
2. With his idea of the moral life as "an act of gratuitous sign-making, he has turned away from both legalism and subjectivism in morality and opened up a new and tantalizing perspective on behaviour as a kind of art, a search for forms that will uncover the interconnectedness of reality" (Williams, *Grace and Necessity,* p. 89).
3. David Jones, "A Christmas Message 1960," in Jones, *The Dying Gaul and Other Writings* (London: Faber & Faber, 1978), p. 167.

ists' dismissal of religion as meaningless. In fact, however, he was already drawn to the idea that religion was the soul's refuge from fear, anxiety, and despair. This intensified during the war and during his time as a schoolteacher in Austria. Influenced by Tolstoy, Kierkegaard, and Dostoyevsky, he sometimes idealized a childlike form of Christian faith, and he often wrote prayers in his journal. At root, he was drawn to the Lutheran idea of faith having the power to exorcise demonic anxieties — that is, to be psychologically helpful. Returning to Cambridge in 1929, he pursued work on the cultural basis of language and a critique of the metaphysical inheritance of philosophy; these subjects were closely related to his thoughts on religion. Many of his recorded comments on religion are sharply critical of conventional apologetics, which claims to defend religion rationally, and of "philosophy of religion," which stands in judgment on religious truth-claims. There are strong echoes of the fideistic tradition of Luther, Pascal, and Kierkegaard: that is, faith is not the product of reasoning but is a response to authority. But Wittgenstein leaves it unclear whether he identifies with this tradition or is simply an interested onlooker.

Partly what makes Wittgenstein's religious thought so difficult to assess is that this existentialist-fideistic theme seems somewhat at odds with his wider, more public thesis about the social and practical nature of language. Or at least the two themes are left unintegrated. His insight into the origin of meaning in shared cultural practices was partly influenced by his reading of anthropology. In 1931 he read Frazer's *The Golden Bough* and was annoyed by the author's rationalist assumptions, his determination to explain the meaning of primitive rituals from a supposedly higher viewpoint. He was spurred into imagining the origin of language in basic cultural practices, or "language games." This was central to his anti-idealist, antimetaphysical agenda: showing that the Cartesian ego was a deeply misleading fiction. It obscures the fact that all meaning is first public and social. Individual thinking is an echo of this, a secondary phenomenon. Language is rooted in meaning-making activities. Much of Wittgenstein's thought is expressed in a note he wrote at the end of his life: he wrote that he wanted to see man as an animal, as a primitive being to which one grants instinct but not ratiocination. As a creature in a primitive state. Any logic good enough for a primitive means of communication needs no apology from us. Language did not emerge from some kind of ratiocination.[4]

Elsewhere he says: "Man is a ceremonious animal."[5] Wittgenstein can seem like the Picasso of philosophy in that he showed primitive communication to be secretly at the heart of civilization. Philosophy is the last aspect of civilization that wants to admit this, for it claims to operate by means of disembodied reason. It must revolutionize its self-understanding and analyze its own urge to escape from basic bodily reality. (Nietzsche had made a similar case, but it was obscured by the fervent rhetoric with which he announced it and his assumption that a particular Promethean narrative was the natural response to the insight.)

The impact on theology is a radical debunking of the whole tradition of treating God as primarily an object of thought, who might, if thinking deems it appropriate, be worshiped. God, as an abstract entity, is epiphenomenal; the practices that generate the idea of God are what is fundamental. Therefore, "Christianity is not a doctrine, not, I mean, a theory about what has happened and will happen to the human soul, but a description of something that actually takes place in human life. For 'consciousness of sin' is a real event."[6] As Fergus Kerr, one of Wittgenstein's most acute theological interpreters, says, "It is because people exult and lament, sing for joy, bewail their sins and so on, that they are able, eventually, to have thoughts about God. Worship is not the result but the precondition of believing in God."[7] In a stunning moving of the goalposts, the question "Does God exist?" be-

---

4. Wittgenstein, *On Certainty*, ed. G. E. M. Anscombe and G. H. von Wright (Oxford: Blackwell, 1969), p. 475.

5. Wittgenstein, *Remarks on Fraser's* Golden Bough, ed. Rush Rhees, trans. A. C. Miles and R. Rhees (Retford: Brynmill, 1979), p. 7.

6. Wittgenstein, *Culture and Value*, ed. G. H. von Wright, in collaboration with Heikki Nyman; trans. Peter Winch (Oxford: Blackwell, 1980), p. 28.

7. Fergus Kerr, *Theology After Wittgenstein* (Oxford: Blackwell, 1986), p. 183.

comes misguided. The only intelligent response to religion is to acknowledge that it is a complex cultural practice. To tackle it at the level of abstract ideas is inept, for it happens elsewhere.

This has allowed theologians to take an *anthropological* view of Christianity, as something rooted in the primary speech-forms and ritual actions of worship. Christianity is a cultural-linguistic tradition; theology reflects on it, "describes" it. But where does this new conception take us? Does it help us understand the complexity of Christian tradition, or does it subtly nudge us toward too simplistic a view? Is there a danger of too strong a location of the essence of Christianity in "the practice of the community"? If each community constructs its own account of truth, does the practice of the community become beyond criticism?[8] Is it not a paradoxical aspect of *this* cultural tradition that it criticizes its own cultural expression? Also, can this model do justice to the theme of tension between faith and reason? Or does it imply that every tradition is its own form of rationality? If meaning is generated by immersion in a community, then the irrationality of faith melts away. The irrational-sounding talk of faith is just another way of being in the world. To say "Jesus is risen" is just a sign of one's participation in this linguistic community. (It is ironic that the cultural-linguistic approach is often called "Wittgensteinian fideism," because it is actually at odds with the fideistic tradition, which is centered on the individual's defiance of reason rather than the community's claim to constitute its own version of reason.) I suggest that most theological uses of Wittgenstein have evaded these complexities and have pointed toward a kind of ecclesial foundationalism.

During the 1970s, Wittgenstein's thought became a steadily growing presence in theology, largely thanks to some English Roman Catholic thinkers and to some theologians at Yale. The latter were also focused on Barth: they deeply admired his rejection of liberal apologetics, but they were a bit detached from his dogmatic approach. For a while the category of narrative was central to their

8. Wittgenstein "strives to show that neither feeling nor reason but *action* is the foundational thing" (Kerr, *Theology After Wittgenstein*, p. 158). Translated into theological terms, this might become a defense of what the church does.

reframing of theology, but the underlying issue was the importing of Wittgenstein's ideas on language and culture. In the 1980s this approach became increasingly central, and one mark of this was George Lindbeck's book *The Nature of Doctrine: Religion and Theology in a Postliberal Age*. It proposed a new view of religious doctrine, distinct from both traditional propositionalism and the "experiential-expressive" approach of liberalism: the new "cultural-linguistic" approach sees doctrines as "communally authoritative rules of discourse, attitude, and action."[9] In the new approach, which is "consonant . . . with the anthropological, sociological, and philosophical studies by which it has been for the most part inspired . . . religions are seen as comprehensive interpretative schemes, usually embodied in myths or narratives and heavily ritualized, which structure human experience and understanding of self and world. . . . Like a culture or language, [a religion] is a communal phenomenon that shapes the subjectivities of individuals rather than being primarily a manifestation of those subjectivities" (pp. 32-33). Doctrines make "intrasystematic rather than ontological truth claims" (p. 80). The new approach is "intratextual": it views the world through the lens of its scriptural text and tradition. "A scriptural world . . . supplies the interpretive framework within which believers seek to live their lives and understand reality" (p. 117). The intratextual model might seem prone to authoritarianism, but in a crucial aside, Lindbeck suggests that it might have more power to resist political violence:

> Liberals start with experience, with an account of the present, and then adjust their vision of the kingdom of God accordingly, while postliberals are in principle committed to doing the reverse. The first procedure makes it easier to accommodate to present trends, whether from the left or the right: Christian fellow travelers of both Nazism and Stalinism generally used liberal methodology to justify their positions. (pp. 125-26)

9. George Lindbeck, *The Nature of Doctrine: Religion and Theology in a Postliberal Age* (Philadelphia: Westminster, 1985), p. 18. Hereafter, page references to this work appear in parentheses in the text.

This approach, he acknowledges, may seem "wholly relativistic: it turns religions, so one can argue, into self-enclosed and incommensurable intellectual ghettos. Associated with this, in the second place, is the fideistic dilemma: it appears that choice between religions is purely arbitrary, a matter of blind faith" (p. 128). This is largely unavoidable, Lindbeck says, yet believers can in a sense argue for their faith by performing it attractively, showing its ability to cope with the complexity of the world. As we shall see, the dominant form of postliberal theology becomes unsatisfied with this and seeks to renew the traditional Catholic approach to faith and reason.

The Communitarian Turn

The 1960s is seen as the decade of the triumph of social liberalism. But, as we have seen, a reaction quickly emerged, most obviously from the religious Right. At the end of that decade of the 1960s, a wider reaction began — in America especially, where many intellectuals began to question liberalism. What chiefly perturbed thinkers was the new profusion of competing claims concerning individual and minority rights. Alongside the religious Right, a more moderate movement emerged, arguing that the rise of secular assumptions was putting the notion of a Christian-based common culture in doubt. Robert Bellah called for a new affirmation of "civil religion," which was the nation's traditional "vital center." Such ideas were largely a rehash of the old cultural Protestantism, but with a new sense of that culture's vulnerability. The old assumption that religion and liberalism were magically fused at America's founding had to be rethought: perhaps secularization had changed liberalism and put it at odds with Christian values. This mood was increased by the *Roe v. Wade* decision in 1973 and the rising strength of civil, women's, and gay rights. Many thinkers began to detect an intrinsic excess — and instability — in liberalism.

On a more theoretical level, the critique of the Enlightenment was becoming more intellectually central, thanks largely to French interpreters of Nietzsche. The concept of liberalism was subjected to new scrutiny. Despite its centrality to the West's self-understanding, in contrast to communism, it was surrounded by an aura of question-ability. Few stepped forward to defend it with the enthusiasm of a John Stuart Mill. One of Britain's foremost public intellectuals, Isaiah Berlin, seemed to give it only two cheers. In an influential essay of 1958, Berlin summed up the problem. Liberalism in the strict sense, "negative liberty," is not a social ideology that people can unite around, he said. It means leaving individuals alone to do what they want, to pursue various — often conflicting — agenda. This "plurality of human values" must be accepted as inevitable: theories that seek to overcome it veer into the dangerous territory of "positive liberty," a strong vision of human liberation that leads to new state oppression. Liberals must modestly settle for "negative liberty," according to Berlin, and guard against the positive aspect of their creed. This is a reworking of Mill's thesis, with a note of realism about incompatible accounts of the good in place of an Enlightenment confidence that all rational agents will desire the general good, defined by utilitarianism. As Berlin put it subsequently, Enlightenment thinkers assume that "reality is a harmonious whole. If this were not so, there is chaos at the heart of things: which is unthinkable."[10] (As discussed with regard to Hegel and Mill, I suggest that the liberal state is necessarily an exercise in positive liberty: it does more than promise to secure individual rights; it tells a story about the positive common ideology that the move away from theocracy brings.)

The problem with "negative liberty," in many eyes, was that it was too close to economic liberalism, and too dismissive of a progressive, egalitarian agenda. It ceded too much ground to thinkers such as Hayek, who argue that economic inequality is a necessary consequence of liberty.[11] This position provoked John Rawls into developing a robustly progressive version of social ethics. In *A Theory of Justice* (1971), he argues that justice is the truly central category for the liberal state: a more just society is a rational objective, in that such a society is what we would all rationally choose if we could lay aside our par-

10. Isaiah Berlin, *Political Ideas in the Romantic Age* (Princeton, NJ: Princeton University Press, 2006), p. 54.

11. Friedrich Hayek, "The Constitution of Liberty" (1960), in Michael J. Sandel, ed., *Liberalism and Its Critics* (Oxford: Blackwell, 1984).

ticular commitments and prejudices and choose from "the original position" or from behind "the veil of ignorance." This conceit provoked others into wide-ranging critiques of philosophical liberalism. They pointed out that, though Rawls claimed to reject philosophical abstraction in favor of a pragmatic approach to social ethics, in practice he renewed Kant's idea of the priority of individual choice. He presupposes the Kantian "notion of a self barren of essential aims and attachments," observes Michael Sandel, "for whom the values and relations we have are the products of choice, the possessions of a self given prior to its ends."[12]

In a later book, *Political Liberalism*, Rawls addresses the question of religion's place in liberal politics more directly. He argues that authentic political discourse, or "public reason," should be intelligible to all citizens and should therefore exclude references to particular religious commitments. Rawls strongly denied that he was advocating "comprehensive" secularism — that is, the privileging of a secular worldview over a religious one. He protested that he was simply sketching rules for the interaction of various contrasting worldviews.[13] But many disagreed, and so he helped to galvanize a theological movement, convinced that liberal neutrality was incipiently secularist.

Alasdair MacIntyre has probably been the most influential proponent of communitarianism. In the 1950s and early 1960s he veered between Marxism and Christianity, and then began formulating a major ethical revisionism. In *After Virtue* (1981) he announced, with prophetic gravitas, that modern ethics lacked substance because it was infected by the Enlightenment belief in abstract rationality, which led to delusions such as human rights: "There are no such rights, and belief in them is one with belief in witches and in unicorns." The cure is

12. Michael J. Sandel, "Liberalism and the Limits of Justice" (1982), in Sandel, *Liberalism and Its Critics*, p. 169.

13. When an interviewer asked whether he was "making a veiled argument for secularism," Rawls strongly denied it: "Consider: there are two kinds of comprehensive doctrines, religious and secular. Those of religious faith will say I give a veiled argument for secularism, and the latter will say I give a veiled argument for religion. I deny both" (Rawls, quoted in Jeffrey Stout, *Democracy and Tradition* [Princeton, NJ: Princeton University Press, 2004], p. 76).

to understand that all meaning is rooted in the particular stories that cultures tell: "Mythology, in its original sense, is at the heart of things." Coherent morality is firmly rooted in a particular cultural context, with a generally agreed narrative of "the good," which is reflected in shared practices as well as narratives. The Aristotelian model of moral thought, centered on the pursuit of virtue, was abandoned in modernity in favor of universal abstractions. The notion that we can shed narrative particularity and escape "into a realm of entirely universal maxims, which belong to man as such . . . is an illusion and an illusion with painful consequences."

The Enlightenment inevitably failed to construct a robust social morality out of abstract concepts; the natural result was Nietzsche's manic individualism. Modern moral discourse cannot admit this: it tries to keep faith with the Enlightenment project and pretends that the lack of a shared narrative tradition does not matter. In fact, however, only a sort of shadowy, unreal moral discourse is possible: "In any society where government does not express or represent the moral community of the citizens, but is instead a set of institutional arrangements for imposing a bureaucratized unity on a society which lacks genuine moral consensus, the nature of political obligation becomes systematically unclear."[14] Ethical debates on abortion, for example, are futile, for resolution could only come from a cultural unity that is lacking.[15] Authentic moral thought must spurn this flawed discourse, must refuse to take its concepts seriously. Like Saint Benedict amid the barbarians, it must affirm smaller forms of community in which the primacy of shared character-forming practices can be affirmed. Essentially, *After Virtue* offers a generalized quasi-religious critique of individualism, of the self "to which the notion of authority is alien and repugnant, so that appeals to authority appear irrational."[16]

After Virtue contains no clear and explicit account of liberalism.

14. Alasdair MacIntyre, *After Virtue: A Study in Moral Theory* (Notre Dame, IN: University of Notre Dame Press, 1981), pp. 67, 201, 206, 236.

15. Jeffrey Stout objects that many modern ethical disputes that seemed interminable have been resolved, such as the abolition of slavery (Stout, *Democracy and Tradition*, p. 123).

16. MacIntyre, *After Virtue*, p. 41.

MacIntyre's next book, *Whose Justice? Which Rationality?* (1988), has a chapter on the issue: there he sees liberalism as the quest for liberation from tradition by means of universal reason. To some extent, it paradoxically becomes a tradition in its own right. But at base it is the philosophical acid of authentic tradition. Is there not much that is good about modern liberal society? Yes, says MacIntyre, but only because the older tradition lives on in various ways: most people may accept "the assumptions of the dominant liberal individualist forms of public life, but [draw] in different areas of their lives upon a variety of tradition-generated resources of thought and action, transmitted from a variety of familial, religious, educational, and other social and cultural sources."[17] This account of liberalism occludes the largely religious emergence of the liberal state, preferring to assume that liberalism is defined by philosophical universalism. This move has become axiomatic in intellectual history, and it has made "liberalism" hard to defend.

Partly influenced by MacIntyre, the Lutheran (and later Roman Catholic) writer Richard John Neuhaus attempted to launch a more theologically serious version of the religious Right. His book *The Naked Public Square: Religion and Democracy in America* (1984) argues that secularism is not just the absence of religion but a positive ideology seeking to remove religion from American public life. The decline of the mainline Protestant churches has allowed this ideology huge new power; thus America's traditional Christian character has to be reasserted. This task could not be left to Protestant fundamentalism, which was too focused on subjective piety. A broader coalition is necessary, and it needs to include Roman Catholicism. Without such opposition, secularism "will lead — not next year, maybe not in twenty years, but all too soon — to totalitarianism." To Neuhaus, the dominant interpretation of the separation of church and state, such as what John F. Kennedy had endorsed in 1960, opens the door to secular liberal usurpation. Religious allegiance must be an unashamed political force, for only religion offers a full and coherent account of the social good.

17. MacIntyre, *Whose Justice? Which Rationality?* (Notre Dame, IN: University of Notre Dame Press, 1988), p. 397.

Neuhaus calls for Christians to show loyalty to America's special role in the world, and to capitalism; he even commends a new "Constantianism."[18] Through his subsequent journalistic work, Neuhaus has been one of the most influential religious writers of recent years.[19] He might be called the spiritual father of George W. Bush's administration.

More politically cautious versions of communitarianism were offered in a collection edited by Robert Bellah entitled *Habits of the Heart* (1985), which noted with some alarm that Americans were fast moving toward individualistic relativism: "Utility replaces duty, self-expression unseats authority."[20] Secular sociology was also turning in a communitarian direction: the questioning of liberal individualism that had been provoked by the late 1960s came to fruition in the 1980s. And theology experienced this turn perhaps more intensely than did any other discipline: whereas secular liberalism still found strong defenders, the same cannot be said of liberal theology.

Stanley Hauerwas has developed such communitarianism in a distinctive direction, and his engaging, straight-talking style has made him the most effective exponent of postliberal theology since the 1980s. He is among the most influential theologians of recent decades because, uniquely among academics, he combines intellectual weight with an accessible reforming radicalism. He was influenced by Barth, Wittgenstein, and MacIntyre — and then by the Anabaptist pacifist theologian John Howard Yoder. Hauerwas decided that pacifism is central to the distinctive witness of the church (a decision that was influenced by Vietnam).[21] He has brought a radical reformation dimension to postliberalism, in which the church must be suspicious

18. Richard John Neuhaus, *The Naked Public Square: Religion and Democracy in America* (Grand Rapids: Eerdmans, 1984), pp. 259, 172.

19. Neuhaus founded the journal *First Things*, which is premised on the need for evangelicals and Catholics to form a common front against secular liberalism and which has renewed the religious Right in recent years (in 2012, two Catholics and a Mormon contended for the Republican Party's nomination).

20. Robert N. Bellah, ed., *Habits of the Heart: Individualism and Commitment in American Life* (Berkeley: University of California Press, 1985), p. 77.

21. Vietnam was "extended training necessary for the development of a more critical attitude toward the government of the United States" (Hauerwas, *Performing the Faith: Bonhoeffer and the Practice of Nonviolence* [Grand Rapids: Brazos, 2004], p. 204).

of all worldly politics and must present its character-forming community as the authentic political practice. American Christians have a particular duty to disown the spuriously Christian superpower they inhabit. The precondition for thinking clearly about the church is a rejection of the ideology of liberalism, which is particularly ingrained in the American story:

> In the absence of any shared history we [Americans] seemed to lack anything in common that could serve as a basis for societal co-operation. Fortunately, liberalism provided a philosophical account of society designed to deal with exactly that problem: A people do not need a shared history; all they need is a system of rules that will constitute procedures for resolving disputes as they pursue their various interests.[22]

So Hauerwas applies the cultural-linguistic approach, learned from Wittgenstein, and the virtue ethics of Aristotle (and MacIntyre) to a radicalized ecclesiology. He goes subtly further than Lindbeck: not only is the language of faith and doctrine particular to the Christian community, but the truth of the Christian idiom must be borne out by the practical political otherness of the church. To say that God redeems the world in Jesus Christ is empty rhetoric unless it is spoken from within a community that actually embodies the new ethic of the kingdom. For Lindbeck, the cultural-linguistic approach does not challenge the conventional idea that the church communicates an ideal of social perfection that it cannot realize. Of course its speech must be backed up by a certain way of life, but this way of life need not be understood as radically distinct from fallen normality. Under the influence of MacIntyre and Yoder, Hauerwas finds this insufficient. The Christian language of absoluteness, of eschatology, of salvation, must be rooted in concrete otherness. What matters is the nurturing of practices that make a concrete difference. Without this difference, Christian talk is dubiously abstract:

22. Hauerwas, *A Community of Character: Toward a Constructive Christian Social Ethic* (Notre Dame, IN: University of Notre Dame Press, 1982), p. 78.

It is my thesis that questions of the truth or falsity of Christian convictions cannot even be addressed until Christians recover the church as a political community necessary for our salvation. What Christians *believe* about the universe, the nature of human existence, or even God does not, cannot, and should not save. Our beliefs, or better our convictions, only make sense as they are embodied in a political community we call church.[23]

It is not enough for the church to speak of salvation: it must constitute it. "The church's main task is to be what we are — God's salvation" (p. 44). And that means being different from "the world." As we saw in chapter 1, the original Anabaptists rejected normal worldly politics in favor of creating a pure community that refuses allegiance to the state. Hauerwas affirms one aspect of such purist separatism (pacifism); on the other hand, he affirms a more mainstream ecclesiology. (He retained his Methodist allegiance for most of his career, gradually moving to Anglicanism; he also emphasizes his strong affinity with Roman Catholicism.) His consistent point has been that liberalism has lulled the church into forgetting that it must be a community of political distinctiveness. "[T]he cultural establishment of Christianity in liberal societies necessarily forced Christians to divorce their convictions from their practices so that we lost our intelligibility as Christians" (p. 24). The churches fatally assumed that liberalism was the modern political expression of Christianity. Because the liberal state allows freedom of religion, and promises to secure social peace, the churches gave it their blessing. The churches thus conspired in the divinization of the modern liberal state: its promise of freedom makes its authority absolute and makes dissenting viewpoints seem illegitimate, threatening.

The principle of freedom of religion is a "subtle temptation," according to Hauerwas. It has led American Christians to think that "their primary religious duty to the state was and is to provide support

---

23. Hauerwas, *After Christendom? How the Church Is to Behave If Freedom, Justice, and a Christian Nation Are Bad Ideas* (Nashville: Abingdon, 1991), p. 26. Hereafter, page references to this work appear in parentheses in the text.

and justification for the state that guarantees freedom of religion" (p. 70). On paper, the state that allows freedom of religion hugely limits its own power — by inviting various forms of Christian critique. But in practice it cunningly induces Christians to forget their nature as a distinctive political community. "We thus become tolerant, allowing our convictions to be relegated to the realm of the private" (p. 71). Churches allowed the liberal Christian state to assume the aura of superchurch, which actual churches should serve. And they consequently lack the power to resist the ideology of liberal individualism, to define Christian identity in contrast to it. "The inability of Protestant churches in America to maintain any sense of authority over the lives of their members is one of the most compelling signs that freedom of religion has resulted in the corruption of Christians who now believe they have the right religiously 'to make up their own minds'" (p. 88). This "shocking" flirtation with reaction is a regular feature of Hauerwas's writing.

The solution is for Christianity to be converted to radical communitarianism and to see every issue in terms of the strengthening of its particular social ethic. For example, it must reject "the presuppositions of political liberalism that assumes sex is fundamentally a private and personal matter" (p. 118). And the idea of liberal neutrality must also be opposed in education. "The very omission of religion from the curriculum of schools in the name of a fictional neutrality speaks loudly about what a society believes and wants its children to believe" (p. 143). Christians must not accept the idea that, whereas science is true, their religion "is an opinion held by some people but not part of the public truth" (p. 143). Such sentiments seem to put him in the ranks of the religious Right, railing against the secular liberal agenda. To resist being put in such company, Hauerwas can produce his pacifism: he does not want a return to stronger establishment, he protests, but a fuller separation of the church from both nationalism *and* liberalism. He seems to have an ideal of Christianity as a robust minority religion, like orthodox Judaism, for example, which rejects dominant liberal norms without incurring the suspicion that it is plotting theocracy. (One of Hauerwas's books, *Resident Aliens,* begins with a direct comparison between the Jewish and Christian predicaments: Christians should learn to resist "assimilation" — as Jews do.)

What is compelling about Hauerwas's position is that it opposes both liberalism and the conventional antiliberalism that calls for a return to a Christian nation. He claims to reject both the old ideal of Christendom and the secular liberal order that has largely replaced it. The church has a clear political vision, distinct from both of these orders, he says. Does this third way exist? It only exists on the basis of the Radical Reformers' rejection of *all politics*. It is only possible to reject both Christendom and the liberal state if you deny the authority of any state and insist that all allegiance should go to the church. There is something unreal about that. In reality, Christianity, being the dominant religion in the West, does not really have the option of claiming minority status. In reality, it must choose between claiming the right to be culturally empowered and affirming the liberal state. There are different ways of opting for each of these, but the basic choice must be made. In real life, a rejection of liberalism means a vote for reaction. Those who claim to reject both Christendom and liberalism are in danger of becoming the "useful idiots" of reactionary religion.[24] For at root there is a choice between desiring the separation of church and state and desiring some form of politically empowered church.

Though he is wrong to reject the liberal state, Hauerwas is right that liberalism, as a wider ideology, subtly claims a sufficiency that it lacks. It implies that a "thick" account of the good, which speaks of the formation of character through community, is less legitimate than a "thin" one, in which the central good is tolerance of universal human rights. Liberalism entails a tacit bias in favor of a minimalist account of social morality, for it enshrines individual rights as the centerpiece of public moral discourse. It does not proscribe the thicker moral discourse of religion, but it marginalizes it. Hauerwas

---

24. Stout implies as much: "Many of Hauerwas's readers probably like being told that they should care more about being the church than about doing justice to the underclass. . . . It was tempting to infer, half-consciously, that following Jesus involves little more than hating the liberal secularists who supposedly run the country, pitying poor people from a distance, and donating a portion of one's income to the church" (Stout, *Democracy and Tradition,* p. 158).

insists that liberalism is therefore the enemy of religion. Because it entails a discourse in which nonreligious assumptions are privileged over religious assumptions, it must be rejected. But I suggest that this either/or approach is unhelpful. It is possible for the church to accept the liberal state and yet to reject what might be called "ideological liberalism" — the assumption that the minimalist morality of the liberal state is sufficient. Admittedly, the churches, especially in America, have found it difficult to pursue this middle way. They have given excessive affirmation to a liberal state with a strong Christian aura. But I suggest that there is no alternative to this nuanced view of liberalism; to see it as a veneer for imperialism is crude.[25]

Hauerwas is still worth listening to on the humanist gravitation of liberal Protestantism.

> The agony of liberal Christianity [is that its] advocates seek to show that Christianity can be made reasonable within the epistic presuppositions of modernity, only to discover, to the extent they are successful, that the very people they were trying to convince could care less. Why should anyone be interested in Christianity if Christians were simply telling them what they already knew on less obscurantist grounds?[26]

Radical Orthodoxy

In the early 1990s a strikingly ambitious Anglo-Catholic thinker began attracting attention. John Milbank strongly imbibed cultural-linguistic Catholicism (partly mediated by Rowan Williams, whom we will consider shortly) and Yale school postliberalism. He also imbibed the Nietzschean tradition of secular postmodernism, which sees all truth claims as veneers for the exercise of power.

25. Soldiers "kill and die to protect our 'freedom.' But what can such freedom mean if the prime instance of the exercise of such freedom is to shop?" (Hauerwas, "September 11, 2001: A Pacifist Response," in Hauerwas, *Performing the Faith*, p. 207.

26. Hauerwas, *Dispatches from the Front* (Durham, NC: Duke University Press, 1994), p. 7.

What defined his early work was a sense that postliberal theology should go further. It was not enough to suggest that Christian tradition could present itself as no less valid than any other practice-based tradition. The demise of Enlightenment-issued universal reason, or "foundationalism," created a space that theology could and should fill. It should revive its claim to be *the* discourse, whose subject matter is not religion but everything. Milbank's first book, *Theology and Social Theory* (1990), urged theologians to reject the tradition of secular social theory, which was marked by Hobbes's idea of original violence. Theology should not choose between liberalism, Marxism, and Nietzscheanism, but should expound its own account of social reality, one rooted in the Augustinian vision of social peace, which the church discloses and embodies. Theology must claim to have — to be — the true social theory: "If theology no longer seeks to position, qualify or criticize other discourses, then it is inevitable that these discourses will position theology: for the necessity of an ultimate organizing logic . . . cannot be wished away."[27] Therefore, theology must deconstruct the tacit pretension of modern secularism to define "natural reality" and show secularism to be an ideology that was "invented," through the adaptation of theological categories such as freedom and justice. The task is to "restore, in postmodern terms, the possibility of theology as a meta discourse" (p. 1). "If truth is social it can only be through a claim to offer the ultimate 'social science' that theology can establish itself and give any coherent content to the notion of 'God'" (p. 6). Milbank sometimes implies that theology must renounce claims to philosophical truth: the truth of the Christian view of the social world cannot be proved; it is "an alternative *mythos* [to Nietzsche's], equally unfounded . . ." (p. 279). Secularism "cannot be refuted, but only out-narrated, if we can persuade people — for reasons of 'literary taste' — that Christianity offers a much better story" (p. 330). Theology asserts an alternative "ontology" of peace, but does not present it philosophically, but rather "as an explication of the doc-

---

27. John Milbank, *Theology and Social Theory: Beyond Secular Reason* (Oxford: Blackwell, 1990), p. 1. Hereafter, page references to this work appear in parentheses in the text.

trine of creation" (p. 432). For Christianity "from the first took the side of rhetoric against philosophy and contended that the Good and the True are those things of which we 'have a persuasion, *pistis,* or faith'" (p. 398). The Christian argument is not abstract but embodied in the practices of the church. The church models the true society, but its otherness belongs to aspiration as well as present reality: "The [Christian] community is what God is like, and He is even more like the ideal, the goal of community implicit in its practices."[28] (Thus does Milbank slightly distance himself from Hauerwas's approach.)

There is a tension between his insistence that theology must refute all other discourses and his awareness that it cannot demonstrate its superiority by any neutral criterion. In his subsequent work the former impulse triumphs over the latter: theology must primarily reestablish itself as the true philosophy. This entails an account of how the true synthesis of theology and philosophy broke down soon after Aquinas, when nominalists launched a new kind of rationality that was implicitly secular, for it included both God and creation in the category "Being." All modern thought inherited this error, most obviously the arid rationalism of deism. So theology's honor must be restored by a bold revival of philosophical theology that might be called postmodern Thomism. This is the antidote to "the secular," the composite ideology that corrodes the medieval Catholic vision of sacramental unity, in which religion, philosophy, politics, art, and culture are one, in which humanity is understood as "participating in God," to use Radical Orthodoxy's favored phrase.[29] Perhaps the core conviction is that Christianity is not just compatible with reason but is the engine of reason; faithless reason is just narrow positivism, or scientism.[30] Without Christianity, the whole tradition of philosophi-

28. Milbank, "Postmodern Critical Augustinianism: A Short Summa in 42 Responses to Unasked Questions," *Modern Theology* 7, no. 3 (1991): 225-37, in John Milbank and Simon Oliver, eds., *The Radical Orthodoxy Reader* (New York: Routledge, 2009), p. 52.

29. He has described the aim as rejecting the ghettoization of theology, "which is partly the result of separating off the biblical from the Greek legacy throughout our Christian culture" (quoted in Milbank and Oliver, *Radical Orthodoxy Reader,* p. 392).

30. He has echoed Pope Benedict's claim that theology affirms the "grandeur of

cal truth crumbles. Why should theology not salvage this tradition through which it can assert its *truth?* This is also confirmed by a recent Milbank essay on apologetics: "We need a mode of apologetics prepared to question the world's assumptions down to their very roots and to expose how they lie within paganism, heterodoxy or else an atheism with no ground in reason and a tendency to deny the ontological reality of reason altogether." A renewed metaphysics must counter the "assumption that the only 'reason' which discloses truth is a cold, detached reason that is isolated from both feeling and imagination, as likewise from both narrative and ethical evaluation."[31]

My argument with this approach is twofold. First, its move toward a synthesis of faith and reason is at odds with the position sketched in chapter 4 above, and subsequently. Protestantism retains a sense of God as ultimately rational, but the emphasis is on "ultimately": it is beyond our fallen powers to square God's rationality with ours. This view is surely biblically warranted: the scandalizing of human reason is more prominent than the idea of the gospel as the answer to philosophy. Our account of modern thought has shown that Christianity is subverted by the desire to reconcile itself with reason. It forgets the primacy of its linguistic and ritual practices. Milbank would reply that this was the wrong sort of reconciliation with reason, which exalted a secular-shaped rationality. People like Pascal and Kierkegaard were thus right, or relatively right, to declare fideistic revolt; but the authentic unity of faith and reason, exemplified by Aquinas and recovered in new terms today, makes such revolts unnecessary. But Protestantism insists that *any* reconciliation of faith and reason is dubious. Theology must stay with the brute fact that Christian witness will be scorned as foolish, unrealistic, irrational. The

---

reason," which should not be confused with "rationalism" (quoted in Rupert Shortt, ed., "Radical Orthodoxy: A Conversation," in Milbank and Oliver, eds., *Radical Orthodoxy Reader*, p. 47). Interestingly, Hauerwas praises the previous pope, John Paul II, for the same sentiment, for claiming that "the Church considers philosophy an indispensable help for a deeper understanding of faith and for communicating the truth of the Gospel to those who do not know it" (Hauerwas, *With the Grain*, p. 235).

31. Milbank, in the foreword to Andrew Davison, ed., *Imaginative Apologetics: Theology, Philosophy and the Catholic Tradition* (London: SCM, 2011), pp. xx, xxii.

urge to expound Christianity in philosophical terms necessarily belittles — and pathologizes — the tradition of faith's defiance of reason. In effect, Milbank uses postmodern theory to construct a new account of rationality that can agree with faith.

The second ground of objection relates to liberalism, which is naturally seen as a basic expression of "secular reason." Adapting the communitarianism of MacIntyre and others (he suggests that his thesis may be seen as a "temeritous attempt to radicalize the thought of MacIntyre"), Milbank presents the church as the truly social vision, the opposite of liberalism.[32] In an essay in his next book he puts the matter this way:

> The universality of the Church transcends the universality of enlightenment in so far as it is not content with mere mutual toleration and non-interference with the liberties of others. It seeks in addition a work of freedom which is none other than perfect social harmony, a perfect consensus in which every natural and cultural difference finds its agreed place within the successions of space and time. In this context it is correct to say that the Church is a "community of virtue" which desires to train its members towards certain ends, rather than a "community of rights" founded upon liberal indifference.[33]

He is right that the church has a fuller social vision than does liberalism, a more ambitious, transformative one. But why should liberalism be seen as a threat, a rival seducing people away from this fuller vision? Why should it not instead be seen as the best possible context in which the ecclesial vision can exist? There seems to be a kind of insecurity at work, a lack of confidence, despite the rhetoric. The value of political liberalism cannot be admitted, for fear that it would take over and undermine the pride of the master discourse. This antipathy toward liberalism is heavily influenced by Marxism: because liberal-

---

32. Milbank, *Theology and Social Theory*, p. 327.
33. Milbank, "The Name of Jesus," in *The Word Made Strange: Theology, Language, Culture* (Oxford: Blackwell, 1997), p. 154.

ism gives such power to capitalism, its idealism is untrustworthy; ultimately, it must serve this power it has unleashed, that of capital. Of
course, Milbank's antiliberalism is also influenced by the Catholic vision, especially the English Catholic vision (of Newman, Chesterton,
Belloc) of medieval paradise lost. This has found expression in the
work of his student and collaborator Catherine Pickstock, who argues
that the modern state, with its "soteriology . . . as guarantor of social
peace and justice" and its strident insistence on the "self-sufficiency
. . . of earthly politics," pushes religion from public centrality. It
"privatizes its relevance and segregates it from the ecclesial sphere of
bodily practice."[34]

Polemical critiques of the liberal state are the stock-in-trade of
the Radical Orthodoxy movement; attacking political liberalism is a
kind of initiation rite into it.[35] Over the last decade Milbank himself
has stepped up his attack on liberalism as the essential expression of
"the secular": "Political liberalism . . . engenders today an increasingly joyless and puritanical world," he announced in 2003; it even exhibits a "totalitarian drift."[36] This he elaborates on in an essay published in 2004:

> Liberalism . . . proceeds by inventing a wholly artificial human be-
> ing who has never really existed, and then pretending that we are
> all instances of such a species. This is the pure individual, thought
> of in abstraction from his or her gender, birth, associations, be-
> liefs and also, crucially, in equal abstraction from the religious or

---

34. Catherine Pickstock, *After Writing: On the Liturgical Consummation of Philosophy* (Oxford: Blackwell, 1998), pp. 152-54. The point is echoed by Graham Ward: "The
price paid [for the birth of the modern secular state] was the separation of religion
from politics; there was private conviction on the one hand, and public debate on the
other" (Ward, *The Politics of Discipleship: Becoming Postmaterial Citizens* [Grand Rapids:
Baker Academic, 2009], p. 264).

35. William T. Cavanaugh claims that the secular state emerged as a new
"*mythos* of salvation," but it has failed to save us (Cavanaugh, in John Milbank,
Catherine Pickstock, and Graham Ward, eds., *Radical Orthodoxy* (London: Routledge,
1999), p. 193.

36. Milbank, *Being Reconciled: Ontology and Pardon* (London: Routledge, 2003),
p. 25.

philosophical beliefs of the observer of this individual as to whether he is a creature made by God, or only material, or naturally evolved and so forth.[37]

Liberalism ascribes a will to such individuals and imagines social order in terms of contracts made between these abstract entities. He goes on to explain that absolutism and liberalism are joined at the hip, for

> they both have to do with the primacy of the will. In the early modern West, the competition of individual wills was only resolved by investing all political rule for the first time in a single sovereign will. This applies whether or not this will was seen as ruling by divine right or by contract or both, and whether it was seen as the will of the king or as the democratic will of the people.[38]

By allowing the complete dominance of the market, liberalism offers only a parody of freedom. "If, for example, the citizens of New York chose to run their city according to that liturgical order which its gothic skyscrapers so strangely intimate . . . with a third of the days off a year for worship and feasting, neither state nor market would permit this. Liberalism allows apparent total diversity of choice; at the same time it is really a formal conspiracy to ensure that no choice can ever be significantly effective." It decrees cultural shallowness: "Under liberalism we no longer really meet each other; establish connections yes, truly make friends, almost never."[39] This sort of critique is, to a certain

---

37. Milbank, "The Gift of Ruling," *New Blackfriars* 85 (1996): 212-38, in Milbank and Oliver, *Radical Orthodoxy Reader*, p. 339.

38. Milbank, "The Gift of Ruling," in Milbank and Oliver, *Radical Orthodoxy Reader*, p. 345. This has been echoed by Milbank's pupil, the "Red Tory" Phillip Blond: "For liberals, autonomy must precede everything else, but such a 'self' is a fiction. A society so constituted would be one that required a powerful central authority to manage the perpetual conflict between self-interested individuals. So the unanticipated bequest of an unlimited liberalism is that most illiberal of entities: the controlling state" (Phillip Blond, *Prospect,* February 28, 2009).

39. Milbank, "The Gift of Ruling," in Milbank and Oliver, *Radical Orthodoxy Reader,* p. 347.

extent, valid: it is true that contemporary culture promotes market-driven superficiality and encourages evasion of big questions of meaning and purpose (safer just to affirm toleration). This is indeed a central aspect of liberal culture: it tacitly implies that a thicker vision of community need not be pursued. It is valid, indeed correct, to point out that cultural liberalism's glass is half-empty. But Milbank goes further and declares it poisoned. He treats liberalism as a comprehensive thing that must be accepted or rejected in toto. In reality, it is a fusion of things, but of two things especially: it is the insistence that the state should establish pluralism, and it is the assumption that such pluralism is enough, that it settles the question of human social meaning. Of course, theology must attack the latter premise; but if it also attacks the former, then it only strengthens the latter. For liberals will be confirmed in their idea that Christians really want to restore premodern Christendom, an idea that Milbank encourages.[40]

A similar attack on political liberalism is basic to the approach of the husband-and-wife team of Oliver and Joan Lockwood O'Donovan, though they are closer to traditional conservatism than to Marx and Nietzsche. In *The Desire of the Nations,* Oliver O'Donovan argues that "early-modern liberalism" was justified in its opposition to feudal Christendom; it sought to develop the Christian natural law tradition for the renewal of true Christian politics. This was an authentically Christian project, for it retained Christian categories. But then the Enlightenment took over, and the dismantling of Christendom acquired an anti-Christian character. The decisive moment was the American Revolution: the new United States Constitution did not understand its own anti-Christian logic. "The paradox of the First Amendment is that a measure first conceived as a liberation for authentic Christianity has become, in this century, a tool of anti-religious sentiment, weakening the participation of the church in society and depriving it of access to resources for its social role." He argues that a liberalism detached

40. "[W]e believe that secular order must be overcome and a new mode of 'Christendom' invented (given that 'Christianity' and 'Christendom' are the same word, and any separation of the two suggests a disincarnate, asocial, acultural, early-modern derived 'belief' that could not possibly be Christian at all)" (Milbank, "Afterword," in *The Radical Orthodoxy Reader,* p. 393).

from its medieval religious roots ceases to make sense; this is most apparent in relation to "rights" that were once based in natural law but have become effectively self-standing. Christians must resist such individualism; they believe that "private purposes have no intelligibility apart from social existence."[41]

Joan Lockwood O'Donovan explains that liberalism is based on "the self-centered, self-owning and self-creating subject, and claims to be able to get from that sovereign individual will to an ordered political community, largely through the mechanism of collective contract, of binding collective agreement. But it never really does arrive at political community, because political community presupposes a shared communicating in a wide range of spiritual goods from the beginning — and that's just what liberalism denies." Through this denial, "it becomes idolatrously overweening and engineering, as the egalitarian welfare state is today."[42] At root, the O'Donovans echo MacIntyre: away from a shared conception of Meaning and Justice, nothing means anything substantial. Because it dispenses with such shared concepts, the "late-modern" secular state is condemned to shallowness and inauthenticity. I should acknowledge that on one level this is true. The preliberal state was more ideologically coherent; and to some extent, the liberal state derives its concepts from its more organic predecessor culture. When secular politicians say "justice" or "the common good," they are using a concept that used to be part of a widely shared theological worldview — whose meaning is now highly debatable. But this transition could be seen as echoing the logic of Christianity, as kenotic. For it could be said that Christianity itself is based in a move away from the organic social context of its predecessor religion. It talks of God's law, but it detaches the concept of divine law — indeed, the concept of God — from a coherent cultural tradition. Of course, the transition from preliberal to liberal politics is very different, but in both cases there is a conceptual reinvention that can be read as a move from organic depth to universalist shallowness.

41. Oliver O'Donovan, *The Desire of the Nations: Recovering the Roots of Political Theology* (Cambridge, UK: Cambridge University Press, 1996), pp. 245, 276.

42. Joan Lockwood O'Donovan, quoted in Rupert Shortt, *God's Advocates: Christian Thinkers in Conversation* (Grand Rapids: Eerdmans, 2005), pp. 252, 253.

Like those in the Radical Orthodoxy movement, the O'Donovans deny the possibility of discriminating between the limited liberalism of the liberal state and liberalism as a general philosophical ideology. Liberalism is one big thing, they say, and it is a threat to Christianity because it claims to have the answers about the good life that only truly come through participation in the church. It should be repeated that the latter concept, ideological liberalism, is indeed corrosive of Christianity. But this is not *the* liberal tradition. Milbank and the O'Donovans are far too dogmatic about all liberalism deriving from the rational Enlightenment, as if Hobbes and Locke were its official founders rather than just a couple of theorists. It also has roots in medieval common law and, as we have seen, in a very Protestant vision of liberty. In Britain it is plainly compatible with a residually medieval constitution. Political liberalism is clearly a mix of traditions: it has various Christian roots that are still alive, and it has post-Christian roots. One would wish to ask Milbank and the O'Donovans an impertinent-sounding question: Is the present British Queen a liberal? She is the head of a state that has long been dominated by political liberalism (and has the strongest claim to have invented it), but she is not exactly a model of rootless individualism.

But don't these theologians have a point — that secular liberalism gravitates toward becoming quasi-religious? They do. Secular liberal culture does indeed idealize certain things, such as tolerance and autonomy, as if they are absolutely good, and as if there is no need for any "thicker" social ideal (one deeply embedded in a distinctive moral way of life). And as the Radical Orthodoxy writer Graham Ward eloquently insists, debased forms of religiosity pervade popular culture. It is hungry for spectacle, for ecstatic experience, for fantasy, and, lacking any sense of the meaning of embodiment, it promotes the dark Gnosticism of virtual reality. The triumph of the free market certainly promotes hedonism and casual cruelty passing as entertainment. Capitalism does indeed spawn an embarrassment of idolatries, with every other advertisement promising some vaguely salvific result, and sport and leisure becoming more cultic (often "ironically," though such irony simply helps people get on with what they know is dubious). Theology should indeed juxtapose the cynical emptiness of liberal culture and the thinness of its "social networks" with what the church offers. It should say that a culture that celebrates atomized individualism is nihilistic, and that its worship of power, money, youth, and sex smells of fascism.

But the newly visible paganism of secular liberal culture does not detract from the virtue of political liberalism. Because he does not accept this, Ward's call for a "post-secular state" and for Christianity to become "public and political" again are unhelpful, because they will confirm liberal suspicions that religion wants to boss people around again.[43] Of course, none of these theologians (some of whom I know to be nice, gentle souls) really wants anything like "theocracy." So why, via simplistic attacks on liberalism, do they flirt with the appearance of it? They seem to feel that only in stark opposition to "liberalism" can the social nature of Christianity be articulated. Like Kierkegaard, they seem to feel that only an extreme case has a chance of being heard. A more nuanced discussion will give the impression that the Church of England, for instance, is still happy to sit at the edge of a post-Christian culture and vaguely affirm it. No, they say, the church is really different from its surrounding culture. Do not be misled by its establishment into thinking that it in any way approves of the dominant culture around it.

One of the very few British theologians to have objected to this antiliberal tendency is Christopher Insole. In *The Politics of Human Frailty* (2004) he explains that "the prevailing wind . . . in the theological academy . . . is to dismiss liberalism as a product of sinful Enlightenment attempts at self-sufficiency and self-determination. From this critique of liberalism there can then be an attempt to leap beyond or behind liberalism to a more enchanted and less 'secular' space." He sees Milbank's antiliberalism as driven by aversion to global capitalism. But "there is a tradition of political liberalism that is much older than global capitalism, and that is conceptually quite distinct from it. Political liberalism is motivated by the desire to preserve the liberties of the individual within a framework of law and fair institutions." In addition, "[i]n political liberalism we have a tradition that

---

43. See Ward, *The Politics of Discipleship*, pp. 264, 296.

acknowledges the dangers and limitations of human projects of self-perfection." Insole defines political liberalism as "the conviction that politics is ordered towards peaceful coexistence (the absence of conflict) and the preservation of the liberties of the individual within a pluralistic and tolerant framework, rather than by a search for truth (religious or otherwise), perfection and unity."[44] Elsewhere, he puts it thus: "I would argue that political liberalism is concerned most of all with the preservation of the liberties of the individual within a pluralistic (not secular or atheist) framework, precisely because of a sense of our fallen condition, characterized by frailty, sin and complexity."

Insole insists that political liberalism is a complex tradition; it should not be hastily identified with the Hobbesian theme of individuals making contracts, for liberal concerns predate the Enlightenment. They are present in Hooker, and many major liberal thinkers, such as Burke and Lord Acton, are deeply suspicious of post-Christian schemes for human betterment. The liberal concern for individual rights should not be seen as a rejection of a social conception of the good; rather, "[t]he individual needs to be the unit of reflection about justice precisely because individuals are precious, fallen and vulnerable."[45] He concludes that the church is called "to an active and vigorous custodianship of the highest ideals of political liberalism."[46]

Welcome as this analysis is, it evades the question of the foundational relationship between Christianity and political liberalism. Insole presents political liberalism as a Christian-based tradition, but is wary of elaborating. He implies that it arises from the general Christian principles of concern for each individual and awareness of fallibility. And by including Hooker among his exemplary liberals, he implies that the seventeenth-century revolution in toleration (discussed in chapter 2) is not decisive, even though it establishes the "pluralistic framework" that is the center of his definition of political liberalism. If this pluralistic framework is so important, it is strange that it is not

44. Christopher J. Insole, *The Politics of Human Frailty: A Theological Defense of Political Liberalism* (Notre Dame, IN: University of Notre Dame Press, 2004), pp. 171, 172, 175.

45. Quoted in Shortt, *God's Advocates*, pp. 61, 62.

46. Insole, *Politics of Human Frailty*, p. 177.

more closely defined. Is Insole, who is a member of the Church of England, wary of giving definition to liberalism that pulls against establishment?

He has recently clarified his position. Theologians should not, he says, offer sweeping, reductive, theoretical accounts of political liberalism (whether to praise or blame it), but should acknowledge that it is a complex set of constitutional *practices*. He sums these up as: "restriction of the use of coercive public power to sustaining peace and justice (giving to each their due) rather than to enforcing ultimate truth or unity of belief; the protection of individuals within a framework of rights and liberties; the separation of powers (between the lawmakers, law-enforcers, and those who interpret the application of the law)," and so on. He also mentions a mixed constitution and representation as the basis of authority. Theology should above all "avoid reductionism" with respect to political philosophy; it should reflect on this untidy tradition of practices.[47] Insole thus takes a strictly nominalist approach: seeking the essence of liberalism leads to bad theology. He illustrates this with a detailed analysis of the mixed constitution as a practice with premodern roots (in the Conciliarist movement to limit papal power). This reminds us that theological traditions tend to underlie liberal practices.

Nuance is a good thing, to be sure, and Insole's attention to detail is an effective rebuke to the postliberals. But we can hardly help summing things up, attempting to create narrative coherence. Nor should we avoid this. If liberalism matters, then contemporary theology's denigration of it should be met with an affirmation of it. And that means taking the risk of essentializing it. Things that matter must be spoken of with some degree of emotive simplicity. By analogy, if we kept on admitting that Christianity was hard to define, we would not get around to proclaiming it. As should already be clear, I suggest that there is an essence of "constitutional liberalism," or "the liberal state." It is the move away from theocracy to religious freedom.

47. Christopher Insole, "Theology and Politics: The Intellectual History of Liberalism," in Christopher Craig Brittain and Francesca Aran Murphy, eds., *Theology, University, Humanities: Initium Sapientiae Timor Dei* (Eugene, OR: Wipf and Stock, 2011), pp. 174-76.

This cannot be neatly identified with a particular constitutional practice, though the defense of every individual's right to freedom of worship is obviously central. It is a slightly vague *narrative*. Significantly,
it is this aspect of constitutional liberalism that Insole refers to first in
his definitions: the state's renouncing of the power to enforce unity of
religion.

A fuller critique of postliberal theology has come from the secular thinker Jeffrey Stout. This movement, which he calls "the new traditionalism," is based on an overabstract view of liberalism as the
invention of certain philosophers. Stout argues that "modern democracy" (a term he prefers to "liberalism") should not be identified
with philosophical liberalism — and its antitraditional universalism.
Instead,

> [d]emocracy . . . *is* a tradition. It inculcates certain habits of rea-
> soning, certain attitudes towards deference and authority in polit-
> ical discussion, and love for certain goods and virtues, as well as a
> disposition to respond to certain types of actions, events, or per-
> sons with admiration, pity, or horror. This tradition is anything
> but empty. Its ethical substance, however, is more a matter of en-
> during attitudes, concerns, dispositions, and patterns of conduct
> than it is a matter of agreement on a conception of justice in
> Rawls's sense.[48]

Democracy is an evolving project in which certain social ideals
are normative. A democratic society is a group "whose members invoke such norms habitually when holding one another responsible
for what they say and do and are" (p. 5). Communitarians have a point
about the need to cultivate virtue, but they overstate the absence of
such virtue-cultivation in modern society. Modern democracy is not
"an inherently destructive, atomizing social force" (p. 11).

Stout offers a more nuanced and restrained version of Rawls's affirmation of the liberal discursive space. Although "the ethical dis-

---

48. Stout, *Democracy and Tradition*, p. 3. Hereafter, page references to this work
appear in parentheses in the text.

course of most modern democracies is *secularized* . . . secularization in this sense is not a reflection of commitment to secularism. It entails neither the denial of theological assumptions nor the expulsion of theological expression from the public sphere . . . [it] just means that the age of theocracy is over, not that the anti-Christ has taken control of the political sphere" (p. 93). The secularization of politics was not the work of ideological secularism, as Milbank claims, but a response to the rise of religious plurality. (I think something more can be said here: a form of Christianity actively promoted this secularization.)

In his discussion of MacIntyre, Stout aims "to show what mischief MacIntyre causes by defining liberal modernity reductively as the social expression of the Enlightenment project's antitraditionalism" (p. 136). But what is liberal modernity? Stout equivocates: it could be seen as the "tailor[ing of] the political institutions and moral discourse of modern societies to the facts of pluralism" (p. 129). Or it could be seen as a complicated configuration of things rather than a single project. "We might even come to think of 'liberalism' as the name for a particular kind of obsolete ideology whose critics and defenders thought there was something worth calling *the* liberal project and who thus engaged in fruitless debates over whether it was a good or a bad thing" (p. 130). Stout opts for this latter view, thus deciding that "liberalism" is too dominated by dogmatic abstract universalism to be salvaged. The thing worth defending is "democracy," which is self-consciously a lived political and cultural tradition that emerged in opposition "to a feudal and theocratic past" (p. 225). He half-acknowledges that its original motivation was Christian:

> The first modern revolutionaries were not secular liberals; they were radical Calvinists. Among the most important democractic movements in American history were Abolitionism and the Civil Rights movement; both of these were based largely in the religious communities. (p. 300)

The current culture war results from forgetfulness about this affinity of religion and democracy, for which secular liberals are partly to blame: "Secular liberalism has unwittingly fostered the decline of the religious Left by persuading religious intellectuals that liberal society is intent on excluding the expression of their most strongly felt convictions" (p. 300). He even suggests that America's future depends on a revival of liberal Christianity: "If the religious Left does not soon recover its energy and self-confidence, it is unlikely that American democracy will be capable of counteracting either the greed of its business elite or the determination of many whites to define the authentic nation in ethnic, racial or ecclesiastical terms" (p. 300). Stout seems almost to be calling for a revival of liberal Christianity on secular grounds: religion is so ingrained in America that a purely secular liberal ideology does active harm by driving religion rightwards, deepening the culture war. Only liberal Christianity can cure the culture war. But this pragmatic, secular defense of liberal Christianity is unlikely to wean theology students away from Hauerwas or Milbank: only a more convincing form of *theology* could do that. And such a form of theology will not be drawn to Stout's idea of democratic tradition, for it is an essentially secular tradition (Emerson and Walt Whitman are treated as its founders). Surely, the task is to reflect on the original affinity of Christianity and the liberal state. For that, "democracy" is not a very helpful category, because it was not a mainstream ideal before de Tocqueville.[49] But Stout is right that the idea of "tradition" must be foregrounded — in response to the postliberals.

Liberal Christianity must present itself as a tradition, a complex and perhaps rather paradoxical one. It is the tradition that gave rise to the liberal state — and to secular liberalism. Liberal Christian identity must entail a mix of pride and penitence at these complex creations (the liberal state is the least bad kind of state, but it continues to do violence). In *After Virtue,* MacIntyre reflects on this area, though

---

49. Insole usefully insists that democracy should be seen as one form of constitutional liberalism rather than the master-concept: "Where democracy — as a form of collective autonomy — is seen as the . . . foundation [of good politics], then it is more than likely to become a danger to other practices of constitutional liberalism. To put it simply: if democracy is the source of truth . . . why bother to preserve . . . certain rights and liberties, if the general will that bestows these things, has determined that they are to be taken away (in the interest of national security, say)?" (Insole, "Theology and Politics," p. 180).

naturally not with respect to liberal Christianity. He criticizes the sort of individualism by which an American denies any complicity in slavery or an Englishman protests that he personally never did any harm to Ireland. This innocence is false, "[f]or the story of my life is always embedded in the story of those communities from which I derive my identity. . . . I find myself part of a history and that is generally to say, whether I like it or not, whether I recognize it or not, one of the bearers of a tradition. . . . A living tradition . . . is an historically extended, socially embodied argument, and an argument precisely in part about the goods which constitute that tradition."[50] Liberal Christianity is such a tradition. To be a liberal Christian is to belong to a huge family that includes embarrassing old uncles such as Luther, Cromwell, Jefferson, Hegel, and the rest. Is it a coherent tradition? No, but there is a golden thread: God wills a new kind of state, in which his gospel can be more fully expressed. Of course, democracy — or secular liberalism — can be defended as a tradition, as Stout insists, but its roots are shallower, and its affinity with antitraditional thought is stronger.

John Gray is a secular thinker whose work usefully reflects on the strange afterlife of liberal theory (though it is not free of "shockingly" postliberal donnish posturing). He builds on Isaiah Berlin's insight that only a modest form of liberalism is defensible, one that accepts the existence of various competing conceptions of the good. This distinguishes Berlin's liberalism "from the panglossian liberalisms that have lately enjoyed an anachronistic revival."[51] As a supreme philosophy, liberalism has failed: it has "failed to establish its fundamental thesis: that liberal democracy is the only form of government that can be sanctioned by reason and morality. It therefore fails to give rational support to the political religion of the contemporary intelligentsia, which combines the sentimental cult of humanity with a sectarian passion for political reform" (p. 246). Although liberal theory has failed, there is a need to defend the practical tradition of freedom that it fostered, which Gray refers to as "civil society," meaning "institu-

50. MacIntyre, *After Virtue*, pp. 205-7.
51. John Gray, *Post-Liberalism: Studies in Political Thought* (London: Routledge, 1993), p. 67. Hereafter, page references to this work appear in parentheses in the text.

tions that are protected by law but independent of the state." This can exist outside of modern liberal democracies, though of course it exists "most stably within them" (p. 246). Government should ensure maximal freedom without pushing a dated ideal of the bourgeois autonomous individual. It should provide "the framework within which different ways of life and styles of thought may compete in peaceful coexistence" (p. 268). But what is the rationale for such an order?

> Allegiance to liberal orders . . . has typically been imposed by secular myths which few of us any longer take seriously. Thus liberalism in France and America was sustained by the historical theodicy of the Enlightenment, with its mythologies of natural rights and global progress. . . . [So] what might sustain a political order that encompasses many traditions and varieties of human identity, if both the traditional and the modern sources of allegiance to such an order are unmistakably on the wane? (pp. 269-70)

We must do without "inspiring mythology" and "the moral solidarity sought by socialists and most conservatives." And yet, in the pursuit of civil society, "we may yet be able to draw on the resource of another kind of solidarity — that of civilized men and women, practitioners of different traditions, who nevertheless have in common a perception of enmity in regard to the totalitarian states and rebarbarizing movements of our time" (pp. 269-70). What Gray means by "civil society" is "the *practice of liberty*" rather than any theory (p. 318). It is "a particularistic form of life, spreading throughout the world, but everywhere threatened by modernist fundamentalisms and atavistic ideologies" (p. 328). What is interesting is that Gray cannot really avoid constructing a myth in which "civil society" defies authoritarianism. He is offering a humble, deregulated version of the narrative of the liberal state.

Since 9/11, Gray's attempt to affirm civil society has been eclipsed by his critique of neoliberalism as a spurious religion. He was inspired by the invasion of Iraq to pose as a secular Niebuhr, warning that naïve Enlightenment optimism has disastrous consequences. On the other hand, he wanted to chide the naïveté of advocates of international justice: in reality, strong states are still needed. Hobbes understood "that freedom is not the normal human condition. It is an artifact of state power. If you want to be free, you need first to be safe." We must therefore "stop demonizing the state."[52] Elsewhere, Gray repeats the point that the state is the only substantial source of liberal values:

> Contemporary liberals think of rights as universal human attributes that can be respected anywhere, but here they show a characteristic disregard of history. Current understandings of human rights developed along with the modern nation-state. It was the nation-state that emancipated individuals from the communal ties of medieval times and created freedom as it has come to be known in the modern world. This was not done without enormous conflict and severe costs.[53]

Gray comes close to affirming the liberal state as the least bad ideology, but then he draws back in fear of seeming naïve: Is not the liberal state the source of the dubious pseudoreligion of liberalism? His desire to seem modishly skeptical of every ideal — beyond Hobbesian realism — seems to outweigh other considerations.

Postliberalism in Practice: Rowan Williams

Rowan Williams, the archbishop of Canterbury from 2002 to 2012, and before that a major influence on British theology, embodies the turn away from liberal Protestant assumptions. He was influenced by Roman Catholic and Russian Orthodox thinkers, but principally by the rich Anglo-Catholicism of the twentieth century that had been quietly bubbling away behind the more attention-grabbing developments of Protestantism. Among those Anglo-Catholics were Charles Gore, William Temple, the liturgical writer Gregory Dix, and Michael Ramsey,

52. John Gray, *Heresies* (London: Granta, 2004), p. 114.
53. John Gray, *Black Mass: Apocalyptic Religion and the Death of Utopia* (New York: Farrar, Straus and Giroux, 2007), p. 169.

archbishop of Canterbury from 1961 to 1974. An essay that Williams wrote on Ramsey in 1995 is a good introduction to his own basic theological assumptions. He explains that Ramsey was influenced by F. D. Maurice "to understand the Church's life as something in which *the nature of God was made manifest.*"[54] This was strengthened by the Russian Orthodox "vision of the Church as 'epiphany': what matters about the Church is not a system of ideas (though doctrine and dogma have their place) nor the structure of an organization competent to deliver authoritative judgements and to require obedience (though order is important in its proper context), but what the bare fact of the Church *shows*" (p. 91). In this conception, "the Church *is* the message . . . to belong in the Church is to know what God wants you to know" (p. 91). This vision is only rescued from authoritarianism, says Williams, if the Eucharist is seen as the central business of the church, and if the church is deeply self-critical, aware of its political fallibility. Ramsey had put forward this robust church-centered theology in the 1930s, "at a time when the faltering responses of classical liberalism to the horrors of war and totalitarianism had prompted a good many to despair of any kind of common rationality as a tool, let alone a source, for theology" (p. 88). Like Barth, then, Ramsey saw the weakness of theological liberalism and made a decisive ecclesial turn (a more Catholic one than Barth, of course). Williams sees himself as maintaining this turn because today, "once again, the resources of liberalism are running thin" (p. 89).

In the 1980s, Williams was a central figure in the critique of Anglican liberalism, the tradition of *Honest to God,* which found new expression in an essay collection of 1977 entitled *The Myth of God Incarnate,* and in the work of Don Cupitt. Williams's critique of theological liberalism (from a cultural-linguistic, Anglo-Catholic angle) overlapped with his critique of political liberalism, rooted in Marxism, but becoming more postmodern-communitarian (again, MacIntyre is an important presence). Barth also influenced him in this direction, as already indicated. Williams was impressed by Barth's claim that theological

---

54. Rowan Williams, *Anglican Identities* (London: Darton, Longman and Todd, 2003), p. 90. Hereafter, page references to this work appear in parentheses in the text.

liberalism is implicated in fascism.[55] These influences led him to argue that the church can only transform the world once it has seen through the illusory gospel of liberalism, a message he passed on to his student John Milbank. Williams can be considered the godfather of the Radical Orthodoxy movement, though its bullishness is not his style.

Williams's post-Marxist communitarianism is evident in an essay he published in 1989. In liberal capitalist societies, all "cultural options . . . are developed and presented as consumer goods . . . [and] religious commitment is reduced to a private matter of style, unconnected with the nature of a person's membership in his or her society."[56] This critique of liberal culture, says Williams, must be central to the church's mission. In another essay of the same year, he explains that the church must have a "primitive and angular separateness" from surrounding culture.[57] (Conveniently this does not preclude the establishment of the Church of England.[58]) What he is clear about is the need to resist the spurious universalism of secular liberalism. Following Augustine, the church should claim to offer the true politics, which no secular state can hope to realize. The church teaches "the pattern of virtues (tangible structures of behaviour, not attitudes alone) characterizing the *polis* of God."[59] This sounds like Hauerwas, but Williams characteristically wants to balance such rhetoric with an insistence on the church's fallibility. Thus he has treated Milbank's thesis with some caution, for example, telling an interviewer that it is

55. "If [theology]'s just, as [Barth] said, talking about man in a loud voice, if it's just uplift or examination of the religious consciousness, well, frankly you're still trapped, you're still under the net of a deeply oppressive and barbaric political system." Only a postliberal theology "can make the challenges to the barbarism of modern politics" (Williams, quoted in Shortt, *God's Advocates*, pp. 14-15).

56. Rowan Williams, "The Judgement of the World," in *On Christian Theology* (Oxford: Blackwell, 2000), p. 35.

57. Rowan Williams, "Incarnation and the Renewal of Community," in Williams, *On Christian Theology*, pp. 233-34.

58. Establishment can witness to "a community without boundaries other than Christ" (*On Christian Theology*, pp. 233-34).

59. Rowan Williams, "Christian Resources for the Renewal of Vision," in Alison J. Eliot and Ian Swanson, eds., *The Renewal of Social Vision* (Edinburgh: Centre for Theology and Public Issues, 1989), p. 3.

questionable to imply that "the church within history achieves the peace it speaks of."[60] On the other hand, he has often echoed the negative aspect of Milbank's thesis, the critique of the secular. Around the time of his appointment to Canterbury, he explained that the secular is not "a space of absence, a benignly untenanted place where citizens can at last relate to each other in innocence of their confessional burdens and prejudices. Secularity is the unreflective world setting its own agenda . . . [a realm of] unspoken violence."[61] Elsewhere, he characterizes "modernity" as "an atmosphere in which people become increasingly *formless,* cut off from what could give their lives in any given moment some kind of lasting intelligibility."[62]

When he was appointed to Canterbury in 2002, Williams was generally hailed as a "liberal" because of his support for reform on the ordination of homosexuals and because of his left-wing politics. The journalists (forgivably) failed to see that his deeper theological identity was determined by this idea of the church as the true universal society and of liberalism as a subtle threat to it — in short, by his radical communitarianism.

It was an interesting time for a postliberal to be appointed to Canterbury. Following 9/11, the big issue — the meta-issue — was the role of religion in public life. To what extent should secular liberalism limit religious expression? For example, should the state fund Muslim schools? (Coincidentally, the government approved the expansion of the faith school sector in 2001.) There was a new wave of secularist anxiety about such developments, soon inflamed by the "new atheism" of Dawkins and others. This was a new situation for Britain, a sudden taste of something like America's culture war. In the past the established church had seemed to ward off such tensions by demonstrating the unity of religion and liberalism. This was now far more difficult due to the rise of non-Anglican religion on the one hand and secularism on the other — and, of course, the steady decline of Angli-

---

60. Rowan Williams, interview with David S. Cunningham, *Christian Century,* April 24, 2002.

61. Rowan Williams, "What Shakes Us," *Times Literary Supplement,* July 4, 2003.

62. Rowan Williams, preface to Duncan Dormor, ed., *Anglicanism: The Answer to Modernity* (London: Continuum, 2003), p. vii.

can allegiance. But Williams had no interest in attempting to revive the old narrative in which the established church reconciles religion and liberalism. His whole career has been geared toward attacking the compromises inherent in the liberal Christian tradition. He has had no interest in reassuring the semi-Christian majority that the national church would underwrite its worldview.

In his very first lecture as archbishop he argued that secular politics gravitates toward a narrow functionalism, balancing competing accounts of the good; only religion can provide "a real questioning of the immediate agenda of a society, the choices that are defined and managed for you by the market."[63] (Incidentally this view of the state is straight out of MacIntyre.) As secular suspicion of religion grew, so did Williams's suspicion of that suspicion. In many public lectures and articles he attacked the idea that the expression of religious allegiance threatened social cohesion. The real threat was an aggressive secularism that sought to exclude religion from the public square. He thus strongly sided with Britain's Muslim minority, reassuring them that their religion was no barrier to full participation in public life. He implied that the role of the established church was now to defend all forms of faith from secularist attack — and to remind the state not to encroach on religious freedom. He insisted that a state that seeks to suppress certain forms of religion as incompatible with "public reason" is on a dangerous path: it marginalizes those who refuse to keep their religious motivation private.

He set out this position with increasing boldness. After London was hit by Islamist terrorists in July 2005, he judged that there was a renewed danger of a secularist backlash. At the same time, France was flexing its ideological secularism by banning school students from wearing religious symbols. In a major lecture of 2006, Williams warns that "programmatic secularism . . . will always carry the seeds, not of totalitarianism in the obvious sense, but of that 'totalizing' spirit which stifles critique by silencing the other."[64] The nation paid

---

63. Rowan Williams, Richard Dimbleby Lecture of 2002, December 19, 2002.

64. Rowan Williams, "Secularism, Faith and Freedom," Rome, November 23, 2006.

little attention to his thesis until February 2008, when he expressed some sympathy with the partial introduction of sharía law into the British legal system. He explained that the Enlightenment idea of equality for all individuals under a single secular law was flawed: "It is not enough to say that citizenship as an abstract form of equal access and equal accountability is either the basis or the entirety of social identity and personal motivation."[65] Williams was defiantly displaying his ideological commitment to postliberal communitarianism, refusing to condone Britain's traditional compromise between religion and liberalism, which has led to nominal Christians with a "thin" concept of the social good and a vague prejudice against fuller religious commitments.

The outcry in the press did not put him off. The next month he implied that Christianity was not so different from Islam: it has always spoken of an alternative "citizenship" — beyond the state. For a Christian, "the community to which you belong is greater than any limited human society." And it is this beyond-secular-political vision that grounds the Christian's belief in the dignity of all human beings. Christians should also affirm the discourse of human rights, but this is no robust alternative, says Williams.

> The human rights culture as it has developed in a competitive, increasingly globalized, boundary-free environment where historic communities are fragmenting is a culture that has rather encouraged the sense that the most important thing about any human individual is that he or she has claims which somebody is able to enforce. And that, while an essential part of a human rights culture within a law-governed society, is of itself a rather slender basis for the understanding of human dignity.

In a healthy society, believers will be free to display their allegiance to their comprehensive vision of human life rather than be pressured to translate it into secular terms.

---

65. Rowan Williams, "Civil and Religious Law in England: A Religious Perspective," Royal Courts of Justice, February 7, 2008.

And one of the signs of slight risk to our social health is the rising presence in our society of some unease about this: an unease about faith schools; an unease sometimes expressed about whether it is right for people who have certain convictions to play a part in government. Against this, we can only say that the risks of a polity which overrules conscience or which seeks to ignore communities of conviction in the public sphere are very high. The coercion of conscience is never a pretty sight, and the exclusion, whether *de facto* or *de jure,* of people with certain convictions from public office is again something for which the precedents are not particularly happy.[66]

What is notable here is the opposition he sets up between the religious view of human dignity and that of international human rights (he refers to the UN Declaration of 1945). This evades the question of the liberal state, which is in practice the enforcer of human rights. It also implies that all forms of religion are united in their desire to operate independently of the liberal state — whereas, as I have argued, liberal Christianity actively affirms the liberal state.

Williams's narrative evades the complexity of British history. It does not, for example, acknowledge that the British state entered its modern phase by imposing a new religious uniformity that proscribed one form of religious allegiance in particular (Roman Catholicism). Both liberalism and the established Church of England originate in the idea that the state has the right to deny a certain kind of public religious expression due to its theocratic tendency. So Williams's argument is misleading in two ways. He suggests that this exclusionary impulse belongs to *secular* liberalism, denying its roots in the modern religious state. And he implies that this exclusionary impulse is never justified; it is based only in secularists' prejudice against religion. The complex reality is that the liberal state *must* marginalize forms of religion that threaten to undermine it. This is how it emerges and survives. When it is strong, it is able to tolerate such forms; but a degree of unease about religious expression that is

66. Rowan Williams, "Faith and Politics," Westminster Abbey, March 18, 2008.

at odds with liberal values remains natural — indeed, is healthy. Williams inverts this: for example, he calls it *unhealthy* that people express "unease about faith schools."

He has often characterized liberal vigilance against religion as incipiently totalitarian. For example, he has warned that the secularist wariness of religious motivations is "dangerous." If believers are subtly pressured to keep their belief partly private, "you have a situation where the state, however you interpret that, ends up dangerously drifting towards a position where it arrogates the right to determine belief itself. We've been there before in our history. We've been there before even within the twentieth century, whether in the near paganism of the Third Reich or the atheism of Soviet Russia and Communist China, and they are not either edifying or successful experiments."[67] Again, this ignores the complexity of British history. The state imposed religious uniformity for the sake of establishing the Church of England, and the church colluded in persecuting dissenters for most of its life. For the leader of a still-established church to act as though innocent of this history and treat secularism as the sole source of theopolitical violence is deeply questionable.

Williams thus washes his hands of the ambiguity inherent in the narrative of the liberal state. He chooses not to see that the established church is implicated in this narrative. What is this narrative? It is the affirmation of liberty as a nation-constituting ideal, a positive vision that unites people. It is ambivalent because it entails the will to discriminate between different forms of religion; it privileges liberal forms of religion over theocratically inclined forms of religion, which it claims the right to curb. This tradition has lost the habit of affirming itself, and yet its basic logic abides, even in twenty-first-century Britain. Forms of religion that seem to threaten liberal values will naturally be frowned upon and marginalized — not because of rationalist secularism, which wants to exclude all religion from public life, but because of this *religion-based* tradition, which privileges liberty-loving religion over the theocratic kind.

---

67. Rowan Williams, "Faith in the Public Square," Lecture at Leicester Cathedral, March 22, 2009.

Williams's postliberal communitarianism claims that all suspicion of religion in the public square comes from the secular Enlightenment and that "liberalism" is a dubiously secular ideology. He has effectively attempted to redefine establishment as a sign of the state's recognition of the legitimacy of all types of religious allegiance. In effect, he has attempted to be what Prince Charles said he intended to be, the defender of *faith* (rather than "the faith"). This may or may not be a noble aim, but it is not the traditional function of the established church, which was to privilege one particular form of religion that was favorable to Britain's tradition of political liberalism. Many of Williams's speeches over the last decade have tried to kill off that model, to make it clear that the church would not collude in the marginalization of awkwardly nonliberal forms of religion, would not pass on the state's message to "tone it down." This is perhaps admirable. But it is at odds with this tradition. In the above, he warns of the state "dangerously drifting towards a position where it arrogates the right to determine belief itself." But is not an established church a form of such determining of belief? For through establishment the state privileges a certain kind of religion, the kind that values social conscience over dogmatic rigor, the kind that worries about climate change rather than contraception or abortion. So there is sharp irony in Williams's throwing his hands up in horror at the idea of the state seeking to influence the nature of public religion while standing in the House of Lords.

The Church of England's establishment is, therefore, deeply muddled. But in a sense it always was. It was England's way of being a liberal state — *and* its way of keeping liberalism in check. It embodied a positive liberal vision of a people united by the rejection of theocracy, the pursuit of liberty. But this vision could only partially accept political liberalism: in a sense the established church fought theocracy with semitheocracy. This arrangement was surprisingly adaptable, as the church, for most of the twentieth century, managed to present itself as a central part of a liberal nation, and to present its premodern aspect as immaterial. The decline of liberal Christianity put that narrative in doubt, and the meaning of establishment was largely evaded. Rowan Williams has presided over the emergence of a new narrative, of the established church as guarantor of the right of all faiths to occupy the public square.[68] This abandons the old ambitious theopolitical vision of Christianity and liberalism in harmony. Instead, it affirms relativism: it says that it is for each religion to supply a grand account of purpose. Citizens are encouraged to be religious, for religion is a force for social good; but they are not encouraged to seek an overall *national* theopolitical narrative. In a strange reversal, the *liberal* is accused of having a dangerously comprehensive vision. Paradoxically, the liberal is more ambitiously "communitarian" than the postliberal communitarian. Nicholas Wolterstorff is alert to this: the liberal, he says, is "not willing to live with a politics of multiple communities. He still wants communitarian politics. He is trying to discover, and to form, the relevant community. He thinks we need a shared political basis; he is trying to discover and nourish that basis." But Wolterstorff thinks that this attempt is "hopeless and misguided. We must learn to live with a politics of multiple communities."[69]

But this is a false alternative; in fact, the liberal simultaneously affirms "a politics of multiple communities" (insofar as the state can accommodate such differences) *and* affirms that liberty is an ultimately social ideal, the means to new cohesion *(e pluribus unum)*. And liberal Christianity affirms this in a "thicker" way than secular liberalism can: it has *faith* in the ultimate harmony of liberty and new social cohesion; it sees this whole project as *God's will*. For only in the liberal state can Christianity's intrinsic love of liberty find full expression. Liberal Christianity imagined, birthed, and sustained such a state, and it must continue to sustain it.

This is really the whole point of my laborious argument. Liberal

---

68. This was recently affirmed by the Queen in an address to an interfaith event that was presumably somewhat scripted by Williams. The church's role, she said, "is not to defend Anglicanism to the exclusion of other religions. Instead, the Church has a duty to protect the free practice of all faiths in this country" (Queen Elizabeth II, Lambeth Palace, February 15, 2012).

69. Nicholas Wolterstorff, "The Role of Religion in Decision and Discussion of Political Issues," in Robert Audi and Nicholas Wolterstorff, *Religion in the Public Square: The Place of Religious Convictions in Political Debate* (New York: Rowman and Littlefield, 1997), p. 109.

Christianity needs to regain pride in its theopolitical vision, which remains the answer to modernity. Milbank's feisty rhetoric about theology's need to ditch its false humility and be the meta-discourse is how *liberal* Christians should learn to speak. For Milbank's idea of a coherent theopolitical vision is a nostalgic fantasy, a posturing tirade against the liberal state that no serious person can honestly deny is basically a good thing (let Milbank spend a year in China; let Hauerwas reside in Iran). Only liberal Christianity has a theopolitical vision that takes account of reality. It is able to tell the truth about the liberal state — that it is good. And it thanks God for it.

Conclusion: Cultic-Liberal Christianity

—⟡⟡⟡—

Perhaps it is futile to call for a "new liberal Christianity" — even if it is billed as "reinvention" — because too much of liberal Christian theology was just too flawed. One cannot risk seeming to advocate such error, and one cannot risk being boxed with religious humanism. But perhaps a new label can affirm the good side of liberalism while closing the door on the ghost of liberalism past. And perhaps it is "cultic-liberal Christianity," which would subordinate liberalism to the thing that liberalism stifled.

Cultic . . .

Cultic comes first. Christianity is cultic. It is, at base, the worship of Jesus Christ — that is, the declaration, or performance, of his divinity. This is a special form of linguistic practice that is at odds with normal discourse. Good theology defends this otherness; bad theology neglects it, implicitly denies it. Liberal Protestantism lost sight of the priority of faith and cult, which must be affirmed together, because it wanted to rethink Christian truth in noncultic terms. It developed a discourse relating Jesus to morality, history, philosophy, and so forth, and it treated this as the main event, implying that worship-speech can be largely left behind.

I am proposing "the cultic" as a central theological principle, like "the Word," "faith," and "church." So what exactly do I mean by it? I mean the ritual communication of Jesus Christ, the performance of his divinity through certain regular practices. These practices are predominantly verbal: God is spoken of — and addressed — in a unique form of language that is set apart from, and above, other uses of language. And there is a particular rite enshrined in the earliest Christian tradition: the Eucharist. By putting huge emphasis on the centrality of this ritual, Christianity locates its essence far away from any kind of rational or quasi-rational discourse. This cult-act is higher than any discourse explaining how things are. Authentic theology defends this cultic core, and refrains from interposing itself, setting itself up as the truth-discourse — which it seems to find difficult. (As I have already hinted, I see philosophical theology and systematic (or dogmatic) theology as guilty of such interposing: in their calm exactitude they implicitly deny that the highest Christian speech is cultic.)

The cultic is rooted in the worship carried on by churches. It is essentially traditional and corporate, but in this tradition it is not statically corporate. It involves dialectical tension between the group and the individual. As I have observed earlier with regard to the Psalms, agonic individualism is central to group worship, and this individualism seeks resolution in communal celebration. This is to say that the dichotomy between inward, private faith and outward, public worship is overcome. For individual faith echoes the public language of worship. In this tradition the cultic cannot be confined to the public sphere; it also takes the form of the most intense individualism. Therefore, the cultic determines the most personal dimension of this religion, which is the reordering of one's mind in response to this rhetoric of authority and truth, a reordering known as faith.

Faith is thus a kind of semiprivate cultic event: believers perform certain ritual dynamics, learned from public worship, in their minds. The practice of solitary prayer is learned from public prayer, but it is not a mere echo of the more authentic corporate thing: solitude is a complementary authenticity. Indeed, it is on the individual level that the dialogical dynamic that we explored in chapter 4 is most vital. Protestant faith is a conversation between the ritual-based language of assent and proclamation, and reflection on this incorporates skepticism. So my category of "the cultic" is an attempt to prioritize both ritual and faith, to see them as inextricable.

My proposed category of the cultic, therefore, enables a balanced account of faith, which has long been a deeply problematic concept. Luther, following Paul, emphasized a conflict between faith and ritual practice; but in both cases this was nuanced, and the essentially cultic nature of faith was taken for granted. Under the influences of deism and Romanticism, Protestantism neglected the true cultic grammar of faith and fetishized a form of individual inwardness that was at odds with the outward cultic tradition and inherited dogmatism. (As we have seen, Harnack used Luther to argue that true faith is detached from ecclesial tradition, an argument continued by Tillich.)

Faith is simply the individual aspect of Christianity's cultic core. But it must not be neglected. And recent theology, in reaction against liberal Protestant errors, has neglected it. Adapting an anthropological approach, it tends to see the cultic purely in terms of public worship, the "practice of the community." As the community is founded on these cultic practices, they acquire a quasi-rational aura. (This approach is evident in the communitarianism of MacIntyre, the post-liberalism of Lindbeck, Kerr's use of Wittgenstein, the feisty ecclesiology of Hauerwas, the postmodernism of Milbank, and so on.) The otherness of the cultic is diminished by these approaches. They open the door to an essentially rational discourse that mediates the cultic, explains it to us. If, on the other hand, individual faith is also an authentic locus of the cultic, there is a new instability or openness. All truth-claiming discourse is vulnerable to disruption by primary Christian speech. All theological systems look pretentious, tottery. The counterrational otherness — and agonic absurdity — of this tradition is unforgettable.

Bonhoeffer saw this: Barth's shiny dogmatic system deprives Christianity of dramatic tension by eclipsing the question of individual faith. Barth and the Confessing Church, he said, "have encouraged us to entrench ourselves persistently behind the 'faith of the church,' and evade the honest question as to what we ourselves really believe.... To say that it is the church's business, not mine, may be a clerical evasion, and outsiders always regard it as such.... We cannot, like the Roman Catholics, simply identify ourselves with the church."[1] Protestantism thrives on tension between faith and reason, and the individual is its arena. For in public worship the tension is mitigated, or disappears altogether: the cultic determines a new common conception of reason, broadly understood. Through a form of safety in numbers, the counterrational otherness, or absurdity, of faith melts away. Bonhoeffer's frustration lies in the fact that Barth had seemed to understand this: his early work staged this (Lutheran, Kierkegaardian) tension, and then his later, more systematic approach veered away from it.

So the cultic, in its fullness, includes this individual-based conflict between faith and reason. It is only here that the acutest antipathy to rational apologetics is born. It is only here that the full otherness of the Word finds expression. Postmodern theology supposes that it has seen through the modern temptation of individualism: it actually neglects the indispensable individual aspect of the cultic.

A final thought on the cultic. The word has a primitive feel. This is intentional. Christianity should be far better at foregrounding its exotic otherness. For it is interesting, and engaging — this business of worship. At least in theory! Why is it that religious worship seems *duller* than more limited cultural expressions such as art and literature? Why is it that people are fascinated by dismembered aspects of religious worship — theater, carnivals, icons, meditation, performance art — but seem to have little desire for the form that integrates these things in a supreme performance of meaning? Why have the churches not learned to become culturally exciting places? A reinvented liberal Christianity needs a new sacramentalism, which should seek the attention of the secular world. Perhaps the medieval feast of Corpus Christi should be the churches' model: worship

---

1. Dietrich Bonhoeffer, *Letters and Papers from Prison* (London: SCM, 2001), p. 144.

should spill out from churches into the streets and nurture busy amateur creativity. Why hasn't this sort of thing happened to any large extent? There remains a strange failure to notice that religious worship is the highest possible site of cultural creativity and also, dare one say, of grown-up *fun*. To some extent, this is surely because of religion's illiberal image, which brings us to the second half of our new coinage.

. . . Liberal

We should not back away from the word "liberal" ("progressive" is regressive). Liberal Christians is what we are if we see the freedom of the liberal state as the proper context for the gospel — and if we dissent from the theocratic-tinged legalism of religious conservatism. But this has become a difficult position to occupy. If you're in favor of secular liberalism, aren't you a rather watered-down kind of Christian? If you are suspicious of moral and ritual rules, isn't your religious identity bound to be far less distinctive?

The liberal Christian is caught up in the benign paradox at the heart of the liberal state. The liberal state rejects a coerced unitive ideology (theocratic or secular totalitarianism) and promotes individual liberty and pluralism. And yet it hopes that liberty will constitute a *positive* ideology that can unite the nation. Of course, nonbelievers can affirm this narrative, but liberal Christians have a special commitment to it. They remember its origins in the vision of a radically tolerant state as God's will.

The liberal Christian is called to affirm this broad political vision — and to remember its Christian roots. Can it be *Christian* to affirm the secular state? Yes. God wills freedom, both because freedom is good and because this is the proper setting for a purer religious culture. The paradox echoes Paul's claim that God wills to be known by those who do not obey his cultic law. This is not a dilution of religious tradition but God's plan — God's *gamble,* it looks like. There is nothing neat and tidy about this. It is no wonder that Christians are inclined to seek clarity elsewhere, and to be more like the other monotheists. But liberal Christians are called to suffer this muddle, and to

325

affirm it as the supreme theopolitics: God wills the state that secures the fullest liberty.

Twentieth-century theology failed to reanimate the liberal state. Its most vital forms were preoccupied with battling the legacy of the Enlightenment — an essential cause, but one that neglected theopolitics, or rather contributed to a reactionary drift. The liberal state was assumed to be part of the problem, something in need of sharp critique, whereas in reality it needed loving concern. At the risk of sounding like a 1950s conservative, I would say that Marxism played a huge role in the undermining of Christian enthusiasm for the liberal state. Barth was never a Marxist, but he was strongly influenced by the Marxist critique of the liberal state, which he transferred into theological terms. And a similar dynamic affected Niebuhr, MacIntyre, Williams, and Milbank. Innovative theology was infected by the assumption that the liberal state was profoundly passé. (As we have seen, Niebuhr moved toward the defense of democratic realism, but somehow he forgot to supply a clear defense of the liberal state.)

In recent years, ambivalence toward the liberal state has intensified due to the bullish response of the United States to the terror attacks on 9/11. Even long before 9/11, European intellectuals tended to resent the implicit American claim that it is the definitive liberal state — the defender of other liberal states. A European culture of suspicion grew: surely the American fusion of liberal idealism and patriotism is a dangerous thing; surely defending liberty is an excuse for capitalist arrogance and imperial belligerence. This suspicion obviously intensified when the United States responded to 9/11 with scant regard for international law and launched an ill-judged war in Iraq. The liberal self-confidence of the United States seemed to find expression in power politics, neglect of human rights, and insecure militarism.

Perhaps enough of the dust has settled for a nuanced response to be possible. Of course, it is right to be critical of an imperial superpower seeking to repair its wounded pride. But it is doubtful that such criticism would spill over into skepticism toward the liberal state. The difficult-for-Europeans-to-stomach fact is that, for all its faults, the United States is the model liberal state, for it has fused liberal idealism with patriotism in a way that the main European states have not quite done. It has an ideological clarity that enables it to assimilate minorities with enviable confidence. America's liberal revolution was simply more effective than the European ones were — in the long run, admittedly. It (slowly) succeeded in putting certain liberal principles beyond politics, making them the basis of national identity. Instead of voicing resentment, critics of the United States should set about trying to bolster other liberal states, so that the global fortunes of political liberalism are not so dependent on one great but fallible power.

But strengthening European anti-Americanism was only one effect of 9/11. It also awoke some of us to the need to rethink theopolitical habits, to confront issues too long evaded. This is one origin of my thesis: I felt the need to look afresh at the question of how Christianity should relate to the state, and to consider the possibility that, despite all that I had been taught about the defunctness of "liberalism," there might be something of stubborn sacred value in the liberal state.

Cultic-liberal Christianity has its work cut out for it. There is a mountain to climb — just in terms of battling prevailing assumptions, pleading not to be misunderstood. A significant revival of liberal Christianity, cultic or not, seems unlikely. Any sociologist of religion will confirm that the huge majority of people want religion to provide a distinctive identity, in contrast to secular normality, and that religious respect for liberalism remains on the wane. How can this megatrend be bucked? How can Christian and liberal idealism be reunited? How can liberal Christianity find the wisdom to affirm political freedom, and reject reactionary religion, without slipping into old habits?

More pressingly, how can liberal Christianity find a whole new style of sacramental practice that reverses the drift of the Protestant centuries? Where can it find new depth and authenticity and the ability to speak to those inoculated against "religion"? (Bonhoeffer's questions abide.) How can it acquire nonreactionary ritual intensity, an immersion in the Christ-cult that engages rather than alienates the secular world? How can it learn a language that combines secular honesty and holy trust? God knows.

Index

329

Index